HOUGHTON MIFFLIN
HISTORY-SOCIAL SCIENCE

★ CALIFORNIA STUDIES ★

 HOUGHTON MIFFLIN   BOSTON

CALIFORNIA

Consultants

Stephen J. Fugita
Distinguished Professor
Psychology and Ethnic
  Studies
Santa Clara University

Douglas Monroy
Professor of History
The Colorado College

Ray Shepard
College Board
New York, New York

Clifford E. Trafzer
Professor of History and
  American Indian Studies
University of California,
  Riverside

Teacher Reviewers

The publisher expresses gratitude to these and the many other California educators who participated in the development of this program.

Dawn Butler
Kingsbury Elementary
Redlands, CA

Charmian Francis
Maie Ellis Elementary
Fallbrook, CA

Melanie Gates
John Burroughs Elementary
Long Beach, CA

Conchita Lizardi
Antelope Meadows
  Elementary
Antelope, CA

Tammy Morici
Piñon Hills Elementary
Piñon Hills, CA

Brian Netzel
Farnham Charter School
San Jose, CA

A. Leigh Scott
Valley Oak Elementary
Davis, CA

Erin Steinhardt
Clovis Elementary
Clovis, CA

Jeannie Tavolazzi
Carryn Elementary
Etiwanda, CA

Kristen Werk
Parkside Elementary
Pittsburg, CA

History-Social Science Content Standards for California Public Schools reproduced by permission, California Department of Education, CDE Press, 1430 N Street, Suite 3207, Sacramento, CA 95814.

Copyright © 2007 Houghton Mifflin Company. All rights reserved.

No part of this work may be reproduced or transmitted in any form or by any means, electronic or mechanical, including photocopying and recording, or by any information storage or retrieval system, without the prior written permission of Houghton Mifflin unless such copying is expressly permitted by federal copyright law. Address requests for permission to reproduce Houghton Mifflin material to School Permissions, Houghton Mifflin Company, 222 Berkeley St., Boston, MA 02116.

Printed in the U.S.A.

ISBN 13: 978-0-618-42392-7
ISBN: 0-618-42392-3

3456789-DW-13 12 11 10 09 08 07 06

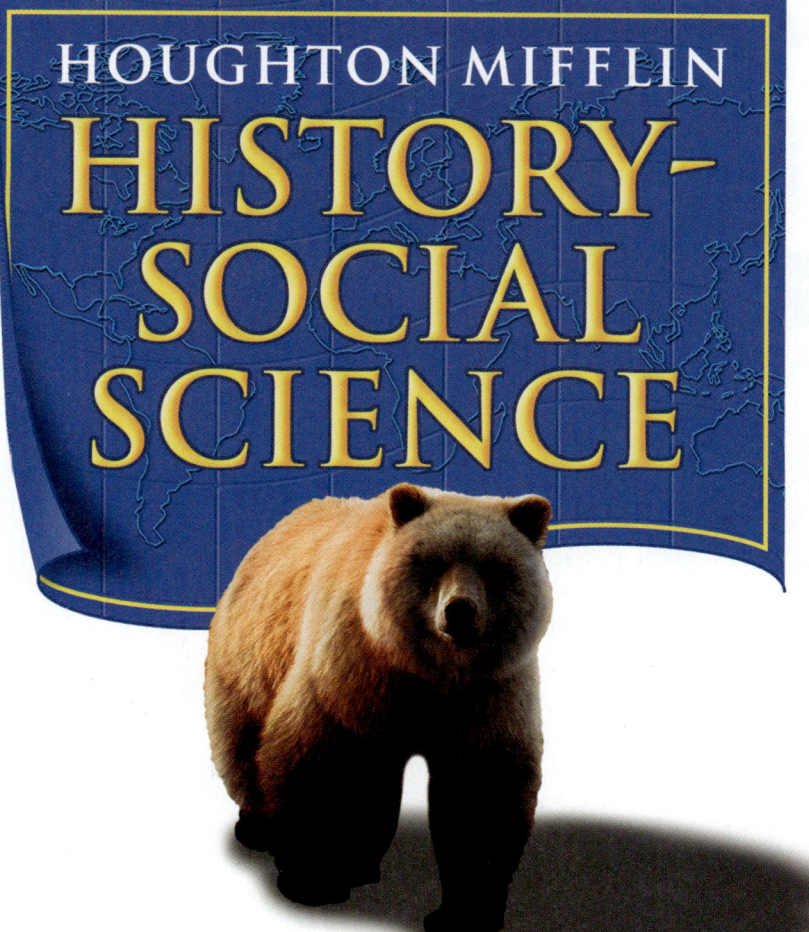

★ AUTHORS ★

Senior Author
Dr. Herman J. Viola
Curator Emeritus
Smithsonian Institution

Dr. Cheryl Jennings
Project Director
Florida Institute of Education
University of North Florida

Dr. Sarah Witham Bednarz
Associate Professor, Geography
Texas A&M University

Dr. Mark C. Schug
Professor and Director
Center for Economic Education
University of Wisconsin, Milwaukee

Dr. Carlos E. Cortés
Professor Emeritus, History
University of California, Riverside

Dr. Charles S. White
Associate Professor, School of Education
Boston University

Consulting Authors

Dr. Dolores Beltran
Assistant Professor
Curriculum Instruction
California State University, Los Angeles
(Support for English Language Learners)

Dr. MaryEllen Vogt
Co-Director
California State University Center for the Advancement of Reading
(Reading in the Content Area)

Welcome!
to History-Social Science

Dear Student and Family,

How did California grow and change to become one of the most vital places in the world? California's past is a story of brave actions, tough decisions, and great ideas, set in a unique and varied geography. Over time, and from all over the world, people have built communities together throughout California, making it an energetic and fascinating place unlike any other.

Welcome to an exciting course:
California Studies

The people and events in your state's history, and how your state has changed—this is what you will study this year. History-Social Science includes history, geography, economics, and civics and citizenship.

Your work, your teacher, your textbook, and the valuable connections you can make at home, will together result in learning success for you.

CALIFORNIA

Helping You Learn

What do you know about the history of California? Who made a difference? What do you need to think about and remember?

The structure of this book will help you answer these questions. Information you need to learn is clearly presented in Core Lessons, and these lessons include a lot of support for building your vocabulary and for reading informational text.

With the sections called "Extends" you can dig deeper—and learn the information in another way—bringing history and ideas to life.

Core Lessons

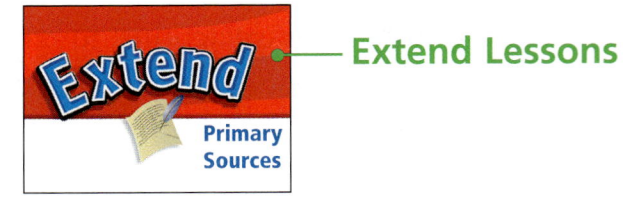 Extend Lessons

Active Reading

You may already know how to be an active reader. First you look ahead at the heading and pictures and think about what the information will be about. As you read, you'll pay attention and ask yourself questions to make sense of what you are reading. After you read, you can go back and reread if you need to. Then you can talk or write about what you have read.

> **Active reading has three main parts:**
> 1. planning or preparing to read,
> 2. actions to take when you are reading, and
> 3. what to do after you read.

 Pages xviii–xxi show the ways your textbook supports your reading, thinking, and understanding of the richness of California's history.

Interactive Learning

What else will help you learn? Interact with the content in the lessons and extends. Look closely at paintings, photographs, documents, and maps. Think about what they show you, ask questions, and use the library or books in your classroom to learn more.

How tall are the trees in my community?

Including history, culture, geography, economics, and citizenship—whew!—as part of your everyday activities will help you remember what you have learned. The more you think and write about the important "big ideas" of History-Social Science, the easier your studies of this subject will become, year to year.

Making Connections at Home

For family members, an important way to help learning is to be involved. Use the checklist provided here for ideas and to help the young learners in your family. Read together and encourage reading. Books and resources that inform, such as newspapers, biographies, and nonfiction topics, are ideal for helping students with History-Social Science and for taking tests.

Home Connections Checklist

☑ Encourage your children to use the library and talk to the librarian about topics of interest.

☑ Locate and share historic quotations, well-known speeches, and important documents, past and present.

☑ Talk together about the news, economic news as well as political events.

☑ Make economic connections: What is needed, what does it cost, how to save? Economics is all around you.

☑ Look for opportunities daily to talk about geography. Use local maps for family errands and activities.

☑ Locate on a map or globe where national and international current events are happening.

☑ Point out natural resources, features of the landscape, and environmental changes in your community.

☑ Share positive stories about your family's history—about people, places, events. Use maps to locate places where you and other family members have lived.

Using Library or Media Resources

Your school library, or library media center, and your public library provide resources for History-Social Science. Different kinds of sources can help you in your studies. Many media centers include Internet connections, videos, DVDs, and other educational media appropriate for the content you are learning.

Resources Checklist

Speeches and historical documents

Books on history and historical fiction

Atlases

Magazines and newspapers

Books about geography

Biographies

Internet links

Videos and DVDs

Helpful Research Tips

The reminders below can help you use a library media center effectively and help you be sure you are choosing reliable resources.

▶ Find more than one book or resource for a topic. Compare the information and facts, and explore different points of view.

▶ Maps can broaden your understanding of a place, such as physical maps showing landforms, a road map, an historical atlas map, or a product map.

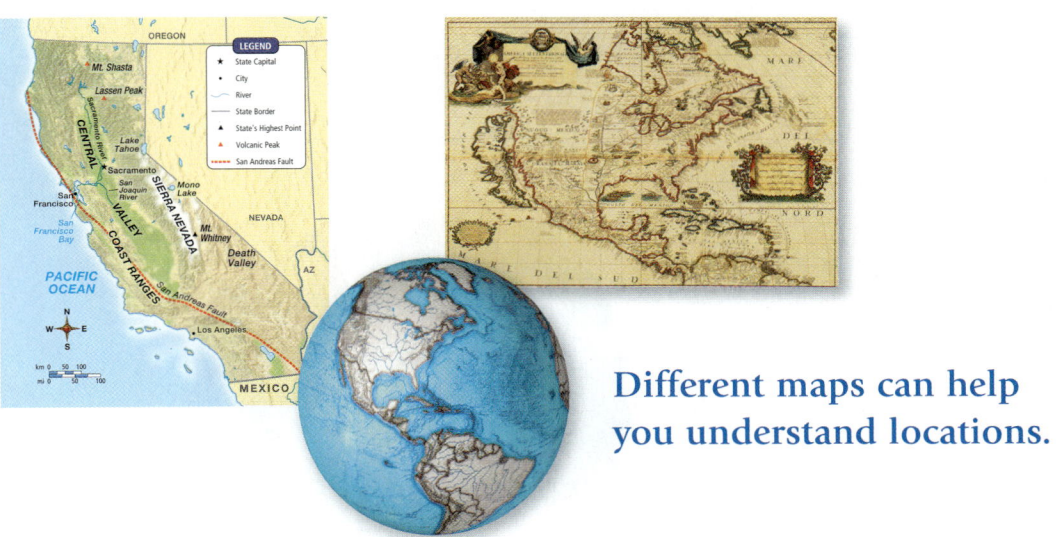

Different maps can help you understand locations.

▶ Look for the most up-to-date resources. Find this symbol (©) with the year printed next to it. This tells you when the source was printed.

▶ Research printed materials as well as electronic or Internet sources.

▶ Use your time well. Focus your research on the information you need. If you need help or have questions, ask your teacher, librarian, or an older student or family member.

▶ Record the sources you use. Use quotation marks around writing or ideas that are not your own.

Achieving Standards

Get to know the content standards. The California Department of Education provides information about standards for all grade levels at this website:

http://www.cde.ca.gov

Standards are learning goals to help you understand who has made a difference in your state's history and why the events of the past are so important. The standards also help you develop geography, economics, and thinking skills.

(See the History-Social Science Standards, Grade 4, California: A Changing State, beginning on page H10.)

Content Standards Worksheet

Fill in this standards support worksheet for each unit. Collecting them will create a standards diary for your achievements this year.

 Read the main content standard. Read the subparts of the standard.

 List the topics included in the standard. Then keep the list on hand as you read a lesson or lessons.

List of the Topics for a Standard

_____

_____

_____

_____

_____

_____

⭐ After reading, ask, *Did I understand the information? Can I repeat it in my own words?*

☐ YES!

⭐ Check your standards list. *Ask, Do I understand what is important to remember about the standard and the information in it?*

☐ YES!

California Content Standards

4.1 Students demonstrate an understanding of the physical and human geographic features that define places and regions in California.

1. Explain and use the coordinate grid system of latitude and longitude to determine the absolute locations of places in California and on Earth.

2. Distinguish between the North and South Poles; the equator and the prime meridian; the tropics; and the hemispheres, using coordinates to plot locations.

3. Identify the state capital and describe the various regions of California, including how their characteristics and physical environments (e.g., water, landforms, vegetation, climate) affect human activity.

4. Identify the locations of the Pacific Ocean, rivers, valleys, and mountain passes and explain their effects on the growth of towns.

5. Use maps, charts, and pictures to describe how communities in California vary in land use, vegetation, wildlife, climate, population density, architecture, services, and transportation.

Los Angeles Skyline

4.2 Students describe the social, political, cultural, and economic life and interactions among people of California from the pre-Columbian societies to the Spanish mission and Mexican rancho periods.

1. Discuss the major nations of California Indians, including their geographic distribution, economic activities, legends, and religious beliefs; and describe how they depended on, adapted to, and modified the physical environment by cultivation of land and use of sea resources.

2. Identify the early land and sea routes to, and European settlements in, California with a focus on the exploration of the North Pacific (e.g., by Captain James Cook, Vitus Bering, Juan Cabrillo), noting especially the importance of mountains, deserts, ocean currents, and wind patterns.

3. Describe the Spanish exploration and colonization of California, including the relationships among soldiers, missionaries, and Indians (e.g., Juan Crespi, Junípero Serra, and Gaspar de Portolá).

4. Describe the mapping of, geographic basis of, and economic factors in the placement and function of the Spanish missions; and understand how the mission system expanded the influence of Spain and Catholicism throughout New Spain and Latin America.

5. Describe the daily lives of the people, native and nonnative, who occupied the presidios, missions, ranchos, and pueblos.

6. Discuss the role of the Franciscans in changing the economy of California from a hunter-gatherer economy to an agricultural economy.

7. Describe the effects of the Mexican War for Independence on Alta California, including its effects on the territorial boundaries of North America.

8. Discuss the period of Mexican rule in California and its attributes, including land grants, secularization of the missions, and the rise of the rancho economy.

 **4.3** Students explain the economic, social, and political life in California from the establishment of the Bear Flag Republic through the Mexican-American War, the Gold Rush, and the granting of statehood.

1. Identify the locations of Mexican settlements in California and those of other settlements, including Fort Ross and Sutter's Fort.

2. Compare how and why people traveled to California and the routes they traveled (e.g., James Beckwourth, John Bidwell, John C. Frémont, Pío Pico).

3. Analyze the effects of the Gold Rush on settlements, daily life, politics, and the physical environment (e.g., using biographies of John Sutter, Mariano Guadalupe Vallejo, Louise Clapp).

4. Study the lives of women who helped build early California (e.g., Biddy Mason).

5. Discuss how California became a state and how its new government differed from those during the Spanish and Mexican periods.

Flag of Mexico from 1822

4.4 Students explain how California became an agricultural and industrial power, tracing the transformation of the California economy and its political and cultural development since the 1850s.

1. Understand the story and lasting influence of the Pony Express, Overland Mail Service, Western Union, and the building of the transcontinental railroad, including the contributions of Chinese workers to its construction.

2. Explain how the Gold Rush transformed the economy of California, including the types of products produced and consumed, changes in towns (e.g., Sacramento, San Francisco), and economic conflicts between diverse groups of people.

3. Discuss immigration and migration to California between 1850 and 1900, including the diverse composition of those who came; the countries of origin and their relative locations; and conflicts and accords among the diverse groups (e.g., the 1882 Chinese Exclusion Act).

4. Describe rapid American immigration, internal immigration, settlement, and the growth of towns and cities (e.g., Los Angeles).

5. Discuss the effects of the Great Depression, the Dust Bowl, and World War II on California.

6. Describe the development and locations of new industries since the turn of the century, such as the aerospace industry, electronics industry, large-scale commercial agriculture and irrigation projects, the oil and automobile industries, communications and defense industries, and important trade links with the Pacific Basin.

7. Trace the evolution of California's water system into a network of dams, aqueducts, and reservoirs.

8. Describe the history and development of California's public education system, including universities and community colleges.

9. Analyze the impact of twentieth-century Californians on the nation's artistic and cultural development, including the rise of the entertainment industry (e.g., Louis B. Mayer, Walt Disney, John Steinbeck, Ansel Adams, Dorothea Lange, John Wayne).

4.5 Students understand the structures, functions, and powers of the local, state, and federal governments as described in the U.S. Constitution.

1. Discuss what the U.S. Constitution is and why it is important (i.e., a written document that defines the structure and purpose of the U.S. government and describes the shared powers of federal, state, and local governments).

2. Understand the purpose of the California Constitution, its key principles, and its relationship to the U.S. Constitution.

3. Describe the similarities (e.g., written documents, rule of law, consent of the governed, three separate branches) and differences (e.g., scope of jurisdiction, limits on government powers, use of the military) among federal, state, and local governments.

4. Explain the structures and functions of state governments, including the roles and responsibilities of their elected officials.

5. Describe the components of California's governance structure (e.g., cities and towns, Indian rancherias and reservations, counties, school districts).

Historical and Social Sciences Analysis Skills

Chronological and Spatial Thinking

1. Students place key events and people of the historical era they are studying in a chronological sequence and within a spatial context; they interpret time lines.

2. Students correctly apply terms related to time, including past, present, future, decade, century, and generation.

3. Students explain how the present is connected to the past, identifying both similarities and differences between the two, and how some things change over time and some things stay the same.

4. Students use map and globe skills to determine the absolute locations of places and interpret information available through a map's or globe's legend, scale, and symbolic representations.

5. Students judge the significance of the relative location of a place (e.g., proximity to a harbor, or trade routes) and analyze how relative advantages or disadvantages can change over time.

Astrolabe

Research, Evidence, and Point of View

1. Students differentiate between primary and secondary sources.

2. Students pose relevant questions about events they encounter in historical documents, eyewitness accounts, oral histories, letters, diaries, artifacts, photographs, maps, artworks, and architecture.

3. Students distinguish fact from fiction by comparing documentary sources on historical figures and events with fictionalized characters or events.

Historical Interpretation

1. Students summarize the key events of the era they are studying and explain the historical context of those events.

2. Students identify the human and physical characteristics of the places they are studying and explain how those features form the unique character of those places.

3. Students identify and interpret the multiple causes and effects of historical events.

4. Students conduct cost-benefit analyses of historical and current events.

Sutter's Mill, California

Contents

Contents v
▶ About Your Textbook xviii
▶ Reading History-Social Science xxii
▶ History-Social Science: Why It Matters xxiv

Bringing the world to your classroom!

UNIT 1 Land and First People

🌐 **Unit Almanac** — Connect to Today 2

CHAPTER 1 The Geography of California 4

Vocabulary Preview **Reading Strategy:** Predict and Infer 4

| Lesson 1 | Core | Where Is California? .... 6 |
| | Extend | Geography — California from Space .... 10 |

Map and Globe Skill Review Map Skills 12

| Lesson 2 | Core | Land and Water .... 14 |
| | Extend | Biography — John Muir .... 18 |

| Lesson 3 | Core | Climate and Regions .... 20 |
| | Extend | Geography — Death Valley .... 26 |

Map and Globe Skill Use Latitude and Longitude 28

| Lesson 4 | Core | California's Resources .... 30 |
| | Extend | Geography — Two Cities .... 34 |

Chapter 1 Review 36

CHAPTER 2 The First Californians 38

Vocabulary Preview **Reading Strategy:** Monitor and Clarify 38

| Lesson 1 | Core | An Ancient Past .... 40 |
| | Extend | Literature — "Mountain-Making" by Jane Louise Curry .... 44 |

| Lesson 2 | Core | Coastal Peoples .... 48 |
| | Extend | Economics — Trade and the Tomol .... 52 |

Study Skill Use Reference Materials 54

| Lesson 3 | Core | Mountain and Valley Peoples .... 56 |
| | Extend | History — Sports and Games .... 62 |

| Lesson 4 | Core | Desert Life .... 64 |
| | Extend | Biographies — Ancient Traditions, Modern Lives .... 68 |

Chapter 2 Review 70

Unit 1 Review **Current Events Project** 72

UNIT 2 — Exploration and Colonization

🌐 **Unit Almanac** — Connect to Today 76

CHAPTER 3 — Spanish California 78

Vocabulary Preview   **Reading Strategy:** Summarize 78

| Lesson 1 | Core | First Europeans in California .... 80 |
| | Extend | **Geography** — Manila Galleons: Using Wind and Water .... 86 |

Map and Globe Skill Make a Map 88

| Lesson 2 | Core | Colonizing California .... 90 |
| | Extend | **Primary Sources** — Alta California Letters ... 94 |

Chart and Graph Skill Read a Timeline 96

| Lesson 3 | Core | California's Missions .... 98 |
| | Extend | **Literature** — "A Day in the Life of a Mission" by Mariah Marvin .... 104 |

| Lesson 4 | Core | Presidios and Settlements .... 108 |
| | Extend | **History** — El Camino Real .... 112 |

Chapter 3 Review 114

CHAPTER 4 — Mexican California 116

Vocabulary Preview   **Reading Strategy:** Question 116

| Lesson 1 | Core | Mexico Wins Independence .... 118 |
| | Extend | **History** — Mexican Independence Day ...... 124 |

| Lesson 2 | Core | Mexico and California .... 126 |
| | Extend | **Biographies** — Stories of Alta California .... 130 |

| Lesson 3 | Core | Ranchos and Pueblos .... 132 |
| | Extend | **History** — Rancho Life .... 136 |

| Lesson 4 | Core | Trails to California .... 138 |
| | Extend | **Readers' Theater** — At Sutter's Fort .... 144 |

Study Skill Write a Report 148

Chapter 4 Review 150

Unit 2 Review   **Current Events Project** 152

UNIT 3 — New Flags for California

🌐 **Unit Almanac** — Connect to the Nation 156

CHAPTER 5 — The Gold Rush Years — 158

Vocabulary Preview **Reading Strategy:** Monitor and Clarify 158

| Lesson 1 | Core | Bear Flag Revolt .... 160 |
| | Extend | **Biographies** — People Who Changed California .... 164 |

| Lesson 2 | Core | The Mexican-American War .... 166 |
| | Extend | **Primary Source** — The Treaty of Cahuenga . 170 |

| Lesson 3 | Core | The Gold Rush .... 172 |
| | Extend | **Primary Sources** — Gold Rush Writings ..... 176 |

| Lesson 4 | Core | Life in the Goldfields .... 178 |
| | Extend | **Technology** — Hydraulic Mining .... 182 |

Citizenship Skill Understand Point of View 184
Apply Critical Thinking 💡

Chapter 5 Review 186

viii

CHAPTER 6 — California Becomes a State ... 188

Vocabulary Preview **Reading Strategy:** Question ... 188

- **Lesson 1**
  - Core — Business Booms ... 190
  - Extend — *Literature* — "The Ballad of Lucy Whipple" by Karen Cushman ... 194

- **Lesson 2**
  - Core — The Thirty-first State ... 198
  - Extend — *Biographies* — Women Who Built California ... 204

- **Lesson 3**
  - Core — New Towns and Cities ... 206
  - Extend — *History* — Arts in the City ... 210

- **Reading and Thinking Skill** Interpret Historical Images ... 212
  Apply Critical Thinking

- **Lesson 4**
  - Core — Land Rights ... 214
  - Extend — *Readers' Theater* — Who Owns This Land? ... 218

Chapter 6 Review ... 222

CHAPTER 7 — Joining with the Nation ... 224

Vocabulary Preview **Reading Strategy:** Summarize ... 224

- **Lesson 1**
  - Core — Linking East and West ... 226
  - Extend — *Geography* — The Pony Express ... 230

- **Lesson 2**
  - Core — A Railroad to California ... 232
  - Extend — *Economics* — The Sledge and Shovel Army ... 238

- **Reading and Thinking Skill** Distinguish Fact from Opinion ... 240
  Apply Critical Thinking

Chapter 7 Review ... 242

Unit 3 Review   Current Events Project ... 244

UNIT 4   California Changes

🌐 **Unit Almanac** — Connect to Today 248

CHAPTER 8 — A Growing State — 250

Vocabulary Preview   **Reading Strategy:** Summarize 250

| Lesson 1 | Core | Newcomers in California .... 252 |
| | Extend | Primary Source — Chinese Newspapers ... 258 |

| Lesson 2 | Core | California Farming .... 260 |
| | Extend | History — The Imperial Valley .... 266 |

| Lesson 3 | Core | Los Angeles .... 268 |
| | Extend | Primary Source — California's Song .... 272 |

Reading and Thinking Skill Summarize 276
Apply Critical Thinking 💡

| Lesson 4 | Core | San Francisco .... 278 |
| | Extend | Geography — Earthquake Safety .... 282 |

Study Skill Identify Primary and Secondary Sources 284
Apply Critical Thinking 💡

Chapter 8 Review 286

CHAPTER 9 — A Stronger California — 288

Vocabulary Preview   **Reading Strategy:** Predict and Infer 288

| Lesson 1 | Core | Time of Reform .... 290 |
| | Extend | Citizenship — The Right to Vote .... 294 |

| Lesson 2 | Core | A Growing Economy .... 296 |
| | Extend | Economics — Making Movies .... 300 |

Chart and Graph Skill Read a Circle Graph 302

| Lesson 3 | Core | The Great Depression .... 304 |
| | Extend | History — The Golden Gate Bridge .... 308 |

Chapter 9 Review 310

Unit 4 Review   **Current Events Project** 312

UNIT 5 Modern California

🌐 **Unit Almanac** — Connect to Today 316

CHAPTER 10 — World War II to the Seventies — 318

Vocabulary Preview **Reading Strategy:** Monitor and Clarify 318

Lesson 1
- Core: California and World War II 320
- Extend: **Literature** — "Journey to Topaz" by Yoshiko Uchida 326

Map and Globe Skill Use a Special Purpose Map 330

Lesson 2
- Core: Peacetime Industries 332
- Extend: **Technology** — The Space Race 336

Lesson 3
- Core: Building New Communities 338
- Extend: **History** — Car Culture 342

Lesson 4
- Core: A Call for Equality 344
- Extend: **Biographies** — Farm Union Leaders 350

Chapter 10 Review 352

CHAPTER 11 — New Steps Forward — 354

Vocabulary Preview **Reading Strategy:** Summarize 354

Lesson 1
- Core: New Neighbors Arrive 356
- Extend: **Citizenship** — The Watts Towers 362

Lesson 2
- Core: Education in California 364
- Extend: **Primary Sources** — School in 1900 368

Lesson 3
- Core: Technology and Trade 370
- Extend: **Economics** — The Pacific Rim 374

Lesson 4
- Core: California's Art and Culture 376
- Extend: **Biographies** — California Creativity 380

Citizenship Skill Make a Decision 382
Apply Critical Thinking 💡

Chapter 11 Review 384

CHAPTER 12 The Twenty-first Century 386

Vocabulary Preview   **Reading Strategy:** Monitor and Clarify......... 386

| Lesson 1 | Core | United States Government .... 388 |
| | Extend | Readers' Theater — Voting Day .... 392 |

Reading and Thinking Skill Draw Conclusions 396
Apply Critical Thinking

| Lesson 2 | Core | State and Local Government .... 398 |
| | Extend | Citizenship — California Firsts.............. 404 |

| Lesson 3 | Core | Californians Today .... 406 |
| | Extend | Economics — Public Servants .... 410 |

| Lesson 4 | Core | The Challenge of the Future .... 412 |
| | Extend | Geography — Water: A Resource for All .... 416 |

Citizenship Skill Resolve Conflicts 418
Apply Critical Thinking

Chapter 12 Review 420

Unit 5 Review   **Current Events Project** 422

References

Citizenship Handbook R2
- **Pledge of Allegiance** R2
- **Character Traits** R4
- **California Databank** R6
- **Immigration Timeline** R8
- **California Governors** R10
- **California Counties** R12
- **Biographical Dictionary** R15

Resources R22
- **Geographic Terms** R22
- **Atlas** R24
- **Gazetteer** R44
- **Glossary** R50
- **Index** R58
- **Primary Source References** R67
- **Acknowledgments** R70

Extend Lessons

Connect the core lesson to an important concept and dig into it. Extend your knowledge!

Geography

California from Space	10
Death Valley	26
Two Cities	34
Manila Galleons: Using Wind and Water	86
The Pony Express	230
Earthquake Safety	282
Water: A Resource for All	416

Readers' Theater

At Sutter's Fort	144
Who Owns This Land?	218
Voting Day	392

Literature

"Mountain-Making" by Jane Louise Curry	44
"A Day in the Life of a Mission" by Mariah Marvin	104
"The Ballad of Lucy Whipple" by Karen Cushman	194
"Journey to Topaz" by Yoshiko Uchida	326

Economics

Trade and the Tomol	52
The Sledge and Shovel Army	238
Making Movies	300
The Pacific Rim	374
Public Servants	410

Citizenship

The Right to Vote	294
The Watts Towers	362
California Firsts	404

Biographies

John Muir	18
Ancient Traditions, Modern Lives	68
Stories of Alta California	130
People Who Changed California	164
Women Who Built California	204
Farm Union Leaders	350
California Creativity	380

Primary Sources

Alta California Letters	94
The Treaty of Cahuenga	170
Gold Rush Writings	176
Chinese Newspapers	258
California's Song	272
School in 1900	368

History

Sports and Games	62
El Camino Real	112
Mexican Independence Day	124
Rancho Life	136
Arts in the City	210
The Imperial Valley	266
The Golden Gate Bridge	308
Car Culture	342

Technology

Hydraulic Mining	182
The Space Race	336

Skill Lessons

Take a step-by-step approach to learning and practicing key skills.

Map and Globe Skills

Review Map Skills	12
Use Latitude and Longitude	28
Make a Map	88
Use a Special Purpose Map	330

Skill Practice: Reading Maps
7, 15, 21, 31, 41, 50, 57, 83, 91, 99, 121, 134, 142, 168, 202, 207, 227, 255, 321, 340, 359

Chart and Graph Skills

Read a Timeline	96
Read a Circle Graph	302

Skill Practice: Reading Charts
23, 49, 174, 199, 366, 407

Skill Practice: Reading Graphs
190, 252, 263, 265, 269, 279, 298, 334, 339, 357

Study Skills

Use Reference Materials	54
Write a Report	148
Identify Primary and Secondary Sources	284
Apply Critical Thinking	

Skill Practice: Primary Sources
91

Skill Practice: Reading Visuals
109, 128, 161, 167, 179, 192, 291, 399

Citizenship Skills

Understand Point of View	184
Apply Critical Thinking	
Make a Decision	382
Apply Critical Thinking	
Resolve Conflicts	418
Apply Critical Thinking	

Reading and Thinking Skills

Interpret Historical Images	212
Apply Critical Thinking	
Distinguish Fact from Opinion	240
Apply Critical Thinking	
Summarize	276
Apply Critical Thinking	
Draw Conclusions	396
Apply Critical Thinking	

Reading Skills/Graphic Organizer

Cause and Effect
    48, 90, 126, 160, 260, 290, 320
Compare and Contrast
    20, 56, 80, 132, 206, 252, 338, 398
Sequence
    166, 198
Problem and Solution
    64, 108, 178, 226, 304, 344, 412
Main Idea and Details
    14, 40, 172, 190, 214, 232, 268, 296, 332, 356, 388, 406
Draw Conclusions
    118, 370
Predict Outcomes
    98, 138, 278
Categorize
    6, 30, 364, 376, 386

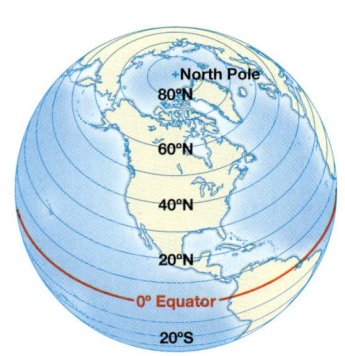

xv

Visual Learning

Become skilled at reading visuals. Graphs, maps, and timelines help you put all of the information together.

Maps

California's Land	2
California and the World	7
California	12
California Landforms	15
Sacramento River	16
California's Climate	21
California Regions	22
Death Valley	27
United States Cities	29
California's Resources	31
Redding and Long Beach	34
California Skill Map	37
Land Bridge	41
Coastal Nations	50
Mountain and Valley Nations	57
Desert Nations	65
California Skill Map	72
Explorers' Routes	76
Routes of Cabrillo and Drake	83
Vizcaíno's Expedition, 1602	84
Manila Galleons Route	87
Serra's Travels	92
Alta California Missions	99
Working Together	110
El Camino Real	113
New Spain, 1810	121
Mexico, 1824	121
Land Grants and Pueblos	134
Explorers' Routes, 1826–1845	142
California Skill Map	152
Land Routes to California, 1850	156
Sonoma	162
Land After the Mexican-American War	168
California Goldfields	173
Routes to California	174
Slave and Free States, 1850	202
Gold Rush Towns and Cities	207
Land in California, 1852	216
Major U.S. Transportation Routes, 1850	227
The Pony Express	230
Transcontinental Railroad	234
California Agriculture, 1920	248
Immigration from Asia	255
Central Valley	261
Imperial Valley	266
Los Angeles Aqueduct	270
The Dust Bowl	305
San Francisco Bay	308
California Immigration	316
Hawaii and the North Pacific, 1941	321
World War II Military Bases	330
Los Angeles Freeways, 1955 and 2005	340
Yosemite National Park	353
Southeast Asia	359
The Pacific Rim	375
California's Water System	414

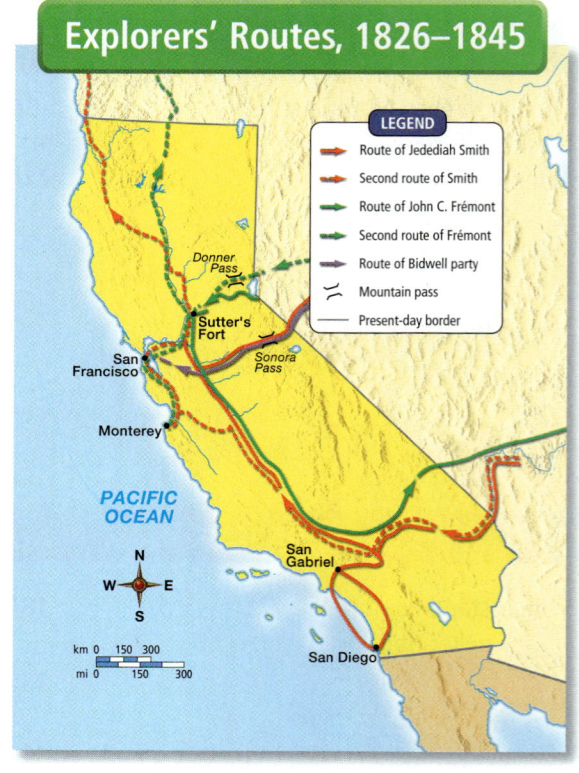

Charts and Graphs

Four Regions	23
Death Valley Temperatures	26
Major Language Groups	42
Using Coastal Resources	49
Reference Materials	55
Sailing to California, 1500s	77
Flying to California Today	77
Population of New Spain, 1800	118
Moving to California by Land 1841–1848	140
California Population, 1850–1870	157
U.S. Population, 1850–1870	157
Travel Routes	174
Value of Gold Mined	178
Average Daily Amount Earned by Miners	180
California Population	190
Governments of California	199
Irrigation, 1919	249
Irrigation Today	249
Immigration to California, 1900	252
California Farmers, 1910	263
California Fruit Shipped East	265
Population of Los Angeles	269
Population of San Francisco	279
California Oil Production	298
Cost of Making a Movie, 1927	300
Jobs in California, 1920	303
Oakland's Industries, 1919	311
Major California Crops, 1909	312
Californians Born in Other Nations, 1940 and 2002	317
Population of Richmond	322
Average Size of California Farms	334
Homes in California	339
California Representatives in U.S. Congress	349
Immigrants to California, 2001	357
University of California System	366
California's Exports	374
Export to Other Countries, 2003	375
California's 10 Largest Cities, 2003	407
State Government Workers	410
Steelhead in the American River	416

Diagrams and Infographics

California Heights	3
Four Questions about Monterey	8
Kinds of Resources	32
An Alta California Mission	100
Supplies for 1 Mile of Track	238
Refrigerated Railroad Car	264
Los Angeles Aqueduct	270
Summarize	276
Make a Decision	382
Draw Conclusions	396
United States and California Constitutions	399
California State Government	401

Timelines

Major Achievements of John Muir	18
European Exploration	96
Voting Rights	294
Major Achievements of the Space Race	336

Unit Preview Timelines
  2, 76, 156, 248, 316
Chapter Preview Timelines
  38, 78, 116, 158, 188, 224, 250, 288, 318, 354
Lesson Timelines
  40, 80, 90, 98, 108, 118, 126, 132, 138, 160, 166, 172, 178, 190, 198, 206, 214, 226, 232, 252, 260, 268, 278, 290, 296, 304, 320, 332, 338, 344
Lesson Review Timelines
  43, 51, 85, 93, 103, 111, 123, 129, 135, 143, 163, 169, 175, 181, 193, 203, 209, 217, 229, 237, 257, 265, 271, 281, 293, 299, 307, 325, 335, 341, 349
Chapter Review Timelines
  71, 115, 151, 187, 223, 243, 287, 311, 353

About Your Textbook

1 How It's Organized

Units The major sections of your book are units.

Meet the people from the unit who've made history.

Use the data for reference.

Your almanac has a map to explore.

Chapters Units are divided into chapters, and each opens with a vocabulary preview.

Get ready for reading.

Four important concepts get you started.

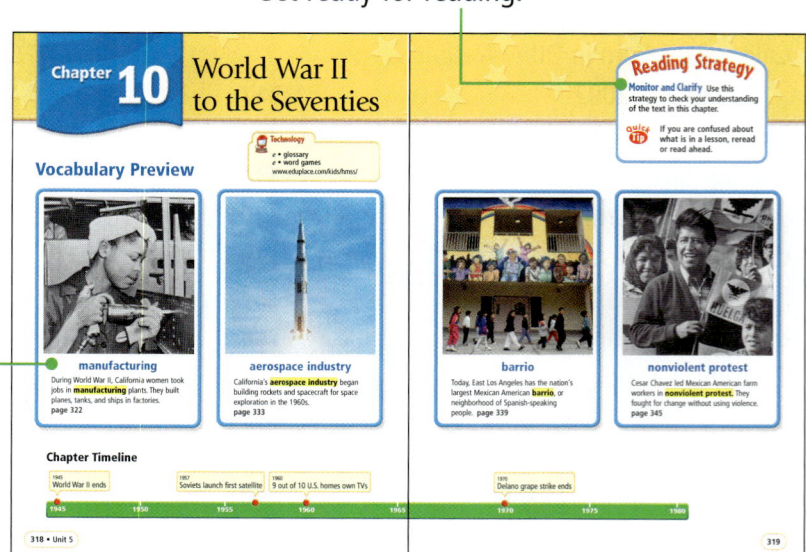

xviii

2 Core and Extend

Lessons The lessons in your book have two parts: core and extend.

Core Lessons

Lessons bring social studies to life and help you meet your state's standards.

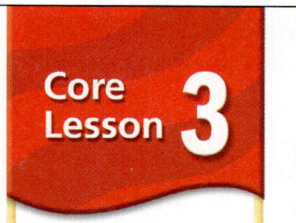

Extend Lessons

Go deeper into an important topic.

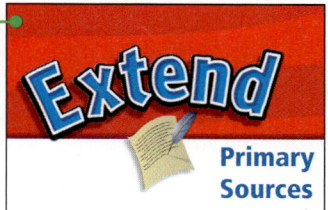

Core Lesson

Vocabulary strategies help with word meanings.

Before you read, use your prior knowledge.

Reading skills support your understanding of the text.

Main ideas for sections state what is important.

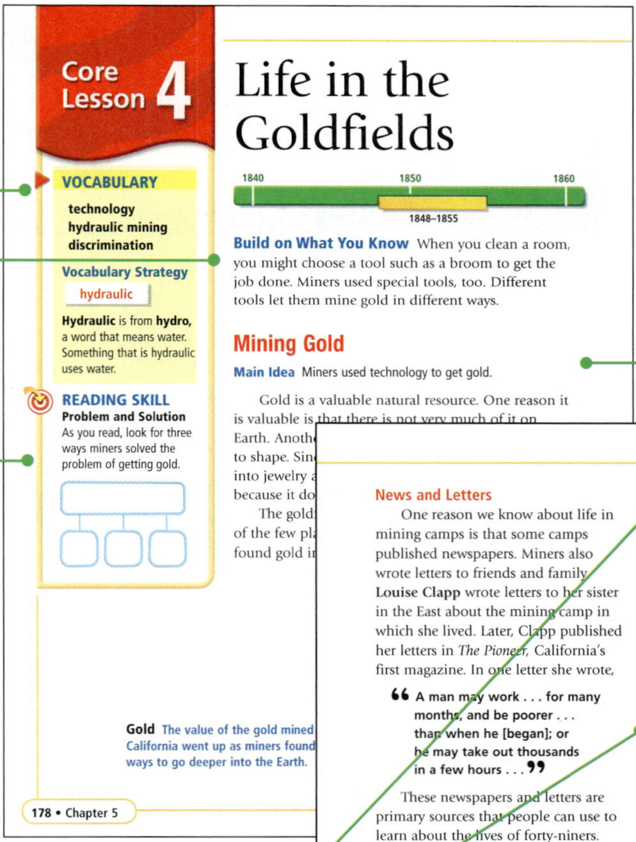

Core Lesson 4

Life in the Goldfields

1840 1850 1860
1848–1855

VOCABULARY
technology
hydraulic mining
discrimination

Vocabulary Strategy
hydraulic

Hydraulic is from **hydro,** a word that means water. Something that is hydraulic uses water.

READING SKILL
Problem and Solution
As you read, look for three ways miners solved the problem of getting gold.

Build on What You Know When you clean a room, you might choose a tool such as a broom to get the job done. Miners used special tools, too. Different tools let them mine gold in different ways.

Mining Gold

Main Idea Miners used technology to get gold.

Gold is a valuable natural resource. One reason it is valuable is that there is not very much of it on Earth. Anoth… to shape. Sin… into jewelry a… because it do…

The gold… of the few pl… found gold i…

Gold The value of the gold mined in California went up as miners found ways to go deeper into the Earth.

178 • Chapter 5

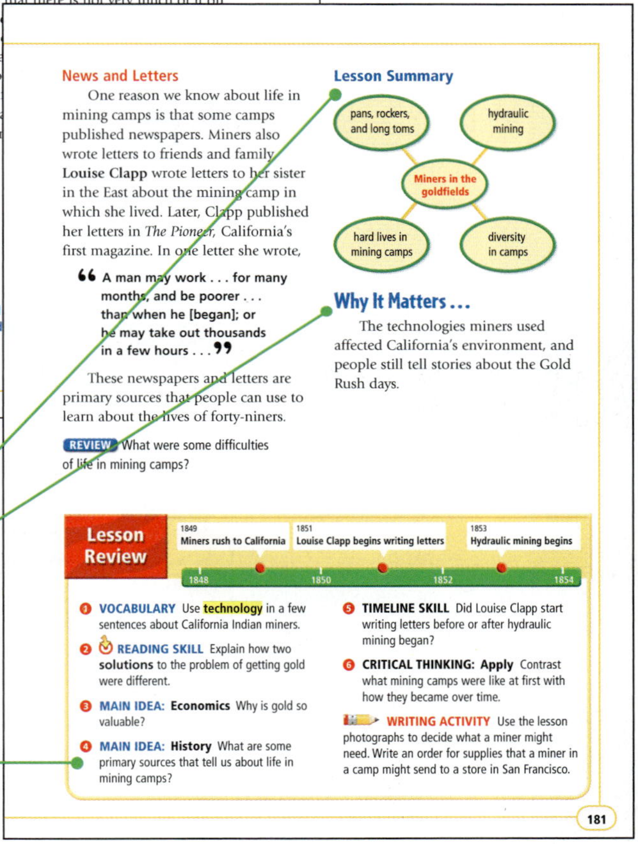

News and Letters

One reason we know about life in mining camps is that some camps published newspapers. Miners also wrote letters to friends and family. **Louise Clapp** wrote letters to her sister in the East about the mining camp in which she lived. Later, Clapp published her letters in *The Pioneer,* California's first magazine. In one letter she wrote,

> "A man may work . . . for many months, and be poorer . . . than when he [began]; or he may take out thousands in a few hours . . ."

These newspapers and letters are primary sources that people can use to learn about the lives of forty-niners.

REVIEW What were some difficulties of life in mining camps?

Lesson Summary

pans, rockers, and long toms
hydraulic mining
Miners in the goldfields
hard lives in mining camps
diversity in camps

Why It Matters . . .

The technologies miners used affected California's environment, and people still tell stories about the Gold Rush days.

Lesson Review

1849 Miners rush to California
1851 Louise Clapp begins writing letters
1853 Hydraulic mining begins
1848 1850 1852 1854

1. **VOCABULARY** Use **technology** in a few sentences about California Indian miners.
2. **READING SKILL** Explain how two **solutions** to the problem of getting gold were different.
3. **MAIN IDEA: Economics** Why is gold so valuable?
4. **MAIN IDEA: History** What are some primary sources that tell us about life in mining camps?
5. **TIMELINE SKILL** Did Louise Clapp start writing letters before or after hydraulic mining began?
6. **CRITICAL THINKING: Apply** Contrast what mining camps were like at first with how they became over time.

WRITING ACTIVITY Use the lesson photographs to decide what a miner might need. Write an order for supplies that a miner in a camp might send to a store in San Francisco.

181

Practice summarizing the lesson.

Studying social studies means asking why ideas are important to remember.

After you read, pull it together!

About Your Textbook

Extend Lesson — Learn more about an important topic from each core lesson.

Look closely. Learn more about primary sources.

Dig in and extend your knowledge.

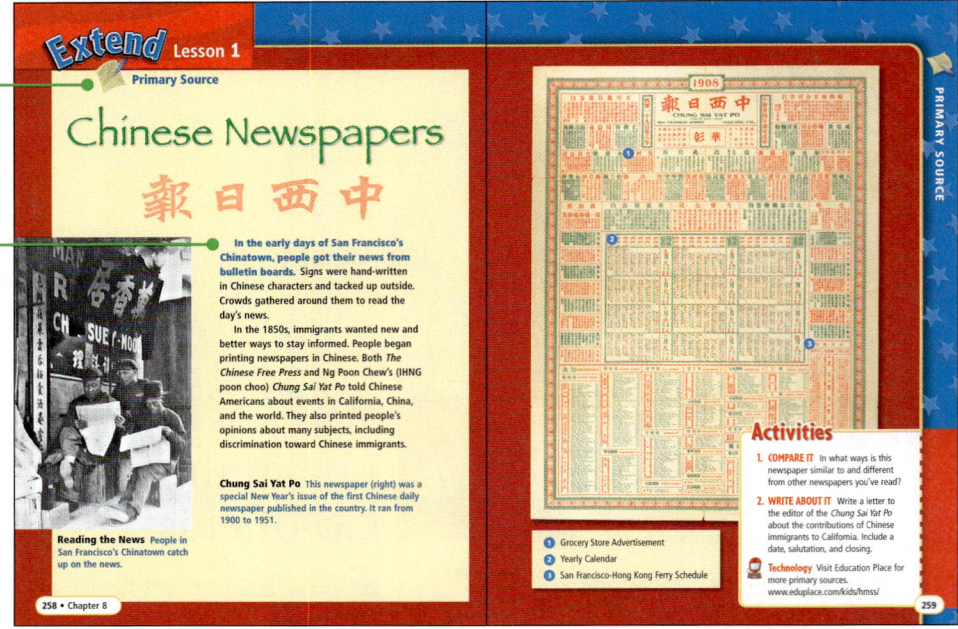

Look for biographies, literature, readers' theater, geography—and more.

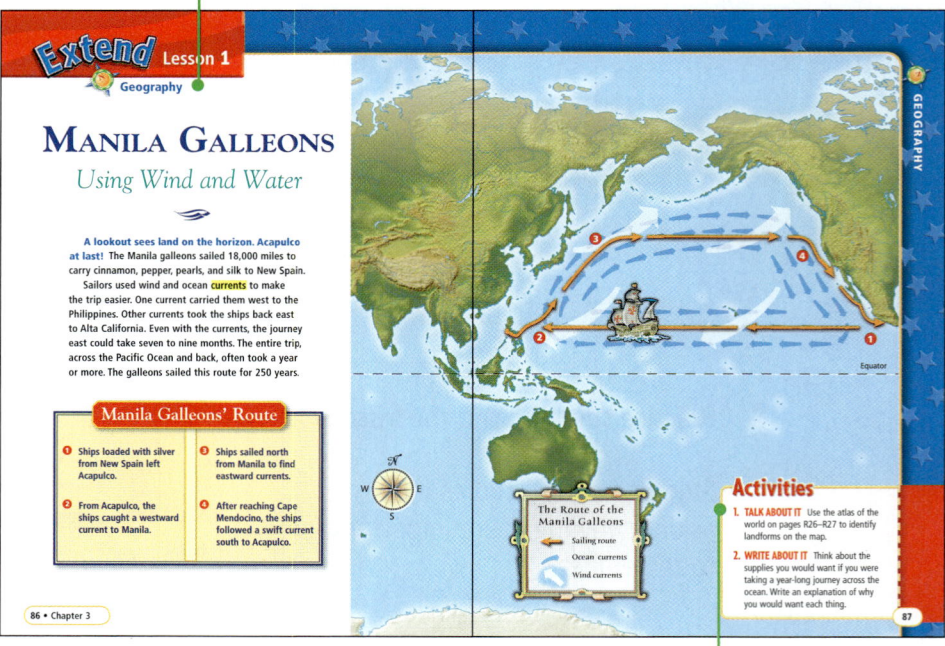

Write, talk, draw, and debate!

3 Skills

Skill Building Learn map, graph, and study skills, as well as citizenship skills for life.

Skill lessons step it out.

Practice and apply a social studies skill.

4 References

Citizenship Handbook
The back of your book includes sections you'll refer to again and again.

Resources
Look for atlas maps, a glossary, and geographic terms.

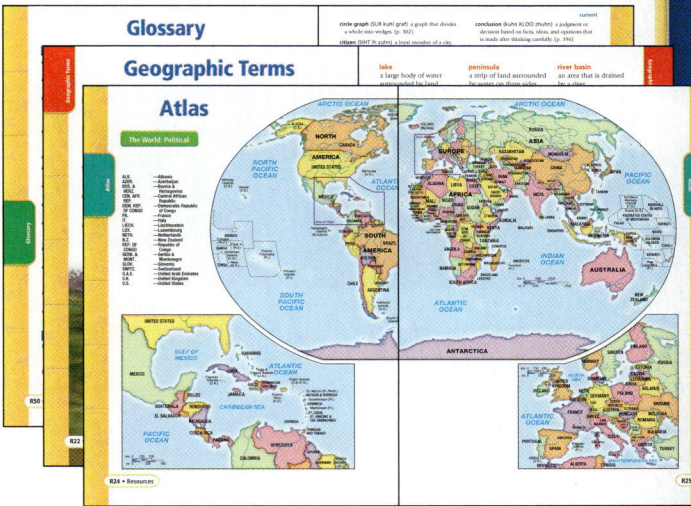

xxi

Reading History-Social Science

Your book includes many features to help you be a successful reader. Here's what you will find:

VOCABULARY SUPPORT

Every chapter and lesson helps you with social studies terms. You'll build your vocabulary through strategies you're learning in language arts.

Preview
Get a jump start on four important words from the chapter.

Vocabulary Strategies
Focus on word roots, prefixes, suffixes, or compound words, for example.

Vocabulary Practice
Reuse words in the reviews, skills, and extends. Show that you know your vocabulary.

READING STRATEGIES

Look for the reading strategy and quick tip at the beginning of each chapter.

Predict and Infer
Before you read, think about what you'll learn.

Monitor and Clarify
Check your understanding. Could you explain what you just read to someone else?

Question
Stop and ask yourself a question. Did you understand what you read?

Summarize
After you read, think about the most important ideas of the lesson.

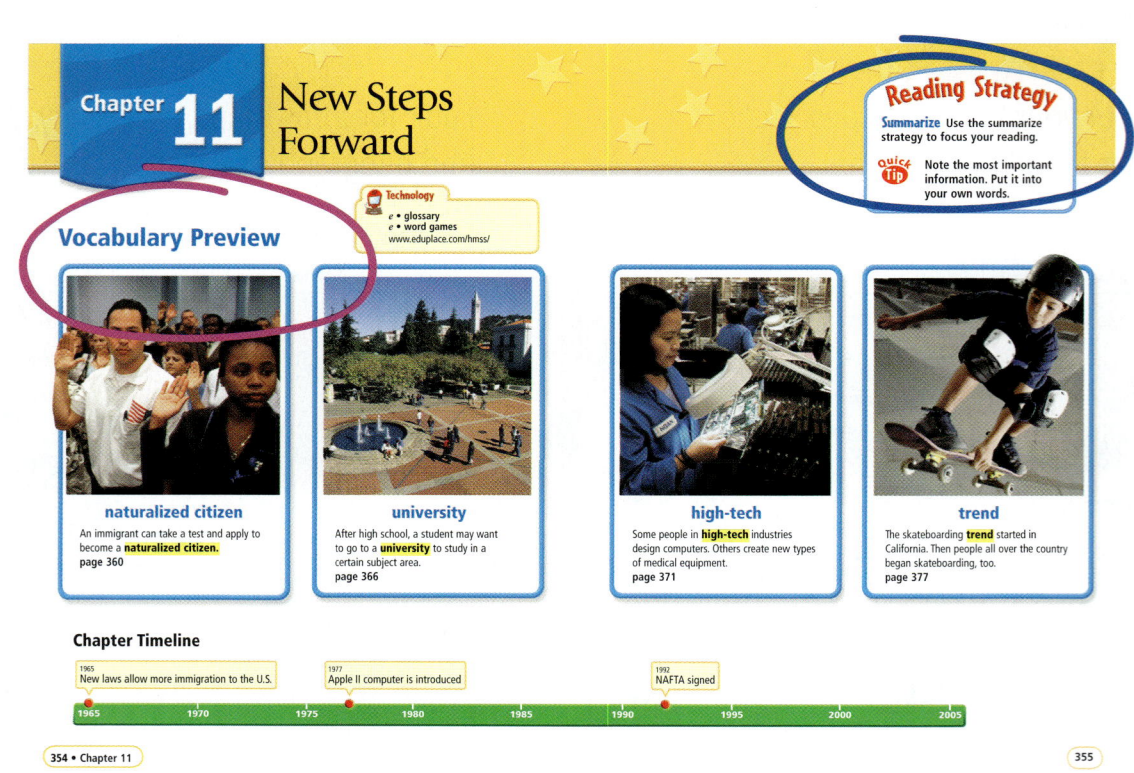

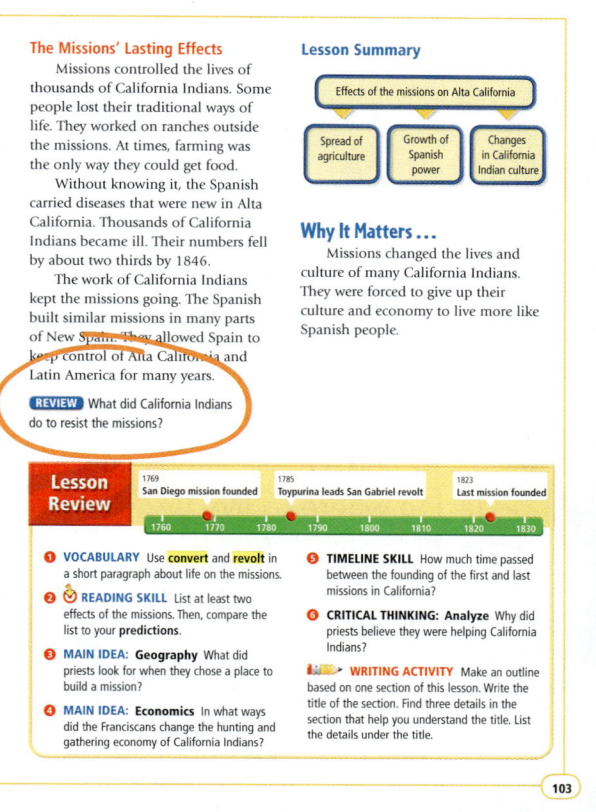

READING SKILLS

As you read, organize the information. These reading skills will help you:

Sequence

Cause and Effect

Compare and Contrast

Problem and Solution

Draw Conclusions

Predict Outcomes

Categorize (or) Classify

Main Idea and Details

COMPREHENSION SUPPORT

Build on What You Know
Check your prior knowledge. You may already know a lot!

Review Questions
Connect with the text. Did you understand what you just read?

Summaries
Look for three ways to summarize — a list, an organizer, or a paragraph.

xxiii

History-Social Science: Why It Matters

Your learning this year will help you know how to get along better in your everyday life, and it will give you confidence when you make important choices in your future.

WHEN I
- decide where to live
- travel
- look for places on a map—

I'll use the geography information I've learned.

WHEN I
- choose a job
- make a budget
- decide which product to buy—

I'll use economic information.

UNIT 1

Land and First People

The Big Idea

What do you like most about the place where you live?

"I firmly believe from what I have seen that [California] is the chosen spot of all this earth."

—from a letter by Luther Burbank

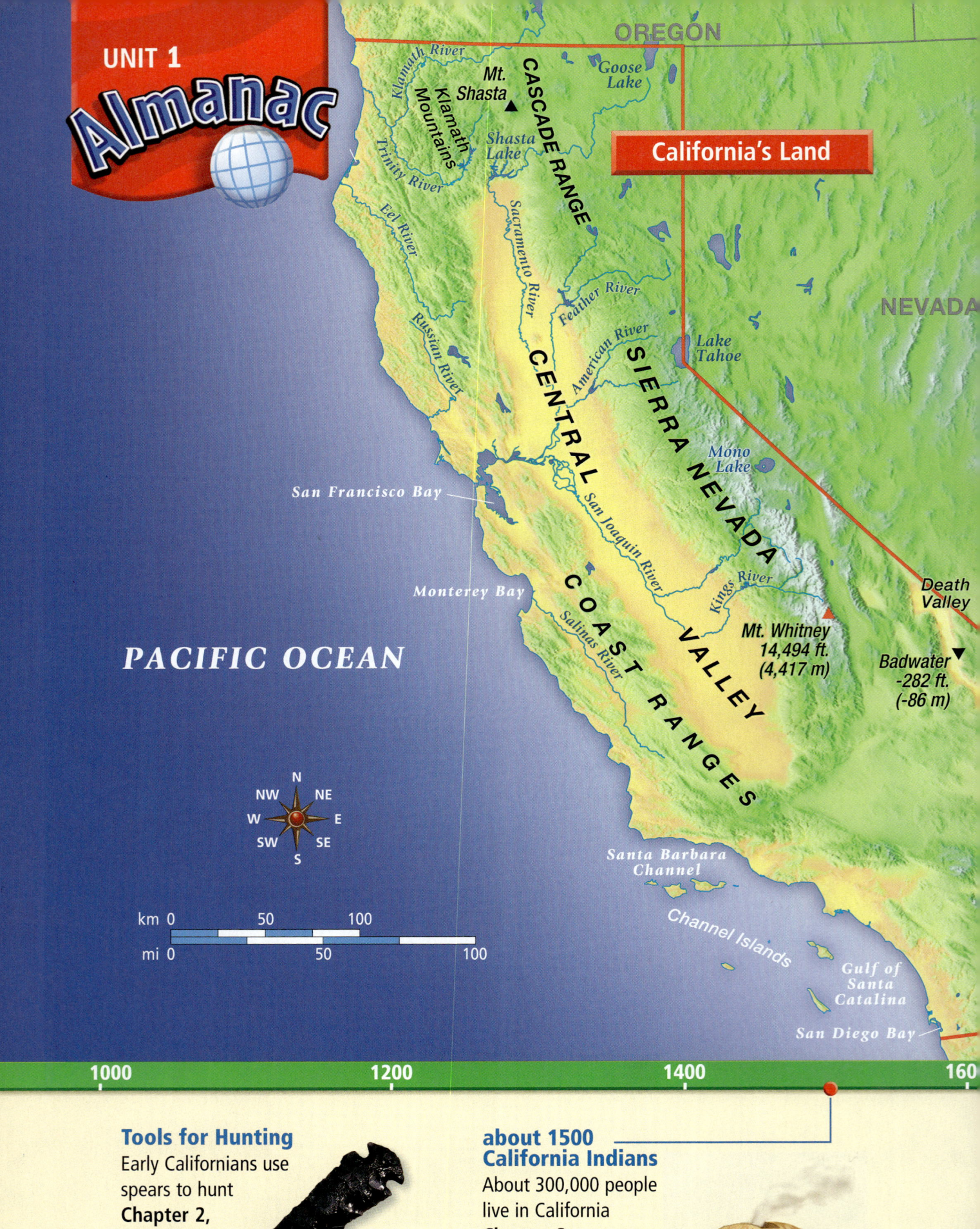

LEGEND
▲ Highest point
▼ Lowest point
— National border
— State border
— California border

UTAH

ARIZONA

MOJAVE DESERT

Salton Sea

Colorado River

SONORAN DESERT

1800 — 2000

2000 Traditions
Some Chumash continue their traditions
Chapter 2, page 48

Connect to Today

California Trees

Tallest tree in the world: 367.5 feet

Oldest tree in the world: 4700 years

California Heights

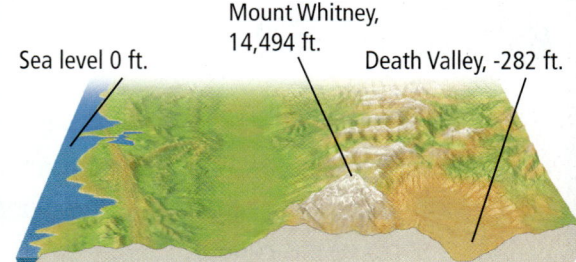

Sea level 0 ft. — Mount Whitney, 14,494 ft. — Death Valley, -282 ft.

What is the difference in the heights of Death Valley and Mt. Whitney?

WEEKLY READER
Current Events

Current events on the Web!
For a selection of social studies articles, go to Education Place.
www.eduplace.com/kids/hmss/

Chapter 1: The Geography of California

Vocabulary Preview

Technology
e • glossary
e • word games
www.eduplace.com/kids/hmss/

hemisphere
California is in the northern **hemisphere.** The state is located in the half of the globe that is north of the equator.
page 7

environment
Air, water, land, plants, and animals are part of California's **environment.** People depend on the environment, but they also change it. **page 17**

Reading Strategy

Predict and Infer Use this strategy as you read lessons in this chapter.

 Look at the pictures in a lesson to predict what you will read about.

region
A desert is a region where little rain falls. A **region** is an area of places that have certain things in common, such as climate.
page 21

natural resource
Californians use their state's **natural resources** every day. They farm its soil, mine its minerals, and drink its fresh water.
page 30

Core Lesson 1

Where Is California?

VOCABULARY

geography
continent
equator
hemisphere

Vocabulary Strategy

geo**graph**y

A **graph** can help you understand something. **Geography** helps you understand Earth and its people.

READING SKILL
Categorize As you read, note what lies to the north, south, east, or west of California.

N	
S	
E	
W	

STANDARDS
Core: HSS 4.1, 4.1.2
Extend support: HSS 4.1

Build on What You Know How would you describe the location of your school? You might say it is near a well-known street. Now, how would you describe the location of California?

California's Location

Main Idea There are many ways to describe the location of California.

Welcome to your state, California! In this book, you will study California's history and geography. **Geography** is the study of peoples and places on Earth.

California has many types of land and water. You can find mountains, beaches, broad valleys, and waterfalls. No state has more varied land than California.

California Poppies California is famous for its wild flowers, like these poppies in the Antelope Valley.

California and the World

Locating California California is at the western edge of North America. **SKILL** Reading Maps What three North American countries are labeled on the map?

California's Place in the World

California is one of the fifty states that make up the United States of America. It is on the continent of North America. A **continent** is a large mass of land on Earth's surface. North America is one of seven continents on the planet.

To study the continents, you can look at a map or a globe. A globe is a model of Earth. Globes are round like Earth. For this reason, globes can show the size and location of continents, islands, oceans, and other features better than a flat map.

The Poles, Equator, and Hemispheres

The point on Earth that is farthest north is the North Pole. The point that is farthest south is the South Pole. The equator is an imaginary line around the middle of Earth. The **equator** is an equal distance from the two poles.

The equator divides the earth into two parts called hemispheres (HEHM ih sfeers). A **hemisphere** is a half sphere, or globe. The Northern Hemisphere lies between the equator and the North Pole. The Southern Hemisphere is south of the equator.

REVIEW In which country, continent, and hemisphere is California located?

7

Geographers Ask Four Questions

Main Idea Geographers describe and analyze places by asking questions.

Geographers, or people who study geography, ask questions about places. Here are four questions they ask.

Where Is It?

Geographers may start studying a place by asking where it is. This is a question about location. How would you describe California's location? You might say it is on the Pacific Ocean. It is north of Mexico, south of Oregon, and west of Nevada and Arizona. What are other ways to answer this question?

What Is It Like There?

Geographers also ask what places are like. Think about where you live. What physical features does it have? Physical features can include hills, mountains, or bodies of water. Other questions that could tell you about where you live are: How many people live there? What kind of work do they do? What plants and animals live there?

What is California like? California has mountains, valleys, and beaches. It is home to many animals, plants, and forests. It has large cities and small towns. People work at farming, making movies, and building computers.

Four Questions about Monterey

Where Is It?
Monterey is on the Pacific Ocean.

What Is It Like There?
Monterey has parks, beaches, and marinas where boats are kept.

Why Is It There?
Sardine canneries led to Monterey's growth.

How Has It Changed?
Monterey was once a small town, but has many homes and businesses today.

Why Is It There?

Geographers also ask why places, people, and plants and animals are where they are. For example, why are certain plants found only in southern California? Geographers would look at the land, water, and weather to find the answer.

They try to understand how land affects people and how people affect land. They might ask why people have built big cities on California's coast.

How Has It Changed?

Geographers also ask how places change over time. Human activities and physical forces can change places. People build roads and bridges, for example. Powerful natural forces such as storms also cause places to change.

REVIEW How might a geographer describe what it is like in California?

Lesson Summary

You can use maps and globes to find a location. Geographers ask questions about places and the people, plants, and animals who live in them.

Why It Matters...

The study of geography helps us understand where we live and how it affects us.

The State Bird The California Quail is found in many parts of the state.

Lesson Review

1. **VOCABULARY** Choose the correct word to complete the sentence.

   equator   hemisphere

   The _____ is an imaginary line around the middle of Earth.

2. **READING SKILL** Review your chart. In what directions do you find other states on California's borders?

3. **MAIN IDEA: Geography** Look at the map on page 7. Describe California's location in at least three ways.

4. **MAIN IDEA: Geography** What is one example of the way places can change?

5. **PLACES TO KNOW** What are the North Pole and South Pole?

6. **CRITICAL THINKING: Cause and Effect** In what way would building a city change land?

 **SPEAKING ACTIVITY** Describe your community's geography by answering the four questions geographers ask.

---

1. HSS 4.1.2 2. HSS 4.1 3. HSS 4.1 4. Analysis Skill CST 3 5. HSS 4.1.2 6. HSS 4.1 Activity HSS 4.1

Extend Lesson 1
Geography

California from Space

Maps and photographs can tell you a lot about California. What do you see in the satellite photo on the opposite page?

You might notice the photo's colors first. Parts of the state are tan, some are a shade of green. These are the colors you would see if you were flying over the land. The forests of northwestern California appear dark green, for example. The long white area in the eastern part of the state are the high, snow-capped mountains of the Sierra Nevada. They divide central California from the dry land east of the mountains.

High in the Sky This satellite flies around, or orbits, Earth, taking pictures of its surface. Scientists study the pictures to learn more about Earth's land and climate.

GEOGRAPHY

1. Channel Islands
2. Mojave Desert
3. Central Valley
4. Sierra Nevada

The Central Valley Look at the land west of the Sierra Nevada. The long green oval is California's Central Valley.

Activities

1. **TALK ABOUT IT** Using a map and this photograph, find the area in which you live. What does it look like from space?

2. **MAKE YOUR OWN** Use the photograph to make your own map of California. Add five new labels for places you think are important, such as the state's highest and lowest points.

Skillbuilder

Review Map Skills

Globes and maps show the shapes of land and water on Earth's surface. A globe is a model of Earth, so it is in the shape of a sphere. A map is a flat picture of all or part of Earth. Maps and globes show where places are located in relation to other places. They can also show features such as cities, mountains, and rivers.

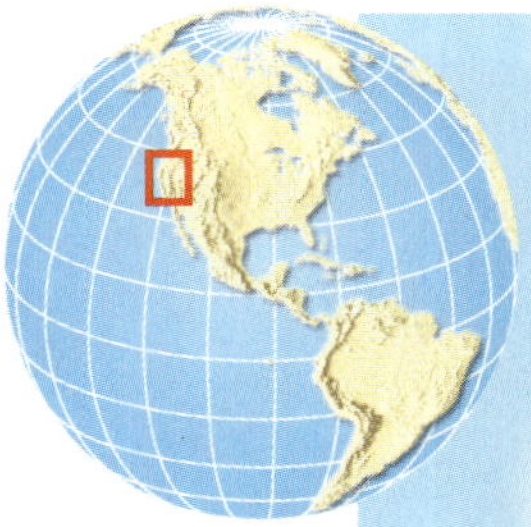

VOCABULARY
legend
compass rose
scale

California

LEGEND
- ★ State Capital
- • City
- ～ River
- — State Border
- ▲ State's Highest Point
- ▲ Volcanic Peak

12 • Chapter 1

STANDARDS Analysis Skill CST 4

Learn the Skill

Step 1: Read the title to find out what the map shows.

Step 2: Study the map legend. The **legend** explains the meaning of the colors, symbols, and lines on the map.

Step 3: Find directions and distances. A **compass rose** shows directions such as west or southeast. A map **scale** shows distance.

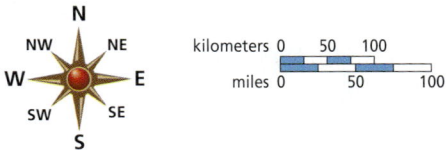

Practice the Skill

Use the map on page 12 to answer these questions.

1. What symbol stands for the state capital? What is the capital of California?
2. Look at the map scale. About how many miles is 100 kilometers?
3. In what direction would you travel to go from Redding to San Jose?

Apply the Skill

Use the map on page 15 to answer the following questions.

1. What is the title of the map?
2. Use the scale on the map to estimate the distance between Mt. Shasta and Lassen Peak.
3. What symbol is used to show a river?

Core Lesson 2

Land and Water

Build on What You Know What is the land like where you live? Some Californians live on the coast and some live on hilly land. The state's varied lands affect where people live.

California's Land

Main Idea California's landforms are always changing. The land affects where and how people live.

California has many types of landforms. A **landform** is a shape or feature on Earth's surface, such as a mountain or a valley. Landforms affect where people choose to live.

California has two major ranges of mountains. The Coast Ranges are near the coast. Most California towns and cities are in the low parts of these mountains. The Sierra Nevada (see EHR uh nuh VAHD uh) is in the eastern part of the state. The Sierra range has many high mountains. It can be difficult to live and travel in the rough, high land there. Fewer people live in the Sierras than in places with more level land.

VOCABULARY

landform
delta
environment

Vocabulary Strategy

environment

The prefix en- means in, or within. People live within the environment, which is made up of all the natural features around them.

READING SKILL
Main Idea and Details
As you read, fill in details about the importance of water in California.

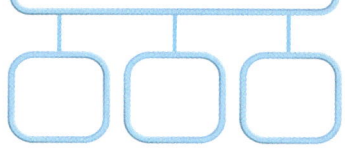

Core: HSS 4.1, 4.1.4, 4.4.9
Extend support: HSS 4.4.9

Mount Shasta
This volcanic peak is over 14,000 feet high.

14 • Chapter 1

Changing Landforms

Long ago, volcanoes created many California mountains. A volcano is an opening in Earth's surface through which lava, ash, and gas can escape. Lava and other materials can build up to form mountains. Lassen Peak and Mount Shasta formed this way.

Earthquakes also reshape the land. They can change the shape of landforms and the course of rivers. Earthquakes are caused by the movement of huge sections of Earth's crust. The line where sections meet is called a fault. The San Andreas (san an DRAY uhs) Fault runs through parts of California. People near the fault build strong buildings to stay safe during earthquakes.

Highs and Lows California's highest point is near its lowest point in Death Valley. **SKILL Reading Maps** About how far apart are Mt. Whitney and Death Valley?

The Effects of Erosion

Erosion also causes landforms to change. Erosion is the wearing away of Earth's surface by wind or water. Over time, erosion carves out canyons and wears down mountains.

Erosion created many of the valleys and mountain passes in California. A mountain pass is a low place in a mountain range. In the 1800s, travelers used passes to cross into California.

REVIEW What are three forces that change California's landforms over time?

Sacramento River This river starts high in the Sierra Nevada. It flows down into the flat farmlands of the Central Valley.

California's Water

Main Idea California's rivers, lakes, and bays have many important uses.

Rivers, lakes, and ocean bays have always been useful to people in California. People use fresh water for drinking, farming, shipping, and other purposes. They fish, travel, and enjoy sports like surfing in the salty ocean.

High in the Sierra Nevada are two lakes created partly by volcanoes. Lake Tahoe (TAH hoh), a freshwater lake, is one of the world's deepest lakes. Mono Lake is very salty, even saltier than the ocean. Salts wash into the lake from the land. When the water evaporates, it leaves the salt behind, so salt builds up in the lake over time.

California's Rivers

The Colorado River flows along the southeastern border of California. Much of its water is used for farming.

The two largest rivers in the state are the Sacramento and the San Joaquin (san wah KEEN). These rivers meet and flow into a delta. A **delta** is a wide, flat, area of land near the mouth of a river. The river delta empties into San Francisco Bay. A bay is a body of water with a wide entrance, partly surrounded by land.

California's long coast has hundreds of bays. Some have deep harbors for ships. Each year, ships move billions of dollars of goods in and out of the Port of Los Angeles in San Pedro harbor.

Protecting Land and Water

Rivers, mountains, and valleys are all part of California's environment. The **environment** is everything that surrounds and affects living things. People get things they need, such as food and water, from the environment. To get these things, they may change the environment. For example, they cut down trees to make space for farms.

Californians have worked hard to protect the state's environment. In the early 1900s, **John Muir** helped to preserve Yosemite (yoh SEHM ih tee) Valley. Photographer **Ansel Adams** worked to protect the environment in another way. His photographs helped people appreciate the beauty of nature and encouraged conservation of the land. Conservation means preserving the environment.

REVIEW What are some differences in the ways people use fresh water and salt water?

Lesson Summary
- Natural forces such as volcanoes, earthquakes, and erosion create and reshape California's landforms.
- California's bodies of water include ocean bays and harbors, rivers, and salt and fresh water lakes.

Why It Matters...

California's land and water affect where people live and what they do.

Margaret Owings
She worked hard to protect California's coast around Big Sur.

Lesson Review

1. **VOCABULARY** Use **landform** in a sentence about California's mountains.

2. **READING SKILL** Use **details** from the lesson to write a paragraph about ways people use water in California.

3. **MAIN IDEA: Geography** What is one way earthquakes affect how people live?

4. **MAIN IDEA: Geography** Name two bodies of water in California and tell ways in which people use them.

5. **CRITICAL THINKING: Evaluate** In what ways do you think landforms and bodies of water might have affected where cities are in California?

MATH ACTIVITY Research California's highest and lowest points. Calculate the difference in elevation between these two points.

1. HSS 4.1.4 2. HSS 4.1.4 3. HSS 4.1 4. HSS 4.1.4 5. HSS 4.1.4 Activity HSS 4.1

Extend Lesson 2

Biography

John Muir
1838–1914

As a teenager, John Muir was an inventor. He invented a machine to tip him out of bed early in the morning so he could read before starting his chores. He also loved to explore the woods near his family's Wisconsin farm.

In 1868, Muir settled in California. He loved the state's ancient forests and valleys and he began to write and speak out about the need to protect forests. Few people at that time thought that places should be preserved just because they were beautiful. Muir helped make sure that the land in Yosemite, Kings Canyon, and Sequoia (si KWOI ah) national parks was protected.

Major Achievements

1890 Helps make Yosemite a National Park.

1892 Starts the Sierra Club.

1894 Publishes *The Mountains of California*.

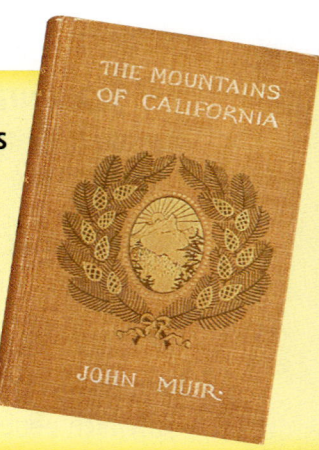

CHARACTER TRAIT: Respect

"Everybody needs beauty as well as bread, [and] places to play in . . . ." —John Muir, from *The Yosemite* (1912)

A Presidential Visit When President Theodore Roosevelt visited Muir in California in 1903, they talked about how to conserve the nation's land and water.

Activities

1. **THINK ABOUT IT** In what ways did John Muir show **respect**?

2. **PRESENT IT** Research Muir's life and travels in California. Create a story map that shows and tells what he did in the state.

 Technology Read more biographies on the Web. Go to www.eduplace.com/kids/hmss/

Core Lesson 3

Climate and Regions

VOCABULARY

climate
region
wetland
desert

Vocabulary Strategy

wetland

Use your knowledge of the words **wet** and **land** to understand **wetland**. A wetland is an area that is wet or even under water.

READING SKILL

Compare and Contrast As you read, compare and contrast two of California's regions.

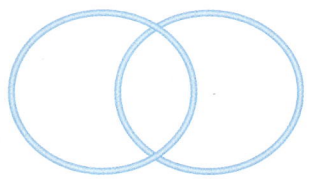

Core: HSS 4.1, 4.1.3, 4.1.5
Extend support: HSS 4.1.3

Build on What You Know Think about the weather where you live. How often does it change? Weather can change from place to place and season to season.

Climate

Main Idea California's climate differs from place to place.

What's the weather like in California? It may be different depending on where you live. In some parts of California, it may be sunny almost every day. In other places, it may often rain. Some areas may have fog every day. Foggy, rainy, and sunny are all weather conditions. Weather is the condition of the air that surrounds a place.

If you follow the weather in different places over a year, you would see that certain places have different climates. **Climate** is the usual weather of a place over time.

Sunny California Outdoor sports are popular in warm southern California.

20 • Chapter 1

California's Climate

LEGEND
- Hot, dry summers with rainy mild winters
- Hot, dry summers with cool winters
- Very hot, very dry summers
- Temperature varies with altitude

Mountain Snow California's high mountains are colder and snowier than land below them.

Climate Regions California's regions can be very dry or quite wet. **SKILL Reading Maps** What is the climate like on the northern California coast during the winter?

What Affects Climate?

Three things affect climate. First is distance from the equator. Places closer to the equator are usually warmer than places that are farther away from it.

Second is distance from the ocean. Water does not change temperature as much as land does. So, the ocean will keep a coastal city such as Eureka warmer in the winter and cooler in the summer than places farther inland.

Third is elevation. Places with higher elevations usually have colder climates than places that are lower. It's colder at the top of the Mount Whitney (14,494 feet) than in Fresno.

Climate Regions

Areas that share a climate are called climate regions. A **region** is made up of places that have certain features that are alike. California has several climate regions. Northern California has a temperate climate. This region gets between 15 and 40 inches of rain every year. Southern California and the Central Valley have a warmer climate with dry summers. The valley's climate makes it possible to grow farm crops almost all year round.

REVIEW Why might southern California be warmer than northern California?

Regions of California

Main Idea Two main regions in California are its coast and mountains.

Regions can be based on features such as climate or landforms. People also use location to describe regions. Many Californians think of their state as having four main regions: the coast, the mountains, the Central Valley, and the desert. Each of these regions is a broad area. They may contain many climates and landforms.

The Coast

A strip of land over 1,300 miles long forms the coast region. It is located between the Pacific Ocean and the mountains of the Coast Ranges.

California's largest cities are in this region. San Francisco is on a large bay. The climate is mild. Cool air comes in from the ocean. When it meets warmer air in the city, fog forms.

Los Angeles is California's largest city. It lies in a basin, a bowl-shaped area of low-lying land. Nearby beaches attract millions of visitors each year.

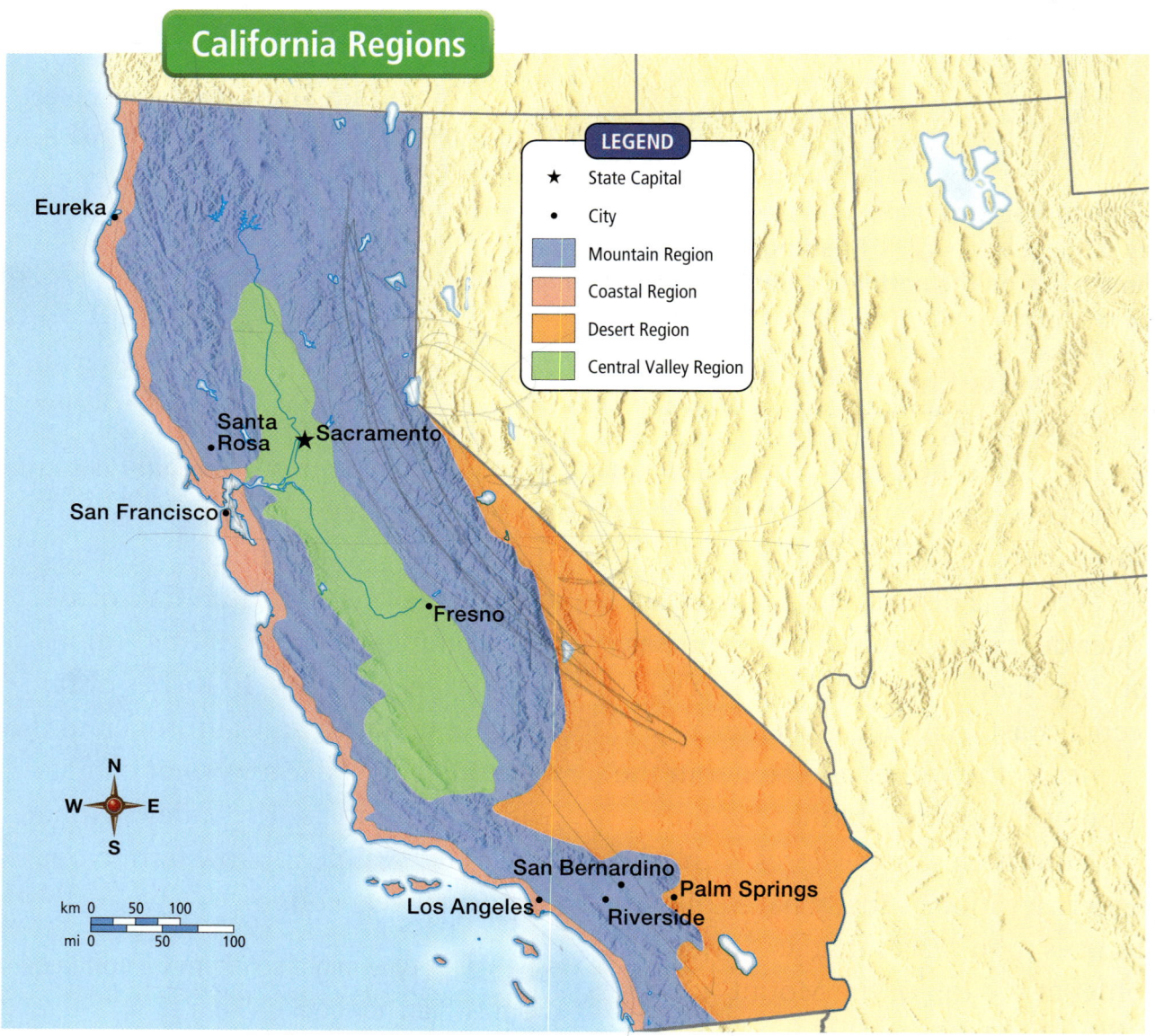

California Regions

22 • Chapter 1

Four Regions

Regions	Wildlife	Vegetation	Land Use
Coast	Black bear, elk, mule deer, turkey	Redwood forest, pine forest, sagebrush	Cities, towns, manufacturing, fishing, ranching, dairy farming, oil
Mountains	Black bear, black-tailed deer, mule deer, quail, trout	Pine forest, oak forest, grassland	Towns, logging, mining
Central Valley	Duck, quail, pheasant, beaver	Oak forest, California prairie	Cities, towns, farming, dairy farming, ranching
Desert	Bighorn sheep, mule deer	Desert shrub	Towns, mining, oil, natural gas

Bighorn Sheep

Using the Land People find ways to use nearly all of California's land. **SKILL Reading Charts** In which region is logging an important kind of land use?

The Mountains

California has many mountain ranges. Most ranges run north to south. The Klamath (KLAY muth) Mountains and the Cascade Range are in northern California. The Sierra Nevada include Mount Whitney, the state's highest peak. The Coast Ranges follow the state's coast from the Oregon border to southern California.

Farther east, the White Mountains are home to 4,000-year-old bristlecone pines. These trees are among the oldest living things in the world. The Transverse Ranges run east to west across southern California. Smaller coastal ranges run south into Mexico.

The northern mountains get lots of rain and snow each year. Melting snow is an important source of water in the state. Water from melting snow flows into rivers and streams. It is used in homes and businesses. It is also used to water crops on farms.

Thick mountain forests are home to wildlife. The largest trees in the world, the sequoias and redwoods, grow in California's mountains.

Fewer people live in the mountains than along the coast. The mountain region has many small cities and towns where people run businesses, dig for minerals, and cut trees for wood.

REVIEW Why is snow in the mountain region important to California?

The Central Valley and Deserts

Main Idea The Central Valley is a farming region, but fewer plants grow in deserts.

The Central Valley is in the center of California. It is surrounded by mountains. Over time, soil has washed down from the mountains. It now forms a thick layer on the valley floor.

Long ago, woods, grasslands, and wetlands covered the Central Valley. A **wetland** is a low area that has water on or near the surface of the land. Today, California's largest wetland is the delta where the Sacramento and San Joaquin rivers meet east of San Francisco. People filled in many of the region's wetlands to make farmland.

Farming the Valley

Most of the Central Valley today is farmland. It has rich soil and a long growing season. Each year, the region grows about half of the fruits, grains, and vegetables produced in the nation.

Because the region has little rain in summer, most farms need more water than they get from rainfall. A system of dams, pipes, pumps, and ditches brings water to fields and orchards.

Most people in the valley live in farming towns and small cities. They work as farm owners and managers, field workers, and store owners. People in the valley have come from all over the world. Many languages are spoken there, including Spanish, Vietnamese, and Hmong (mahng).

The Central Valley Over 400 miles long, this is one of the world's largest valleys.

The Desert

California is separated from states to the east by a wide area of mountains and deserts. A <mark>desert</mark> is a region that gets little rain. California's deserts mostly lie to the east of the mountains. Some of the mountains are also in the desert. Tall peaks block rainclouds as they blow east from the ocean. Little rain falls east of the mountains.

The Mojave (moh HAHV ee) Desert is California's largest. It includes Death Valley, which has little water, few plants, and very hot summers. Almost no one lives there. Death Valley has the lowest land in the United States. It lies 282 feet below sea level.

REVIEW What kinds of work do people in the Central Valley do?

Lesson Summary

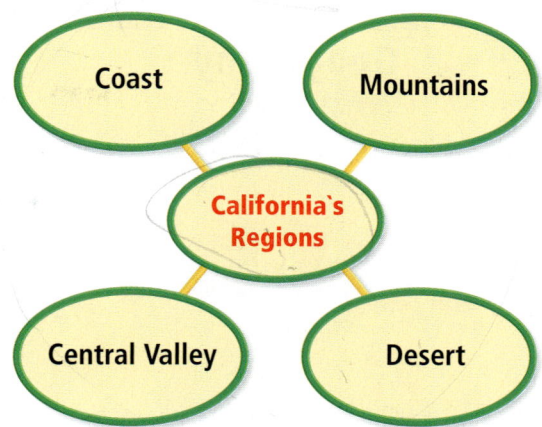

Why It Matters...

California's resources, regions, and climates have attracted many people to live and work in the state.

Joshua Trees These trees need little water to survive in the desert.

Lesson Review

❶ **VOCABULARY** Use <mark>wetland</mark> in a sentence about California's rivers.

❷ **READING SKILL** Write a paragraph to contrast the regions you chose.

❸ **MAIN IDEA: Geography** Compare the cities of the coast and mountain regions.

❹ **MAIN IDEA: Geography** Tell how the Central Valley has changed over time.

❺ **CRITICAL THINKING: Evaluate** Of the four regions of California that you've read about, in which would a surfer most like to live? Explain why.

ART ACTIVITY Choose one kind of vegetation from each region using the chart on page 23. Research them and draw pictures of each in their natural setting.

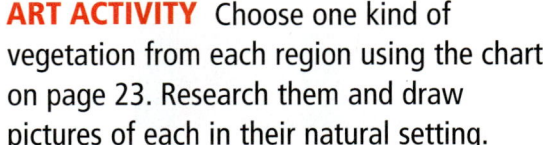

1. HSS 4.1.3 2. HSS 4.1.3 3. HSS 4.1.3 4. HSS 4.1.5 5. HSS 4.1.3 Activity HSS 4.1.5

Extend Lesson 3
Geography

Death Valley

It is the lowest, hottest, and driest place in North America. Some years, no rain falls at all. Welcome to Death Valley, California's driest desert!

Around 600 kinds of plants have adapted to Death Valley's **climate.** Some have roots 10 times as long as a person's height. These roots go deep into the soil to find water. Other plants gather moisture with roots that spread widely near the surface.

Animals have adapted, as well. Coyotes, foxes, and bobcats hunt kangaroo rats and antelope squirrels. Some animals avoid the blazing heat by sleeping during the day. After dark, the desert cools off quickly.

Lizards in the desert cool their feet by lifting them off the ground, one or two at a time.

Death Valley Temperatures

Long ago, there was a lake at the bottom of Death Valley. Today, the water is gone and the floor of the valley bakes in the sun.

GEOGRAPHY

Activities

1. TALK ABOUT IT What advice would you give people planning a hike in Death Valley? Think about food, clothing, and the time of year.

2. CHART IT Keep track of the high and low temperatures at your home for five days. Create a bar graph to record your findings and compare them to the temperatures in Death Valley.

Map and Globe Skills

Skillbuilder

Use Latitude and Longitude

VOCABULARY
latitude
longitude
prime meridian

Where is California? One way to find out is to use lines of latitude and longitude on a globe or a map. Lines of latitude measure distances from the equator. Lines of longitude measure distances from the prime meridian. The prime meridian is a line of longitude.

Learn the Skill

Step 1: Study the lines of latitude circling the globe (right). Lines of latitude measure distance in degrees north or south of the equator. The equator is a line of latitude located at 0° (zero degrees) latitude. The tropics are the areas between the Tropic of Cancer and the Tropic of Capricorn.

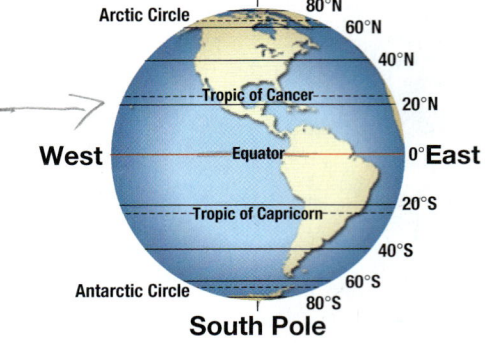

Step 2: Look at the longitude lines circling the second globe. Lines of longitude measure distance in degrees east or west of the prime meridian. The prime meridian is located at 0° longitude.

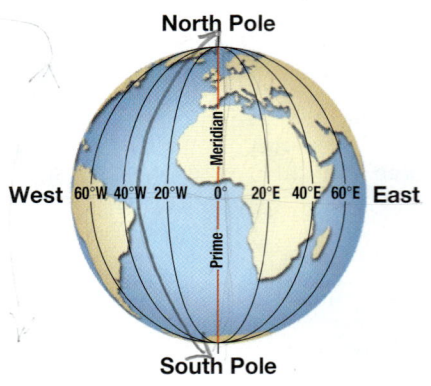

Step 3: Look at the next map. You can find the absolute location of a place by finding its latitude and longitude. Absolute location is a place's exact spot on Earth. For example, Santa Cruz, California, is at 37°N, 122°W.

STANDARDS HSS 4.1.1, Analysis Skill CST 4

Practice the Skill

Use the map above to answer these questions.

1. What city is located at 30°N, 90°W?
2. What is the location of Denver, Colorado?

Apply the Skill

Use your school library or other resources to locate the center of Death Valley. Give its location using latitude and longitude.

Core Lesson 4

California's Resources

VOCABULARY

natural resource
renewable resource
nonrenewable resource
flow resource

Vocabulary Strategy

natur**al** resource

The suffix **-al** means "of." **Natural** means "of nature." Natural resources are found in nature.

READING SKILL

Categorize Fill in a chart with different kinds of California's resources.

STANDARDS

Core: HSS 4.1, Analysis Skill HI 2
Extend support: HSS 4.1.5

Coachella Valley This area between Palm Springs and the Salton Sea has the right natural resources for growing date palm trees.

Build on What You Know What is your desk or table made of? The wood or metal parts come from things found in nature. What else do you see in your classroom that was made from natural materials?

A Land of Resources

Main Idea California's four regions have a variety of natural resources.

California is rich in natural resources. A **natural resource** is anything from nature that people use. Air and water are natural resources. So are minerals such as stone, sand, salt, coal, and petroleum, or oil. Even sunshine and wind are natural resources. People use natural resources to produce many of the things we need and want, such as food, shelter, and clothing. They use natural resources to heat and cool buildings and to fuel cars, buses, and airplanes.

Desert and Coast Resources

Each of California's regions has natural resources. The Colorado River flows through the desert. The river is a natural resource that supplies water to Los Angeles and other cities and to farmers in the Coachella and Imperial valleys. Desert areas also have mineral resources such as boron. Boron is used to make glass.

Rich resources can also be found along California's coast. Workers pump oil and natural gas from underground sources near Santa Barbara and Long Beach. North of San Luis Obispo, Douglas fir and redwood trees are an important source of wood.

Mountain and Valley Resources

Forests in mountain regions are resources that provide wood. They also help conserve California's water resources. Rain that falls on forests soaks slowly into the ground rather than flowing quickly away. Pipelines and channels carry water from the wetter north to the state's drier areas.

The rich soil and warm climate of the Central Valley are resources that allow farmers to grow crops almost all year long. The Central Valley is the leading region in the United States for growing fruits, nuts, and vegetables.

REVIEW What are two California resources and where are they found?

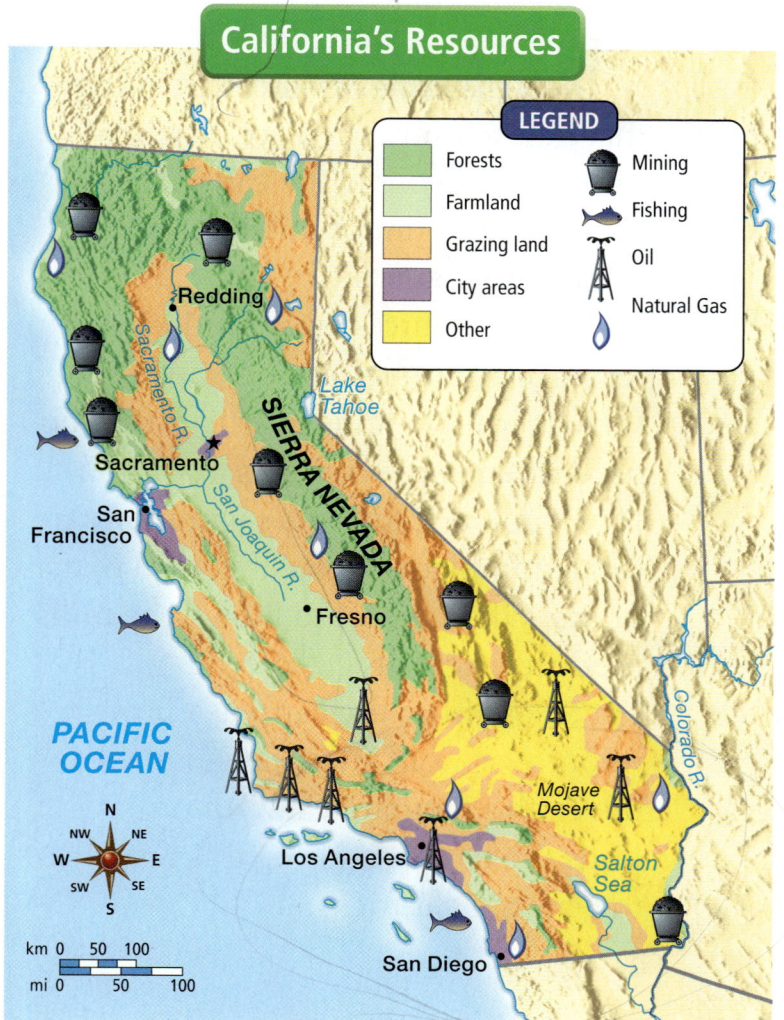

Many Resources California is rich in resources, but different parts of the state have different resources.

SKILL Reading Maps What are two resources found in southern California?

Kinds of Resources

Renewable   **Nonrenewable**   **Flow**

Bees that produce honey are a renewable resource.

Once oil is taken from nature, it cannot be replaced.

Flow resources such as wind cannot be used up.

Using Resources

Main Idea There are different kinds of resources, but each should be used wisely.

Natural resources can affect the work people do. People who live in an area with rich soil may work on farms. Those who live in an area rich in minerals may work in mining.

Renewable resources can be replaced after people use them. Plants are one example of renewable resources. When people pick oranges, new ones can grow.

However, renewable resources must be used wisely. If too much of a resource is used, it cannot renew itself. So many sea otters were once killed for fur that they nearly died out.

Nonrenewable and Flow Resources

Nonrenewable resources are things that nature cannot replace or renew once they are used. The earth has only a limited amount of mineral resources such as gold and oil.

Flow resources are a third kind of resource. A **flow resource** is something such as wind or sunshine that must be used when and where it is available. For example, California's windmills are located in places where the wind often blows. When the wind blows, the mills produce electricity.

Steam from the earth is a flow resource as well. The steam is made by the earth's natural heat. California leads the nation in using this resource to generate electricity.

Using Resources Wisely

People need natural resources. People should be careful to conserve them. Scientists and ordinary people are finding new ways to use and conserve resources. For example, solar energy, which comes from sunlight, might be used in place of oil and gas. Families and schools could recycle paper, metals, and plastics. Conserving natural resources of all kinds can help make them last.

REVIEW Why do renewable resources need to be used carefully?

Lesson Summary

California is rich in natural resources. Renewable resources can be replaced. Nonrenewable resources cannot be replaced. Flow resources need to be used where they are found.

Why It Matters...

Californians will want resources in the future, so people today must use them wisely.

Bicycles People conserve oil when they ride bikes rather than driving cars.

Lesson Review

1. **VOCABULARY** Write a pair of sentences using **renewable** and **flow resources.**

2. **READING SKILL** Review your chart and choose two resources. Write a short paragraph comparing the way people use each resource.

3. **MAIN IDEA: Geography** What uses do people have for natural resources?

4. **MAIN IDEA: Geography** Tell the difference between renewable and nonrenewable resources.

5. **CRITICAL THINKING: Infer** In what ways do the natural resources of the Central Valley affect how people use the land?

WRITING ACTIVITY Think of a way to protect natural resources in your area. Write a speech to share your ideas with others.

1. HSS 4.1 2. HSS 4.1 3. HSS 4.1 4. HSS 4.1 5. HSS 4.1.3 Activity HSS 4.1

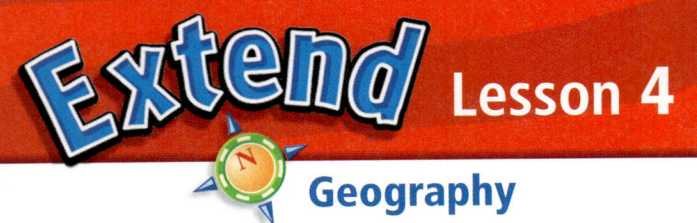

Extend Lesson 4
Geography

Two Cities

California's communities differ, just as its regions do. Redding and Long Beach are examples. Redding is at the north end of the Central Valley, which is known for its agriculture. Long Beach, near Los Angeles, has one of the busiest ports in the United States. Look at the photos and charts to compare these two California cities.

Redding

Redding, California

Population
80,865

Density
1,385 people per square mile

Climate
Average temperature: 62°F
Average Annual Rainfall: 33.3 inches

Land Use
Forest products; mining; farming; homes and businesses; recreation

Transportation
16 local bus routes

Services
113 police officers;
7 fire stations;
46 public schools

Long Beach

Long Beach, California

Population
487,100

Density
9,813 people per square mile

Climate
Average temperature: 64.3°F
Average Annual Rainfall: 11.8 inches

Land Use
Industries; shipping; tourism; homes and businesses

Transportation
38 local bus routes
Long Beach Airport

Services
934 police officers;
23 fire stations;
95 public schools

Activities

1. **TALK ABOUT IT** Name two similarities between Redding and Long Beach.

2. **CHART IT** Create a chart that lists important facts about your community. Include information about climate and resources.

Chapter 1 Review

Visual Summary

1–4. 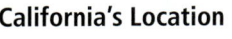 Write a description for each of the items shown below.

California's Location

_____
_____
_____
_____

California's Land and Water

_____
_____
_____
_____

California's Regions

_____
_____
_____
_____

California's Resources

_____
_____
_____
_____

 STANDARDS 1. HSS 4.1 2. HSS 4.1 3. HSS 4.1.3 4. HSS 4.1.3

Facts and Main Ideas

Answer each question or statement below.

5. **Geography** Describe California's location in two different ways.

6. **Geography** Name three types of landforms in California.

7. **Culture** Give two examples of the way California's climates and landforms affect where people live.

8. **Economics** List four of California's natural resources. What is a way that people use each one of them?

5. HSS 4.1.2 6. HSS 4.1.3 7. HSS 4.1.4 8. HSS 4.1.3

Vocabulary

Choose a word from the list below to complete each sentence.

desert, p. 25
delta, p. 16
wetland, p. 24

9. Many _____ areas were filled in and turned into farmland.

10. A _____ is an area where a river meets a larger body of water.

11. An area that receives very little rain in most years is called a _____.

9. HSS 4.1.3 10. HSS 4.1.3 11. HSS 4.1.3

36 • Chapter 1

Apply Skills

✓ **Map Skill** Use what you have learned about maps to answer each question.

12. In which direction would you travel to get from San Francisco to Fresno?
    A. south
    B. northwest
    C. southwest
    D. southeast

13. What latitude and longitude is Los Angeles closest to?
    A. 38°N, 124°W
    B. 38°N, 118°W
    C. 34°N, 118°W
    D. 34°N, 124°W

12. Analysis Skill CST 4   13. Analysis Skill CST 4

Critical Thinking

✓ Write a short paragraph to answer each question below. Use details from the chapter to support your response.

14. **Cause and Effect** What are two California landforms that were shaped by erosion? Explain the way erosion affects these landforms.

15. **Draw Conclusions** Why does California have many climate regions?

16. **Infer** Why is conserving natural resources important?

14. HSS 4.1.4   15. HSS 4.1.3   16. HSS 4.1.3

Activities

 Speaking Activity Describe California's landforms as though you were seeing them from an airplane.

 Writing Activity Write a personal essay telling what you like about the climate where you live in California. Support your statements with details.

Activities HSS 4.1.3, HSS 4.1.3, W 1.2

 Technology
Writing Process Tips
Get help with your writing at
www.eduplace.com/kids/hmss/

37

Chapter 2 — The First Californians

Vocabulary Preview

Technology
e • glossary
e • word games
www.eduplace.com/kids/hmss/

oral history
California Indians, like people everywhere, share stories from the past. These stories form an **oral history**.
page 41

trade
When people exchange goods, they take part in **trade**. Baskets were one item traded by California Indians.
page 50

Chapter Timeline

| 12,000 years ago | 10,000 years ago — Early people in California | 8,000 years ago — Californians grind seeds for food | 6,000 years ago |

Reading Strategy

Monitor and Clarify As you read, use this strategy to check your understanding.

 Ask yourself if what you are reading makes sense. Reread if you need to.

culture
A nation's **culture** is carried on through stories, songs, and other activities. Making canoes is part of Chumash culture.
page 56

agriculture
Corn was a common American Indian food. The Cahuilla and Mohave used their skills in **agriculture** to grow it.
page 65

500 years ago
More than 300,000 California Indians

4,000 years ago   2,000 years ago   Today

Core Lesson 1

An Ancient Past

10,000 years ago–500 years ago

Build on What You Know Getting used to a new place is part of moving. When people first came to California, they had to get used to the environment they found here.

California's First People

Main Idea Scientists think that people first came to California by crossing a land bridge from Asia.

Between 10,000 and 30,000 years ago, Earth was colder than it is now. Animals such as mammoths and mastodons roamed the land. Sheets of ice called glaciers covered large areas. So much water was frozen that the seas were lower. Lower levels of water made a land bridge between Asia and North America.

La Brea Tar Pits The tar pits in Los Angeles have models of the animals that once lived nearby.

VOCABULARY

oral history
adapt
diversity

Vocabulary Strategy

oral *history*

A **history** tells about the past. An **oral history** is a history told in speech.

READING SKILL
Main Idea and Details
Note details that support the second main idea.

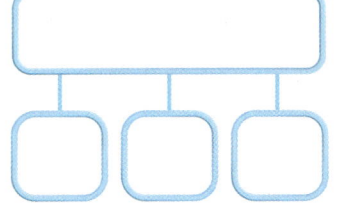

Core: HSS 4.2, 4.2.1
Extend support: HSS 4.2.1

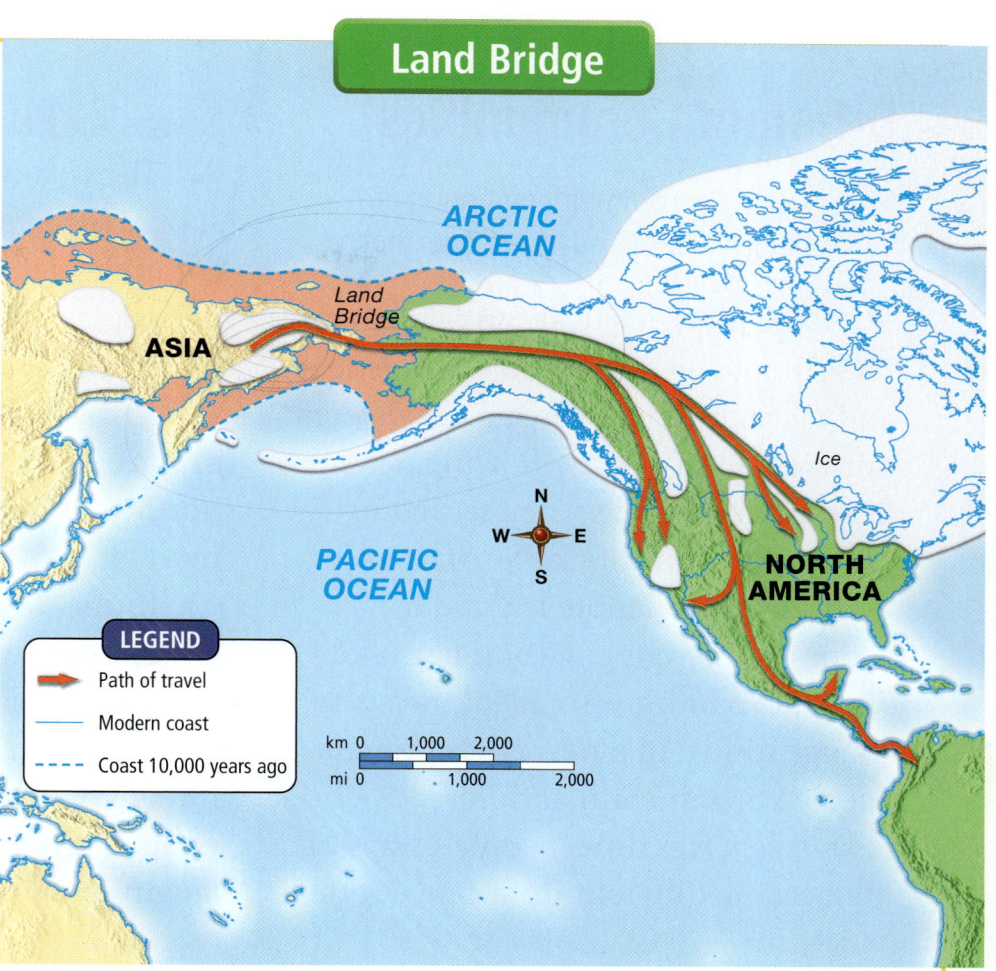

Crossing to California
This map shows one route that people might have taken to get to North America thousands of years ago.

SKILL **Reading Maps**
What two continents did the land bridge connect?

Ancient California

Many scientists think the first humans arrived in North America by walking across this land bridge. Others think people sailed to North America from Asia or Europe. People may have come by more than one route.

Many California Indians have different ideas about how people first arrived. They say that human beings have lived in California since the beginning of time. Elders tell oral histories about how human beings were created in California. An **oral history** is an account of events that is told through speaking.

Scientists think that people have lived here for at least 10,000 years. Back then, California was colder than it is today. It had more wetlands. Lakes covered areas that are now desert. The land was full of plant and animal life.

Camels, giant sloths, mammoths, bison, and mastodons roamed the land. Such animals were a source of food and clothing for ancient people. They hunted with spears made of wood and stone. When the herds moved, the hunters followed.

REVIEW What effect did cold temperatures have on the ocean 10,000 years ago?

Different Communities

Main Idea People in different parts of California lived differently from one another.

Over the years, California changed. The climate warmed. The ocean rose and lakes dried up. Large animals died out. People stopped following herds from place to place. They settled in different regions of California.

Groups of people learned to adapt to different environments and start communities. To **adapt** means to change to live in a new environment. Each environment had different resources. Over time, people's ways of life became different from one another.

Towns and Nations

The rich resources of California supported large numbers of people in communities. A community is a group of people who live in the same place under the same laws.

By about 500 years ago, as many as 3 million people may have lived north of modern-day Mexico. Probably more than 300,000 people lived in California. Most lived in small towns. Groups of towns led by the same chief formed a nation. There was great diversity among nations of California Indians. **Diversity** is variety. These nations spoke about 100 different languages.

Major Language Groups

Language	Nations That Spoke It	Word for *Deer*
Hokan	Chumash, Pomo, Yana, Shasta	In Chumash: *wï*
Penutian	Miwok, Yokut, Maidu, Modoc	In Miwok: *choyekke*
Yukian	Wappo, Yuki	In Wappo: *kecu*
Uto-Aztecan	Kawaiisu, Cahuilla, Tongva	In Kawaiisu: *tïhïya*
Athapascan	Cahto, Hupa, Tsnungwe, Tolowa	In Cahto: *iintc'ee'*
Algic	Yurok, Wiyot	In Yurok: *puuktek*

Language Groups California Indian languages are part of six major language groups. A language group is a number of languages that are related.

Using Resources

California Indians built homes along the coast, on mountains, in valleys, and in deserts. They changed the environment to meet their needs. People trimmed trees to make them grow stronger. They planted oaks and burned grassland to make the soil better and help new plants grow.

The Tongva first settled in the area that is now Los Angeles because it had fresh water, warm weather, and food resources. People from Spain and Mexico who later founded the city of Los Angeles chose the site for the same reasons.

REVIEW Why did the Tongva choose to settle in the area that is now Los Angeles?

A Food Resource Many California Indians ate acorns, which grew on oak trees found in most regions of California.

Lesson Summary

By about 500 years ago, more than 300,000 people lived in California. Most of them lived in small towns. People adapted to and changed the environment around them.

Why It Matters...

Hunters who followed herds of large animals may have become the first Californians.

Lesson Review

10,000 years ago — People in California
500 years ago — More than 300,000 California Indians
12,000 years ago — 9,000 — 6,000 — 3,000 — Today

1 VOCABULARY Use **adapt** and **diversity** in a paragraph about California Indians.

2 READING SKILL Use **details** to explain why people who lived in different regions had different ways of life.

3 MAIN IDEA: History What was the climate like when people first arrived?

4 MAIN IDEA: Geography Name two ways that California Indians changed the land.

5 TIMELINE SKILL When did people probably first come to be in California?

6 CRITICAL THINKING: Evaluate Why do you think people who live in separate areas might develop separate languages?

RESEARCH ACTIVITY Find out about the California Indians who lived in your area. Write a paragraph explaining what they did to adapt to or change their environment. Be sure to use facts and details.

1. HSS 4.2.1 2. HSS 4.2.1 3. HSS 4.2.1 4. HSS 4.2.1 5. HSS 4.2 6. HSS 4.2 Activity HSS 4.2.1

Mountain-Making

by Jane Louise Curry,
from *Back in the Beforetime*

California Indians told stories about the world around them. In some stories, animals act like people. The author of this story put together stories from several California Indian nations to tell how bird and animal people created the Sierra Nevada.

    Back in the Beforetime, in the days after the Sun was put in the sky, the animal people could see at last how wide and empty the World was. The plains stretched north, south, east, and west to the sky's edge. In all the World there were no landmarks but the white-teepee mountain Shasta and the lake that was called Tulare.

    Coyote was still full of his own cleverness. Had not his Sun been a great success? Even Crane said so. But before long, the animal people took to turning away when they spied him coming. "Troublemaker," they called him. "Old Nosy." And "Sneak," because of his silent step as he sidled close to listen to the plans and secrets of others. For Coyote snooped and gossiped and meddled. And always he knew better than anyone else.

But then Coyote turned his tongue's mischief on Eagle, chief of all the bird and animal people. Coyote whispered this, and whispered that. He stirred up trouble happily.

"Did you hear what Eagle said about Crane?"

"Is it true that Eagle ate Cottontail's cousin?"

"I hear old Eagle is blind in one eye, and others must do his hunting."

At last Eagle could stand it no more.

"No more!" Eagle shrilled. "I must find somewhere to live where Coyote cannot spread his nonsense."

But where? Coyote wandered everywhere but under the waters of Tulare Lake or on the high mountain slopes.

A mountain! Now there was an idea, thought Eagle.

At once he called the animal people together—all of them but Coyote—to make his announcement. "I am moving away," said Eagle. "Away from the mischief Coyote makes with his meddling and tale-telling. And you shall help me. All of you."

"Tell us what to do," said Bear.

"And where you will live," added Jackrabbit.

LITERATURE

Eagle nodded. "Coyote travels the foothills and plains. I must live in the mountains, where he will not go. So you must build me mountains. High mountains, away to the east, where I can make the highest mountaintop home."

Eagle was a good chief, so the bird and animal people did as he asked. With digging sticks they dug earth to fill their burden baskets, and when their baskets were full they slung them on their backs and set out toward the east. At the place where the mountains were to be, they emptied the baskets and returned for more. Beaver went, and Bear. Fox and Weasel, Cottontail and Caribou worked side by side. Mouse and Mountain Lion and Deer came, and Crow and Pelican, Quail and Rail and Owl, Badger, Otter, and Skunk. Hundreds came. Even Hummingbird, and Ant and all of his people.

As the earth was heaped higher and higher, the mountains rose. Bit by bit they grew until at last they were so tall that the snow began to fall on their crests.

"Enough!" called Eagle. "Enough!"

The bird and animal people stopped at the mountain foot and emptied there on the ground the baskets of earth left over. When they looked up at the mountains they had mounded up, they raised a cheer. Such ridges and ranges! Such fine pointed peaks!

And the round mounds you still may see along the foothills of the Sierras? They are the earth from the baskets left over from building Eagle's new home.

Activities

1. **THINK ABOUT IT** Why do you think the bird and animal people were willing to build mountains for Eagle?

2. **WRITE ABOUT IT** Write a version of this story from Coyote's point of view. As you write, think about what you read in this story and other legends.

Core Lesson 2

VOCABULARY

goods
service
trade
economy
barter

Vocabulary Strategy

service

Service comes from the word **serve**. A service is work that serves others.

READING SKILL
Cause and Effect Chart the effects life near the ocean had on people.

Cause	Effect

STANDARDS
Core: HSS 4.2.1
Extend support: HSS 4.2.1

Coastal Peoples

Build on What You Know Why do some people choose to live near the ocean today? In California long ago, one reason people lived near the ocean was to hunt for fish and other food resources in the water.

Living on the Coast

Main Idea Coastal California Indians used the resources of the ocean and the land around them.

Five hundred years ago, the coast of California was home to many nations. California's long coast stretches from warm, dry areas in the south to thick forests in the north. Each part of the coast had different resources that affected the way people lived.

Some resources were found in many parts of California. For example, most California Indians ate acorns, the nuts of the oak tree. Women ground and rinsed acorns to get rid of their bitter taste. They made acorn breads and soups. Other resources, such as seals and whales, were found only along the coast. Coastal peoples built boats to use the sea's resources.

Tomol Chumash people have made and paddled tomol canoes for hundreds of years.

48 • Chapter 2

Using Coastal Resources

	Northern Coast	Central Coast	Southern Coast
Nation	Yurok	Miwok	Chumash
Houses	rectangular houses made of cedar or giant redwood boards	cone-shaped houses made of wooden poles and covered with grass	dome-shaped houses made of wooden poles and covered with grass
Foods	salmon, sea lions, seals, eels, seaweed, deer, elk, acorns	salmon, shellfish, rabbits, squirrels, acorns	tuna, sea lions, porpoises, shellfish, deer, elk, acorns

Different Ways of Life The Yurok, Miwok, and Chumash all lived along the coast, but they used different resources.

SKILL Reading Charts What food did all three nations eat?

Food and Shelter

The ocean was a source of food for all coastal people. The Yurok, who lived in small towns in the north, gathered shellfish. They also caught salmon in nearby rivers. In the south, the Chumash used boats to hunt tuna, porpoises, and other sea animals.

People used materials around them to build homes. In the north, they used wood from cedar or giant redwood trees. Along the southern coast, people used smaller trees, tough grasses, and marsh plants to make their houses. Up to 70 people could live in a Chumash house.

Goods and Services

Coastal people made goods from natural resources. **Goods** are objects that satisfy people's wants. They can be bought and sold. For example, people made baskets of reeds and branches. Some were big enough to store 1,000 pounds of acorns. The Pomo wove baskets that were tight enough to hold water. People even cooked in baskets by putting hot rocks into soups.

People who wove baskets provided a useful service. A **service** is work people do for others to satisfy wants.

REVIEW What is one way coastal people used resources from the ocean?

Trading Resources

Main Idea Coastal peoples exchanged resources to meet their needs.

Some regions of California lacked certain resources, goods, or services. Coastal Indians used trade with people in other areas to get goods and services that they wanted. **Trade** is the exchange of resources, goods, or services.

An economy based on trade grew in California. An **economy** is the way in which a group uses its resources to make, buy, and sell things. Resources may include natural resources, tools, or people's work. Some coastal people grew wealthy through trade.

Coastal nations traded with people in the valleys and deserts to the east. They exchanged food, baskets, and beads. Along the southern coast, the Chumash also traded with people of the Channel Islands, including Santa Cruz and Santa Catalina. Steatite, a soft stone from the islands, was a prized resource. It was carved into bowls, pipes, and ornaments. Island people traded steatite and fish for mainland goods such as acorns.

Goods traded to one group could then be traded to another group for something else. Resources and goods traveled throughout present-day California and beyond its borders.

Near the Ocean Many California Indians lived along the coast and on the Channel Islands (above).

SKILL Reading Maps Which nation lived farthest south?

Using Money

People in California used barter to trade goods. **Barter** is trade without the use of money. About 800 years ago, however, the Chumash began using money made from a type of shell that was hard to find. Beads made of these rare shells were strung together. A long string of beads was worth more than a short string.

Money made trade easier. People who did not have goods to barter could use shell money instead. They bought stone knives, animal hides, and other items. They also used money to buy services, such as the help of a healer. By about 500 years ago, other California nations, such as the Yurok and the Ohlone (oh LOW nee), were also using shell money.

REVIEW Why did the people of the Channel Islands trade with people on the mainland?

Lesson Summary

- California Indians used a variety of resources.
- They did not have all the resources they wanted.
- People traded resources to meet their needs.

Why It Matters...

The largest cities in California today are in areas where coastal California Indians settled.

Lesson Review

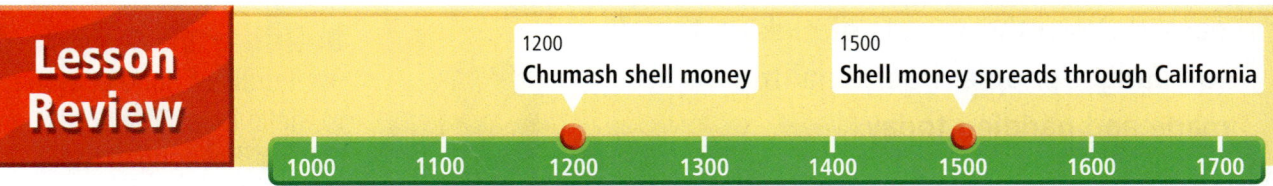

1200 — Chumash shell money
1500 — Shell money spreads through California

1000 1100 1200 1300 1400 1500 1600 1700

1. **VOCABULARY** Explain the difference between **goods** and **services**.

2. **READING SKILL** Make an outline showing the **effects** that living near the ocean had on the Chumash economy.

3. **MAIN IDEA: Culture** Why did people in different environments use different materials for their houses?

4. **MAIN IDEA: Economics** Why did groups in California trade with each other?

5. **CRITICAL THINKING: Evaluate** Based on what you have read, what do you think people who did not live on the coast would have used for money? Explain your answer.

HANDS ON **ART ACTIVITY** Make a display of ocean resources that coastal nations used. Use information from the lesson or find out more at the library.

1. HSS 4.2.1 **2.** HSS 4.2.1 **3.** HSS 4.2.1 **4.** HSS 4.2.1 **5.** HSS 4.2.1 Activity HSS 4.2.1

Extend Lesson 2

Economics

Trade and the Tomol

Chumash canoes have crossed the Santa Barbara Channel for hundreds of years. Long ago, *tomols,* or canoes, were part of the Chumash trading **economy.** Traders loaded tomols with seeds, acorns, bows, and arrows. They sailed to the Channel Islands, and came home with goods such as shells, beads, baskets, and stone tools.

To make tomols, Chumash builders used the resources of the coast. Older builders passed down the secrets of making tomols to younger people. Traditional tomols are made and paddled today.

1 **Building** The Chumash used drills of bone or stone to make holes in wooden planks. They looped ropes made of plants through the holes and tied the planks together.

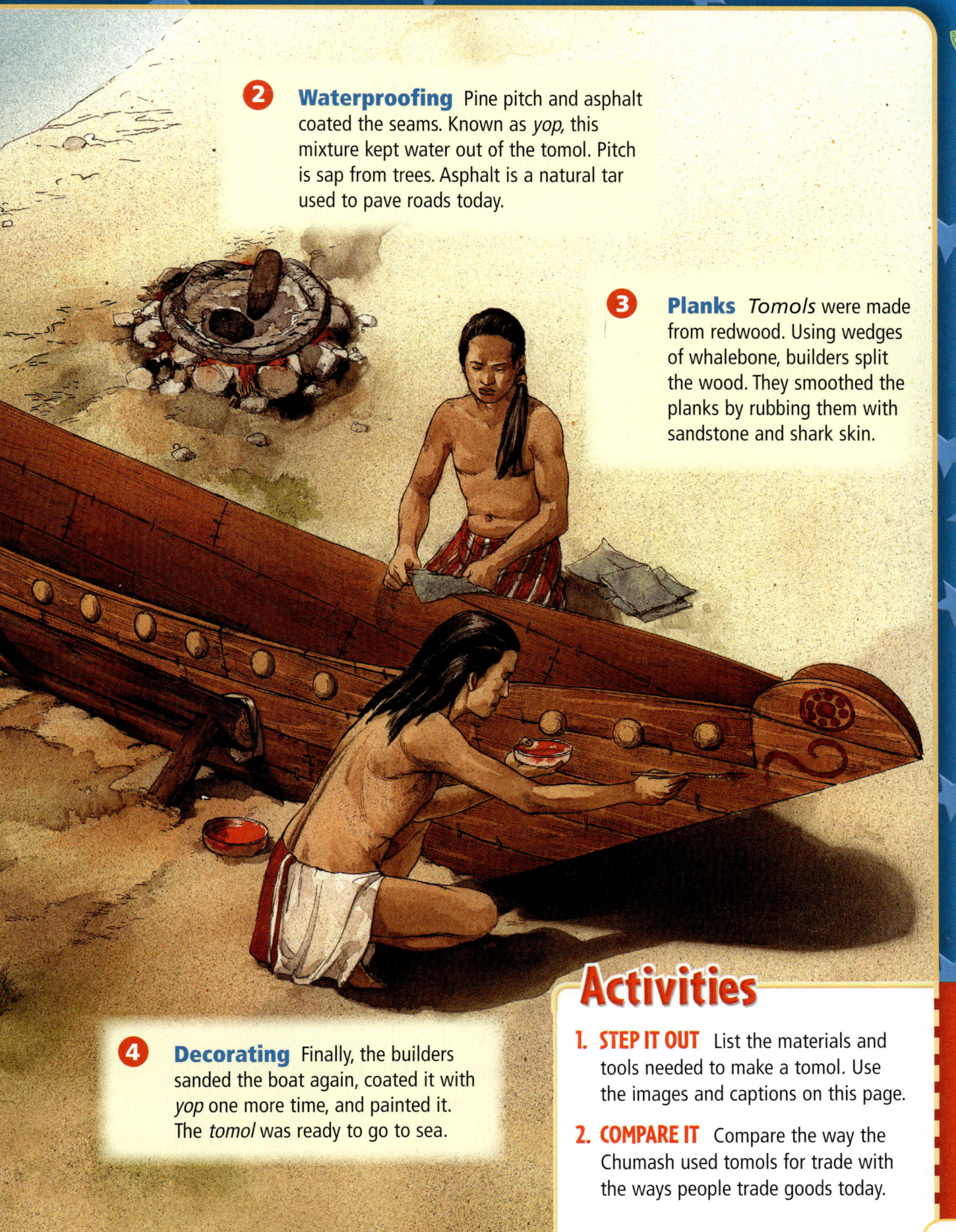

2 **Waterproofing** Pine pitch and asphalt coated the seams. Known as *yop*, this mixture kept water out of the tomol. Pitch is sap from trees. Asphalt is a natural tar used to pave roads today.

3 **Planks** *Tomols* were made from redwood. Using wedges of whalebone, builders split the wood. They smoothed the planks by rubbing them with sandstone and shark skin.

4 **Decorating** Finally, the builders sanded the boat again, coated it with *yop* one more time, and painted it. The *tomol* was ready to go to sea.

Activities

1. **STEP IT OUT** List the materials and tools needed to make a tomol. Use the images and captions on this page.

2. **COMPARE IT** Compare the way the Chumash used tomols for trade with the ways people trade goods today.

Skillbuilder

Use Reference Materials

VOCABULARY
atlas
index
encyclopedia
Web site
search engine

Use reference materials to find out more about California Indians. Reference materials include books or electronic materials, such as encyclopedias, atlases, and dictionaries. Nonfiction books, newspapers, magazines, and the Internet are other sources of information. You can find these in your library.

Learn the Skill

Step 1: Write some questions you want to answer. For example: What do people use tomols for today?

Step 2: Underline the topic or key words in your question. Key words are the most important words. The key words in the question above are "tomol" and "today."

Step 3: Choose reference materials or other sources that might have the information you need.

Step 4: Use the key words to look up information in the sources you chose.

STANDARDS Analysis Skill REPV 2

Reference Material	How to Find Information
An **atlas** contains many different kinds of maps. 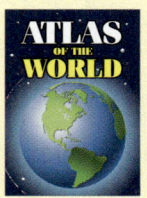	Look in the index for the location you want to find. The **index** is in the back of the atlas. It is an alphabetized list of locations included in the book.
An **encyclopedia** has information about people, places, and events. 	Find the volume that includes the first letter of the topic. If your topic isn't listed, think of a bigger idea that your topic might be a part of.
An Internet **Web site** is a source of information that can be found online by using a computer. 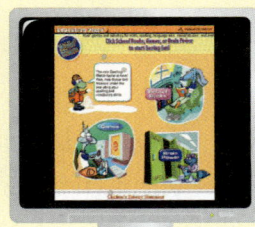	Type your topic into a search engine. A **search engine** is a Web site that helps you find other Web sites. A search engine will show you a list of Web sites related to the topic.

Practice the Skill

1. What are the key words in the question "What did the Yurok use to make their houses?"

2. Which reference source do you think would be most helpful in locating the Channel Islands off the California coast?

3. Suppose you want to find out more about the baskets that California Indians made. Which reference materials and sources do you think would be most helpful? How would you use them?

Apply the Skill

Review the information in Lesson 2, pages 48–51. Think of a topic that you would like to know more about. Use one or two of the reference materials named above to learn about the topic. Write a short paragraph about your findings.

55

Core Lesson 3

Mountain and Valley Peoples

VOCABULARY

culture
ceremony
tradition

Vocabulary Strategy

tradition

A synonym for **tradition** is **practice**. Both are ways of life passed down by members of a group.

READING SKILL
Compare and Contrast
Note ways in which life in the mountains differed from life in the valleys.

STANDARDS
Core: HSS 4.2.1
Extend support: HSS 4.2.1

Miwok House The Miwok built houses from wood and other materials found in the area.

Build on What You Know How did you learn how to celebrate special days or events in your life? Among California Indians of the mountains and valleys, older people taught children how to celebrate.

Valley and Mountain Life

Main Idea People used the resources of river valleys and mountains.

Over time, people who settled in the Central Valley and the Sierra Nevada developed different cultures. A **culture** is the way of life, including beliefs, language, and foods, of a group of people. The cultures of this region included the Maidu, the Miwok, the Karuk, and the Yokut.

Each culture included several nations, and each nation had a number of towns. People who shared a culture had similar languages and beliefs, but they did not act as one. People of one Yokut nation did not feel they belonged to the same group as any other Yokut nation.

56 • Chapter 2

Mountain Life

Many Yokut, Miwok, and Maidu lived in the foothills of the Sierra Nevada. Their lives were different from those of the same culture groups who lived in the valley. Mountain people built shelters as protection from cold winter weather. They covered their cone-shaped houses with tree bark. The thick bark kept out the wind and kept in the heat from fires. In the summer, they built shelters out of reeds for shade from the sun.

Each year mountain people left their towns and moved up or down the hills to find the best sources of food. They ate acorns and fish. Acorns were a major food source in the foothills. People also gathered rye grass, pine nuts, and other plants. They hunted for large animals such as deer, elk, and bears. Hunters also caught rabbits, quail, and other small animals.

REVIEW In what ways did people use resources in the mountains?

Living in Different Regions
Some nations were in the Central Valley, while others were located in the mountains around it.

SKILL Reading Maps Which nations lived near the Kawaiisu?

Central Valley Life

Main Idea California Indians in the Central Valley had plentiful resources.

Miwoks and Yokuts in the Central Valley lived in an almost ideal place. The climate was mild. Many rivers flowed into the valley and brought a steady supply of fresh water. Plants grew well in the good soil. Fish, birds, and land animals made homes there.

People in the Central Valley depended on the resources around them, and with so many resources, they did not have to travel far for food or shelter. Some groups stayed in one place all year long.

Food in the Valley

The Central Valley had plentiful food resources. The northern valley's oak trees supplied acorns. Gathering acorns was a common yearly activity among Miwoks and northern Yokuts. People also gathered wild grasses, nuts, and roots for food.

Miwoks and Yokuts hunted for elk, rabbits, and birds. Fish were another valuable source of food in the valley. Some Yokut towns were built near the marshy wetlands of the southern valley. People in these southern towns used boats made of reeds to fish for trout. Yokuts in the northern valley trapped salmon with nets.

Resources in the Valley This image shows an artist's idea of how the Central Valley's plant and animal life might have looked 500 years ago.

Building Homes

People in the Central Valley wove reeds and grasses to make their houses. The weather there was usually warm. In the northern Central Valley, houses were dug into the earth.

In the southern Central Valley, people built towns that they lived in all year round. Some of their houses held one family. Other houses were very long, and held ten or more families. In such houses, each family had its own fireplace and door.

Miwoks and Yokuts also built special structures for ceremonies. A **ceremony** is a formal act held to honor an event or belief. These ceremonies included prayers and songs.

Living by Traditions

California Indian traditions guided what people wore, the way they married, and what they believed. A **tradition** is a way of life that is handed down over many years.

Some traditions affected how people gathered food. For example, Miwok tradition allowed people to own oak trees. They ate acorns from their own oaks. However, Miwok traditions also said that people could not eat certain foods, such as eagle. The valley offered many other food resources they could eat instead.

REVIEW What resources did people in the Central Valley have available?

California ground squirrel

California Indian Religions

Main Idea California Indians passed down religions, beliefs, and stories over many years.

Like other nations, mountain and valley peoples held special ceremonies. Such ceremonies were often based on people's religion. Dancing was part of many religious ceremonies. For example, the Maidu danced during ceremonies to honor the grizzly bear and the coming of spring.

Shamans often led ceremonies. A shaman is a healer and a religious leader. Some of the ceremonies told stories about gods. The Maidu held ceremonies to honor the god World Maker, as well as other beings.

The Miwok, Maidu, Karuk, and Yokut all had stories about powerful beings or animals, such as Coyote and Eagle. In some stories, Coyote creates the first people. He was not always helpful, however. In other stories, he makes trouble by hiding the sun or creating mountains.

Children learned about their culture and religion from parents and grandparents. Through songs, oral histories, ceremonies, and art, they learned to live as their ancestors had. An ancestor is a relative who lived a long time ago. People learn about their culture this way today as well.

Stories and Culture A California Indian storyteller shares a story with children. The feather skirt on the right was worn for Miwok dances.

Living Cultures

Today, California Indians are teachers, builders, and government officials. Like many Californians, they keep their culture alive by practicing their traditions and speaking the language of their ancestors.

The Maidu still dance to celebrate spring and to honor the grizzly bear. Some Miwoks practice traditions such as making baskets and playing games.

REVIEW What do California Indians do to carry on their traditions?

Lesson Summary

California Indians living in mountains and valleys used nearby resources for food and housing. Their cultures included ceremonies, dances, and games. People carry on these cultures today.

Why It Matters...

Like people today, the California Indians of the Central Valley depended on resources for food and shelter.

Lily Baker She is a Maidu who weaves baskets from thin willow branches.

Lesson Review

1. **VOCABULARY** Write a paragraph about California Indian life, using the words **culture** and **tradition**.

2. **READING SKILL** Make a diagram to **compare** and **contrast** the foods eaten by people in the Central Valley and the Sierra Nevada.

3. **MAIN IDEA: Geography** Why did people in the Central Valley and the Sierra Nevada live in different kinds of houses?

4. **MAIN IDEA: Culture** What are two features of Miwok culture?

5. **CRITICAL THINKING: Synthesize** What changes might people from the Sierra Nevada have made to their way of life if they had moved to the Central Valley?

WRITING ACTIVITY Write a summary of information in the lesson about the traditions of California Indians of the Central Valley and Sierra Nevada.

1. HSS 4.2.1   2. HSS 4.2.1   3. HSS 4.2.1   4. HSS 4.2.1   5. HSS 4.2.1   Activity HSS 4.2.1

Extend Lesson 3
History

SPORTS and GAMES

Two teams face each other, ready to play. The ball drops and the game begins. Players dash from one end of the field to the other, knocking the ball towards the other team's goal with their sticks. This is a traditional Yurok game that is played today.

Games are a tradition in many **cultures.** Some games played by children and adults hundreds of years ago are still enjoyed today. Among those played by California Indians are *peon*, *ama'ty*, and hoop games. What traditional games do you play?

Hoop and Pole

Yokuts and other California Indian nations played team hoop games.

- A hoop made of tree bark was rolled back and forth between two teams.

- Players tried to throw poles through the hoop.

- A team won two points every time a player threw a pole through the hoop.

- Players laughed, yelled, and tried to distract the other team.

62 • Chapter 2

Peon

Guessing games were popular in many parts of California. In one common game, players guessed in which hand another player held a marked stick or bone. This game was known as *peon* (PAY own) in southern California.

- Players from one team held small deer bones in their hands, one in each fist.

- Each player held one bone that was marked with a piece of string.

- A player on the other team tried to guess which hands held the marked bones.

Ama'ty

Miwok and Maidu women played *ama'ty* in teams.

- Players used small baskets to throw and catch a ball.

- They aimed to throw the ball between the other team's goalposts.

- The first team to score a goal won the game. However, scoring one goal could take hours.

Activities

1. DRAW IT Make a picture of people playing one of the games described on these pages.

2. WRITE IT What natural resources were used to make the equipment on this page? Do research to find out how objects were made. Report on what you find.

63

Core Lesson 4

Desert Life

Build on What You Know Your community has leaders, such as a mayor. Long ago, California Indian communities and towns had leaders, too.

Adapting to the Desert

Main Idea California Indians adapted to life in the desert.

Much of southern and eastern California is desert. Summer days are blazing hot, but temperatures fall at night. The Cahuilla (ka HWEE ya), Kumeyaay (KOO may eye), Mohave (moe HAH vee), and other peoples adapted to these desert areas.

Like other California Indians, desert peoples were hunter-gatherers. **Hunter-gatherers** collected food by hunting animals and gathering plants. They moved from place to place to harvest ripe plants or to find water when wells and streams dried up. The Cahuilla, however, built towns near steady springs or streams. Hunter-gatherers brought food to the town.

Desert Home The Cahuilla lived in places where water could be found, such as Palm Canyon, near Palm Springs.

VOCABULARY

hunter-gatherer
agriculture
government
leadership

Vocabulary Strategy

government

Find the word **govern** in **government**. A government is a person or group that governs.

READING SKILL
Problem and Solution
List problems of desert life and ways people met each challenge.

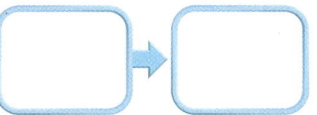

Core: HSS 4.2.1
Extend support: HSS 4.2.1

64 • Chapter 2

Dry Lands The deserts in California's southeast have been home to nations such as the Cahuilla, who used arrowheads such as these to hunt.

Desert Nations

Gathering in the Desert

People found resources even in the desert. In the mountains and hills, which got more rain, they gathered more than 100 types of roots, seeds, berries, and nuts. They fished in the streams. In the dry lower desert, people gathered cactus fruit and the seedpods of mesquite trees. They ground up the pods to make a food of mush or cakes. To hunt, the Cahuilla used nets, sticks, and bows and arrows. They caught rabbits and other desert animals.

For shelter during the summer, people built homes without walls. A roof held up by poles gave them shade. For colder weather, they built houses using brush, wood, and bark.

Farming in the Desert

Unlike most California Indian nations, desert people used agriculture. **Agriculture** is farming. The Cahuilla, for example, grew crops such as melons, squash, beans, and corn. They dug deep wells in places where water was hard to find. They carried well water to their crops in clay jars.

The Mohave lived near the Colorado River. Each year, the river flooded. Floods left soft mud on the land beside the river. Crops grew well in this rich soil. The Mohave planted pumpkins, beans, and corn on these flood areas.

REVIEW What did California Indians in the desert do to find water?

Government

Main Idea Most California Indian communities were led by chiefs.

Like other nations, people in the desert worked together. That way, they could collect enough food and water for everyone. To organize themselves, desert people set up governments. A **government** is a system for making and carrying out laws for a group of people.

In California, chiefs usually led family groups or towns. Among the Cahuilla, the job of chief was handed down from father to son. Other groups chose their leaders. In some nations, women were chiefs. People expected chiefs to provide honest, wise leadership. **Leadership** is guidance.

Chiefs and Councils

Chiefs were usually wealthy and did not need to farm or hunt. People paid chiefs with items such as food and blankets. In return, they expected chiefs to share their wealth by helping people in need. If a chief did not show good leadership or did not share wealth, he or she might be replaced.

Cahuilla chiefs decided when people would gather or hunt. They settled arguments about property. They also met with other chiefs to decide if their people would go to war. Councils helped chiefs make big decisions. The council was usually a group made up of respected older people. Today, Cahuilla nations have governments organized into councils of five people.

Modern Leaders The council of the Agua Caliente Band of Cahuilla Indians in Palm Springs meets to discuss issues that affect their future.

Social Organization

Most California Indians were part of a family, town, or another small group. Many organized themselves by clans. A clan is a large group of people who share an ancestor. The Cahuilla had about twelve clans.

Small groups of desert people usually governed themselves. However, Mohave groups also worked together in ways that groups in other nations did not. They saw themselves as one large nation. During wars, Mohave towns fought together against their enemies. By working together, they protected themselves.

REVIEW What reasons did people have for working together in desert communities?

Lesson Summary

- Hunter-gatherers moved around to find food and water in the desert.
- Some groups, such as the Cahuilla and Mohave, grew food.
- People set up governments, usually led by chiefs, so that they could work together.

Why It Matters...

California Indians living in the desert showed us how people can adapt to a dry climate.

Californians Today These Kumeyaay girls are among the California Indians that live in the state's desert areas.

Lesson Review

1. **VOCABULARY** Write a sentence telling what **hunter-gatherers** did.

2. **READING SKILL** Compare the **solutions** the Cahuilla and Mohave found for the **problem** of watering their crops.

3. **MAIN IDEA: Geography** What resources did desert people use for food, tools, and shelter?

4. **MAIN IDEA: Government** What was the job of a chief in California Indian desert communities?

5. **CRITICAL THINKING: Analyze** What skills do you think the chief of a desert community would need to be admired and followed? Explain your answer.

WRITING ACTIVITY Summarize the information on pages 66–67, explaining what California Indian nations in the desert did to organize themselves. Be sure to include the main ideas and details.

Extend Lesson 4

Biographies

Ancient Traditions, Modern Lives

From scholars to artists, more than 300,000 California Indians live and work in our state today. Like other people, they take part in modern California culture but also pass on their own cultures. The people in this lesson use art or teaching to share their cultures.

Mitchell E. Robles, *Painter*

"I've spent a lot of time cycling through mountains, forests and deserts," says Mitchell Robles. Like his Chumash ancestors, he shows the natural world in his art. His family has lived near Santa Barbara for hundreds of years. Robles uses images from American Indian culture, such as the shape of an eagle or a buffalo, in his colorful paintings.

CHARACTER TRAIT: Civic Virtue

Katherine Siva Saubel, *Scholar*

Katherine Siva Saubel (SEE vah SOH bell) grew up near San Diego. She learned to speak Cahuilla from her parents. Saubel has written grammar books and a dictionary of the Cahuilla language. A book she wrote about her own life is called *A Dried Coyote Tail*. Saubel helped start the Malki Museum, a museum about American Indians of southern California and the Great Basin. She is a member of the National Women's Hall of Fame.

David Risling, *Community Leader*

David Risling, a Hupa, was one of the first California Indians to graduate from a university. He taught Native American studies and set up education programs for American Indians. He also led the Native American Rights Fund, which offers legal help to American Indians. In 1992, the University of California at Davis gave David Risling an award for his work in American Indian education.

Activities

1. **TALK ABOUT IT** Discuss what the people in this lesson have done that shows **civic virtue**.

2. **REPORT IT** Find out more about one person from this lesson. Prepare a report telling what you learned.

  Biographies Visit Education Place for more biographies. Go to www.eduplace.com/kids/hmss/

Chapter 2 Review

Visual Summary

1–3. Write a description of each item shown below.

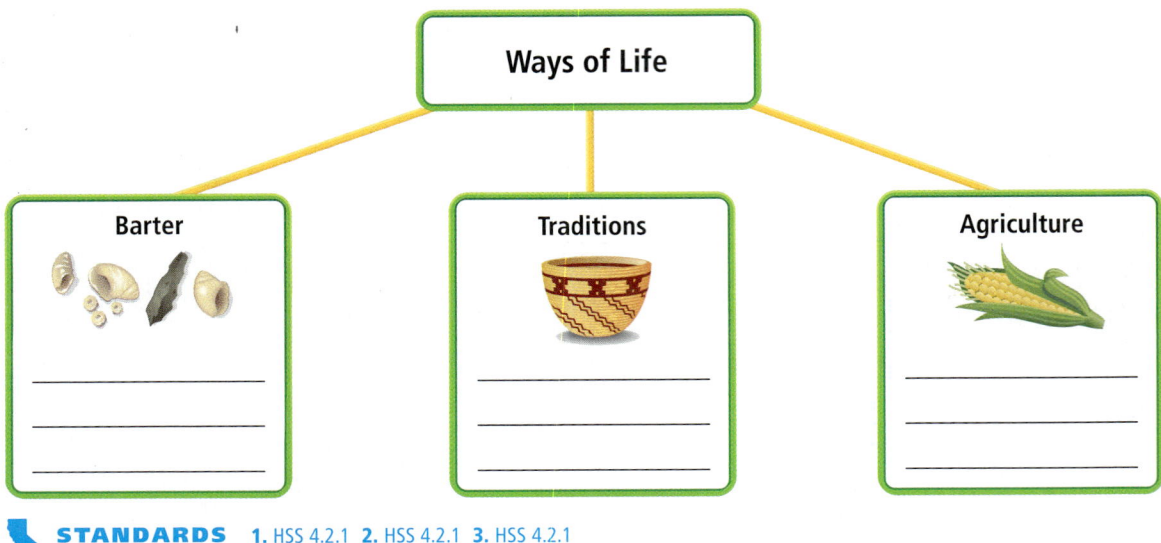

STANDARDS 1. HSS 4.2.1 2. HSS 4.2.1 3. HSS 4.2.1

Facts and Main Ideas

Answer each question below.

4. **Geography** What do scientists believe life was like for people in California 10,000 years ago?

5. **Economics** What was one of the goods traded by California Indians? What was one of the services?

6. **Geography** Why did California Indians in different regions collect and eat different foods?

7. **Government** Why were chiefs and councils important in desert communities?

4. HSS 4.2.1 5. HSS 4.2.1 6. HSS 4.2.1 7. HSS 4.2.1

Vocabulary

Choose the correct word from the list below to complete each sentence.

adapt, p. 42
economy, p. 50
tradition, p. 59

8. Some modern California Indians, including the Maidu, carry on the _____ of making baskets.

9. People in different parts of California were able to _____ to their environment.

10. The Chumash used both barter and shell money in their trading _____.

8. HSS 4.2.1 9. HSS 4.2.1 10. HSS 4.2.1

CHAPTER SUMMARY TIMELINE

- 10,000 years ago — People in California
- 500 years ago — More than 300,000 California Indians

12,000 years ago | 9,000 years ago | 6,000 years ago | 3,000 years ago | Today

Apply Skills

Use Reference Materials Use what you have learned about reference materials to answer each question.

11. Which source would you look at first to find out general information about California Indians?

    A. newspaper
    B. photo album
    C. encyclopedia
    D. dictionary

12. What would be the best way to find out whether a book titled *American Indians of the West* has information about the Yurok?

    A. Look up "Yurok" in the index.
    B. Read the book cover.
    C. Use a search engine to look for the book.
    D. Look at the pictures.

11. Analysis Skill REPV 2 12. Analysis Skill REPV 2

Critical Thinking

Write a paragraph to answer each question below.

13. **Analyze** In what way did living in the desert affect the ways of life of the Cahuilla and Mohave?

14. **Evaluate** Why do you think most California Indians were hunter-gatherers, while desert peoples used agriculture to grow food?

Timeline

Use the Chapter Summary Timeline above to answer the question.

15. About how many people lived in California 500 years ago?

13. HSS 4.2.1 14. HSS 4.2.1 15. HSS 4.2.1

Activities

Science Activity Find out about one resource California Indians used. Make a display showing where it could be found and why it was useful.

Writing Activity Write a description of trade between the Chumash and Channel Island people.

Activities HSS 4.2.1, HSS 4.2.1, W 2.4

Technology
Writing Process Tips
Get help with your writing at www.eduplace.com/kids/hmss/

71

UNIT 1 Review

Vocabulary and Main Ideas

Write a sentence to answer each question.

1. Name some things people do that affect the **environment.**

2. Describe what the **climate** of the Central Valley is like.

3. Why do people have to use **nonrenewable resources** wisely?

4. In what ways did California Indian nations **adapt** to life in different areas?

5. What was the purpose of trade in the California Indian **economy?**

6. Give a reason why some California Indians may have farmed instead of being **hunter-gatherers.**

Critical Thinking

Write a short paragraph to answer each question.

7. **Apply** Compare the landforms and resources of the coast and desert.

8. **Synthesize** Do you think it was harder for California Indians to adapt to the mountains or the desert? Explain your answer.

Apply Skills

Use the map of California below and what you have learned about map skills to answer each question.

9. Which of the following cities is farthest north?

    A. Los Angeles
    B. Sacramento
    C. Bakersfield
    D. Redding

10. About how many miles is it from San Francisco to Sacramento? Use the map scale to find the answer.

    A. 25 miles
    B. 50 miles
    C. 100 miles
    D. 350 miles

STANDARDS 1. HSS 4.1.3 2. HSS 4.1.3 3. HSS 4.1.3 4. HSS 4.2.1
5. HSS 4.2.1 6. HSS 4.2.1 7. HSS 4.1.3
8. HSS 4.2.1 9. Analysis Skill CST 4
10. Analysis Skill CST 4 **Activity** HSS 4.1.3, W 1.1

Unit Activity

Create a Guidebook

- List the features of a region or city in California that interests you.
- Find or create pictures, maps, and photographs that show the place you chose.
- Prepare a booklet that would show someone what the place is like.

WEEKLY READER
Current Events

Connect to Today

Create a display about a traditional activity that takes place today.

- Find information about a traditional activity that takes place today, such as a harvest or other seasonal festival.
- Write a description that explains why the activity began, and why it is still carried on today.
- Find pictures of the traditional activity.
- Create a display with the information and pictures you find.

 Technology
Weekly Reader online offers social studies articles. Go to:
www.eduplace.com/kids/hmss/

At the Library

You may find these books at your school or public library.

Uniquely California by Stephen Feinstein
Symbols, songs, flags, landmarks, and even recipes make California unique.

The Bone Man: A Native American Modoc Tale by Laura Simms
Nulwee's grandmother tells him he is destined to defeat the terrifying Bone Man.

Read About It

Look in your classroom for these Social Studies Independent Books.

73

UNIT 2

Exploration and Colonization

The Big Idea

Why do people move to a new land?

"[here is] a country... with fine forests in the north; the waters filled with fish, and the plains covered with thousands of herds of cattle..."

—from *Two Years Before the Mast* by Richard Henry Dana American trader, 1841

Francis Drake
1540(?)–1596

Drake loaded his ship with so much treasure it almost sank. He stopped in California to make repairs and claimed the land for England. **page 83**

History Makers

Maria Ontiveros Yorba
1833–1894
Yorba's ranch stretched for 25 miles along the Santa Ana River. Rancheras like her earned their living by raising cattle.
page 133

James Beckwourth
1798–1867
Beckwourth traveled all over the West, trapping and trading. He was so well known and respected that the Crow people made him a chief. **page 139**

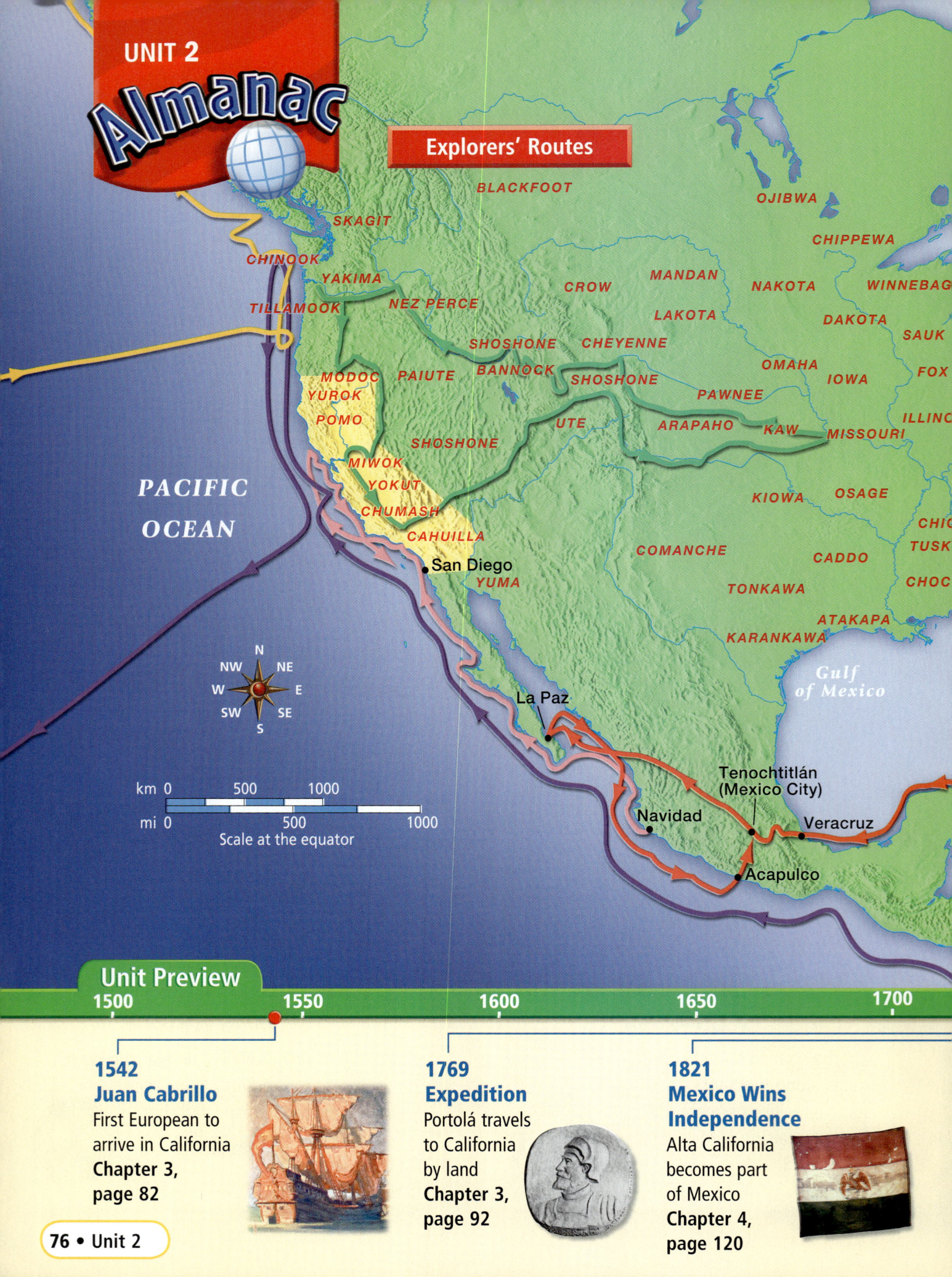

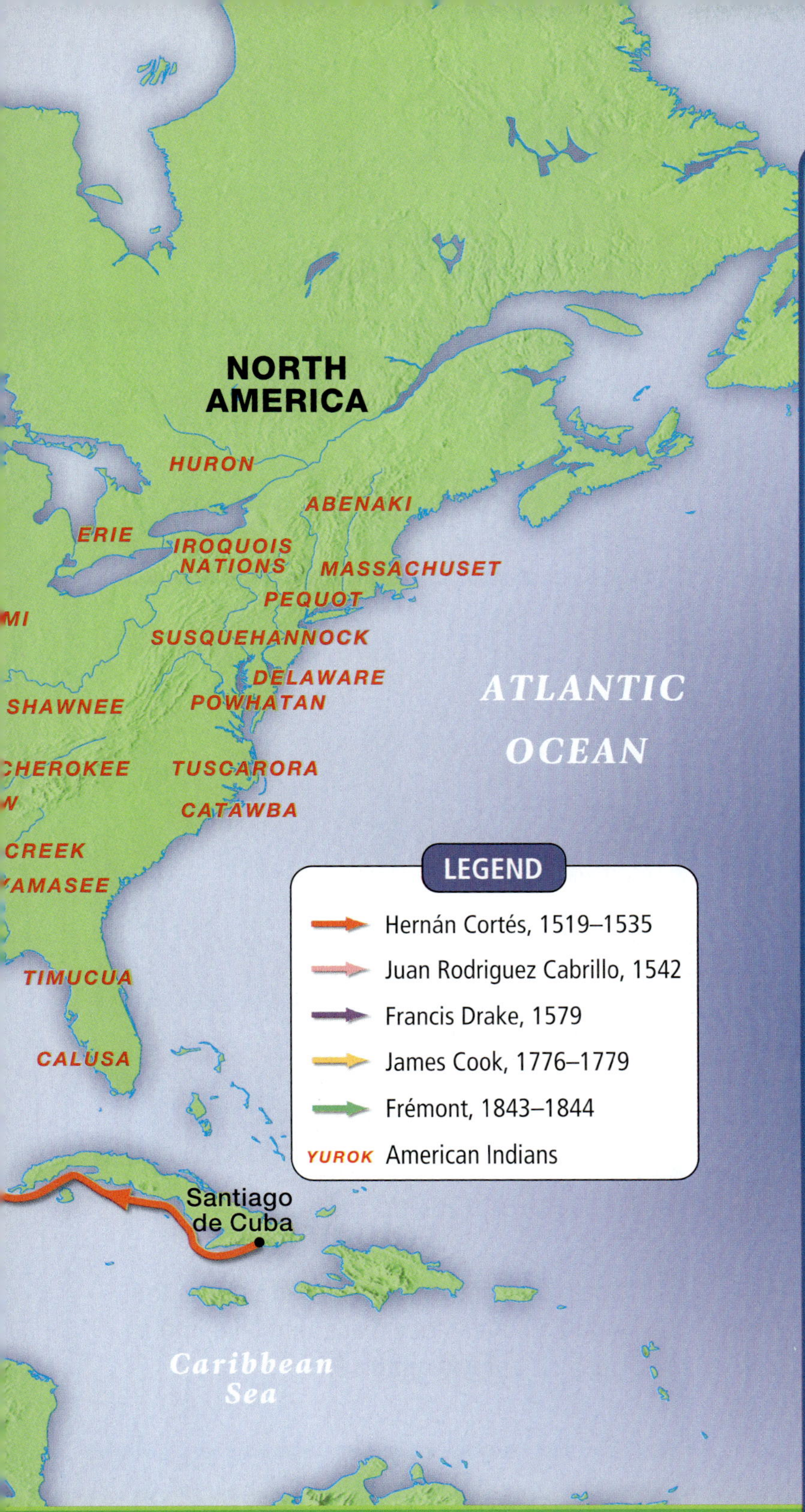

NORTH AMERICA

HURON
ABENAKI
ERIE
IROQUOIS NATIONS
MASSACHUSET
PEQUOT
MI
SUSQUEHANNOCK
DELAWARE
SHAWNEE
POWHATAN

ATLANTIC OCEAN

CHEROKEE
TUSCARORA
CATAWBA
CREEK
YAMASEE
TIMUCUA
CALUSA

LEGEND
→ Hernán Cortés, 1519–1535
→ Juan Rodriguez Cabrillo, 1542
→ Francis Drake, 1579
→ James Cook, 1776–1779
→ Frémont, 1843–1844
YUROK American Indians

Santiago de Cuba

Caribbean Sea

1750 — 1800 — 1850

1841
Bidwell Party
Settlers from the United States arrive in Alta California
Chapter 4, page 140

Connect to Today

Sailing to California, 1500s

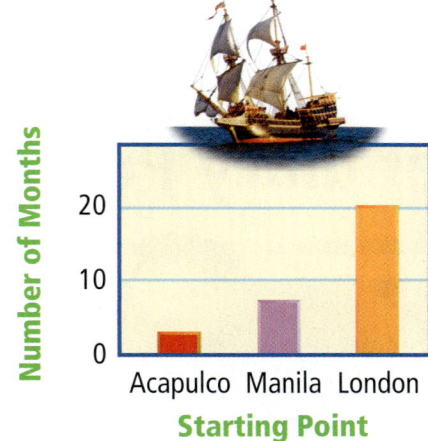

Number of Months
Acapulco Manila London
Starting Point

Flying to California Today

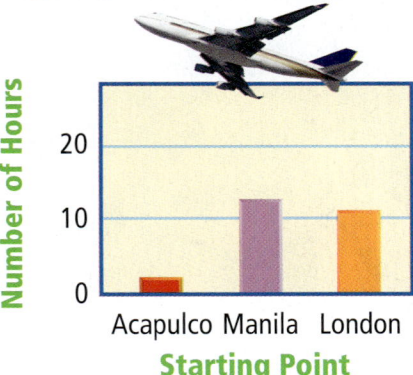

Number of Hours
Acapulco Manila London
Starting Point

What route had the longest travel time by ship? What route has the longest travel time by plane? Why are the answers to these questions different?

WEEKLY READER
Current Events

Current events on the web!
For a selection of social studies articles about current events, go to:
www.eduplace.com/kids/hmss/

77

Chapter 3
Spanish California

Vocabulary Preview

Technology
- e • glossary
- e • word games
www.eduplace.com/kids/hmss/

conquistador
Hernán Cortés was a **conquistador.** He took control of large areas of what is now Mexico. **page 81**

colony
Spain sent priests, settlers, and soldiers to Alta California. They made that land into a Spanish **colony.** **page 91**

Chapter Timeline

1542 Cabrillo reaches Alta California

1579 Drake lands in northern California

1500 — 1550 — 1600 — 1650

Reading Strategy

Summarize As you read, use the summarize strategy to focus on important ideas.

 Review the main idea. Then look for details that support the main idea.

missionary
Junípero Serra was the first **missionary** in Alta California. He wanted to teach his religion to California Indians. **page 92**

presidio
The Spanish built **presidios** along the coast of Alta California. Soldiers in these forts guarded the colony. **page 109**

1769 Portolá explores California by land

1823 Last mission founded

1700 — 1750 — 1800 — 1850

Core Lesson 1

First Europeans in California

VOCABULARY

conquistador
peninsula
current

Vocabulary Strategy

current

Two synonyms for **current** are **flow** and **stream**. All of these words are related to water.

 READING SKILL
Compare and Contrast Note similarities and differences among early explorers.

 **STANDARDS**

Core: HSS 4.2, 4.2.2, Analysis Skill HI 1
Extend support: HSS 4.2.2

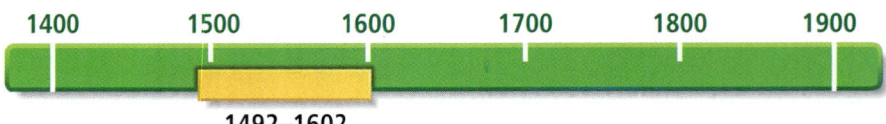

1492–1602

Build on What You Know How long do you think it would take travelers from Asia or Europe to reach California by jet today? In the 1500s, it took explorers many months on small ships.

A Search for Riches

Main Idea European explorers found California when they looked for a way to reach Asia.

In 1492, a sailor named **Christopher Columbus** sailed west across the Atlantic Ocean from Spain. He hoped to find a new trade route to Asia so that he could trade for spices, gold, and other Asian goods. Instead, he landed in North America. Europeans at that time did not know about this continent.

Christopher Columbus
Born in Italy, Columbus explored the Atlantic Ocean for Spain on his journey in 1492.

Hernán Cortés He met with the Aztec leader in 1519. Later, Cortés defeated the Aztecs and took their land for Spain. A Spanish helmet from the time is shown on the right.

Explorers from Europe

Spain's rulers sent conquistadors to North America to find gold and new lands. The word **conquistador** means conqueror in Spanish. Conquistadors took large areas of land from the American Indians already there.

A Spanish conquistador named **Hernán Cortés** (ehr NAN kohr TEHS) conquered the Aztec people of present-day Mexico in 1521. The lands he took from the Aztecs he called New Spain. Cortés sent a group of explorers up the Pacific coast. He hoped that they would find a waterway through North America. Such a waterway would help shorten the distance that ships had to sail between Europe and Asia.

Naming California

In 1535, the explorers found land they thought was an island. They called it California. A book of the 1500s spoke of an imaginary island called California.

The land the Spanish named California was not an island, however. It was a peninsula. A **peninsula** is land surrounded by water on three sides.

The Spanish called the peninsula Baja (BAH hah) California. *Baja* means "lower" in Spanish. They called the land to the north Alta California. *Alta* means "upper." Alta California is now the state of California in the United States. Baja California is in Mexico.

REVIEW Why did Spain's rulers send conquistadors to North America?

81

Exploring the Coast

Main Idea In the 1500s, sailors from Spain and England explored the coast of California.

In 1542, **Juan Rodríguez Cabrillo** (wahn roh DREE gehz cah BREE oh) led an expedition from New Spain. An expedition is a trip taken for a reason. The reason Cabrillo sailed was to look for a waterway through North America. He took about 250 sailors. Some in his crew were enslaved American Indians and Africans.

Cabrillo sailed north up the coast of Baja California. After months of sailing, he came to the area where San Diego is today. He became the first European sailor to visit Alta California.

Alta California

Cabrillo met people of different California Indian nations, including the Kumeyaay, Tongva, and Chumash. Cabrillo wrote that the Chumash had "many very good canoes." Some of the Chumash, including the woman who was their leader, canoed to his ship. The Chumash gave the sailors wood, water, and fish.

The expedition sailed most of the way up the coast of California. Farther north, rough waters forced the ships to turn back. The expedition returned to Navidad, New Spain, the next year. There was no waterway through North America, but Cabrillo's ships were the first to explore Alta California's coast.

Cabrillo's Arrival Juan Rodríguez Cabrillo led the first European expedition to land ships in Alta California.

Routes of Cabrillo and Drake

Sailing to California Cabrillo and Drake both reached Alta California by sailing north.

SKILL Reading Maps Where did Cabrillo begin his journey?

The Manila Galleons

In the 1500s, the Spanish were more interested in Asia's wealth than in California. They had captured some Pacific islands that were rich in spices. They named them the Philippines after Spain's king, **Philip II**. Manila was the islands' largest Spanish port.

By the late 1500s, Spanish ships known as galleons carried silver from New Spain to Manila. Traders bought spices, silk, and other goods in Manila. Sometimes Filipinos joined the galleon crews and sailed with them back to New Spain. The ships became known as Manila galleons.

Elizabeth I, Queen of England, wanted to stop the Manila galleons because they made Spain richer. Spain and England were enemies at this time.

Drake's Voyage

Queen Elizabeth sent **Francis Drake** to the Americas to keep treasure away from Spain. Drake captured Spanish ships loaded with treasure.

By 1579, Drake's ship carried so much treasure that it was sinking. Drake stopped to fix his ship along the Alta California coast, perhaps near Drakes Bay. He spent 36 days with the people there, probably the Coast Miwok. Drake said Alta California belonged to England, but Spain still felt it owned the land.

After Drake's voyage, the Spanish sent more ships to Alta California. They wanted to keep ships from other countries away from Alta California.

REVIEW What did Cabrillo and Drake find when they came to Alta California?

Vizcaíno's Expedition, 1602

Seeking a Harbor This map shows some of California's natural harbors. Vizcaíno (above) thought Monterey was one of them.

A Dangerous Coast

One sailor described Alta California's coast this way:

"There are mountains that reach the sky, and the sea beats upon them. When sailing along near the land, it seems as if the mountains would fall upon the ships."

In 1602, **Sebastián Vizcaíno** (seh bahs tee AHN vihz kah EE noh) led another expedition to Alta California. He sailed up the coast, naming places as he went. He named Santa Barbara, Santa Catalina Island, and San Diego.

Vizcaíno watched for good harbors. Harbors that protected ships from wind and waves were hard to find. As Vizcaíno sailed north, he thought he saw a harbor that was "sheltered from all the winds." He named the place Monterey Bay.

Barriers To Travel

Main Idea Getting to California was difficult for Europeans because of physical barriers.

Sailors traveling to Alta California from other parts of New Spain faced problems. They had to sail against wind currents from the northwest. A **current** is a flow of something, such as wind or water. The crews also had to steer against water currents that flowed from north to south.

Desert Barrier Crossing the dry Sonoran Desert was one of the many challenges of reaching Alta California by land.

Exploration Ends

As it turned out, Vizcaíno was wrong about Monterey Bay. Winds blew right into the bay. Ships were not protected there.

After Vizcaíno's voyage, the government of New Spain stopped sending explorers to Alta California. It was too difficult to reach by sea. Traveling there by land was also very difficult. Deserts and high mountains blocked the way from towns in New Spain. The challenge of reaching Alta California kept the Spanish from settling there for more than 150 years.

REVIEW Why did the Spanish stop exploring Alta California after Vizcaíno's expedition?

Lesson Summary

- Conquistadors searched for riches and for a water route to Asia.
- Explorers sailed up the California coast and made contact with Chumash and Miwok Indians.
- The Spanish stopped exploring Alta California after Vizcaíno's 1602 expedition.

Why It Matters...

Early explorers gave many places along the coast the names they still have today, such as San Diego.

Lesson Review

1. **VOCABULARY** Write a few sentences about early exploration of California using the words **expedition** and **current.**

2. **READING SKILL Compare** Vizcaíno's voyage with Drake's. Which voyage do you think was more successful? Why?

3. **MAIN IDEA: Economics** Why did explorers want to find a sea route to Asia?

4. **MAIN IDEA: Geography** What made exploring California difficult?

5. **TIMELINE SKILL** Which expedition came first, Cortés's or Cabrillo's?

6. **CRITICAL THINKING: Analyze** Make a chart to categorize the different reasons explorers sailed to Alta California.

ART ACTIVITY Reread the quote about the coast of California on page 84. Make an illustrated map of what the coast might have looked like to early explorers.

1. HSS 4.2.2 2. HSS 4.2.2 3. HSS 4.2.2 4. HSS 4.2.2 5. HSS 4.2.2 6. HSS 4.2.2 Activity HSS 4.2.2

Extend Lesson 1
Geography

MANILA GALLEONS
Using Wind and Water

A lookout sees land on the horizon. Acapulco at last! The Manila galleons sailed 18,000 miles to carry cinnamon, pepper, pearls, and silk to New Spain.

Sailors used wind and ocean currents to make the trip easier. One current carried them west to the Philippines. Other currents took the ships back east to Alta California. Even with the currents, the journey east could take seven to nine months. The entire trip, across the Pacific Ocean and back, often took a year or more. The galleons sailed this route for 250 years.

Manila Galleons' Route

1. Ships loaded with silver from New Spain left Acapulco.

2. From Acapulco, the ships caught a westward current to Manila.

3. Ships sailed north from Manila to find eastward currents.

4. After reaching Cape Mendocino, the ships followed a swift current south to Acapulco.

86 • Chapter 3

Equator

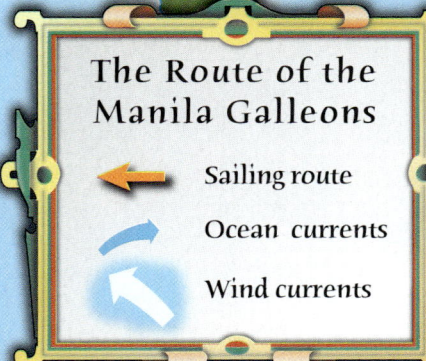

The Route of the Manila Galleons

→ Sailing route
⇢ Ocean currents
⇢ Wind currents

Activities

1. **TALK ABOUT IT** Use the atlas of the world on pages R26–R27 to identify landforms on the map.

2. **WRITE ABOUT IT** Think about the supplies you would want if you were taking a year-long journey across the ocean. Write an explanation of why you would want each thing.

Map and Globe Skills

Skillbuilder

Make a Map

VOCABULARY
symbol

Maps with symbols helped you understand the exploration of California. A **symbol** is a simple picture that stands for something. When you make a map, you can use symbols to show buildings and towns, rivers and mountains, or routes. Making a map with symbols can help you understand your community or the whole world.

Learn the Skill

Step 1: Decide what kind of map you want to make and how it will be used. Think of a title for your map. Write the title on the map.

Step 2: List the details you want to include on the map. These may be buildings, cities, land, water, or other things.

Step 3: Draw the outline of your map.

Step 4: Put your details on the map in the correct location. Use clear labels or symbols. Include a legend that explains any symbols you use.

Map Of Francisco De Ulloa's Voyage, 1539

1. Pacific Ocean
2. Gulf of California
3. New Spain
4. Baja California
5. Acapulco
6. La Paz

88 • Chapter 3

Practice the Skill

STANDARDS HSS 4.1.2, Analysis Skill CST 4

Follow the directions below to make a map of your community.

1. List the places you would like to include on the map, such as your school and your home. Think of a title and write it on your map.

2. Name any natural features in the area. Think of other details you want to add, such as major roads and parks.

3. Draw an outline of your community. Add details from your list to the map. Use labels or symbols. Create a legend to explain any symbols or colors you used.

Apply the Skill

Use what you have learned to make a map of the world. Label the seven continents and four oceans, as well as the equator, prime meridian, tropics, and North and South Poles.

Core Lesson 2

Colonizing California

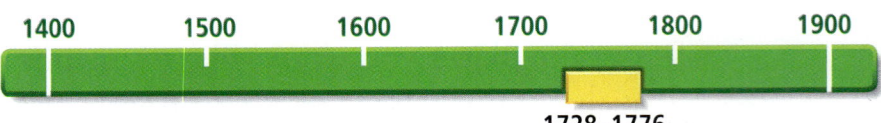

1728–1776

Build on What You Know Can you picture what your town might have looked like 300 years ago? When explorers arrived in Alta California in the 1700s, they found a vast land full of wildlife.

Seeking New Routes

Main Idea After Russia explored the northern Pacific Ocean, the Spanish decided to start a colony in Alta California.

In the early 1700s, people in Europe knew little about large areas of the world. Some wondered about land or water routes from North America to Asia. They set out to explore the northern Pacific Ocean.

Vitus Bering explored for Russia. In 1728, he found a narrow body of water between Asia and North America. It is now known as the Bering Strait. Later, Bering sailed to present-day Alaska, where he saw seals and other fur-bearing animals. Russian fur traders soon built trading posts along Alaska's coast.

VOCABULARY

colony
settler
missionary
mission

Vocabulary Strategy

settl**er**

The suffix **-er** describes a person. A **settler** is a person who settles. Other words with this suffix are painter or banker.

READING SKILL

Cause and Effect As you read, note causes and effects of the expedition led by Portolá and Serra.

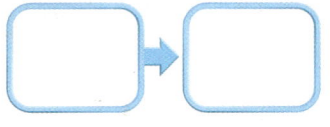

Core: HSS 4.2.2, 4.2.3
Extend support: HSS 4.2.3

Bering Reaches Alaska
Bering found seals, otters, and sea lions living in the cold waters of Alaska.

California Island This map from the 1600s shows California as an island.
SKILL **Primary Sources** What areas of land do you recognize on this map?

The British Explore

Britain also wanted to find an easy water route to Asia. The government offered a reward to anyone who could find a water route through North America. A famous British sailor, Captain **James Cook,** explored the northern Pacific in 1778. He never found the water route he was looking for, because it did not exist. However, he did map the Pacific coast.

News of European exploration near Alta California alarmed Spanish leaders. They especially feared Russia would start a colony there. A **colony** is a land ruled by another country.

Spain Plans a Colony

José de Gálvez, a leader in New Spain, took action. In 1769, he sent settlers to start a Spanish colony in Alta California. A **settler** is a person who moves to a new area. Gálvez hoped the settlers could keep other European countries out of California.

Gálvez planned for an expedition from Baja California to Monterey Bay, which **Sebastián Vizcaíno** found in 1602. Gálvez split the expedition into groups. Three ships sailed north to San Diego. Two groups marched by land to meet them. From San Diego, the expedition would continue north.

REVIEW Why did Gálvez decide to set up a colony in Alta California?

91

A Major Expedition

Main Idea Soldiers and priests took part in the expedition to colonize California.

An officer named **Gaspar de Portolá** (gas PAHR deh pohr toe LAH) led the expedition planned by Gálvez. **Junípero Serra** (hoo NEE peh roh SEHR ah) joined Portolá. Serra was a Roman Catholic priest. He wanted to go to Alta California as a missionary. A **missionary** is a person who travels to an area to teach a religion. Other missionaries went with him.

Soldiers, sailors, and settlers also joined the expedition. Some of the settlers were Spanish. Others came from American Indian or African families. Baja California Indians took care of the pack animals on the trip.

The First Mission

The journey to San Diego was hard. One ship got lost and took three months to get there. One ship sank. The groups traveling by land crossed rugged hills and harsh deserts. About one-third of all the people on the expedition died.

The groups reached San Diego by July 1769. Portolá left some people there to care for the sick. He led others to search for Monterey. A priest named **Juan Crespí** went along. He kept a diary of the group's travels.

Serra stayed behind to set up his first mission, San Diego de Alcalá. A **mission** is a settlement built for people who want to teach a religion and for those they want to teach. Serra planned more missions in California.

A Long Trip Junípero Serra left Europe to work as a missionary in New Spain. In 1769, he went to Alta California.

Finding Monterey

Portolá marched north with his group. When they reached Monterey Bay, though, they did not recognize it. They kept going farther north.

In October, the group came to a large inland body of water. Crespí called it a "very noble and very large harbor." This was San Francisco Bay. They were the first Europeans to see it.

The next year, Portolá led another expedition that found Monterey Bay. Serra set up the new mission of San Carlos Borromeo there. By 1776, Spanish missions stood in San Diego, San Gabriel, Santa Barbara, Monterey, and San Francisco. The purpose of the missions was to make California Indians adopt the culture and religion of Spanish people.

REVIEW Where did Gaspar de Portolá's expedition go?

San Francisco Bay Portolá's expedition came to this bay in 1769.

Lesson Summary

After Bering explored the northern Pacific, Russians set up trading posts along the Alaskan coast. José de Gálvez sent an expedition led by Gaspar de Portolá to Alta California. Junípero Serra and other missionaries built missions in the colony.

Why It Matters...

Several of the settlements Gálvez planned are among the largest cities in California today.

Lesson Review

1728 Bering Strait discovered
1769 Portolá's expedition begins

1. **VOCABULARY** Write a paragraph about Portolá's journey using **mission** and **colony**.

2. **READING SKILL** Explain the **effect** of Vitus Bering's exploration on the expedition of Portolá and Serra.

3. **MAIN IDEA: Geography** What did Bering find on his exploration of the northern Pacific Ocean?

4. **MAIN IDEA: History** Who took part in Portolá's expedition to Alta California?

5. **TIMELINE SKILL** How long after the Bering Strait was discovered did Portolá's expedition begin?

6. **CRITICAL THINKING: Synthesize** In what way was Portolá's expedition different from those of Drake, Cabrillo, and Vizcaíno?

WRITING ACTIVITY Write a narrative about one of the expeditions in this lesson. Use concrete details from the lesson and from the maps and pictures.

1. HSS 4.2.3 2. HSS 4.2.2 3. HSS 4.2.2 4. HSS 4.2.3 5. HSS 4.2.3 6. HSS 4.2.3 Activity HSS 4.2.3

Extend Lesson 2
Primary Sources

ALTA CALIFORNIA Letters

Juan Crespí sits down to write a diary entry. Crespí, a **missionary,** had traveled to Alta California with Junípero Serra and Gaspar de Portolá. Crespí and Serra left written records of the journey. Thanks to their diary entries and letters, we know about the events of the trip.

Juan Crespí (1721 – 1782)

In one diary entry, Crespí described a friendly meeting with the Chumash in the Santa Barbara area.

"*Shortly after, the [California Indians] from the towns arrived with roasted and fresh fish, seeds, acorns, atole [corn meal], and other kinds of food. They urged us to eat. . . . [T]he soldiers traded with them and obtained various objects, such as baskets, feather headdresses, and pelts. The entire area along the route, as well as that which can be seen from the camp, is extremely beautiful. . . . [T]he area is covered with live-oak, willow, and other trees.*"

—From a diary entry by Juan Crespí

Junípero Serra
(1713 – 1784)

After starting the mission of San Carlos Borromeo in Monterey, Serra wrote a letter describing how the mission was founded.

"*Our arrival was greeted by the joyful sound of the bells suspended [hung] from the branches of the oak tree. . . . [W]e shouted at the top of our voices, "Long live the Faith! Long live the King!" All the time the bells were ringing, and our rifles were being fired, and from the boat came the thunder of the big guns. . . . Thus our dear College [group of missionaries] may now count this new mission as one more on the list.*"

—From a letter by Junípero Serra

Activities

1. **DRAW IT** Draw a picture of the founding of San Carlos Borromeo, using Father Serra's description.

2. **COMPARE IT** Make a chart showing ways in which the primary sources of Crespí and Serra are alike and different.

 **Technology** Visit Education Place for more primary sources.
www.eduplace.com/kids/hmss/

Skillbuilder

Read a Timeline

Timelines are a social studies tool. People use them to organize and remember the dates of events. A timeline shows events in the order in which they happened. They are usually divided by years, decades, or centuries. A **decade** is a period of 10 years. A **century** is a period of 100 years.

VOCABULARY
decade
century

Learn the Skill

Step 1: If the timeline has a title, read it. The title will tell you the subject of the timeline.

Step 2: Look at the beginning date and the ending date. How much time does the timeline cover?

Step 3: Look at the events shown on the timeline. Read the dates to find out when the events happened. Events on the left side of the timeline happened before events on the right. Think about how much time passed between the events. Ask yourself whether some events caused others.

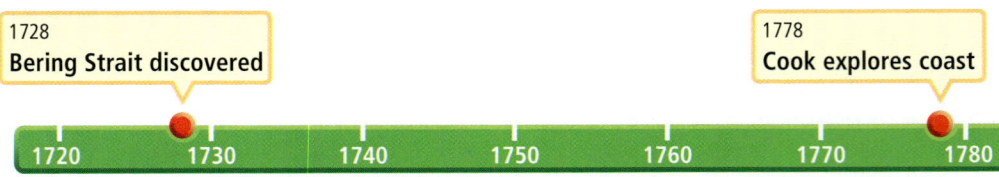

96 • Chapter 3

STANDARDS Analysis Skill CST 1, Analysis Skill CST 2

Practice the Skill

Use the timeline on page 96 to answer the questions.

1. How many decades are covered in the timeline?
2. Which event came first?
3. What event took place in 1778?

Apply the Skill

Make your own timeline. Reread Chapter 3, Lesson 1 on pages 80–85. Choose four events from the lesson. Then create a timeline that shows when those events took place.

Core Lesson 3

California's Missions

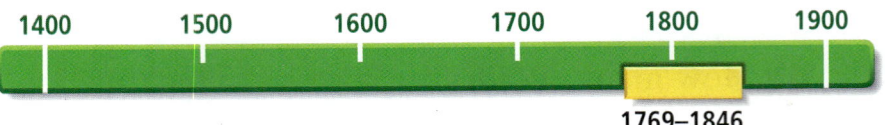
1769–1846

VOCABULARY

convert
adobe
revolt

Vocabulary Strategy

revolt

Revolt comes from a word meaning "overturn." A revolt overturns, or removes, people in power.

READING SKILL

Predict Outcomes As you read, predict the outcome of the building of missions in California.

PREDICTION
↓
OUTCOME

 **STANDARDS**

Core: HSS 4.2.4, 4.2.6
Extend support: HSS 4.2.5

Build on What You Know If you live on California's coast, there may be a mission near you. The Spanish built many missions along the coast, from San Diego to the present-day Bay Area.

A Chain of Missions

Main Idea The mission system brought the power of Spain and the Catholic Church to California.

Spain's rulers had several goals in the late 1700s. They wanted Spain's power and wealth to grow. They also wanted to keep other European countries out of New Spain. Building missions along the coast of Alta, or upper, California helped them meet these goals.

Spanish missionaries also had a reason to settle in Alta California. They wanted to convert California Indians to Roman Catholic beliefs. To **convert** means to change a religion or belief.

Mission in San Diego
The first Alta California mission was San Diego de Alcalá, built in 1769. It was moved in 1774.

98 • Chapter 3

Mission Chain This map shows the 21 missions of Alta California. Junípero Serra founded the first mission in 1769.

SKILL **Reading Maps** Which missions were founded after 1800?

Alta California Missions

- San Francisco Solano de Sonoma, 1823
- San Rafael Arcángel, 1817
- San Francisco de Asís, 1776
- Santa Clara de Asís, 1777
- San José de Guadalupe, 1797
- Santa Cruz, 1791
- San Juan Bautista, 1797
- San Carlos Borromeo, 1770
- Nuestra Señora de la Soledad, 1791
- San Antonio de Padua, 1771
- San Miguel Arcángel, 1797
- San Luís Obispo, 1772
- La Purísima Concepción, 1787
- Santa Inés, 1804
- Santa Barbara, 1786
- San Buenaventura, 1782
- San Fernando Rey de España, 1797
- San Gabriel Arcángel, 1771
- San Juan Capistrano, 1776
- San Luís Rey de Francia, 1798
- San Diego de Alcalá, 1769

Land for Missions

Priests used missions as places to convert California Indians. As they mapped new missions, they chose places where many people lived. Economic factors helped decide where to build missions. They had to be in areas where they could grow food and support many people. Missionaries looked for areas with fresh water, good soil, and resources for building.

California Indians did most of the work of building missions. The first missions were built of wood. Later, adobe was used. **Adobe** is a brick made of dried clay and straw. It can last for a long time.

The missions took land that California Indians had used for hunting and gathering. Without that land, some Indians had to go to the missions for food. Soldiers brought some as well. Some people came to missions by choice and others were brought by force.

As time went on, fewer people came to missions by choice. However, the mission system kept growing. By 1823, there were 21 missions in Alta California. The last mission to be founded was San Francisco Solano, in present-day Sonoma.

REVIEW Why did the Spanish leaders and missionaries build missions in California?

Life at a Mission

Main Idea Missions changed the way many California Indians lived.

The missionaries who traveled to Alta California were Franciscans, who were a group of Roman Catholic priests. They worked to spread their religion and make other people live more like Europeans. For example, the Franciscans wanted California Indians to become farmers. The missionaries believed that farming was a better way of life than hunting and gathering. They also wanted California Indians to grow food for the missionaires and the soldiers.

Using Skills

California Indians did more than build the missions. When missionaries first arrived, they needed the skills of California Indians to help them survive. California Indians knew how to gather food and how to use herbs for medicine. They guided priests who were moving north and showed them sites for new missions.

As the mission system expanded, mission life changed. Farms grew more food. Priests did not want food collected by hunting and gathering. They forced people to work on the mission farms. They tried to control people's lives.

Mission Buildings Although each mission was different, all had churches, workshops, and housing.

100 • Chapter 3

Learning New Skills

Missionaries taught California Indians skills such as herding cattle and making new goods. California Indians learned to make goods used in Europe, such as cloth, bricks, and iron tools.

The Spanish brought plants from Europe, such as wheat, oats, and citrus fruits. Missions grew these new crops. They grew North American plants such as corn and cotton as well.

California Indians also raised animals from Europe. Cattle were the most common. People raised them for meat, horns, hides, and tallow. Tallow, or fat, was used in candles and soap.

A Changing Economy

California Indians who moved to the missions had to learn a new way of life. Their economy changed from hunting and gathering to agriculture and herding. They had to convert to Catholicism. They also had to speak Spanish and wear Spanish clothes.

Some California Indians kept their traditional cultures and customs. They practiced the religion of their ancestors. They spoke their own languages. Some priests allowed them to practice their traditions. Other priests wanted them to completely change their way of life.

REVIEW What kind of work did California Indians do on missions?

An Alta California Mission

1. Mission church
2. Courtyard with fountain
3. Workshops, storage, and living area for priests and soldiers
4. California Indian houses
5. Fields and orchards for growing food for mission
6. Water for fields
7. Pasture for cattle, sheep, and horses
8. More workshops and storage

Resisting the Missions

Main Idea Some California Indians fought back against the mission system.

Missionaries used different ways of making California Indians convert to Catholicism and act like Spanish people. Sometimes they used gifts and kindness. Other times, though, they used harsh treatment, including whipping and heavy chains. Soldiers were often cruel to California Indians. For those who suffered bad treatment, the missions were places of misery.

A priest at Mission San Miguel protested to the government in New Spain about this treatment. However, his complaint was ignored.

California Indians Revolt

Many California Indians resisted the missionaries. Some worked slowly. Some broke their tools and equipment. Thousands fled. Soldiers often forced the people who fled to return. Some California Indians planned revolts. A **revolt** is an uprising against a ruler. The Tongva, Ohlone, and others attacked missions. They hoped to get rid of missionaries and soldiers.

The first revolt was at the San Diego mission in 1774. In 1785, **Toypurina** led a revolt at the San Gabriel mission. She said she felt the missionaries "were trespassing on the land of my forefathers."

San Gabriel Mission This mission near modern-day Los Angeles was started in 1771. A statue of Junípero Serra stands in front. Bells (right) were used in missions to tell people the time.

The Missions' Lasting Effects

Missions controlled the lives of thousands of California Indians. Some people lost their traditional ways of life. They worked on ranches outside the missions. At times, farming was the only way they could get food.

Without knowing it, the Spanish carried diseases that were new in Alta California. Thousands of California Indians became ill. Their numbers fell by about two thirds by 1846.

The work of California Indians kept the missions going. The Spanish built similar missions in many parts of New Spain. They allowed Spain to keep control of Alta California and Latin America for many years.

REVIEW What did California Indians do to resist the missions?

Lesson Summary

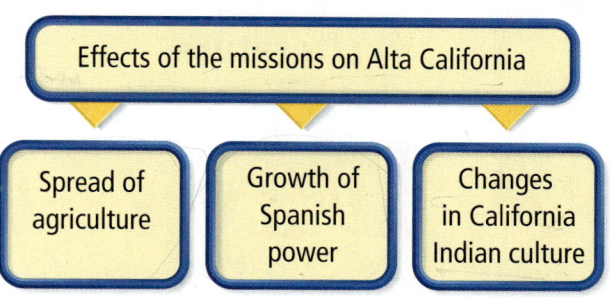

Why It Matters...

Missions changed the lives and culture of many California Indians. They were forced to give up their culture and economy to live more like Spanish people.

Lesson Review

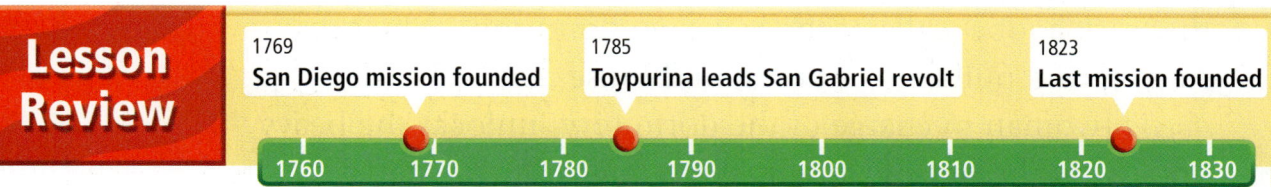

1. **VOCABULARY** Use **convert** and **revolt** in a short paragraph about life on the missions.

2. **READING SKILL** List at least two effects of the missions. Then, compare the list to your **predictions**.

3. **MAIN IDEA: Geography** What did priests look for when they chose a place to build a mission?

4. **MAIN IDEA: Economics** In what ways did the Franciscans change the hunting and gathering economy of California Indians?

5. **TIMELINE SKILL** How much time passed between the founding of the first and last missions in California?

6. **CRITICAL THINKING: Analyze** Why did priests believe they were helping California Indians?

WRITING ACTIVITY Make an outline based on one section of this lesson. Write the title of the section. Find three details in the section that help you understand the title. List the details under the title.

1. HSS 4.2.4 2. HSS 4.2.4 3. HSS 4.2.4 4. HSS 4.2.6 5. HSS 4.2.4 6. HSS 4.2.4 Activity Analysis Skill HI 1

Extend Lesson 3
Literature

A Day in the Life of a Mission

by Mariah Marvin, from *Cobblestone Magazine*

The ringing of a bell marked the beginning, middle, and end of the mission's day. Hundreds of California Indians lived at Mission La Purísima Concepción (pyoo REE see muh cuhn sep see OWN). These stories tell what life might have been like for a young woman, a man, and a boy living at the mission in 1816.

Dawn

The girl hears the faint *clung* of the mission bell through the thick adobe walls of the *monjerio* [dormitory]. She rises sleepily and pulls on a homespun blouse and skirt. The *dueña* [woman in charge of the dormitory] unlocks the heavy door from the outside and it creaks open. Dueña María is strict, but she comes from the girl's mother's village, and sometimes gives her special treats from the storeroom. Through the opening the girl can see the first-light sky.

The sound of the bell is now loud through the open door. It calls them all to church.

The girl has learned many things in her years at the mission. She has learned to sow seeds and tend the plants. She has learned to weave on the mission looms. She knows how to make candles. She can bake bread in the mission's outdoor ovens shaped like beehives. She likes to learn, and she takes pride in how quickly her hands gain new skills. But sometimes she worries that she is forgetting the skills of her own people. Her mother had woven beautiful baskets, baskets so tight that they could be used to store water.

If she were married, she could move out of the monjerio and into a house. Living in a traditional house, with a family of her own, she thinks she might not remember so clearly the edge of the river where the soldiers took her from her mother and brought her to the mission.

Morning

He stops the plow when he reaches the end of the long furrow. He looks back along the long, straight line of broken earth. This is not the way the world was. The earth did not make long straight lines, as far as he can remember. In his Indian world, plants were not sown in long straight lines and told to grow there, one against the other. The Chumash knew where each kind of plant liked to grow, and when. Sometimes they scattered seeds where it was convenient, or burned meadows so new grasses would grow. They took fish from the sea and the river, too. Sometimes they would kill a deer with their arrows or take a wild goose from the lagoon.

The river valley usually gave them enough to eat. But then the strangers at the mission began taking some of the land, and there were a few years of dry weather. His family had been hungry, and he had come to the mission for food. He had walked into another world, and then found he was not allowed to leave.

Night

The boy lies in the dark, listening. Through the smoke hole in the roof, the boy watches the stars. His father died at the old mission, on the other side of the river. . . but the boy feels his father is not far. He seems to hear his voice. "Remember the quiet, open places," his father says. "Remember the grass by the river. Remember the soft feathers. . ." And the boy falls asleep.

Activities

1. **TALK ABOUT IT** In what ways are the three people you read about alike? In what ways are they different?

2. **WRITE ABOUT IT** Write a paragraph explaining what life is like for the girl in the story.

Core Lesson 4

Presidios and Settlements

VOCABULARY

presidio
governor
pueblo
alcalde

Vocabulary Strategy

g**over**nor

Find **over** in **governor**. A governor is a person who rules over others.

READING SKILL
Problem and Solution
Chart ways in which the Spanish tried to solve the problem of feeding their soldiers in Alta California.

Problem:	Solutions:

Core: HSS 4.2.3, 4.2.5
Extend support: HSS 4.2.5

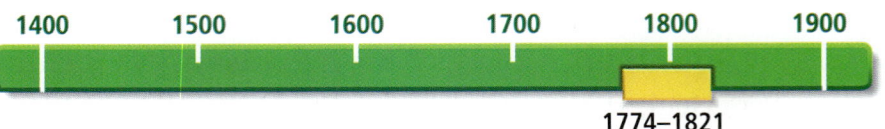

1774–1821

Build on What You Know Soldiers need to eat, but they do not usually have farms. They can't eat unless other people grow food for them. Spanish soldiers in Alta California needed to have farmers nearby.

A Growing Colony

Main Idea Spain sent soldiers to Alta California to build forts and guard the colony.

Spanish leaders wanted more settlers in Alta California. Yet the journey from other parts of New Spain was dangerous. Many people died, whether they tried to make the trip by land or by sea.

In 1774, a young soldier set off to find a better route. **Juan Bautista de Anza** crossed the Sonoran Desert from southern New Spain to Alta California. He reached Mission San Gabriel in three months. The next year, Anza led 240 settlers across the desert to Alta California. The trip was hard, but Anza's group reached Monterey. He led some of them north to start a new settlement at San Francisco.

Juan Bautista de Anza His first expedition was lost in the Sonoran Desert for a month.

108 • Chapter 3

California's Presidios Soldiers in presidios guarded Alta California. The picture shows an artist's idea of how a presidio might have looked.

SKILL Reading Visuals Why is the presidio built with a wall around it?

Spanish Forts

Spain built presidios along the coast of California. A **presidio** is a fort. California Indians did most of the work of building forts in San Diego, Monterey, San Francisco, and Santa Barbara. The Spanish chose sites they could defend. Some presidios were built near ports to protect against attacks by sea. Each presidio also needed a source of fresh water nearby.

Soldiers traveled from one presidio to another on a road that linked the missions and presidios. The road was known as El Camino Real (ehl cah MEE noh reh AHL). Its name means "The Royal Highway." Like everything else in the colony, it belonged to the king of Spain.

Presidio Life

Soldiers in presidios protected missions against revolts by California Indians. Sometimes soldiers captured California Indians who fled from missions. They also explored the land, guarded the colony from sea attacks by other European countries, and carried mail along El Camino Real.

Life in the presidios was hard for soldiers and their families. Presidio buildings were crowded and needed repairs most of the time. Soldiers did not have enough food, supplies, or money. Sometimes they were not paid for years. Their weapons were in poor condition and gunpowder was scarce. There were no schools for soldiers' children to attend.

REVIEW Why did the Spanish build presidios in Alta California?

Starting Pueblos

Main Idea Spanish settlers in Alta California started towns and raised food.

In 1775, Felipe de Neve (feh LEEP de NEH veh) became governor of Alta California. A **governor** is a person who leads a colony or state. Neve wanted more settlers in Alta California. He wanted them to grow food for soldiers. Neve also hoped they would raise families and make the colony grow.

Neve gave 14 families land to start the pueblo of San José in 1777. A **pueblo** is a town or village. Four years later, eleven families with children received land to found the pueblo of Los Angeles. The founders of Los Angeles had a mix of Indian, African, and Spanish ancestors.

Daily Life

Many of the first settlers were farmers, miners, and traders from other areas of New Spain. California Indians and soldiers also settled in pueblos. Many settlers hired California Indians to work for them.

Settlers received land, tools, and money from Spain. They were given farm animals such as cattle. In return, they built houses and raised food. They sold their extra food to the presidios. Pueblo life could be difficult. Settlers faced bad harvests and lack of water.

Each pueblo had an alcalde (ahl CAHLD eh). An **alcalde** was the leader of a pueblo. Alcaldes had the powers of a mayor and a judge. The governor chose the first alcaldes. Later, people in pueblos chose their leaders by voting.

Spanish Settlements
Missions, presidios, and pueblos were all parts of Spain's colony in Alta California.

The Colony's Economy

The number of people in the pueblos grew, but not very quickly. For example, 139 people lived in Los Angeles in 1790. Ten years later, 315 people lived there.

People in presidios, missions, and pueblos each had jobs to do. Soldiers defended the colony. Missionaries tried to convert California Indians and teach them Spanish ways of life. Settlers in pueblos grew food and raised families.

REVIEW What did Spain do to make people want to settle in Alta California?

Pueblo Life Early settlers lived in adobe houses such as this one in San José.

Lesson Summary

- The presidios protected Alta California for Spain.
- Soldiers led a hard life without enough food or supplies.
- Felipe de Neve sent settlers to start pueblos at San José and Los Angeles.

Why It Matters...

Some early pueblos, such as Los Angeles and San José, later became centers for trade in Alta California.

Lesson Review

1769 San Diego presidio founded
1777 San José pueblo founded
1781 Los Angeles pueblo founded

1760 — 1770 — 1780 — 1790

❶ **VOCABULARY** Write a short description of life for settlers in Alta California using **pueblo** and **alcalde.**

❷ **READING SKILL** Use the information in your chart to explain what pueblos did to **solve** the **problem** of feeding soldiers.

❸ **MAIN IDEA: History** Why was life in presidios hard for soldiers?

❹ **MAIN IDEA: Government** What did Felipe de Neve do to make the colonies in California grow?

❺ **TIMELINE SKILL** When was the pueblo of San José founded?

❻ **CRITICAL THINKING: Decision Making** What were the costs and benefits of becoming a settler in Alta California?

WRITING ACTIVITY Write an outline to summarize the information on pages 108–109. Include the main idea and supporting details.

1. HSS 4.2.5 2. HSS 4.2.5 3. HSS 4.2.5 4. HSS 4.2.5 5. HSS 4.2.5 6. HSS 4.2.5 Activity Analysis Skill HI 1

Extend Lesson 4
History

El Camino Real

A messenger on horseback races down a narrow, dusty road. What news does he carry? Messengers used El Camino Real, the Royal Highway, to travel through Alta California. They warned of attacks and announced important news, such as the death of the King of Spain.

El Camino Real connected Alta California's missions. The road did not look much like a highway. Rainy weather would turn the dirt road to mud. The route of El Camino Real is still used today. Paved roads follow its path. Signs such as the one on page 113 mark the route of the original El Camino Real.

Travelers
Priests, settlers, soldiers, and California Indians used the road to travel.

News
A messenger on a galloping horse could spread news to all the missions in less than four days.

HISTORY

LEGEND
- El Camino Real
- Mission
- Presidio

- San Francisco Solano de Sonoma
- San Rafael Arcángel
- San Francisco de Asís
- Presidio de San Francisco
- San José de Guadalupe
- Santa Clara de Asís
- Santa Cruz
- Presidio de Monterey
- San Juan Bautista
- San Carlos Borromeo
- Núestra Señora de la Soledad
- San Antonio de Padua
- San Miguel Arcángel
- San Luis Obispo de Tolosa
- La Purísima Concepción
- Santa Inés
- Santa Barbara
- Presidio de Santa Barbara
- San Buenaventura
- San Fernando Rey de España
- San Gabriel Arcángel
- San Juan Capistrano
- San Luis Rey de Francia
- San Diego Alcalá
- Presidio de San Diego

Pacific Ocean

Supplies
Carts carried supplies from Baja California to the missions.

Activities

1. MAP IT Look at a map of California today. Which missions are now sites of towns or cities?

2. WRITE IT Describe a trip that someone might have taken along El Camino Real in Spanish California. Use details about people and places.

113

Chapter 3 Review

Visual Summary

1–3. Write a description for each of the items shown below.

Spanish Settlements in California	
 Missions	
 Presidios	
 Pueblos	

STANDARDS 1. HSS 4.2.4 2. HSS 4.2.3 3. HSS 4.2.5

Facts and Main Ideas

Answer each question below.

4. **History** Why did the Spanish first send expeditions to Alta California in the 1500s?

5. **History** What was the purpose of Portolá and Serra's expedition in 1769?

6. **Economics** In what ways did life change for California Indians who moved to the missions?

7. **Geography** What kinds of locations did the Spanish look for when they built missions?

4. HSS 4.2.2 5. HSS 4.2.3 6. HSS 4.2.5 7. HSS 4.2.4

Vocabulary

Choose a word from the list below to complete each sentence.

peninsula, p. 81
mission, p. 92
alcalde, p. 110

8. A(n) _____ acted as a mayor and judge for each pueblo.

9. Cortés thought Baja California was an island, but it is actually a(n) _____, surrounded by water on only three sides.

10. Junípero Serra founded the first _____ in Alta California at San Diego.

8. HSS 4.2.5 9. HSS 4.2.2 10. HSS 4.2.3

114 • Chapter 3

CHAPTER SUMMARY TIMELINE

1542 Cabrillo explores California
1769 First Spanish settlements
1785 San Gabriel revolt

1500 — 1550 — 1600 — 1650 — 1700 — 1750 — 1800 — 1850

Apply Skills

Read a Timeline Read the timeline above. Then use your timeline skills to answer each question.

11. About how many years after Cabrillo explored Alta California did the Spanish start their first settlements?

    A. 158 years
    B. 227 years
    C. 363 years
    D. 418 years

12. Suppose you wanted to add the founding of the San José pueblo in 1777 to this timeline. Where would you place it?

    A. at the beginning
    B. at the end
    C. after the first Spanish settlements
    D. before Cabrillo explores California

13. Which of these titles would be best for the timeline?

    A. Spain Settles Alta California
    B. Drake and Cabrillo
    C. Daily Life in New Spain
    D. The Causes of Spanish Exploration

11. Analysis Skill CST 1   12. Analysis Skill CST 1   13. Analysis Skill CST 1

Critical Thinking

Write a short paragraph to answer each question below. Use details from the chapter to support your response.

14. **Analyze** In what ways were missions, presidios, and pueblos different?

15. **Evaluate** Why do you think missions helped Spain control Alta California?

Timeline

Use the Chapter Summary Timeline above to answer the question.

16. About how long after the Spanish started their settlements was the revolt at Mission San Gabriel?

14. HSS 4.2.5   15. HSS 4.2.3   16. HSS 4.2.3

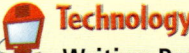

 **Map Activity** Trace routes of three explorers on an outline map of North America. Use different colors for each route. Include a map legend.

 Writing Activity Summarize the story of how the Spanish made Alta California a colony. Include main ideas and important details from the lessons.

Activities HSS 4.2.2, HSS 4.2.3, W 2.4

Technology
Writing Process Tips
Get help with your writing at
www.eduplace.com/kids/hmss/

Chapter 4 Mexican California

Technology
e • glossary
e • word games
www.eduplace.com/kids/hmss/

Vocabulary Preview

republic

After winning freedom from Spain, Mexicans wanted to choose their leaders. They made their government a **republic**.
page 120

rancho

An Alta California **rancho** could cover 75 square miles. Cattle, horses, and sheep grazed on these huge ranches.
page 129

Chapter Timeline

1810 Mexican War for Independence begins

1826 Jedediah Smith reaches California

1810 — 1820 — 1830

116 • Unit 2

Reading Strategy

Question To make sure you understand what you read, ask yourself questions.

 From time to time, test yourself to see if you understand what you read.

fiesta
Californios held a **fiesta** to celebrate special events such as weddings or cattle roundups. They invited many guests to these parties. **page 133**

pioneer
Pioneers crossed deserts and mountains for land and opportunities. They were some of the first people from the United States to reach Alta California. **page 140**

1841
Bidwell party

1850
Beckwourth Pass discovered

1840 — 1850

Core Lesson 1

Mexico Wins Independence

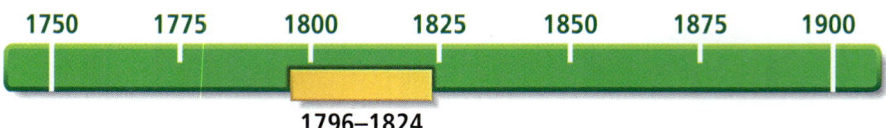
1796–1824

VOCABULARY

republic
constitution
import
export

Vocabulary Strategy

import, **ex**port

The prefix **im-** means into, and the prefix **ex-** means out. Imports are goods that come into a country. Exports go out.

READING SKILL
Draw Conclusions
Chart facts that lead to the conclusion that Californios had to trade with other countries.

STANDARDS
Core: HSS 4.2, 4.2.7, 4.3.1
Extend support: HSS 4.2.7

Build on What You Know Think about a time when you saw something you thought was unfair. Many people in New Spain felt that their government was not fair to them, and they decided to change it.

Fighting for Freedom

Main Idea People in New Spain fought to change the way they were governed.

In the early 1800s, Alta California was part of New Spain, a Spanish colony. The king of Spain governed the colony, but he lived far away. A viceroy, or governor, ruled New Spain for the king.

Many people in New Spain were unhappy with Spanish rule. Unjust laws gave most of the power to rich people from Spain. People born in New Spain, especially American Indians, had fewer legal rights and little money. They wanted more rights and more power. Some wanted to be free from Spain.

New Spain In the early 1800s, most people in New Spain were American Indians.

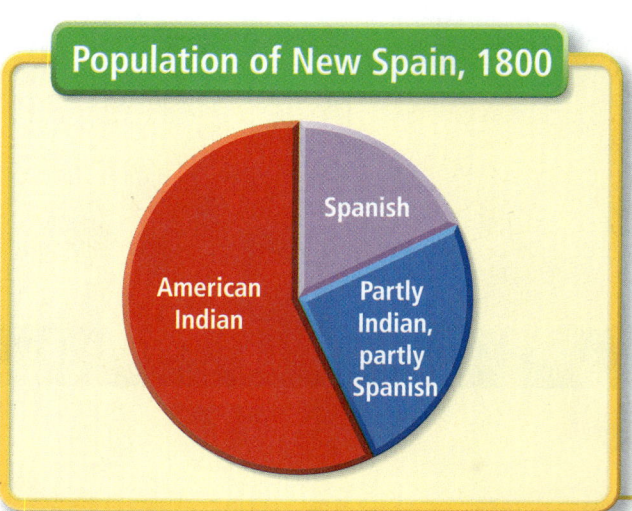
Population of New Spain, 1800

118 • Chapter 4

The Cry of Dolores

In 1810, a priest named **Miguel Hidalgo y Costilla** rang the church bells in Dolores, a town in what is now Mexico. As people gathered, he asked them to start a revolt against the government. People called Hidalgo's speech the "cry of Dolores." Thousands chose to follow him. They wanted to change New Spain's government.

Hidalgo gathered an army of about 50,000 people. Spanish soldiers defeated his army, but Hidalgo's "cry of Dolores" grew into a war for freedom from Spain. Today the war is known as the Mexican War for Independence. Independence is freedom from rule by another country.

Hidalgo was killed, but many others led the war against Spain, including **José María Morelos** and **Vicente Guerrero**. The fighting was fierce. The soldiers who fought for Spain had better weapons and training, but the people who revolted were determined to win. After 11 years of war, the Spanish gave up control of New Spain.

Although Alta California was part of New Spain, no battles took place there. Mountains and deserts cut the region off from the rest of New Spain. The government of Spain paid little attention to Alta California. People there did not hear much about the war.

REVIEW Why did some people in New Spain want independence from Spain?

Dolores Hidalgo Today, the town of Dolores is called Dolores Hidalgo, after Miguel Hidalgo (right).

The Republic of Mexico

Main Idea Mexico's government changed after it won independence from Spain.

The people of New Spain won independence in 1821. They called their nation Mexico. News of the victory did not reach Alta California until months later.

In 1822, a group of Mexican leaders arrived at Monterey's presidio. As Californians watched, the flag of Spain came down. Up went a green, white, and red flag with an eagle in the center. Alta California was declared part of the free nation of Mexico.

The new nation needed a new government. At first, Mexico had a government that was similar to Spain's. An emperor would rule. An emperor is a ruler of a group of lands or nations.

A New Nation The flag of Mexico flew over Monterey for the first time in 1822.

The Mexican Constitution

A former officer named **Agustín de Iturbide** (ah goo STEEN deh ee tuhr BEE deh) became emperor. Iturbide had fought for Spain, but changed sides in 1821. His leadership helped Mexico win its freedom. He did not rule Mexico for long, though. Many Mexicans found his rule too harsh. After less than a year, they forced him to leave his job.

Mexico's leaders met to create a new government. Instead of a single ruler, they wanted a republic. A **republic** is a government in which citizens elect lawmakers. In 1824, Mexico's leaders wrote a constitution. A **constitution** is a written plan for a government. The people who wrote the new Mexican constitution used the constitution of the United States as a model.

The constitution created a congress to be elected by voters. A congress is a group of people who make laws. The republic also had an elected president and a system of courts similar to that of the United States.

During the war, Spain had given up Florida to the United States. When Mexico won the war, it took control of all of Spain's land in North America.

REVIEW Why did Mexicans create a new government in 1824?

New Spain, 1810

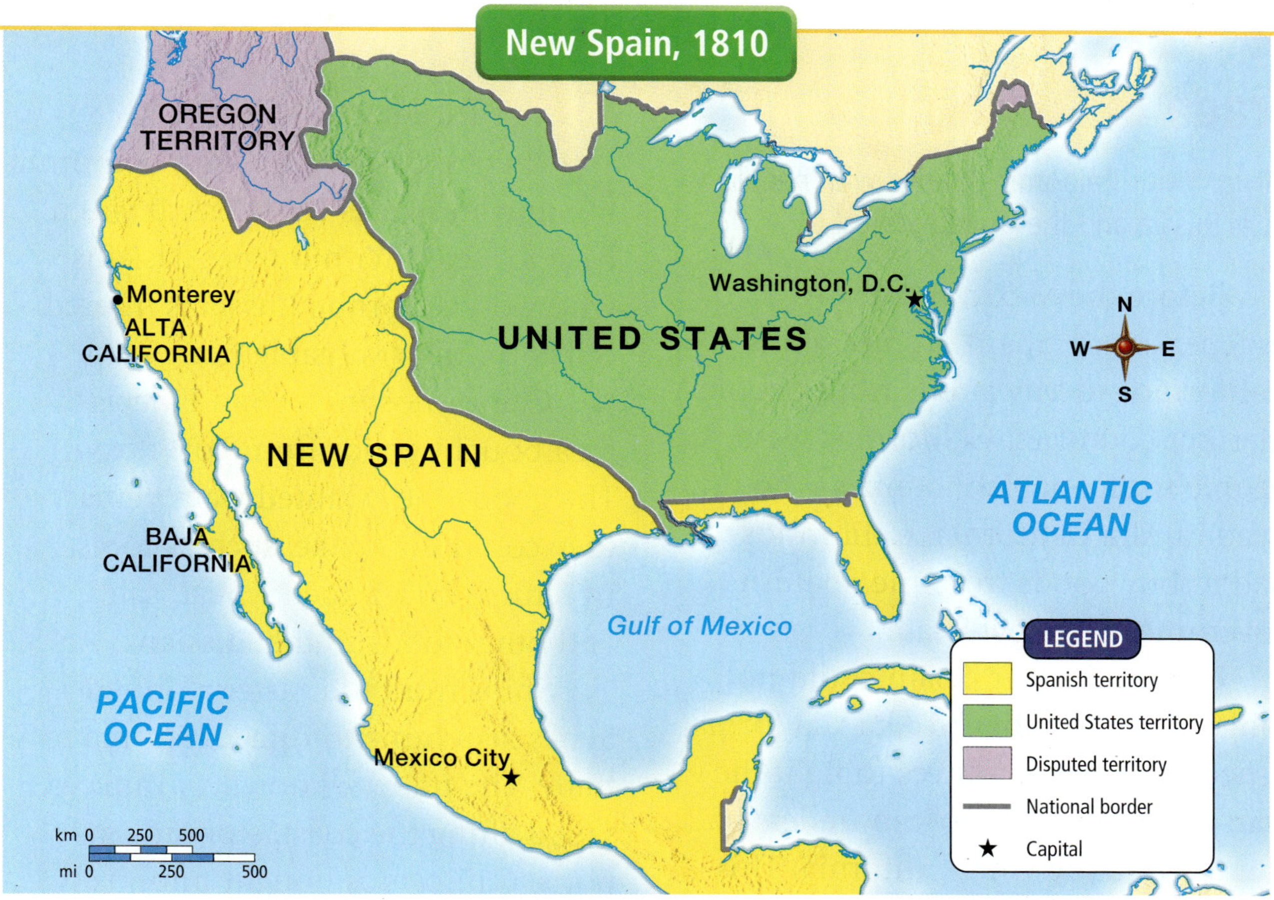
OREGON TERRITORY
Monterey
ALTA CALIFORNIA
BAJA CALIFORNIA
NEW SPAIN
UNITED STATES
Washington, D.C.
Mexico City
Gulf of Mexico
PACIFIC OCEAN
ATLANTIC OCEAN
N
W
E
S
km 0 250 500
mi 0 250 500
LEGEND
Spanish territory
United States territory
Disputed territory
National border
Capital

Mexico, 1824

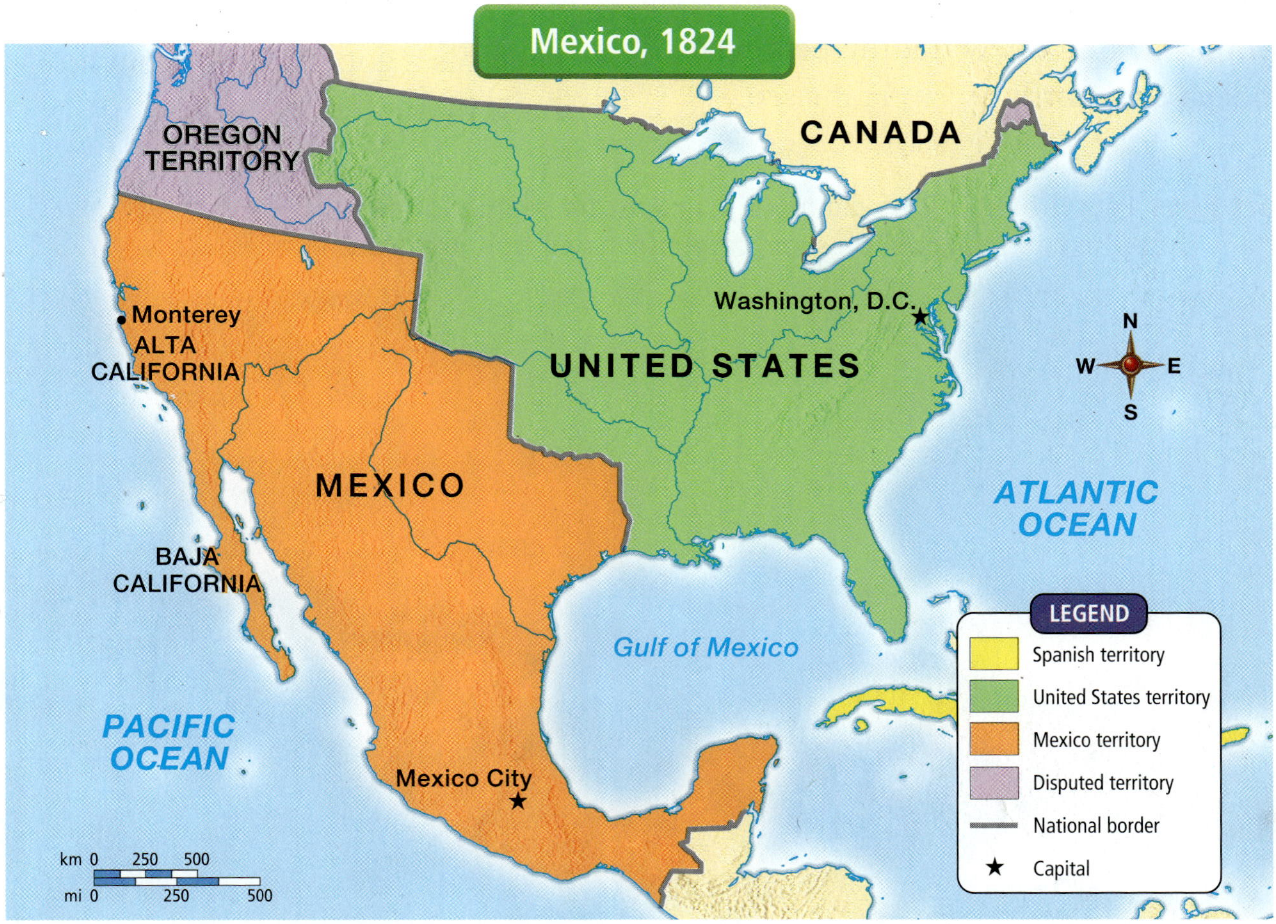
OREGON TERRITORY
CANADA
Monterey
ALTA CALIFORNIA
BAJA CALIFORNIA
MEXICO
UNITED STATES
Washington, D.C.
Mexico City
Gulf of Mexico
PACIFIC OCEAN
ATLANTIC OCEAN
N
W
E
S
km 0 250 500
mi 0 250 500
LEGEND
Spanish territory
United States territory
Mexico territory
Disputed territory
National border
Capital

SKILL **Reading Maps** Describe how borders in North America changed between 1810 and 1824.

Trade in California

Main Idea Californios traded with people from Russia and the United States.

Before the Mexican War for Independence, Spain did not allow Californios to buy goods from people in other countries. Californios were people from Spanish families who lived in Alta California. Californios had to buy goods from the Spanish government in New Spain.

During the war, Spain could no longer send supplies to Alta California. It needed all its resources to fight the war. Russian and American traders had wanted to trade with California. This was their chance. In 1812, a Russian company built a new trading post near Bodega Bay, north of San Francisco.

Russian Traders at Fort Ross

The Russian post in Alta California became known as Fort Ross. It was a base for sea otter hunters. Alaskans who worked for the Russians hunted otters for their valuable fur.

Californios in the San Francisco area bought goods from Fort Ross. The goods they wanted were items they could not make, such as tools. In return, they traded wheat, salt, and other foods to the Russians.

Ships from the eastern United States also came to Alta California to trade. The traders, known as Yankees, sailed along the coast, stopping at ports. Californios bought imports such as cloth and lace from them. An **import** is a good bought from a business in another country.

Fort Ross People at Fort Ross did more than hunt for seals and sea otters. They also had a blacksmith shop, carpenters, and fruit orchards.

The Hide and Tallow Trade

Californios sold exports to the traders from the United States. An **export** is a good sold to a business in another country. The main exports of Alta California were cow hides and tallow, or fat. Hides were used to make shoes and other leather goods. Tallow was used to make candles. Trade in these goods became a source of wealth in Alta California.

REVIEW In what way did trade in Alta California change during the Mexican War for Independence?

Lesson Summary

- Unjust laws and few legal rights led the people of New Spain to revolt.
- Mexico won independence from Spain in 1821.
- The people of Mexico created a government that was a republic.
- Californios traded hides and tallow during the war.

Why It Matters...

The Mexican War for Independence led to freedom for Mexico, which included Alta California.

Yankee Traders Ships such as this one sailed from the United States to Alta California.

Lesson Review

Timeline: 1810 Mexican War for Independence begins — 1821 Mexican War for Independence ends (1810–1825)

1. **VOCABULARY** Write a sentence to explain the purpose of the **constitution** in the **republic** Mexicans created in 1824.

2. **READING SKILL** Explain why the facts you wrote support the **conclusion** that Californios had to trade with other countries.

3. **MAIN IDEA: Government** What two kinds of government did Mexico have after winning independence?

4. **MAIN IDEA: Economics** For what kinds of goods did Californios trade?

5. **TIMELINE SKILL** How long did the Mexican War for Independence last?

6. **CRITICAL THINKING: Evaluate** Why do you think Mexicans first chose to have an emperor after they became independent?

WRITING ACTIVITY Rewrite the three main ideas of this lesson in your own words. List two details under each main idea to support or explain it.

1. HSS 4.2.7 2. HSS 4.2.7 3. HSS 4.2.7 4. HSS 4.2.7 5. HSS 4.2.7 6. HSS 4.2.7 Activity Analysis Skill HI 1

Extend Lesson 1

History

Mexican Independence Day

On September 16, 1810, Father Hidalgo called on Mexicans to fight for their freedom. Today, Mexicans and Mexican Americans celebrate the anniversary of his speech. It marks the beginning of Mexico's work toward independence, good government, and equality. These values are part of the culture of the United States as well.

California is home to millions of people of Mexican heritage. Many cities and towns hold festivals to mark September 16. Such festivals are a chance for everyone to celebrate the spirit of freedom and equality.

Mariachis, the famous street musicians of Mexico, play for the crowds. Folk dancers spin and twirl. The smell of tamales and other traditional Mexican foods fill the air.

Many people in California also celebrate Cinco de Mayo, or the Fifth of May. This festival marks the day when a Mexican army defeated a French army in 1862.

Celebrate! Dancing, singing, and marching are a part of celebrations for Mexican Independence Day.

Activities

1. **TALK ABOUT IT** What does Mexican Independence day have in common with July 4, the Independence Day of the United States?

2. **WRITE ABOUT IT** Describe the sights, sounds, and smells of September 16. Use details from the photos and text.

Core Lesson 2

Mexico and California

1821–1846

VOCABULARY

secularization
land grant
rancho

Vocabulary Strategy

land **grant**

A **grant** is something that is given. A land grant is land that is given to someone.

 READING SKILL
Cause and Effect Note ways a new government affects Alta California.

1	
2	
3	
4	

 **STANDARDS**
Core: HSS 4.2.7, 4.2.8
Extend support: HSS 4.2.8

National Palace This Mexico City building has been the center of Mexico's government since independence.

Build on What You Know When you go to a new school or get a new teacher, the rules might change. When Mexico gained its independence, the new government changed some rules in Alta California.

Change in Alta California

Main Idea The Mexican government changed the laws that governed Alta California.

While people fought a war for freedom in some parts of New Spain, Alta California stayed peaceful. The people there were cut off from the rest of New Spain by mountains and deserts. Little news of the war reached them. When the war ended, Californios accepted Mexico's new government and constitution.

Mexico's New Laws

Mexico's new constitution made all of its people citizens. A citizen is a member of a city, state, or nation. Mexico's citizens included the people of Alta California.

Mexico's laws said that all citizens would be equal. Although the laws recognized California Indians' equal rights, the laws were ignored.

The government of Mexico paid little attention to Alta California. It changed the region's government, but it did not make people follow all of the laws.

Changes in Government

In 1822, **Luís Antonio Argüello** (loo EES ahn TOE nee oh ar GWEH yo) was chosen to lead Alta California, but he was not actually the governor. Mexico did not choose a new governor until 1825. In the meantime, Argüello set up a diputación in Monterey. The diputación was an assembly, or group of citizens, that made laws. Citizens of Alta California chose the members of the diputación.

The diputación had little power. It gave the governor advice, but only met when the governor wanted it to.

REVIEW What changes did Mexico's rulers make to the laws of Alta California?

Luís Antonio Argüello He was the first leader of Alta California to have been born there.

The End of the Missions

Main Idea The Mexican government closed the missions and gave their land away.

Land was a source of wealth in Alta California. Under Spain's rule, the missions had owned the land that was best for raising cattle. Many Californios now wanted the missions closed. Some hoped to give California Indians who had been forced to live at the missions their freedom. Others hoped to get the mission lands.

The government of Mexico began a process of secularization in 1833. During **secularization,** the government took control of property that belonged to the missions. Church property and lands were given away. The missions lost most of their wealth and power.

Mexico's leaders wanted to make Alta California's economy stronger. Half the former mission lands were to go to people who would start farms and ranches that would bring trade to California. The other half of the lands were supposed to go to California Indians.

Very little land went to California Indians, however. Most land grants went to Californios and new settlers. A **land grant** is an area of land that is given away.

To get a land grant, people drew a map, called a diseño, of the land they wanted. Unless someone else owned the land, the person who wanted it could have it. Some Californios and settlers bought land from California Indians. Others cheated them to get it.

Diseño This hand-drawn map shows the land that someone wanted for a rancho.

SKILL Reading Visuals What geographic features does this diseño show?

128 • Chapter 4

Land Grants and Trade

Between 1834 and 1846, officials made about 700 land grants. They gave away more than eight million acres of land. Many land grants became part of ranchos. A **rancho** was a cattle ranch.

Some California Indians who had farmed and herded on the missions stayed to work on ranchos. Others tried to return to their old ways of life.

Mexico allowed ranchos to trade with people from other countries. The ranchos exported cattle hides and tallow, or fat, which brought money into Alta California. Through this trade, the ranchos made the region's economy stronger.

REVIEW What did Mexico's leaders do to make Alta California's economy stronger?

Lesson Summary

Alta California became part of Mexico. The Mexican government closed the missions. Most of the mission land went to rich Californios. Many California Indians worked on ranchos, raising cattle for the hide and tallow trade.

Why It Matters...

As farming and ranching grew in Alta California, so did trade with people in other countries.

Cattle Ranchos kept large herds of cattle.

Lesson Review

1821 Mexican independence
1824 Mexican constitution
1833 Secularization begins

1820 — 1825 — 1830 — 1835

1 VOCABULARY Use **secularization, land grant,** and **rancho** in a paragraph that explains changes in land ownership.

2 READING SKILL Describe the **effects** of Mexican rule on California Indians.

3 MAIN IDEA: Government What was the job of Alta California's diputación?

4 MAIN IDEA: Economics Who received most of the land grants after the missions were closed?

5 TIMELINE SKILL Did secularization begin before or after the writing of Mexico's constitution?

6 CRITICAL THINKING: Evaluate Why do you think the Mexican government decided to give away mission lands?

MAP ACTIVITY Draw a diseño of your school. Make sure to include important features so that someone else could understand the area you show.

1. HSS 4.2.8 2. HSS 4.2.8 3. HSS 4.2.8 4. HSS 4.2.8 5. HSS 4.2.8 6. HSS 4.2.8 Activity HSS 4.2.8

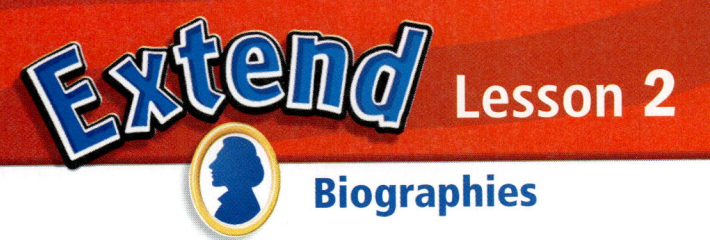

Extend Lesson 2
Biographies

Stories of ALTA CALIFORNIA

Who were the people of Alta California? Some were visitors from distant lands, such as Britain and Russia. Others lived their whole lives in Alta California. Frederick Beechey and Concepción Argüello were two people whose stories we can read about today.

Frederick W. Beechey
(1796 – 1856)

In 1825, Frederick Beechey explored the coast of Alaska. He was a British sailor searching for a water route through North America. Cold weather forced him to take shelter in a harbor farther south. He sailed his ship, *Blossom*, into San Francisco Bay in 1826.

Beechey thought Alta California was beautiful. However, he also saw problems there. Beechey wrote that California Indians were often treated cruelly in missions. He believed that the Mexican government ignored Alta California. His stories about his visit were published in 1831. People who read his book learned what life was like in Alta California.

CHARACTER TRAIT: Caring

Maria de Concepción Argüello
(1791 – 1857)

Concepción Argüello (kohn sehp see OHN ar GWEH yo), was the daughter of the head of San Francisco's presidio. In 1806, Count Nikolai Rezanov (NEE kuh LIE ryeh ZAH nuv) sailed into San Francisco Bay. He was a Russian explorer looking for supplies. He met Argüello, and the two fell in love.

Rezanov had to return to Russia. He promised to come back and marry Argüello, but he died on his journey. Many other men asked Argüello to marry them. She always said no. Instead, Argüello spent her life helping people and teaching her religion. In Mexican Alta California, she became known among the poor as "La Beata," which means "The Blessed One."

Activities

1. **TALK ABOUT IT** Compare the ways Concepción Argüello and Frederick Beechey showed **caring** for people in Alta California.

2. **WRITE IT** Find out more about someone who lived in Spanish or Mexican California. Write a one-page summary of this person's life.

 Biographies Visit Education Place for more biographies. www.eduplace.com/kids/hmss/

Core Lesson 3

Ranchos and Pueblos

VOCABULARY

vaquero
rodeo
fiesta

Vocabulary Strategy

vaquero

The Spanish word **vaquero** comes from **vaca**, or cow. Vaquero means cowhand.

READING SKILL
Compare and Contrast
Fill in a Venn diagram to compare life on ranchos and pueblos.

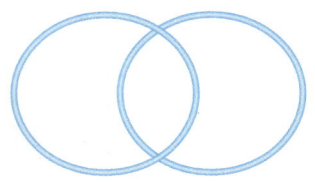

Core: HSS 4.2.5, 4.2.8, 4.3.1
Extend support: HSS 4.2.5

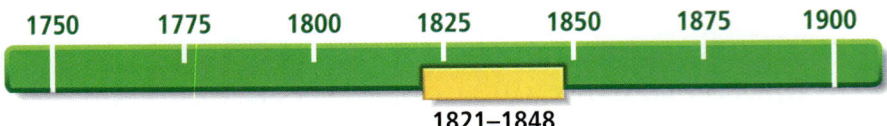
1821–1848

Build on What You Know Is there one kind of business in your area in which many people work? In Mexican California, ranchos were big businesses, and many people worked for them.

The Rise of the Ranchos

Main Idea Cattle ranching made some Californio families very wealthy.

After Mexico became independent, people in Alta California could trade with people in other countries. Traders from the United States and Britain sailed to Alta California to buy hides and tallow. People in those countries did not have many cattle. Rancheros and rancheras grew wealthy in this trade. A ranchero was a man who owned a rancho. Women who owned ranchos were called rancheras.

Rancho Culture The music on ranchos was influenced by Spanish culture.

132 • Chapter 4

Vaqueros The cowhands of Alta California were some of the most skilled riders in the world. They watched over thousands of cattle on ranchos.

Rancheros and Rancheras

Major land grants, which began in 1834, created some huge ranchos. One famous ranchero, **Mariano Guadalupe Vallejo** (gwah dah LOO peh vah YEH hoh), owned most of the Sonoma Valley. **Maria de los Delores Ontiveros Yorba** (awn tee VEHR ohs YOR buh) lived on a rancho of more than 65,000 acres. Wealthy rancheros and rancheras such as Yorba owned thousands of cattle. Whole families took part in running ranchos.

Dozens or hundreds of other people worked on ranchos. They were gardeners, farmers, weavers, cooks, and hunters. Vaqueros herded the cattle. A **vaquero** is a cowhand. Many workers, including the vaqueros, were California Indians.

Rodeos and Fiestas

The ranchos were so large that their cattle roamed free. There were no fences to keep them in. Herds from different ranchos could get mixed. Twice a year, ranchos held rodeos to sort the cattle. **Rodeo** means roundup in Spanish. During the spring rodeo, vaqueros put brands on calves to show who owned them.

Once the rodeo was over, it was time for a fiesta. A **fiesta** is a party or celebration. At fiestas, vaqueros showed off their skills at riding and roping. Families entertained visitors who stayed for days. Close friends and strangers were welcomed.

REVIEW What was the rancho economy based on?

Living in a Pueblo

Main Idea Pueblos differed from ranchos, but the people in them shared many customs.

As ranchos grew, so did pueblos, or towns. Rancho owners stored hides and tallow in warehouses in pueblos near the coast. That way, when ships from the United States arrived, traders did not have to visit every rancho. Pueblos such as Santa Barbara and San Luis Obispo became centers of business.

Traders sold Californios goods in exchange for hides and tallow. When a trade ship docked at a pueblo, people gathered to see the shoes, spices, cookware, and other goods it carried. The trading went on for days. There was often music and dancing.

Fiestas were a part of pueblo life, just as they were on ranchos. The arrival of a trade ship brought people together for a big party. Weddings and holidays also called for fiestas. Ranchos and pueblos had other customs in common. People in both ranchos and pueblos shared their homes and food with visitors.

Homes in pueblos were made of adobe. Their floors were made of packed earth, and the roofs were made of straw. Government officials, soldiers, skilled workers, and some rancho workers lived in pueblos.

The voters of each pueblo chose an alcalde and a council. Alcaldes acted as mayors and judges. They tried to solve most arguments among people in pueblos. The council gave advice to the alcalde.

A Cattle Economy Ranchos and pueblos along the coast both played a part in the trade in hides and tallow.

SKILL Reading Maps Why do you think most ranchos and pueblos were near the coast?

Choices for California Indians

In the 1830s, after the Mexican government closed the missions, many California Indians had to decide what to do. They knew how to farm, but had no land. They needed to find work. Some moved to pueblos. There, they had to do heavy labor for little pay.

Many California Indians stayed on the land that once belonged to the missions. These lands were now ranchos. On ranchos, California Indians often worked in exchange for clothing, food, and a house. They did jobs such as growing crops and tanning cattle hides. Some organized and supervised the other workers.

REVIEW In what ways were pueblos and ranchos alike?

Lesson Summary

Ranchos	Pueblos
Large areas of land	Trading towns
Big houses	Small houses
Cattle herders	Many different jobs
California Indian workers	California Indian workers

Why It Matters...

Ranchos and pueblos created a busy trading economy in hides and tallow in Alta California.

Lesson Review

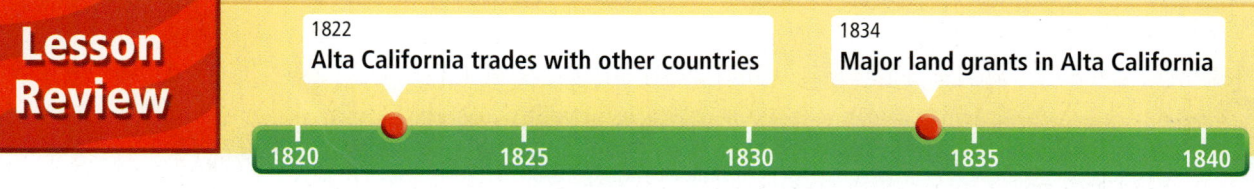

1822 — Alta California trades with other countries
1834 — Major land grants in Alta California

1820   1825   1830   1835   1840

❶ **VOCABULARY** Fill in the blanks:
 fiesta rodeo vaquero
 After a _____, people living on a rancho held a _____.

❷ **READING SKILL** In a paragraph, **compare** the importance of the hide and tallow trade in the ranchos and pueblos.

❸ **MAIN IDEA: Economics** Name three kinds of work done on ranchos.

❹ **MAIN IDEA: Government** Which members of the government did voters in pueblos choose?

❺ **TIMELINE SKILL** When did major land grants begin in California?

❻ **CRITICAL THINKING: Analyze** Write a statement about the decisions California Indians living at the missions had to make as the missions closed.

MATH ACTIVITY In 1834, a cow hide was worth about two dollars—a lot of money then. Ranchos could produce 80,000 hides in one year. How much would the hides have been worth?

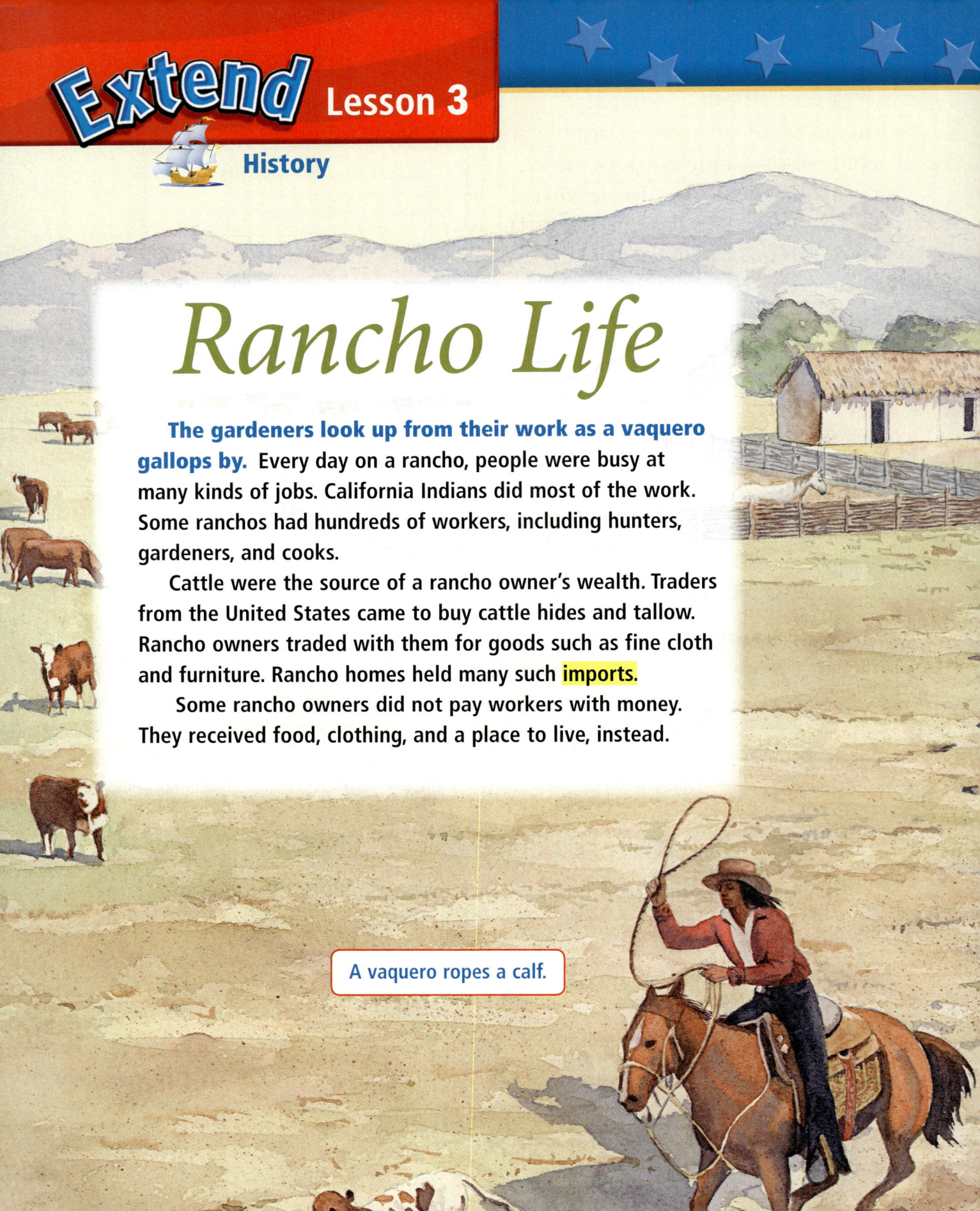

Extend Lesson 3
History

Rancho Life

The gardeners look up from their work as a vaquero gallops by. Every day on a rancho, people were busy at many kinds of jobs. California Indians did most of the work. Some ranchos had hundreds of workers, including hunters, gardeners, and cooks.

Cattle were the source of a rancho owner's wealth. Traders from the United States came to buy cattle hides and tallow. Rancho owners traded with them for goods such as fine cloth and furniture. Rancho homes held many such imports.

Some rancho owners did not pay workers with money. They received food, clothing, and a place to live, instead.

A vaquero ropes a calf.

The rancho house can hold many guests.

Workers grow vegetables for rancho meals.

The ranchera watches over work on the rancho.

Activities

1. **TALK ABOUT IT** Discuss the different jobs you see people doing on the rancho.

2. **WRITE IT** Find out what rancho owners bought from traders. Write an agreement for trading hides and tallow for imports.

Core Lesson 4

Trails to California

VOCABULARY

frontier
trapper
pioneer

Vocabulary Strategy

trapper

Find the word **trap** in **trapper**. A trapper is a person who traps animals for their fur.

READING SKILL
Predict Outcomes
Predict what will happen when Americans find land routes to Alta California.

PREDICTION
|
OUTCOME

 **STANDARDS**
Core: HSS 4.1.4, 4.3.1, 4.3.2, 4.3.3, Analysis Skill REPV 2
Extend support: HSS 4.3.2

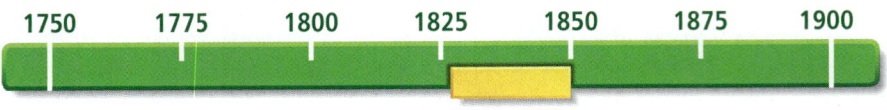
1826–1850

Build on What You Know You know that if something new is going to be done, someone has to be the first to do it. Settlers crossed the high Sierra Nevada to become some of the first people from the United States to move to Alta California.

Explorers Cross the Frontier

Main Idea In the 1820s, people from the United States explored the mountains and valleys of Alta California.

Sea traders from the United States who went to Alta California came home with stories about what they had seen. One trader, **Richard Henry Dana,** told of a land with a warm climate and plentiful resources. Such stories made some explorers want to cross the western frontier and reach Alta California. A **frontier** is an area of land into which settlers start moving.

Richard Henry Dana His book, *Two Years Before the Mast*, made many people want to go to Alta California.

138 • Chapter 4

Beckwourth Pass Beckwourth Pass was easier to cross than other passes in the Sierra Nevada because it was the lowest pass through the mountains. It was named after James Beckwourth (right).

Jedediah Strong Smith

Some explorers from the United States who went west were trappers. A **trapper** hunts animals for their fur. Trappers hoped to hunt animals in the West. In 1826, **Jedediah Strong Smith**, a trapper, became the first American to reach Alta California by land.

With help from California Indians, Smith crossed the Mojave Desert to the mission of San Gabriel. From there, he went north to the Central Valley. The next year, Smith returned east by going over the Sierra Nevada. He was the first person from the United States to cross those rugged mountains.

After his trip, Smith wrote about the rich wildlife of the Central Valley. His reports caused other trappers to look for routes to Alta California.

Frémont and Beckwourth

In 1844, **John C. Frémont** led mapmakers to the San Joaquin Valley. Frémont was an army officer who explored the West. He returned the next year to map other areas and mountain passes. A mountain pass is a low gap between mountains. Finding passes through the Sierra Nevada would make it easier to get to Alta California from the United States.

Five years later, a trapper and trader named **James Beckwourth** found the lowest pass through the Sierra Nevada. Beckwourth had been exploring the West since he was a young man. The pass was named for him.

REVIEW Why did trappers from the United States explore the western frontier?

Pioneers Move West

Main Idea Trappers were followed by settlers moving to Alta California.

Even though Alta California was part of Mexico, a few people from the United States moved there in hopes of finding land to farm. The Mexican government was too weak to stop them from settling.

Most pioneers used land routes to reach Alta California. A **pioneer** is one of the first from a group or a country to enter or settle a place. Going by land cost less than travelling by sea from the eastern United States.

Pioneers had to cross prairies, deserts, and the Sierra Nevada to get to Alta California. They did not have paved roads. Instead, they followed the routes that earlier explorers had taken.

The Bidwell-Bartleson Party

John Bidwell organized one of the first pioneer groups to reach Alta California. Bidwell, a teacher, had read about California. He decided to move there although he had no experience crossing mountains. His wagon train, or group of wagons, left Missouri in May 1841. At first **John Bartleson** led the group, but Bidwell later took over.

Bidwell's party, or group, faced difficulties. Their wagons broke, and tired animals slipped on rocky paths. In the Sierra Nevada, they had to abandon most of their goods. They had barely enough food left.

The hungry pioneers reached the San Joaquin Valley about six months after leaving Missouri. The route they used became known later as the California Trail.

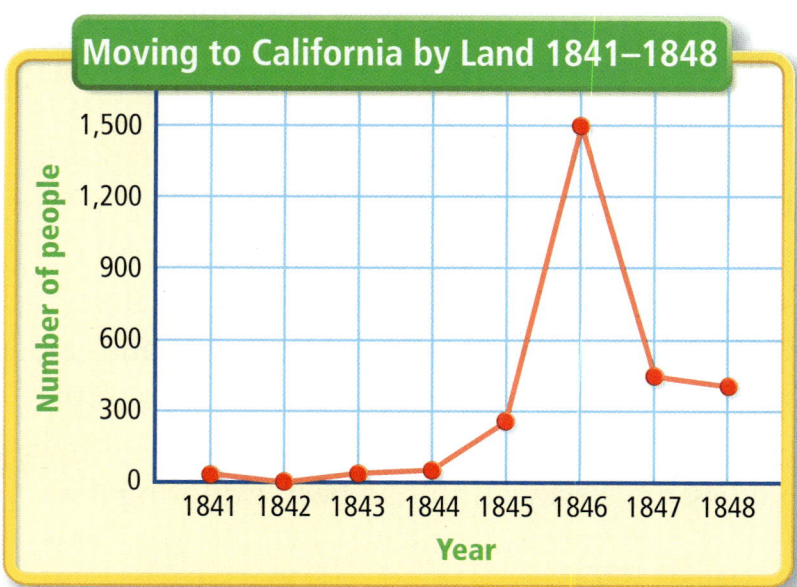

Moving West The number of people moving to Alta California grew until 1846, when more pioneers went to Oregon instead.

The Donner Party

Not all pioneers arrived safely. In 1846, the Donner family left Illinois for Alta California. Other families joined them until the wagon train grew to include 87 people. None of them knew the best way to cross the Sierra Nevada. Winter came while they were high in the mountains. As the weather grew colder, food ran out. They were trapped in snow up to 22 feet deep.

Seven people managed to cross the mountains. One of these seven was a young woman named **Mary Graves**.

Mary wrote about the challenges of the trip in her diary:

> We would sit or lie in the snow, and rest our weary frames [bodies]. We would sleep, only to dream of something nice to eat, and awake again to disappointment.

Mary Graves and the others sent back help to the starving group. The Donner party spent four months in the snow before being rescued. Only about half of them survived the winter.

REVIEW What made crossing the Sierra Nevada difficult for pioneers?

Pioneers This painting shows a wagon train of pioneers heading to Alta California around 1850.

Sutter's Fort

Main Idea Sutter's Fort grew as Mexican control of Alta California weakened.

One of Alta California's most famous pioneers was **John Augustus Sutter**. Sutter was a business owner from a Swiss family. He arrived in Alta California in 1839 and asked for a land grant. The government gave him 50,000 acres in the area where the city of Sacramento is today. Sutter called his land New Helvetia, which means "New Switzerland." He built a fort, which he named Sutter's Fort.

Mexico made Sutter the alcalde of New Helvetia. In return, they wanted him to help protect Alta California from attacks by California Indians. They also wanted his help keeping out trappers from the United States.

New Helvetia grew. It became a stop for pioneers who crossed the Sierra Nevada. They could rest and get new supplies there. Sutter welcomed them, though the government did not. He gave jobs to some pioneers, including John Bidwell. Sutter also sent rescuers to the Donner party.

In 1841, when the Russians decided to give up their trading post at Fort Ross, Sutter bought the fort. He brought everything he could use from the fort to New Helvetia.

Explorers' Routes, 1826–1845

LEGEND
- Route of Jedediah Smith
- Second route of Smith
- Route of John C. Frémont
- Second route of Frémont
- Route of Bidwell party
- Mountain pass
- Present-day border

Explorers This map shows the routes of some of California's first explorers from the United States.

SKILL Reading Maps What places on the map did Frémont visit during his explorations?

Mexico Reacts

The leaders of Alta California did not trust the pioneers from the United States as much as they did Sutter. They worried that the United States might take over Alta California. The Mexican government was losing control of the region. Wealthy rancheros fought with the governor.

In 1845, a ranchero named **Pío Pico** became governor. He moved the government from Monterey to Los Angeles. Pico wanted the pioneers to become Mexican citizens, but most settlers ignored him. He even suggested giving France or Britain control of Alta California to keep United States settlers out. Pico couldn't stop pioneers from coming to Alta California, however.

REVIEW Why was Sutter's Fort important to pioneers?

Governor Pío Pico He became governor after rancheros forced the earlier governor to leave.

Lesson Summary

- In the 1820s, people from the United States began to cross the frontier to reach Alta California.
- Sutter's Fort became a stopping point for pioneers.
- The Mexican government feared that settlers from the United States would take over the region.

Why It Matters...

Explorers and pioneers found routes that led the way for others to move to and settle in Alta California.

Lesson Review

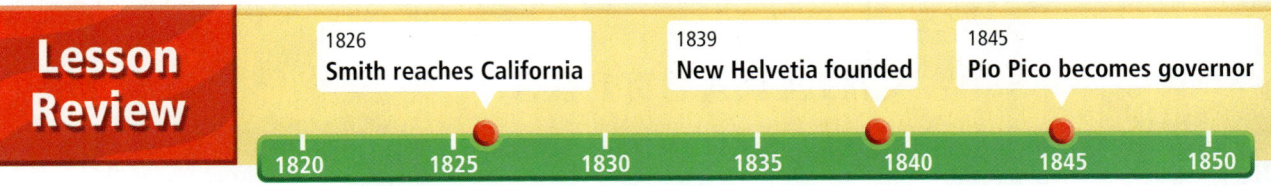

1826 Smith reaches California
1839 New Helvetia founded
1845 Pío Pico becomes governor

1. **VOCABULARY** Use **trapper** and **pioneer** in a paragraph explaining why people from the United States came to Alta California.

2. **READING SKILL** Compare your **prediction** to what actually happened when explorers found land routes to Alta California.

3. **MAIN IDEA: Geography** What did pioneers use mountain passes for?

4. **MAIN IDEA: History** Why was John Sutter asked to help protect Alta California?

5. **TIMELINE SKILL** When did Jedediah Smith reach Alta California by land?

6. **CRITICAL THINKING: Apply** Think about the reasons that Smith, Frémont, and Bidwell traveled to Alta California. In what ways were their reasons alike and different?

WRITING ACTIVITY Write a description of the challenges trappers and pioneers faced in trying to reach Alta California. Use concrete sensory details.

1. HSS 4.3.2 2. HSS 4.3.2 3. HSS 4.1.4 4. HSS 4.3.3 5. HSS 4.3.2 6. HSS 4.3.2 Activity HSS 4.3.2

Extend Lesson 4
Readers' Theater

At Sutter's Fort

California at last! The Brown family has spent months traveling to California from their home in Missouri. After the dangerous journey across the Sierra Nevada, they have arrived at Sutter's Fort. This morning is the start of their first full day at the fort, and there is much for them to see.

Taipa Bigriver

Characters

Moses Greene, guide

Charles Brown, pioneer

Kathleen Brown, pioneer

Joe Brown, 9-year-old son

Amelia Brown, 11-year-old daughter

Taipa Bigriver, vaquero

Emilio Navarro, vaquero

Eliza Fox, baker

144 • Chapter 4

Moses Greene: Good morning! Did you sleep well?

Charles Brown: After all that time in the mountains, getting to sleep in a warm, dry room was better than any fancy hotel! Thank you.

Kathleen Brown: We are grateful you brought us here safely. I don't even mind that we had to leave so many things by the side of the trail.

Taipa Bigriver: We welcome you. I am one of the cowhands here. Mr. Sutter likes to help the people Mr Greene brings to the fort.

Joe Brown: Look at the sunshine, Mother!

Kathleen Brown: Yes. It seems like the sun here is much brighter than back home.

Amelia Brown: Can we look around?

Moses Greene: We will give you a tour. You didn't see much last night.

Emilio Navarro: Along the front wall are storage rooms, the store, and the cooper's shop. Our cooper makes barrels for shipping Mr. Sutter's grain.

Charles Brown: I hadn't heard that Mr. Sutter was a farmer.

Emilio Navarro: Yes, he was given a great deal of land by the Mexican government.

Amelia Brown: That's why the fort flies the Mexican flag!

Taipa Bigriver: Exactly. Across the courtyard is a blanket factory. We raise sheep for wool and spin it into yarn. Then people weave it into blankets.

Charles Brown

Joe Brown: What smells so good?

Emilio Navarro: That's our bakery. Our bakers make all the bread we need. We grind our own flour at the mill here in the fort.

Eliza Fox: Holá. Hot bread, coming out!

Amelia Brown: That's an oven?

Eliza Fox: It's called an orno. What does it look like to you?

Joe Brown: A big beehive.

Eliza Fox: That's right. It's made of bricks that hold heat well. I'd better get these loaves inside! You'll be joining us for breakfast, won't you?

Amelia Brown: Breakfast!

Kathleeen Brown: We'll finish our tour and then we'll eat.

Moses Greene: At harvest, the cooks have to feed as many as 200 people. Mostly, though, it's just 30 or 40.

Kathleen Brown: Every day? I cooked for 30 people at a time on my parents' farm during harvest. It's a lot of work.

Amelia Brown: Look, another tower, Papa.

Moses Greene: We keep watch on the area from them. This is a fort, and we are able to protect ourselves. But let me show you this.

Joe Brown

Amelia Brown

Amelia Brown: A woodsmith's shop?

Charles Brown: Just like back home.

Taipa Bigriver: You're a carpenter?

Charles Brown: Yes. I trained in Saint Louis, back in Missouri.

Emilio Navarro: Impressive! The carpenters here make everything from spoons to shingles. They are almost as important as the blacksmith, whose shop is next door.

Kathleen Brown: It sounds as if the fort can take care of itself very well.

Moses Greene: We can make many of the things we need, and we grow our food—not just wheat, but barley, peas, and beans, too.

Emilio Navarro: Outside of the fort we keep the livestock. And there are homes for vaqueros, and for recently arrived people.

Joe and Amelia Brown: Can we see the animals?

Kathleen Brown: Joe and Amelia have a way with animals.

Taipa Bigriver: Is that right? Well, perhaps you two would like to be my helpers while you're here. I take care of the animals at the fort. Mr. Sutter owns hundreds of horses and mules and thousands of cattle and sheep. Extra hands are always welcome.

Moses Greene: But first, we should make sure you get some breakfast. There is plenty to do here at Sutter's Fort—plenty for everyone.

Moses Greene

Activities

1. **TALK ABOUT IT** What do you think the Browns will do next? Discuss the things they might do or see at Sutter's Fort.

2. **MAP IT** Make a map of what Sutter's Fort might have looked like, using the descriptions in the text. Research more details to add to the map.

Skillbuilder

Write a Report

You may want to learn more about pioneers in Alta California. Who else made the trip? Where did they go? One way to learn more about a topic is to research it and write a report. A **report** is a piece of writing that provides information about a topic.

VOCABULARY
report

Learn the Skill

Step 1: Choose a topic. What would you like to know about it? Write questions that you would like answered.

Step 2: Use reference materials to find answers to your questions.

Source: American National Biography
Who was Joseph Walker?
trapper, trader, and explorer
lived 1798–1876

Step 3: Take notes as you read. Write the name of each source. Organize your notes according to main idea and details.

Step 4: Write your report. Let your opening paragraph tell the reader what it is about. Then, write one paragraph for each main point. Use details to support the main points. Finally, write a closing paragraph to summarize your points.

Many people from the United States found routes to California. One of the most famous was Joseph Walker. Joseph Walker was a trapper, trader, and explorer from Tennessee who lived in the 1800s.

Practice the Skill

STANDARDS Analysis Skill HI 1

Choose a pioneer or group of pioneers who traveled to Alta California. Then answer the following questions.

1. What are some questions I want to answer about these pioneers?
2. What sources can I use to find the answers?

Apply the Skill

Write a report about the pioneers you chose. Find at least two sources about them. Take notes and write a short report that answers your questions. Check to make sure you have written the information from your sources in your own words.

Chapter 4 Review

Visual Summary

1–4. Write a description for each of the items shown below.

Pueblo
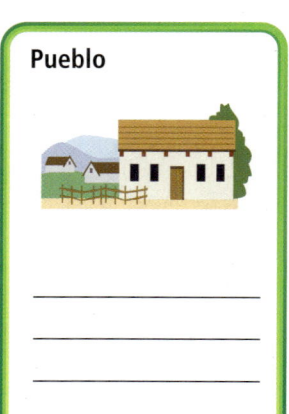

Independence

Rancho

Sutter's Fort

STANDARDS 1. HSS 4.2.5 **2.** HSS 4.2.7 **3.** HSS 4.2.5 **4.** HSS 4.3.1

Facts and Main Ideas

Answer each question below.

5. Economics Why did Californios trade with people from other countries during the Mexican War for Independence, even though it was against the law?

6. Government In what way did the Mexican government change the mission system in Alta California?

7. Economics Explain why cattle were important to the rancho economy.

8. Geography What problems did pioneers who traveled to California face?

5. HSS 4.2 **6.** HSS 4.2.8 **7.** HSS 4.2.8 **8.** HSS 4.3.2

Vocabulary

Choose the correct word from the list below to complete each sentence.

import, p. 122
vaquero, p. 133
pioneer, p. 140

9. Crossing the Sierra Nevada could be very dangerous for a(n) _____ trying to reach Alta California.

10. Shoes were a(n) _____ many Californios bought from traders.

11. A(n) _____ helped take care of the cattle on a rancho.

9. HSS 4.3.2 **10.** HSS 4.2.8 **11.** HSS 4.2.5

150 • Chapter 4

CHAPTER SUMMARY TIMELINE

- 1821 Mexican Independence
- 1826 Smith arrives by land
- 1845 Pío Pico becomes governor

1810 — 1820 — 1830 — 1840 — 1850

Apply Skills

Write a Report Read the passage below. Then use what you have learned about writing a report to answer each question.

> John Bidwell wrote a book of advice for pioneers who wanted to come to California. He told them to pack all their belongings into wagons and make sure they had enough food. They also needed to reach the Sierra Nevada before winter came. Otherwise, they could be trapped in the mountains by heavy snow.

12. What is the main idea of this passage?
    - A. John Bidwell's trip to California
    - B. California's mountain passes
    - C. John Bidwell's advice to pioneers
    - D. Secret wagon train routes

13. Which of the following new details would help support the main idea?
    - A. Pioneers should not pack too much, or they will move too slowly.
    - B. The Mojave Desert is located in southeastern California.
    - C. Some Alta California ranchos covered 75 square miles.
    - D. Pío Pico became governor in 1845.

12. Analysis Skill HI 1 13. Analysis Skill HI 1

Critical Thinking

Write a couple of sentences to answer each question.

14. **Evaluate** What effect did the Mexican War for Independence have on Alta California?

15. **Analyze** Compare the ways people traveled to Alta California and the kinds of routes they used.

Timeline

Use the Chapter Summary Timeline above to answer the question.

16. Was Mexico independent by the time Pío Pico became governor?

14. HSS 4.2.8 15. HSS 4.3.2 16. HSS 4.3

Activities

Citizenship Activity After winning independence, Mexicans wrote a new constitution. Think of one law you would include in a new country's constitution.

Writing Activity Write a story about a child pioneer on a wagon train going to Alta California.

Activities Analysis Skill CST 3, HSS 4.3.2, W 2.1

Technology
Writing Process Tips
Get help with your writing at
www.eduplace.com/kids/hmss/

UNIT 2 Review

Vocabulary and Main Ideas

✔ Write a sentence or two to answer each question.

1. What did **missionaries** hope to do in Alta California?

2. Why did people in the **pueblos** of Alta California begin trading with people from other countries?

3. What **imports** did people in Alta California want?

4. In what way did **secularization** change the lives of California Indians who had lived on missions?

5. What challenges did people from the United States face as they crossed the **frontier** to reach Alta California?

Critical Thinking

✔ Write a short paragraph to answer each question.

6. **Apply** What changes did Mexico's independence from Spain bring to the government of Alta California?

7. **Analyze** In what ways were the Spanish settlers in pueblos and pioneers from the United States alike? In what ways were they different?

Apply Skills

✔ Use the map below and what you have learned about making maps to answer each question.

8. Which of the following would you add to the legend to show the route taken by an explorer or pioneer?

   A. a compass rose
   B. a ship symbol
   C. a colored line with the person's name
   D. a symbol to show mountains

9. Which symbol would you use to add California cities to the map?

   A. ●
   B. ➡
   C. ★
   D. 🏰

STANDARDS 1. HSS 4.2.3 2. HSS 4.2.7 3. HSS 4.2.5 4. HSS 4.2.8
5. HSS 4.3.2 6. HSS 4.2.7 7. HSS 4.3.2
8. Analysis Skill CST 4 9. Analysis Skill CST 4
Activity HSS 4.3.2, W 1.1

Unit Activity

Create a "Why I Came to California" Cartoon

- Choose an explorer or pioneer.
- Draw a three- or four-frame cartoon for younger children showing this person in Alta California.
- Use speech balloons to explain why the person came to Alta California.

At the Library

You may find these books at your school or public library.

Rosalba of Santa Juanita: A Story of Early California by Clara Stites

Rosalba and her family face questions about their land under a new government.

When the Mission Padre Came to the Rancho by Gare Thompson

In 1834, a visiting padre tells stories of times when California belonged to Spain.

WEEKLY READER
Current Events

Connect to Today

Find information about missions that people can visit in California.

- Choose one mission to read about.
- Write notes about the mission's history and what visitors can do there.
- Make an illustrated report that tells about the mission in the past and in the present.

 Technology
Weekly Reader online offers social studies articles. Go to:
www.eduplace.com/kids/hmss/

Read About It

Look in your classroom for these Social Studies Independent Books.

UNIT 3

New Flags for California

The Big Idea

What happens when people move to a new place?

"All the kitchen that I have is four posts stuck down into the ground and covered over the top with a factory cloth…"

From an 1852 letter by Mary Ballou, boarding house manager

Eliza Steen Johnson
1824–1899

For Johnson, who was born in Ireland, moving to California was a chance to try something new. Her San Francisco clothing store was a great success. **page 192**

History Makers

Manuel Dominguez
1803–1882

Why did Manuel Dominguez want to help plan the government of the new state of California? He wanted to be sure the rights of Californios were protected. **page 200**.

Peter Lester
c1814–?

In the 1850s, Lester owned a boot and shoe store in San Francisco. He worked for equal opportunities for African Americans in California. **page 208**

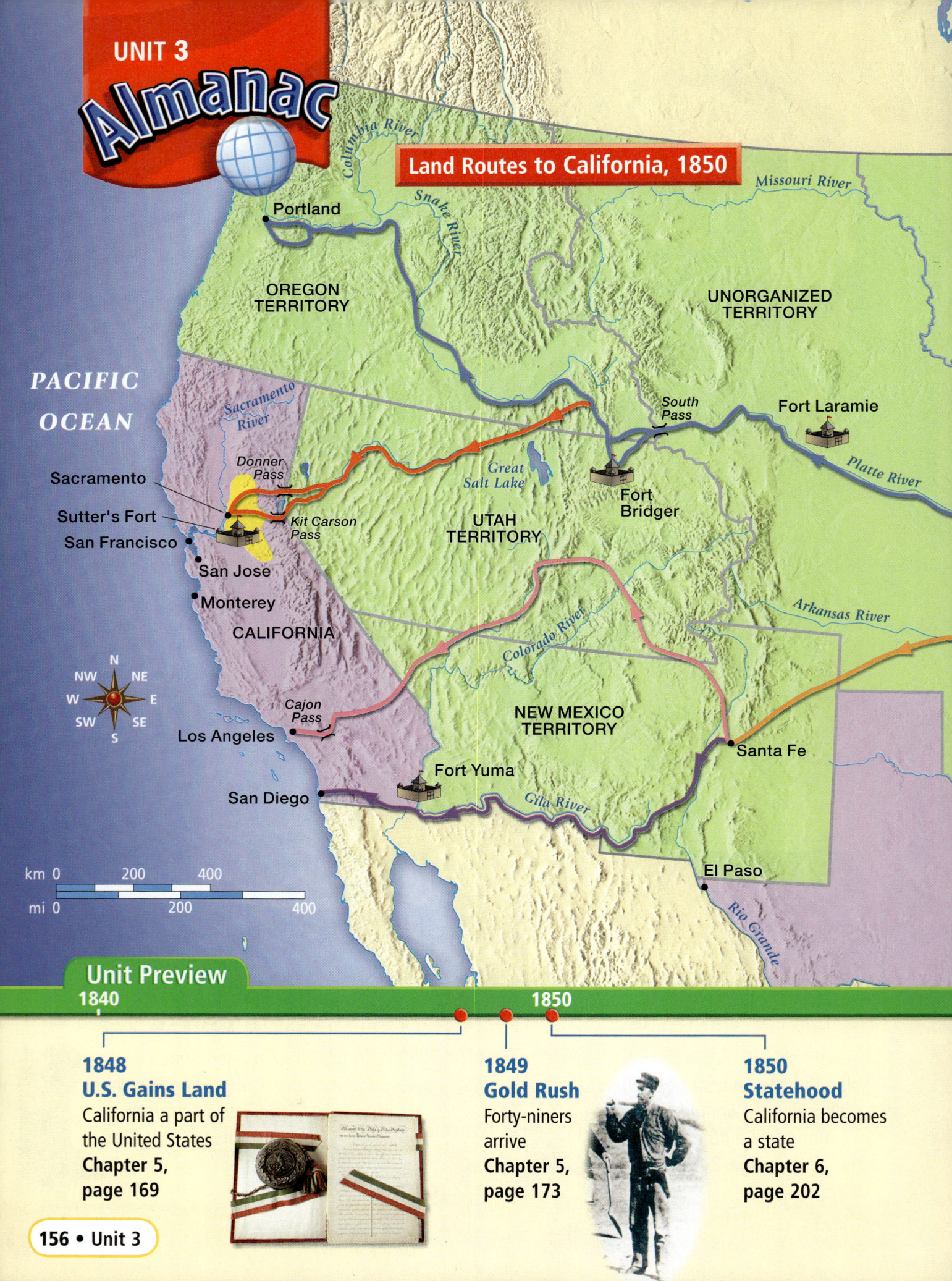

LEGEND

- Oregon Trail
- California Trail
- Santa Fe Trail
- Old Spanish Trail
- Gila River Trail
- United States
- U.S. Territory
- Gold Rush region
- Fort
- Mountain pass
- Territory border

Connect to The Nation

California Population, 1850–1870

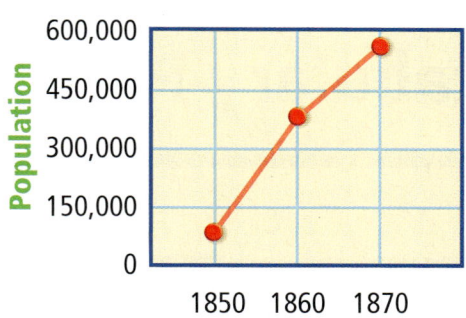

About how many more people lived in California in 1860 than in 1850?

U.S. Population, 1850–1870

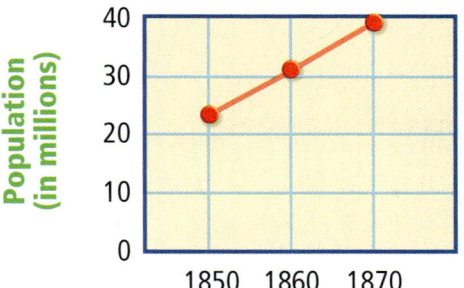

Which line on the two graphs is steeper? What does this tell about how California's population grew?

WEEKLY READER Current Events

Current events on the web!

For a selection of social studies articles about current events, go to:

www.eduplace.com/kids/hmss/

1861 Telegraph Messages reach California
Chapter 7, page 229

1869 Transcontinental Railroad Tracks completed
Chapter 7, page 235

157

Chapter 5

The Gold Rush Years

Vocabulary Preview

Technology
e • glossary
e • word games
www.eduplace.com/kids/hmss/

treaty
This **treaty** made California part of the United States. Mexico and the United States signed the agreement in 1848. **page 169**

isthmus
One way to California was to sail to the **Isthmus** of Panama, cross this narrow strip of land, and then board another ship to sail northwest. **page 174**

Chapter Timeline

- 1846 Bear Flag Revolt
- 1848 Gold found at Sutter's Mill
- 1849 Forty-niners go to California

1845 — 1847 — 1849

Reading Strategy

Monitor and Clarify Check your understanding of events in this chapter as you read.

 Ask yourself whether you understand what you have read. Reread, if necessary.

forty-niner

A **forty-niner** was someone who rushed to California in 1849, joining more than 80,000 in search of gold.
page 173

technology

In the first years of the Gold Rush, miners used simple tools to find gold. As gold became harder to find, miners needed more complicated **technology.** page 179

1853
Hydraulic mining begins

1851 — 1853 — 1855

Core Lesson 1

Bear Flag Revolt

1840 — 1845 — 1850 — 1855 — 1860

1840–1846

Vocabulary

official
military
headquarters

Vocabulary Strategy

official

A meaning of **office** is a job in government. An **official** is someone with a government job.

READING SKILL

Cause and Effect List events that caused the Bear Flag Revolt.

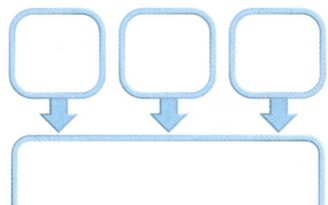

Core: HSS 4.2, 4.3, 4.3.4
Extend support: HSS 4.3

Build on What You Know Our state was first home to California Indians. Next, Spain ruled it. Later, it was part of Mexico. Then some groups wanted it to become part of the United States.

American Interest in California

Main Idea The United States wanted control of California.

By the mid 1840s, about 7,000 Californios lived in California. Most were Mexican citizens by birth. Under the laws of Mexico, only Mexican citizens could own land.

Some people from the United States became Mexican citizens so they could own land in California. **Abel Stearns** was an example. Stearns came to California in 1829. After becoming a Mexican citizen, he married a Californio, **Arcadia Bandini**. They owned a large rancho in Los Angeles, where Stearns became a government official. An **official** is someone in charge of a certain area.

Arcadia Bandini Her land and fortune gave her influence in the Los Angeles area.

160 • Chapter 5

Moving to California
This painting by William Smith Jewett shows a family from the United States arriving in California in 1846.

SKILL Reading Visuals What details show what kind of future the painter thinks the people in the painting might have?

Manifest Destiny

By 1845, about 1,000 settlers had come to California from the United States. Most of them did not want to become Mexican citizens as Abel Stearns had. Some were trappers or merchants. Others ranched or farmed, though Mexican law did not allow them to own land.

Pío Pico (PEE oh PEE koh), the Mexican governor of California, grew worried. Many of the new settlers from the United States believed in "Manifest Destiny." Manifest Destiny was the idea that the United States should stretch across North America, from the Atlantic to the Pacific Ocean. The new settlers from the United States wanted Mexico to give up California.

President Polk

James K. Polk became President of the United States in 1845. Polk believed in Manifest Destiny and wanted California to be part of the United States. He wanted ports such as San Francisco to increase trade and to protect the United States from other countries, such as Great Britain.

In a speech, President Polk said that he would protect the "right of the United States to . . . our [land] that lies beyond the Rocky Mountains." That included California. He promised to protect people who had come from the United States to settle there.

REVIEW Why did President Polk want the United States to control California?

The Bear Flag Republic

Main Idea Settlers from the United States rebelled against Mexican California.

In the spring of 1846, a group of new settlers called the Bears was ready to rebel. To rebel means to refuse to obey people in charge. The Bears wanted to end Mexican government in California.

John C. Frémont was mapping land in California for the United States military. A **military** is a group of people paid and trained by a government to fight. Frémont and **Ezekiel Merritt**, a leader of the Bears, made a plan to capture the pueblo of Sonoma.

Control of Sonoma

Sonoma was the headquarters of part of the Mexican army in northern California. **Headquarters** means a central place. Colonel **Mariano Vallejo** (vah YEH ho), a Californio, was in charge of Sonoma, but he had only a few soldiers there. Like the Bears, Vallejo felt that Mexico was not doing a good job of governing California.

In the early morning of June 14, 1846, General Vallejo awoke to a surprise. Merritt and 32 other rebels were pounding on the door of his home. Instead of fighting, Vallejo invited them in. He agreed to give them control of Sonoma.

The Bears at Sonoma This illustration shows the Bears raising a new flag to replace the Mexican flag.

The Republic of California

Though the Bears controlled just one town, they declared California free from Mexico. They claimed it was now the Republic of California. The Bears quickly created a flag. One of them painted a star, a grizzly bear, and the words "California Republic" on the flag. The event is now known as the Bear Flag Revolt.

The Bear Flag The symbols and words of the Bear Flag became part of the state flag of California.

The Republic of California lasted less than one month. An event had already taken place that would change California forever. The United States had declared war on Mexico.

REVIEW What happened at Sonoma during the Bear Flag Revolt?

Lesson Summary

- More and more California settlers came from the United States.
- Many newcomers wanted California to be part of the United States.
- The Bears rebelled against the Mexican government at Sonoma.

Why It Matters...

The Bear Flag Revolt was the first step on a path that would end 25 years of Mexican government in California.

Lesson Review

1842 — 7,000 Californios in California
1845 — 1,000 U.S. settlers in California
1846 — Bear Flag Revolt

❶ **VOCABULARY** Explain the meaning of **official.** Give an example of one.

❷ **READING SKILL** Use your notes to write three sentences explaining the **causes** of the Bear Flag Revolt.

❸ **MAIN IDEA: Culture** Why was Pío Pico worried about new settlers from the United States in California?

❹ **MAIN IDEA: History** What was the Bear Flag Revolt?

❺ **TIMELINE SKILL** Write a sentence about each of the events on the timeline.

❻ **CRITICAL THINKING: Evaluate** Why do you think General Vallejo chose to give the Bears control of Sonoma?

ART ACTIVITY Make a picture that compares the original flag of the Bear Flag Revolt with the current flag of California.

1. HSS 4.3 2. HSS 4.3 3. HSS 4.2 4. HSS 4.3 5. HSS 4.2 6. HSS 4.3 Activity HSS 4.3

Extend Lesson 1
Biographies

People Who Changed California

They lived during exciting changes in California, and they helped make them. Today we can read about their lives.

Mariano Guadalupe Vallejo
(1808–1890)

In 1835, Mariano Vallejo founded the pueblo of Sonoma, where he raised his family. Vallejo was an official in the Mexican government of California, but he wanted people in California to have more say in their government. He tried to work with newcomers from the United States, although this could be difficult. Recalling the Bear Flag Revolt, Vallejo wrote,

"at dawn on the fourteenth of June they surrounded my house located on the plaza at Sonoma."

— from a book by Mariano Guadalupe Vallejo

164 • Chapter 5

John Charles Frémont
(1817–1890)

John Frémont was a mapmaker in the U.S. Army. He explored western frontiers, including California. Later, he was a military leader who fought to add California to the United States. Later he represented the state of California in the U.S. Senate. In 1887, his wife Jessie Benton Frémont published a book about his life.

Jessie Benton Frémont
(1824–1902)

Jessie Benton used the power of words throughout her life. She was a confident writer and speaker. After marrying John Frémont, she wrote books about his expeditions that sold thousands of copies. Her popular stories and articles about the West made many people want to go there.

Activities

1. **REPORT IT** Report two facts you learned from reading one of these biographies.

2. **CHART IT** Research one of the people in these biographies and create a timeline of important events in the person's life.

 **Technology** Read other biographies for this unit at Education Place. www.eduplace.com/kids/hmss/

Core Lesson 2

The Mexican-American War

VOCABULARY

slavery
armed forces
treaty
territory

Vocabulary Strategy

territory

Terra means earth, or land. A **territory** is an area of land.

READING SKILL

Sequence List in order events in California during the Mexican-American War.

STANDARDS
Core: HSS 4.3
Extend support: HSS 4.3

1840 1845 1850 1855 1860

1846–1848

Build on What You Know What are some reasons neighbors fight? The United States and Mexico were once neighboring countries at war.

Neighbors at War

Main Idea Disagreements about borders between the United States and Mexico led to war.

By 1846, Mexico and the United States had disagreed many times about the borders between them. In April of that year, they fought on land both said was theirs. President **James Polk** wanted to go to war against Mexico. Some groups in the United States said a war would just be an excuse to take land from Mexico. People who were against slavery were against the war, too. **Slavery** is the practice of buying and selling people and forcing them to work without pay. Laws allowed slavery in some states, but not in all of them. People who were against slavery worried that it would be allowed in land gained through war.

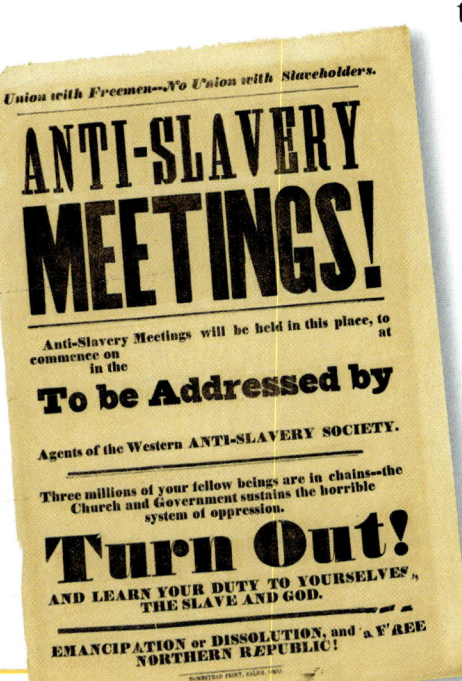

Anti-Slavery Poster
Groups against slavery held large meetings to build support.

166 • Chapter 5

Marines Landing at Monterey Marines like these traveled by sea and fought on land.

SKILL **Reading Visuals** Describe what is happening in the boats and on land.

War Begins

President Polk said he wanted to go to war to "acquire [get] California." In May 1846, the United States declared war on Mexico. Today the war is called the Mexican-American War.

Commodore **John D. Sloat**, who was in charge of United States Navy ships along the Pacific coast, had orders to take California ports from Mexico as soon as the United States declared war. The message that war had been declared took more than a month to travel from Washington, D.C., to California.

In early July, Sloat heard that the war had started. He landed his armed forces at the port of Monterey on July 7. **Armed forces** are groups organized to protect a country with weapons. Sloat's forces raised the American flag at Monterey. They said the town belonged to the United States.

Sloat sent orders to another ship to capture Yerba Buena and San Francisco Bay. Commodore **Robert Stockton** captured San Diego and Los Angeles.

REVIEW Why were some people in the United States against war with Mexico?

California and the War

Main Idea The Mexican-American War made California a part of the United States.

Other battles in California took place on land. General **Stephen Watts Kearny** led United States Army troops in from the east. At about the same time, more United States forces landed in Los Angeles. Kearny and Stockton joined forces. Meanwhile **John Frémont** led other troops down from the north. He arrived in Santa Barbara in January of 1847.

The Treaty of Cahuenga

While in Santa Barbara, Frémont met **Bernarda Ruiz** (roo EEZ). Ruiz, a Californio, had sons in the Mexican army. She told Frémont that he would win support from Californios if he made peace with the Mexican Army.

Ruiz also spoke to General **Andrés Pico** (PEE koh), a Californio leader in the Mexican army. Frémont and Pico worked out a peace treaty that allowed the Mexican troops in California to go home safely. A **treaty** is a written agreement between countries.

New Boundaries When the war ended, Mexico gave up almost half its land to the United States.

SKILL **Map Skill** Name three bodies of water in the territory gained from Mexico.

Land after the Mexican-American War

The War Ends

The Treaty of Cahuenga (kah WEN ga) ended the fighting in California. For more than a year after that, the war continued in other places. After the United States defeated Mexico, both sides signed the Treaty of Guadalupe Hidalgo (gwah dah LOO peh ee DAHL goh).

This treaty forced Mexico to give the territory of California to the United States. A **territory** is land that belongs to a country. The territory included present-day California, Nevada, and Utah, as well as parts of four other present-day states.

REVIEW Why did fighting in California stop before the Mexican-American War ended?

Lesson Summary

The United States went to war with Mexico to gain land. Fighting in California ended with the Treaty of Cahuenga. After the Mexican-American War, California became part of the United States.

Why It Matters...

After the Mexican-American War, the United States included most of the land that it has today.

Andrés Pico He was one of the signers of the Treaty of Cahuenga.

Lesson Review

Timeline:
- 1846 Mexican-American War begins
- 1847 Treaty of Cahuenga
- 1848 Treaty of Guadalupe Hidalgo

❶ **VOCABULARY** Explain what a **treaty** is. Give an example from this lesson.

❷ **READING SKILL** Use your chart of the **sequence** of events to write a paragraph telling what happened in California during the Mexican-American War.

❸ **MAIN IDEA: Culture** What were some reasons people in the United States gave for and against a war with Mexico?

❹ **MAIN IDEA: History** What did John Frémont do in the Mexican-American War?

❺ **TIMELINE** What happened before the Treaty of Cahuenga?

❻ **CRITICAL THINKING: Apply** Compare and contrast the two treaties in this lesson.

✏️ **WRITING ACTIVITY** Choose one of the people mentioned in the lesson to research. Write a two-paragraph biography of the person you choose.

1. HSS 4.3 2. HSS 4.3 3. HSS 4.3 4. HSS 4.3 5. HSS 4.3 6. HSS 4.3 Activity HSS 4.3

Extend Lesson 2
Primary Source

The Treaty of Cahuenga

Bernarda Ruiz wanted to stop a war. How would she get both sides in the Mexican-American War to stop fighting in California? Ruiz met with Commander John Frémont, a leader of the United States military in California. She helped him write a treaty in Spanish and in English. She also convinced General Andrés Pico, leader of the Mexican military in the region, to meet with Frémont.

Both leaders signed the treaty on January 13, 1847, at the Campo de Cahuenga. This ended the fighting in California. The treaty guaranteed that citizens of California would have the same rights as citizens of the United States. It also set free prisoners of war on both sides.

One artist imagined the signing of the Treaty of Cahuenga this way.

PRIMARY SOURCE

This is one page of the Spanish treaty. Leaders signed their names to the English and Spanish treaties.

The names of Andrés Pico and John Frémont are on the Treaty of Cahuenga.

Activities

1. NOTICE IT Describe a detail that you notice in the painting or in the copy of the treaty page.

2. WRITE ABOUT IT List things that you think both Frémont and Pico would have wanted written in a treaty they agreed to sign.

 Technology Visit Education Place for more primary sources. www.eduplace.com/kids/hmss/

171

Core Lesson 3

The Gold Rush

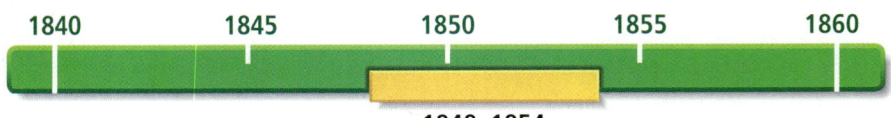
1848–1854

VOCABULARY

gold rush
forty-niner
isthmus

Vocabulary Strategy

forty-nine*r*

Forty-niners were named for the year most of them went to California—1849.

READING SKILL

Main Idea and Details As you read, note details about different routes to California.

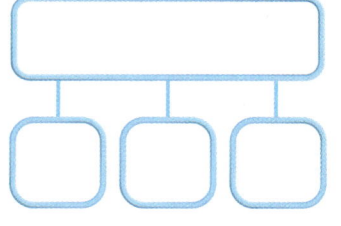

STANDARDS
Core: HSS 4.4.2, 4.4.3
Extend support: HSS 4.4.2, Analysis Skill REPV 2

Sutter's Mill This sawmill was built to cut logs into boards. Gold was discovered here.

Build on What You Know When have you seen people rush to get something? That's what people did when they got news of gold in California.

News of Gold

Main Idea The discovery of gold led to the Gold Rush.

In January 1848 California Indians and other workers were building a new mill for **John A. Sutter.** The mill was near the Maidu village of Coloma on the American River. According to one story, the workers found a shiny lump in the mud and took it to the carpenter in charge, **James Marshall.** Later, he recalled,

> " It made my heart thump, for I was certain it was gold. "

Marshall and Sutter tested the shiny rock in secret. Marshall was right. It was gold.

172 • Chapter 5

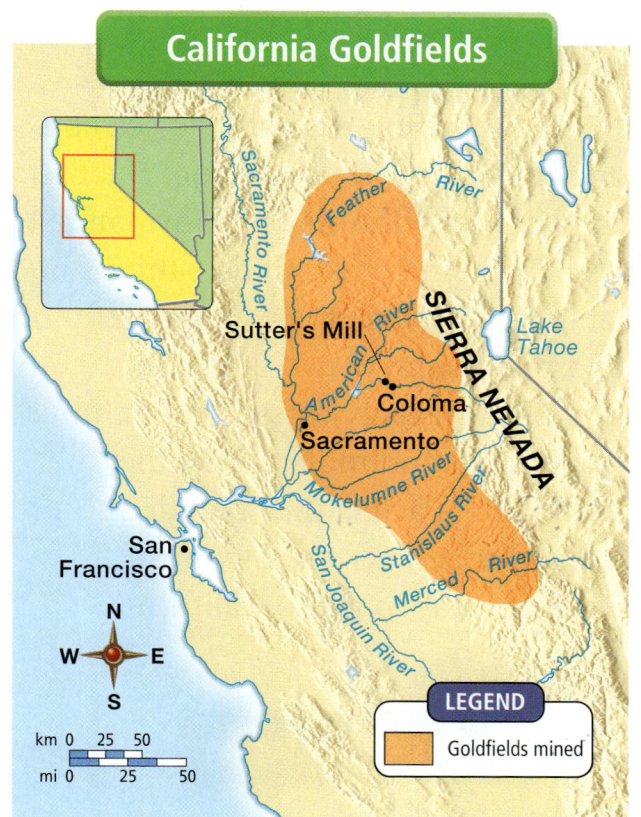

Goldfields The richest goldfields were in the river valleys west of the Sierra Nevada. Newspapers around the country printed stories that brought forty-niners to California.

The Word Spreads

The discovery of gold did not stay secret for long. **Sam Brannan** found out about it. He thought he could sell shovels to eager miners. He walked through San Francisco with a bottle of gold dust, calling,

> " Gold! Gold! Gold from the American River. "

Others also spread the word, starting a gold rush. A **gold rush** happens when lots of people hurry to a place to look for gold. Many of the first miners were Californios from other parts of California. Nearly half were California Indians hired to work for other miners.

The Forty-niners

At first, people outside California did not believe the stories of gold. Then, in December 1848, President **James Polk** said in a speech that there really was a lot of gold in California.

When newspapers reported on Polk's speech, thousands of people got "gold fever." They left their homes and headed for California. In 1849, about 80,000 people joined the California Gold Rush. They became known as forty-niners. A **forty-niner** was someone who went to California in 1849 to look for gold.

REVIEW What were two ways that people learned about the discovery of gold?

173

Three Routes

Main Idea Forty-niners took three main routes to California.

Forty-niners came from many places, especially the eastern United States. The most popular route from the East to California was by land. This overland journey cost the least money, but it took the longest time. Travelers spent six months crossing rivers and mountains in wagons. They faced harsh weather, hunger, and thirst.

The second-most popular route was by boat. Passengers sailed around the tip of South America and then to California. Boat tickets cost more than traveling by wagon, but sailing was less difficult than taking an overland route.

Gold Rush Routes The map and chart compare routes.

SKILL **Reading Charts** Which route cost the least?

Travel Routes	Cost	Time
Overland	$200–500	6–9 months
Sea	$500–700	4–6 months
Land and Sea	$800–1200	1–3 months

The Fastest Route

The third route combined sea and land travel. People sailed from the East Coast to Central America. Most landed in Panama and crossed the Isthmus of Panama. An **isthmus** is a narrow strip of land that connects two larger land areas. They usually crossed the isthmus by riverboat and mule. When they reached the Pacific, they boarded ships to California. This was the most expensive way to get to California.

Routes to California

174 • Chapter 5

Miners Come to California They came from all over the United States and from many other countries. This miner probably came from China.

Thousands of Immigrants

Sailors spread news of the Gold Rush to other countries. Between 1848 and 1854, about 300,000 people came to California. About 75,000, or one-fourth of them, were immigrants. An immigrant is a person who leaves one country to live in another.

Immigrants spoke Chinese, English, French, Spanish, Russian, and many other languages. They brought customs and religious practices from around the world. Gold Rush immigrants added to California's diversity.

REVIEW What three routes brought miners from the East Coast to California?

Lesson Summary

In 1848, gold was discovered near the American River in California. Although travel to California was slow, difficult, and expensive, forty-niners rushed to California from across the country and around the world.

Why It Matters...

The Gold Rush changed California by bringing many people from many places into the state very quickly.

Lesson Review

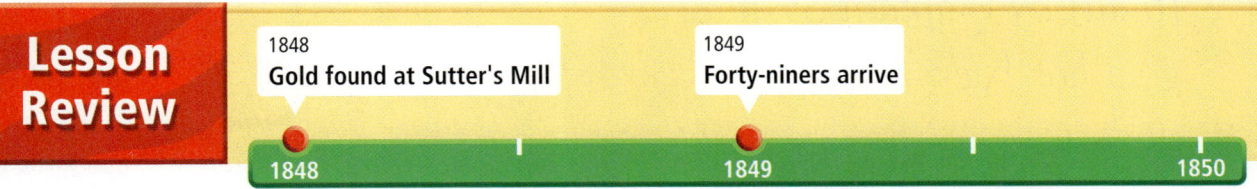

1848 Gold found at Sutter's Mill
1849 Forty-niners arrive

1. **VOCABULARY** Use **forty-niner** and **isthmus** in sentences about the Gold Rush.

2. **READING SKILL** Compare **details** about the different routes. Which way seems best to you?

3. **MAIN IDEA: History** What did President Polk do that spread "gold fever"?

4. **MAIN IDEA: Geography** What were the advantages and disadvantages of traveling overland to California in 1849?

5. **PLACES TO KNOW** Which route on the map on page 174 includes Cape Horn?

6. **TIMELINE SKILL** How many years are shown on the timeline?

7. **CRITICAL THINKING: Analyze** What were some reasons immigrants might have come for the Gold Rush?

WRITING ACTIVITY Write a dialogue between two people who disagree about whether to join the California Gold Rush.

1. HSS 4.4.3 2. HSS 4.4.3 3. HSS 4.4.3 4. HSS 4.3.2 5. HSS 4.3.2 6. HSS 4.4.3 Activity HSS 4.4.2

Extend Lesson 3
Primary Sources

Gold Rush Writings

"Gold Mine Found." These words in a San Francisco newspaper announced the discovery of gold at Sutter's Mill. Journals, letters, books, and photographs also recorded what life was like during the Gold Rush.

> "In the newly made raceway of the Saw Mill recently erected [built] by Captain Sutter . . . gold has been found."
>
> - from *The Californian*, March 15, 1848

John Sutter (left) owned the mill where gold was discovered in 1848.

176 • Chapter 5

> "I met a man to-day from the mines in patched buckskins, rough as a badger from his hole, who had $15,000 in yellow dust [gold] swung at his back."
>
> - from *Three Years in California*, by Walter Colton

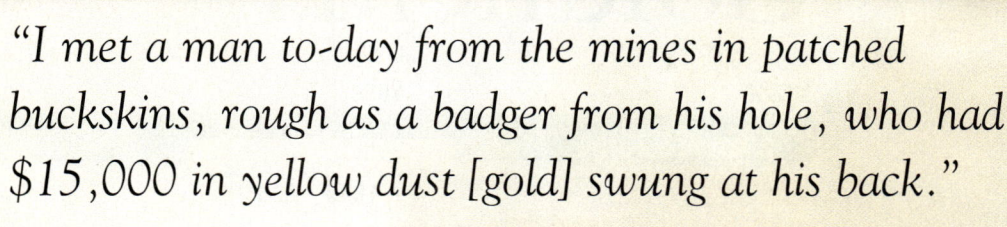

Photographs such as this one can tell us about Gold Rush miners and their tools.

Activities

1. **DESCRIBE IT** Write a short description of what you can tell about miners from the photograph.

2. **CHART IT** Make a chart to compare and contrast the kinds of information you can get from the primary sources in this Extend.

Technology Read more primary sources at Education Place.
www.eduplace.com/kids/hmss/

Core Lesson 4

Life in the Goldfields

VOCABULARY

technology
hydraulic mining
discrimination

Vocabulary Strategy

hydraulic

Hydraulic is from **hydro**, a word that means water. Something that is hydraulic uses water.

READING SKILL
Problem and Solution
As you read, look for three ways miners solved the problem of getting gold.

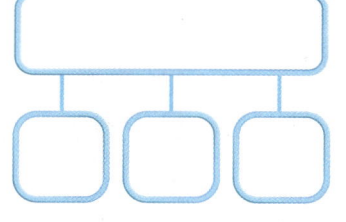

STANDARDS
Core: HSS 4.1, 4.3.3, 4.4.2
Extend support: HSS 4.3.3

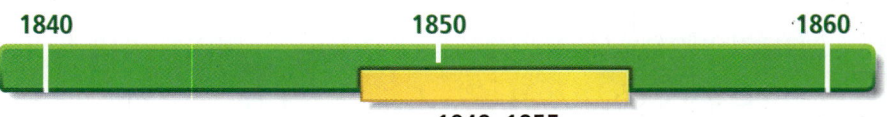
1848–1855

Build on What You Know When you clean a room, you might choose a tool such as a broom to get the job done. Miners used special tools, too. Different tools let them mine gold in different ways.

Mining Gold

Main Idea Miners used technology to get gold.

Gold is a valuable natural resource. One reason it is valuable is that there is not very much of it on Earth. Another reason people value it is that it is easy to shape. Since ancient times, people have shaped it into jewelry and coins. Finally, gold is valuable because it does not rust or decay.

The goldfield area along the Sierra Nevada is one of the few places in the world where people have found gold in large amounts.

Gold The value of the gold mined in California went up as miners found ways to go deeper into the Earth.

178 • Chapter 5

Mining in the Goldfields These miners are using a long tom. Pouring water down the long trough helps separate out the gold.

SKILL **Reading Visuals** Name tools in the photograph and explain their uses.

Taking Gold from the Ground

Gold forms deep in the ground. When erosion wears away the rock over gold, water carries gold flakes, dust, or nuggets into rivers and streams. Miners used technology to separate gold from mud and gravel in rivers and streams. **Technology** is the use of tools and knowledge to produce goods or services.

California Indians used the knowledge that gold was heavier than other materials in sand and gravel. Their tools were baskets and blankets that trapped gold flakes. Mexicans used the same knowledge to let heavy gold settle in pans and bowls after the lighter sand and soil were poured off.

Early forty-niners learned from California Indian and Mexican miners. Forty-niners also used rockers and long toms, which are wooden troughs used to separate gold from other materials.

Within a few years, most of the gold in streams and rivers was gone. Miners began using hydraulic mining to go deeper underground. **Hydraulic mining** is the use of powerful jets of water to break apart earth and find gold.

Miners used other technologies to find gold deeper below ground. They dug tunnels and holes into the ground and used gunpowder to blast and break up rocks.

REVIEW What were three tools forty-niners used?

Life in Mining Camps

Main Idea Miners had hard lives and some comforts.

Most miners were men whose families and homes were far away. These miners did not plan to stay long enough to build homes. After mining from sunup to sundown, they were truly tired. Their meals were very plain. There were few places to buy food, and few types of food to buy.

Early miners lived in tents on land they claimed as their own. These plots of land were called claims. Some claims were just ten feet wide. Claims could be right next to each other, allowing fires to spread quickly from tent to tent. Fires destroyed many mining camps.

Diversity in Mining Camps

Much of the earliest successful mining was done by Chinese, Mexican, and California Indian miners. Jealous white miners practiced discrimination against these miners. **Discrimination** is unequal treatment of people who belong to a certain group.

For example, California Indian miners who worked for mining companies were paid less than other, less-skilled, miners. Threats and attacks pushed Chinese and African American miners into separate camps.

In some camps, however, people from many cultures lived and worked together peacefully. Over time, miners built houses. Camps became towns with shops, restaurants, and public buildings.

Hard Work In 1849, miners like this one earned money from the gold they mined. By 1852, most miners were paid wages to work for mining companies.

Average Daily Amount Earned by Miners

- 1848: $20
- 1849: $16
- 1850: $10
- 1851: $8
- 1852: $6

News and Letters

One reason we know about life in mining camps is that some camps published newspapers. Miners also wrote letters to friends and family. **Louise Clapp** wrote letters to her sister in the East about the mining camp in which she lived. Later, Clapp published her letters in *The Pioneer,* California's first magazine. In one letter she wrote,

> A man may work . . . for many months, and be poorer . . . than when he [began]; or he may take out thousands in a few hours . . .

These newspapers and letters are primary sources that people can use to learn about the lives of forty-niners.

REVIEW What were some difficulties of life in mining camps?

Lesson Summary

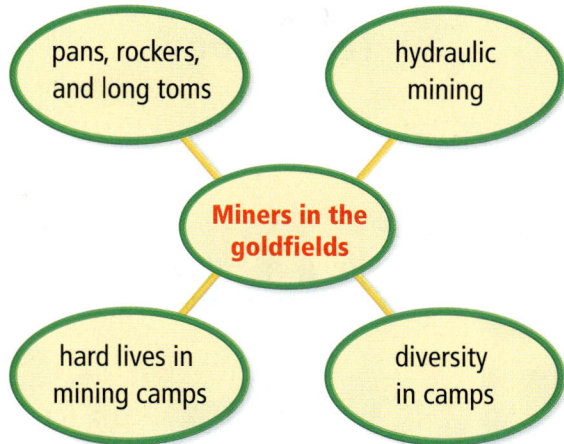

Why It Matters . . .

The technologies miners used affected California's environment, and people still tell stories about the Gold Rush days.

Lesson Review

1. **VOCABULARY** Use **technology** in a few sentences about California Indian miners.

2. **READING SKILL** Explain how two **solutions** to the problem of getting gold were different.

3. **MAIN IDEA: Economics** Why is gold so valuable?

4. **MAIN IDEA: History** What are some primary sources that tell us about life in mining camps?

5. **TIMELINE SKILL** Did Louise Clapp start writing letters before or after hydraulic mining began?

6. **CRITICAL THINKING: Apply** Contrast what mining camps were like at first with how they became over time.

WRITING ACTIVITY Use the lesson photographs to decide what a miner might need. Write an order for supplies that a miner in a camp might send to a store in San Francisco.

1. HSS 4.4.2 2. HCC 4.4.2 3. HSS 4.3.3 4. Analysis Skill REPV 2 5. HSS 4.3.3 6. HSS 4.3.3 Activity HSS 4.3.3

Extend Lesson 4
Technology

Hydraulic Mining

The jets of water could knock over miners standing 200 feet away. The water ripped into river banks and hillsides. Millions of tons of loosened soil and rock fell into long ditches. After miners separated out the gold, ditches carried off masses of mud and gravel.

Miners in California probably took out over $100 million in gold. They also destroyed forests and choked the rivers and streams of the Sacramento Valley. Boats couldn't travel on clogged waterways. Rivers flooded towns and farms.

Farmers were unhappy because floods ruined their crop land. In 1883, a judge stopped hydraulic mining in California.

1. **Building Pressure** As water sped down pipes, pressure increased in the hose.
2. **Nozzles** Miners swiveled nozzles on hoses to direct water to different spots.
3. **Tearing Away Land** Water tore into hillsides. Gravel, sand, mud, and gold washed downhill.
4. **Water** The extra water overflowed rivers and streams. Farms, businesses, and homes were ruined.

TECHNOLOGY

Activities

1. **TALK ABOUT IT** Technology is the use of tools and knowledge to get things done. Describe the tools and knowledge used in the photograph.

2. **ANALYZE IT** Make a chart to show the costs and benefits of hydraulic mining. Write a persuasive speech that uses the chart to support your view of hydraulic mining.

183

Skillbuilder

Understand Point of View

▶ **VOCABULARY**
point of view

People in California had different points of view about life during the Gold Rush. A **point of view** is the way someone sees an issue, event, or person. Understanding different points of view can help you understand the decisions of others. Part of being a good citizen is listening to and respecting other points of view.

Learn the Skill

Step 1: Read or listen to the statement carefully. Note the person's name and what the statement is about.

Step 2: Look for words that signal the point of view. Words that express emotions such as happiness or anger are clues.

Step 3: Ask yourself questions about the experiences that might have shaped the person's point of view.

Step 4: Summarize the writer or speaker's point of view in your own words.

Apply Critical Thinking

STANDARDS Analysis Skill REPV 2

> From here, one has a charming view…a most sunny spot…nestled lovingly in the embracing curve of a hill…like some sheltered nook [*corner*] …
>
> —Louise Clapp, letter to sister, October 29, 1851

> Our feet are wet all day, while a hot sun shines down upon our heads, and the very air parches [*dries*] the skin like the hot air of an oven… After our days of labor, exhausted and faint, we… [*lie*] down in our clothes.
>
> —Daniel B. Woods, journal, July 10, 1851

Practice the Skill

Read the passages about living in California during the Gold Rush. Then answer these questions.

1. Summarize Louise Clapp's point of view.
2. What words express her emotions?
3. Summarize Daniel B. Woods' point of view. In what ways is it different from Clapp's point of view?

Apply the Skill

Read the "Letters to the Editor" section of a daily newspaper. Choose one letter and write a question about the writer's point of view. Then write a paragraph that answers your question.

185

Chapter 5 Review

Visual Summary

1–3. Write a description of each item named below.

The Bear Flag Revolt

_____
_____
_____
_____

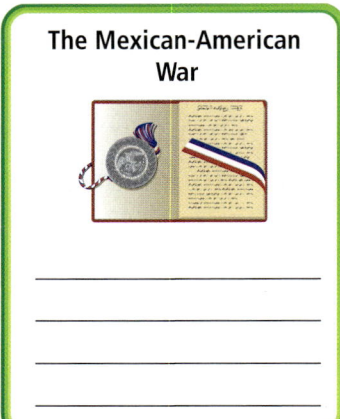

The Mexican-American War

_____
_____
_____
_____

The Gold Rush

_____
_____
_____
_____

1. HSS 4.3 **2.** HSS 4.3 **3.** HSS 4.3.3

Facts and Main Ideas

Answer each question below.

4. **History** After which war did California become part of the United States?

5. **Geography** What three main routes did forty-niners from the United States take to get to California?

6. **Technology** Describe technology of Mexican miners before the forty-niners came.

7. **Economics** What did most forty-niners do to earn money?

8. **Culture** What did Louise Clapp do during the Gold Rush?

4. HSS 4.3 **5.** HSS 4.4.4 **6.** HSS 4.4.2 **7.** HSS 4.4.2 **8.** HSS 4.3.3

Vocabulary

Choose the correct word from the list to complete each sentence.

treaty, p. 162
isthmus, p. 174
hydraulic mining, p. 179

9. The United States and Mexico signed a(n) _____ to end the Mexican-American War.

10. Miners used _____ to remove earth so they could uncover gold.

11. A narrow strip of land that connects two larger areas of land is a(n) _____.

9. HSS 4.2 **10.** HSS 4.4.2 **11.** HSS 4.4.3

CHAPTER SUMMARY TIMELINE

- 1846 Bear Flag Revolt
- 1847 Treaty of Cahuenga
- 1849 Gold Rush
- 1853 Hydraulic mining begins

Apply Skills

Point of View Read the statements below. Then use what you have learned about point of view to answer the questions that follow.

Miner: There's little gold left in the streams to pan or sift with rockers. Hydraulic mining lets us get gold from hillsides. To make a living, we must mine this way.

Farmer: Hydraulic mining clogs the rivers and floods our land and crops. It must stop.

12. In what way are both statements alike?
    - A. Both are about panning for gold.
    - B. Both are about hydraulic mining.
    - C. Both are about farming.
    - D. Both are about mining and farming.

13. Which sentence describes how the two points of view are different?
    - A. The miner wants hydraulic mining and the farmer doesn't mind.
    - B. The miner wants hydraulic mining, and the farmer wants to pan.
    - C. The miner wants hydraulic mining, and the farmer wants it to stop.
    - D. The farmer wants hydraulic mining and the miner wants it to stop.

12. Analysis Skill REPV 2   13. Analysis Skill REPV 2

Critical Thinking

Write a short paragraph to answer each question below. Use details to support your response.

14. **Analyze** Tell ways that John Frémont and Mariano Vallejo were alike and different.

15. **Synthesize** In what ways did the Gold Rush change California?

Timeline

Use the chapter summary timeline to answer the question.

16. What agreement was signed before the Gold Rush?

14. HSS 4.3   15. HSS 4.4.4   16. HSS 4.3

Activities

Music Activity Choose an event on the timeline. Then use what you have learned about the event to write four lines of a song about it.

Writing Activity Write a letter that a miner might have written to a parent about work and life in the goldfields.

Activities Analysis Skill CST 1, HSS 4.3.3, W 2.1.a

Technology
Writing Process Tips
Get help with your writing at:
www.eduplace.com/kids/hmss/

Chapter 6 California Becomes a State

Vocabulary Preview

Technology
e • glossary
e • word games
www.eduplace.com/kids/hmss/

entrepreneur

Mifflin Gibbs was an **entrepreneur** during the Gold Rush. He started a shoe store and a newspaper in San Francisco. **page 192**

delegate

Californians chose people to represent them at a meeting to plan California's new government. Robert Semple was a **delegate** to the meeting. **page 200**

Chapter Timeline

| 1848 | 1849 | 1850 | 1851 |

- 1849 Constitutional convention
- 1850 California becomes a state
- 1851 Land Act creates Land Commission

Reading Strategy

Question As you read the lessons, list your questions about important ideas and events.

 When you finish reading, go back to find answers.

justice

Some people had jobs to carry out **justice** in the new state of California. They were supposed to make sure that people were protected equally by laws. **page 208**

property right

Californios showed picture maps to judges to prove they had **property rights** to land they owned.
page 214

| 1852 | 1853 | 1854 |

1854
Sacramento becomes state capital

Core Lesson 1

Business Booms

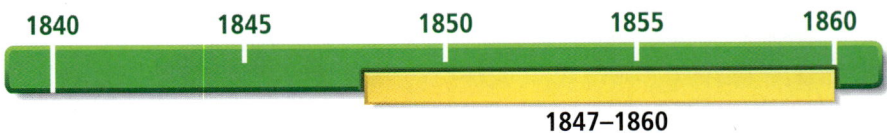
1847–1860

Build on What You Know Think of some goods and services that you buy. Gold Rush miners also bought goods and services.

Businesses Grow

Main Idea Businesses grew during the Gold Rush because miners bought goods and services.

Businesses boomed during the Gold Rush. A business sells goods or services to earn a profit. A **profit** is the money left over after all the costs of running a business are paid. During a boom, many new businesses start and succeed, and older businesses earn more money. One reason businesses did well during the Gold Rush was that between 1848 and 1852, more than 200,000 people came to California. Nearly all of these people were consumers. A **consumer** is someone who buys goods or services.

VOCABULARY

profit
consumer
supply
entrepreneur

Vocabulary Strategy

consumer

To consume means to use. A **consumer** is someone who uses goods.

READING SKILL
Main Idea and Details
List three details about businesses started by entrepreneurs during the Gold Rush.

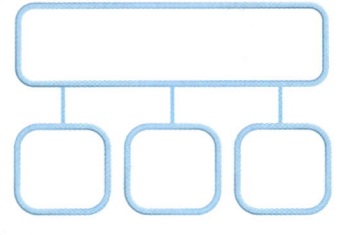

STANDARDS

Core: HSS 4.3.3, 4.4.2
Extend support: HSS 4.3.3

SKILL Reading Graphs In what year was the population count close to 100,000?

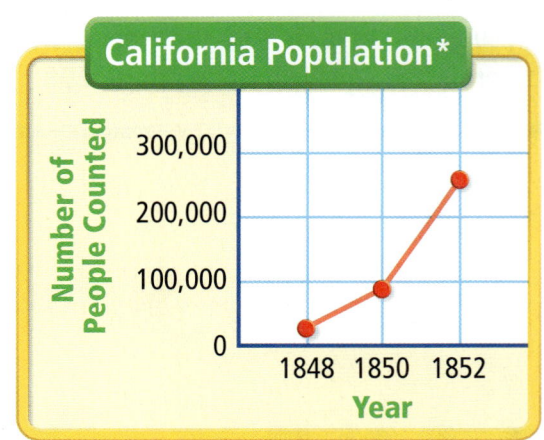

*These figures did not include California Indians.

190 • Chapter 6

Feeding the Miners

One thing miners needed was food. To produce a supply of food, people started farms, grocery stores, bakeries, and restaurants. A **supply** is the amount of a good or service businesses will produce at a certain price. New shops sold miners goods such as food, tools, blankets, and clothes. Laundries and blacksmiths sold services that miners needed.

Businesses in mining towns could charge high prices. Mining towns were far from other businesses that sold goods and services at lower prices. For example, **Sam Brannan** bought all the pans he could find in San Francisco for about 30 cents each. Then he sold them in mining camps for $15 apiece!

Mining Town Trees from nearby hills were cut down to build the town of Placerville.

The Business of Mining

Mining was also a business, and it changed quickly. In the first years of the Gold Rush, gold was easy to find along rivers or streams. Miners worked alone or in small groups. They did not need costly tools or equipment.

When most of the surface gold was gone, miners dug deeper. Some bought expensive equipment, such as hoses for hydraulic mining. Some started mining companies and hired over a hundred miners. If mining companies didn't earn a profit, they closed. Workers moved on, and businesses that sold things to miners closed or moved on too. They left empty buildings, or ghost towns, behind.

REVIEW What were some types of businesses that sold things to miners?

Gold Rush Entrepreneurs

Main Idea Some Gold Rush entrepreneurs started businesses that still exist.

During the Gold Rush, many entrepreneurs started businesses to serve consumers. An **entrepreneur** is a person who takes a risk to start and run a business.

One entrepreneur, **Domenico Ghirardelli** (gihr uhr DEH lee), was a candy maker from Italy. He was one of many forty-niners who came to mine but didn't find much gold. Instead, he started a company that became known for its chocolates.

Levi Strauss was an entrepreneur who never tried mining. His family sold cloth and other goods in New York City.

Successful Businesses

In 1853, Strauss opened a branch of the family business in San Francisco. Most of Strauss's customers were business people who bought cloth and supplies to sell in the goldfields. His business grew. Twenty years later, his company created the popular work pants now called blue jeans.

Eliza Steen Johnson, who came from Ireland, ran a successful clothing store in San Francisco. Other entrepreneurs did well cleaning clothes, taking pictures, or selling food. **Lucy Stoddard Wakefield** baked 240 pies in a week and sold them for $1 each. In this way, she could earn more each week than many miners earned.

Levi Strauss His company found ways to make work pants stronger. **SKILL Reading Visuals** What do the words and pictures tell about the product?

Room and Board

Many Gold Rush entrepreneurs started restaurants, hotels, or boarding houses. Boarding houses offered board, or meals, along with a bed. **Luzena Stanley Wilson** built a hotel called El Dorado in Nevada City. About 200 people paid $25 a week to sleep and eat there. Wilson wrote,

> The miners were glad to get something to eat, and were always willing to pay for it.

Entrepreneurs gained skills from their Gold Rush businesses. Later on, they used the skills in other businesses.

REVIEW Tell three ways entrepreneurs earned money during the Gold Rush.

Jane Bushton Allen She came from Australia and started a boarding house in Monterey.

Lesson Summary

- Gold Rush businesses boomed because thousands of miners bought goods and services.
- Entrepreneurs took risks and had success during the Gold Rush.

Why It Matters...

The Gold Rush made California's economy grow. Some businesses continued to grow after the Gold Rush.

Lesson Review

1849 Ghirardelli's store
1850 Luzena Wilson's hotel
1853 Levi Strauss's store

1 VOCABULARY Write two sentences to explain why **businesses** need **consumers**.

2 READING SKILL Write a short paragraph about entrepreneurs of the Gold Rush using **details** from your chart.

3 MAIN IDEA: Economics Why did business boom during the Gold Rush?

4 MAIN IDEA: Economics What did Lucy Stoddard Wakefield do to earn money during the Gold Rush?

5 TIMELINE SKILL Write sentences that explain the first and second events on the timeline.

6 CRITICAL THINKING: Analyze Why would some people choose to sell food rather than to mine during the Gold Rush?

MATH ACTIVITY Suppose Sam Brannan bought 100 tin pans for $.30 each. He sold all of them to miners for $15 each. How much profit did he earn?

1. HSS 4.4.2 2. HSS 4.4.2 3. HSS 4.4.2 4. HSS 4.3.2 5. 4.4.2 6. 4.3.3 Activity HSS 4.2

The Ballad of Lucy Whipple

from a novel by Karen Cushman

Hundreds of boom towns in the goldfields went "bust." Sometimes the gold ran out. Sometimes fire swept through town, burning the buildings and tents.

Lucy lives in a mining town called Lucky Diggins with her mother and her sisters, Prairie and Sierra. This excerpt takes place a few weeks after a terrible fire.

The middle of June it began to rain, but by then everyone had shelter—a tangle of cabins and lean-tos, unpainted board shacks, and tents of canvas, of blankets, of brush, of potato sacks and old shirts. It looked a lot like the Lucky Diggins I had seen some years before from above the ravine, but smaller, dirtier, poorer, and certainly no prettier.

We reckoned that soon a pack train or something would clear a path through the charred remains of the woods and reach Lucky Diggins. We could then eat a real meal and replace our pots and pans, buckets, linens, bushels of oats and wheat and dried apples. Funny how fast what little we had here in Lucky Diggins began to seem like luxuries.

Mama and I gathered pigweed, plums, and acorns to trade for meat and flour. Prairie and Sierra sifted through the ashes of the town for gold dust and nuggets. At night we baked acorn-meal biscuits and doughy little crabapple pies to sell to the miners. Then for a few hours we slept on scratchy brush and branches, dreaming of what we no longer had, of hairbrushes and soap, forks and baskets and table spreads, ribbons and trimmings on caps and hats, flannel, cotton, wool, and featherbeds.

The town was gone, the game was gone, and the miners were finding that even the far diggings were pretty much worked out, and many of them moved on into the mountains. Others took to digging tunnels, called coyote holes, in the gritty banks of the river. There was talk about breaking the gold out of rocks, but that was beyond the miners' resources. Gloom hung in the air.

Real summer came at last. On a powerful hot day, while I sat with my feet dangling in the tepid shallows of the river, Snowshoe Ballou came by, his big feet stirring up the dust like an unlucky wind. I feared more bad news.

"Saying good-bye, little sister. Moving on." He tipped his hat and turned to go.

"Wait, Snowshoe. Wait. Where are you going and why?"

Two questions—it looked for a moment like they might be too much for Snowshoe, but finally he swallowed hard and answered. "Farther into the mountains. Me and Hennit and his kin. Too many folks around here lately. Done caught all the fish, killed the game, dammed the rivers, cut down the trees, scattered the acorns, then burned it all down. Indians can't live here no more, and neither kin I." He looked up into the woods.

"Too bad. Mighty purty country once, afore it was fished and logged and mined to death. Me and Hennit, we got to go. Up there, where is more game and less people."

After this longest speech of his life, he tipped his hat again and left. I watched him climb up the ravine path to the edge of the woods, where he joined a group of Indians, backs laden with skins and packs and babies. I waved until I couldn't see them anymore.

Walking home, I whispered, "Know many, trust few, always paddle your own canoe." That's what Snowshoe wanted—his own canoe again. I hoped he'd find it.

Activities

1. **THINK ABOUT IT** What was one of the problems for the town and what did people do to try to solve it?

2. **WRITE ABOUT IT** What might Lucy and her family do next? Write two paragraphs telling what you think.

Core Lesson 2

The Thirty-first State

1848–1854

VOCABULARY

convention
delegate
compromise

Vocabulary Strategy

convention

The prefix **con-** in **convention** means together. People come together in a convention.

READING SKILL

Sequence List events that led to California becoming a state.

1	
2	
3	
4	

Core: HSS 4.3.3, 4.3.4, 4.3.5, 4.5.2
Extend support: HSS 4.3.4

Build on What You Know What are some rules in your classroom that might be different from rules in a first-grade classroom? When California became a state, some rules changed.

Reasons for a State

Main Idea Many people who came to California during the Gold Rush wanted it to become a state.

California became a part of the United States in 1848, but it was not a state. People in California did not vote for a governor the way people in states could. The United States Army put military governors in charge of the new territory. California had five different governors in one year. Pueblos were still governed by alcaldes, or mayors who had been appointed during Mexico's government.

Bennett Riley He was the sixth military governor appointed to California.

198 • Chapter 6

Governments of California

Colony of Spain 1769–1821	Territory of Mexico 1821–1848	State of U.S. 1850
King of Spain	President and Congress of Mexico	President and Congress of the United States
Governor appointed by Spanish government	Governor appointed by Mexican government	Governor and representatives chosen by voters
Alcaldes appointed by Spanish government or pueblo council	Alcaldes appointed by Mexican government or pueblo council	Mayor chosen by voters

Changing Governments The chart compares governments of California at different times in its history.

A Call for Change

The Gold Rush brought thousands of newcomers to California during each month of 1849. People from other parts of the United States soon outnumbered Californios in Los Angeles and the pueblos of northern California. These people set up town governments like those where they had come from.

These newcomers had chosen leaders of their towns and home states. They saw this as a right, or freedom, they had as citizens of the United States. They also wanted to vote for leaders to represent them in the United States Congress. For these reasons, they wanted California to become a state.

Californios Take Part

In most of southern California, Californios were still in charge. Most wanted to end military government. Some wanted California to become a state. Some were against it. Others felt that they did not have much choice. The large numbers of newcomers from the United States were powerful.

In April 1849, **General Bennett Riley**, became the sixth military governor. Riley agreed that California needed a better system of government. He called a group of Californians together to discuss a plan that would let the people in California govern themselves.

REVIEW Why did many people in California want to form a state?

A Constitutional Convention

Main Idea Delegates met and decided on a plan for their state government.

In June 1849, General Riley called for a convention. A **convention** is a meeting that brings people together for a common purpose. The purpose was to write a constitution, or a plan of government. The meeting was called a constitutional convention.

Riley first called for elections in twelve different parts of California. People in each part would vote for delegates for the convention. A **delegate** is a representative chosen to speak or act for others.

The Convention Begins

On September 1, 1849, forty-eight delegates, all men, met in Colton Hall in Monterey. Forty were born in the United States. Eight delegates were Californios.

Robert Semple wanted Californios to agree that California should become a state. He had met Californio delegate **Mariano Vallejo** during the Bear Flag Revolt. The two men walked together to the front of the hall. Their walk showed that Californios and people from other parts of the United States could get along. The walk helped delegates agree that they wanted California to become a state.

The Convention at Colton Hall

Voting and Borders

Next the delegates discussed who would be allowed to vote. Most did not want California Indians to vote.

However, many worried that if California Indians could not vote, Californios would not be able to vote. Most Californios had Indian ancestors. **Manuel Dominguez**, a delegate, had already been denied some rights because he looked like a California Indian. Delegates agreed that all Californios, including Dominguez, would be allowed to vote because they were citizens.

Delegates also had to decide on California's eastern border. They chose a border along the Sierra Nevada and the Colorado River. This is where the state border is today.

California's Constitution

Delegates also agreed that slavery would not be allowed in California. At that time, slavery was allowed in some states. The decisions about borders, slavery, and other issues were written into a new state constitution.

The 1849 constitution begins with a "Declaration of Rights." A declaration states important ideas. The Declaration of Rights protected freedom of religion and freedom of speech. These are rights that are protected by the Constitution of the United States.

The California Constitution also included some rights that were not in the United States Constitution or the laws of other states. One was the traditional Spanish right of married women to own property such as land.

REVIEW What was the purpose of California's constitutional convention?

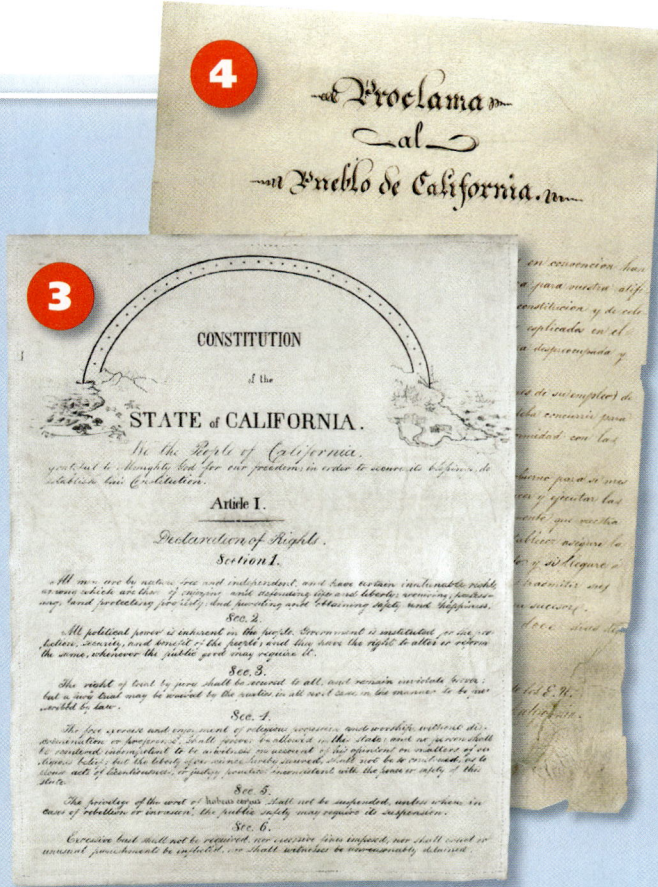

"All political power is... in the people."

– from **Declaration of Rights, California Constitution.**

❶ **Robert Semple** He led the meetings at the convention.
❷ **Colton Hall** Delegates met in this room.
❸ **English** This is the first page of the state constitution in English.
❹ **Spanish** This is the first page of the state constitution in Spanish.

201

Statehood

Main Idea California became a state after a compromise in the United States Congress.

The new constitution was ready. The delegates told the United States Congress that California wanted to become a state.

Some people in Congress did not want California to become a state. In 1849, fifteen southern states allowed slavery. They were known as slave states. Fifteen northern states did not allow slavery. They were called free states. People in slave states did not want another free state. If there were more free states, Congress might vote to stop slavery in the whole country.

After almost a year, the two sides in the United States Congress reached a compromise. A **compromise** is an agreement that gives something to both sides. The southern states agreed to accept California as a free state. The northern states agreed to the Fugitive Slave Law, which required northerners to turn in slaves who already had escaped.

This compromise was called the Compromise of 1850. It led to California becoming the 31st state on September 9, 1850. The compromise changed the lives of African Americans who had been enslaved in other states and then came to California. One of these was **Bridget "Biddy" Mason**. She won her freedom in an important court case about people's rights.

North and South The map helps locate and identify the slave states and free states.

Slave and Free States, 1850

202 • Chapter 6

A State Capital

Delegates at the first constitutional convention decided on a capital, or central place for the work of state government. The state capital they chose was San Jose. Later, they moved it to Vallejo, and then to Benicia.

The state government had to decide finally on one place. The city of Sacramento offered buildings to the government. The city also offered a plan for more buildings. In 1854, Sacramento became the state capital, as it still is today.

REVIEW What did southern states agree to in the Compromise of 1850?

Lesson Summary

- Many people in California wanted to vote for their own leaders after California became part of the United States.
- Delegates at the constitutional convention wrote a plan for state government.
- California became a state after the United States Congress agreed to the Compromise of 1850.

Why It Matters...

The government created by the California Constitution was the start of California's government today.

News of the 31st State
Some people in California celebrated by adding an extra star to their flags.

Lesson Review

1849 — Constitutional convention
1850 — California becomes a state

1849 ———— 1850 ———— 1851

1 VOCABULARY Use **delegate** and **convention** in a short paragraph about the constitutional convention.

2 READING SKILL Write a paragraph that summarizes the **sequence** of events that led to California becoming a state.

3 MAIN IDEA: Culture What were two reasons people in California wanted California to become a state?

4 MAIN IDEA: Government What were three questions that delegates discussed as they wrote the California constitution?

5 TIMELINE SKILL Write sentences that explain the connection between the first and second event.

6 CRITICAL THINKING: Cause and Effect What were some effects of the Compromise of 1850?

CHART ACTIVITY Make a chart that organizes information you learned about the California constitution.

1. HSS 4.3.5 2. HSS 4.3.5 3. HSS 4.3.5 4. HSS 4.5.2 5. HSS 4.5.2 6. HSS 4.3.5 Activity HSS 4.5.2

Extend Lesson 2

Biographies

Women Who Built California

Women who came to California had opportunities they hadn't had before. They used their skills and energy to write books, earn money, and have adventures. As they did so, they changed California. They helped make the state what it is today.

Helen Hunt Jackson
(1830-1885)

Writer Helen Hunt Jackson knew that California Indians had been treated unjustly by the United States government. She came to California to learn more. She used what she saw to write *Ramona*, a novel about a California Indian woman. Many people read the novel and learned about California's history.

204 • Chapter 6

CHARACTER TRAIT: Responsibility

Bridget "Biddy" Mason
(1818-1891)

Biddy Mason came to California as an enslaved person. After she learned that California's constitution outlawed slavery, she went to court and won her freedom. With the money she earned as a nurse, she bought and sold land in Los Angeles. She used the money she earned to give people food, shelter, and care.

Louise Clapp
(1819-1906)

Louise Clapp came to the goldfields in 1851. She wrote long letters with rich details and funny comments to her sister in Massachusetts. Two years later, Clapp published her letters in a magazine. The letters became popular and were later published as a book.

This illustration is from Clapp's book.

Activities

1. **TALK ABOUT IT** Explain what you think one of these three women did that showed **responsibility**.

2. **RESEARCH IT** Find five more facts about one of the people on these pages. Write three paragraphs that include those facts.

 **Technology** Read other biographies at Education Place.
www.eduplace.com/kids/hmss/

BIOGRAPHIES

Core Lesson 3

New Towns and Cities

VOCABULARY

capitol
justice
vigilante

Vocabulary Strategy

capit**o**l

Capitol, the main building of a government, is spelled with an **o**. Capital, the government city, is spelled with an **a**.

READING SKILL
Compare and Contrast
List facts about what California was like before and after the Gold Rush.

STANDARDS
Core: HSS 4.1.3, 4.1.5, 4.4.2, 4.4.3, 4.4.4
Extend support: HSS 4.4.2

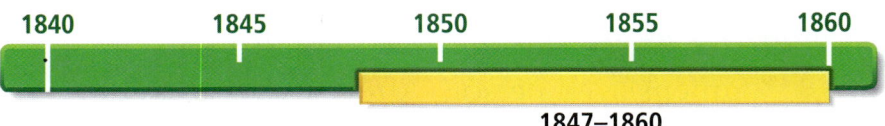
1847–1860

Build on What You Know Today California has many big cities. Perhaps you live in one. Which ones do you think became cities because of the Gold Rush?

Building Towns

Main Idea Cities grew and new towns sprang up near the goldfields of northern California.

Some of the mining camps built during the Gold Rush became towns after California became a state. Some places that had been small towns before the Gold Rush grew into cities. Until 1847, San Francisco was a village called Yerba Buena. Only a few hundred people lived there. When the Gold Rush began, ships brought thousands of forty-niners to San Francisco. By 1850, about 25,000 people lived in the quickly growing city.

San Francisco Most ships from other countries and the rest of the United States came to California through San Francisco Bay.

206 • Chapter 6

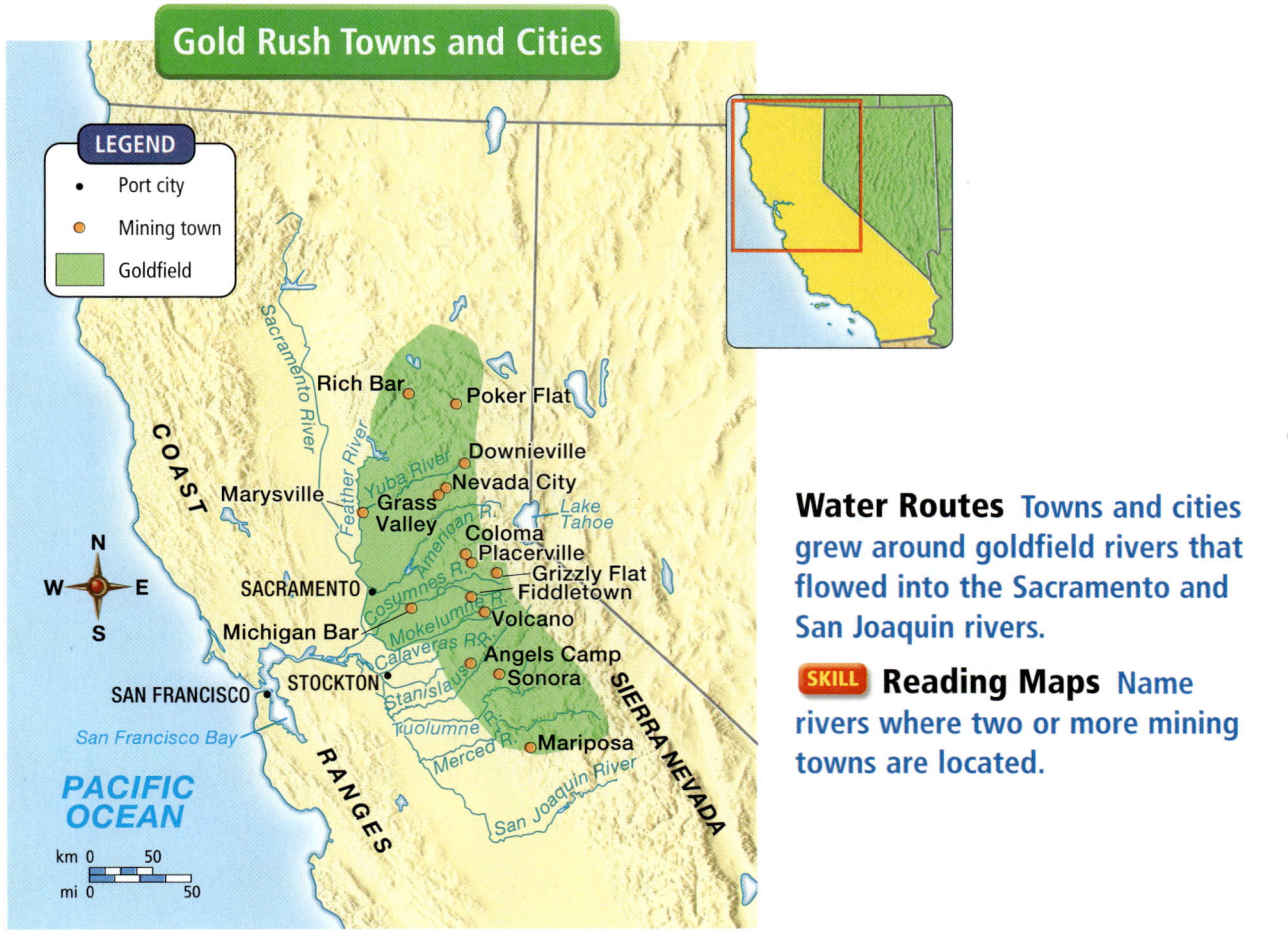

Gold Rush Towns and Cities

Water Routes Towns and cities grew around goldfield rivers that flowed into the Sacramento and San Joaquin rivers.

SKILL Reading Maps Name rivers where two or more mining towns are located.

Port Cities

San Francisco grew because ships brought mining supplies and other products. Merchants traded these goods for gold and items made in California. By 1860, San Francisco was a busy city of about 60,000 people.

Another port city that started during the Gold Rush was on the San Joaquin River. Boats from San Francisco sailed to a camp called Mudville to get closer to goldfields.

Charles Weber, an immigrant from Germany, bought land in Mudville. Instead of looking for gold, he rented out land for shops, hotels, and other businesses. He named the growing town after **Robert Stockton**, a United States Navy leader he admired.

Sacramento

At the start of the Gold Rush, **John Sutter** built a road from his fort to the Sacramento River. As ships full of gold seekers arrived, the little port grew. **Sam Brannan** opened a store that sold supplies to miners. Brannan's store and other businesses boomed as more forty-niners arrived. The port became the lively town of Sacramento.

In 1854, when Sacramento became the state capital, it grew as the center of government. The capitol, which was completed in 1855, had meeting rooms and offices. A **capitol** is the main building for government work.

REVIEW Why did San Francisco and Stockton grow during the Gold Rush?

Seeking Success

Main Idea People who came to California found new opportunities and problems.

The Gold Rush brought together people from all over the world. By the 1850s, the population of California was very diverse, or varied. Some people came to get rich any way they could. Others wanted new opportunities and were willing to work hard.

Mifflin Wistar Gibbs came to California to try mining. He didn't find gold, but he opened a shoe store with **Peter Lester**. In 1855, Gibbs began to publish *Mirror of the Times*. It was California's first newspaper written by and for African Americans.

Gibbs wrote and spoke against the discrimination that many African Americans faced. Throughout his life, he worked for justice. **Justice** is fair and equal treatment under the law. Gibbs wrote that

> "determination holds the key to success."

He later became a lawyer and a judge.

Not everyone in California cared about justice. Many criminals also came during the Gold Rush. They thought that it would be easy to steal gold, money, and land in California. Gold miners did not always stay in one place long enough to set up strong governments and fair laws.

Mifflin Gibbs He started a newspaper as well as a meeting place in San Francisco for African Americans to share ideas.

Organizing Governments

To stop criminals, some people became vigilantes. **Vigilantes** are people who punish and even kill others without proving they have broken any laws. Vigilantes claim to fight crime, but they often commit crimes themselves. Vigilantes attacked immigrants, African Americans, Mexicans, and American Indians. They were often cruel and unjust.

In time, people organized local governments and systems of laws. They set up police forces and courts. The new laws protected citizens from both criminals and vigilantes.

REVIEW What did Mifflin Gibbs do in California?

San Francisco Police Chief, P. Crowley Cities such as San Francisco formed police forces.

Lesson Summary

During the Gold Rush, San Francisco grew into a city. New towns sprang up along rivers near goldfields. Most people came to do honest work, but crime was a problem.

Why It Matters...

Many of California's modern cities had their beginnings as trade and business centers during the Gold Rush.

Lesson Review

1850	1855	1860
San Francisco has 25,000 people	Gibbs starts newspaper	San Francisco has 60,000 people

1848 — 1850 — 1852 — 1854 — 1856 — 1858 — 1860

1. **VOCABULARY** Use **justice** and **capitol** in two sentences about government.

2. **READING SKILL** Write a sentence to **contrast** San Francisco before and after the Gold Rush.

3. **MAIN IDEA: Geography** How did ports help towns or cities grow during the Gold Rush?

4. **MAIN IDEA: Government** Why did many mining camps lack fair laws?

5. **TIMELINE SKILL** In what year did San Francisco have 60,000 people?

6. **CRITICAL THINKING: Synthesize** Why do you think Charles Weber decided to rent his land to businesses?

RESEARCH ACTIVITY Choose a town or city from the lesson. Do research to learn more and report on what this place was like during the Gold Rush.

1. HSS 4.4.2 2. HSS 4.4.2 3. HSS 4.4.2 4. HSS 4.4.2 5. HSS 4.4.3 6. HSS 4.4.2 Activity HSS 4.4.4

Extend Lesson 3
History

ARTS in the CITY

The Gold Rush changed San Francisco and other California towns. People built theaters, concert halls, and museums to bring the arts to the city. The Metropolitan Theatre in San Francisco was one of the first of these new buildings. Actors, dancers, and musicians came from far away to perform.

Catherine Norton Sinclair was director of the Metropolitan Theatre, which opened in December 1853.

Edwin Booth was one of the famous actors who came to San Francisco to perform in plays.

Posters like this one brought customers to the theater for drama, dance, and many kinds of musical performances.

Activities

1. **DESCRIBE IT** Look at these two pages. How can you tell the Metropolitan Theatre was important to San Francisco?

2. **WRITE IT** Write a letter about an evening at the theater. Mention and describe at least three things pictured on these pages.

Skillbuilder

Interpret Historical Images

To interpret means to explain. When you interpret a historical image, you explain what it tells you about a time or place. Look carefully at this photograph of San Francisco during the 1850s. Use it to practice the skill of interpreting historical images.

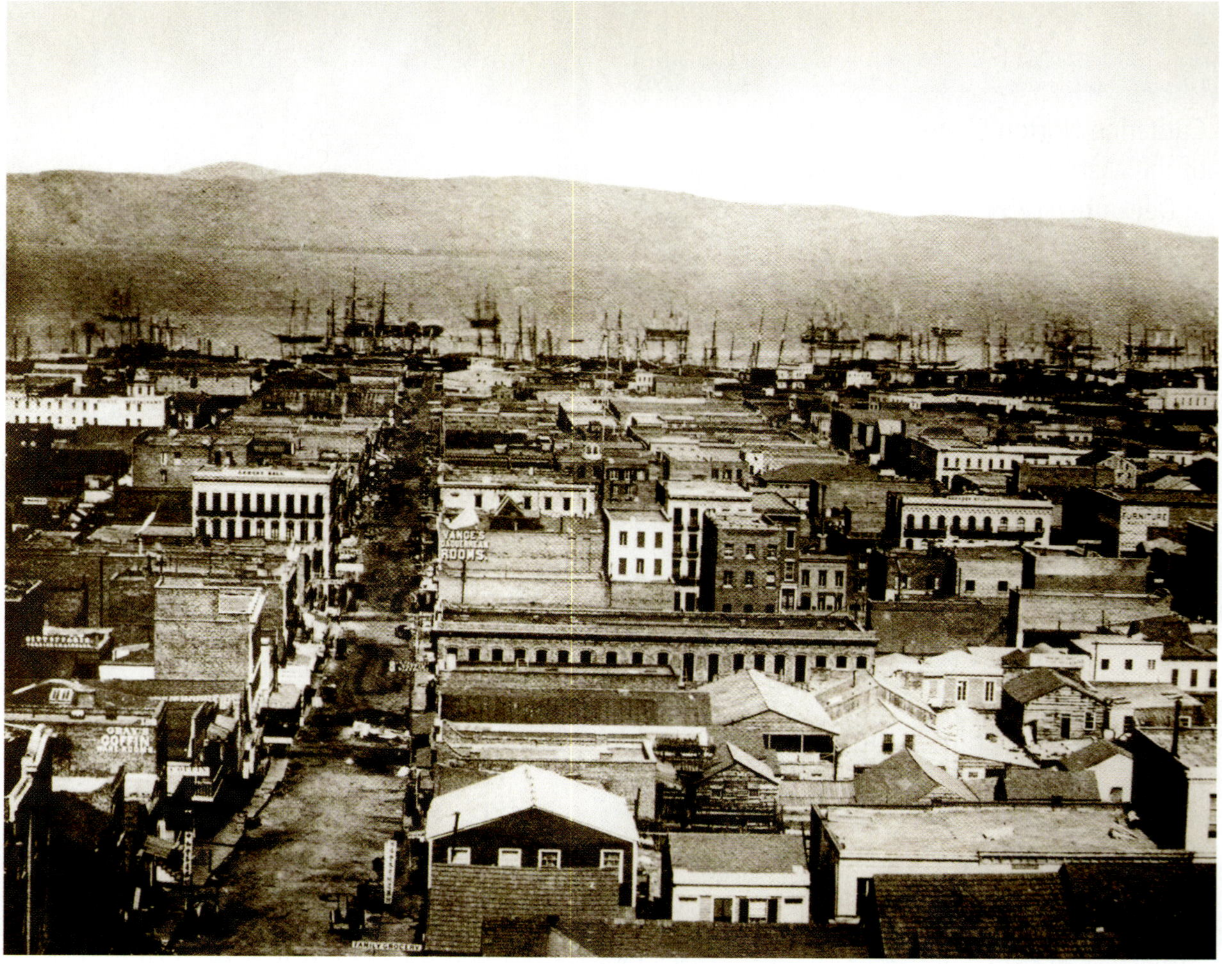

A View Down Sacramento Street in San Francisco, 1856 The photograph was taken from Dupont Avenue. Later, Dupont Avenue was named Grant Avenue.

Apply Critical Thinking

Learn the Skill

Step 1: Read the title and the caption of the picture. Think about what you already know about the event or time period.

Step 2: Look at the picture carefully. What kind of information does it give you? What can you tell about early San Francisco?

Step 3: Ask yourself what you have learned from the picture. What can you see in the image that helps you understand how San Francisco grew into a city?

Practice the Skill

Use the picture on page 212 to answer the questions below.

1. What does the caption tell about the time and place of the photograph? What else does the caption tell you?
2. Describe two different kinds of buildings in the photograph. What were some ways that people might have used the buildings?
3. What do you see in the photograph besides buildings?

Apply the Skill

Choose a picture from a part of this textbook you have already studied. Write a short paragraph to explain what the picture shows you. Then write three questions you could ask to better understand the picture.

Core Lesson 4

Land Rights

1851–1873

Build on What You Know Think of a shirt or book you own. Can you prove that you own it? Californios had to prove that they owned their land.

Californio Lands

Main Idea Californios had to prove that they owned the land on which they lived and ranched.

The Treaty of Guadalupe Hidalgo made everyone in California, including California Indians and Californios, citizens of the United States. The treaty also protected their religious and property rights. A **property right** is a person's right to own and control possessions such as land or other property.

VOCABULARY

property right
squatter
commission
reservation

Vocabulary Strategy

reservation

Reserve means to set aside. **Reservations** were lands set aside for American Indians.

READING SKILL
Main Idea and Details
List details that support the first main idea in the lesson.

 STANDARDS
Core: HSS 4.4.2, 4.4.3
Extend support: HSS 4.4.3

The Land Commission

Most Californio landowners had owned their land since California was part of Spain. Others were granted land by the Mexican government. Newcomers from other parts of the United States wanted Californio lands. Some moved onto the land and became squatters. A **squatter** lives on land without the owner's permission.

Squatters said the land they lived on was theirs. Some fought Californio landowners with guns and knives. To deal with the conflicts, the United States Congress passed the Land Act of 1851. This law set up the Land Commission to settle conflicts over land in California. A **commission** is a group that meets to solve a problem.

The commission told Californios to prove they owned their lands. Yet the commission did not accept certain papers from earlier Spanish or Mexican governments of California as proof. Most Californios had no other papers.

The Land Commission looked at more than 800 cases. Most of the cases were not decided for many years. Californios won more than half the cases, but many had to sell their land to pay the costs of lawyers.

One Californio, **Maria Amparo Ruiz de Burton,** wrote, "It makes me heartsick to think how unjustly the native Californians [Californios] have been treated."

REVIEW What was the job of the Land Commission?

Juan and Martina Ontiveros This family and others who owned ranchos had to sell large amounts of their land to pay lawyers.

Reservations

Main Idea California Indians were forced to move to reservations.

The Treaty of Guadalupe Hidalgo made California Indians citizens with property rights. During the Gold Rush, however, forty-niners mined California Indian lands. Others came and started farms or businesses on these lands.

To stop conflicts over land, the United States set up the Commission for Indian Reservations. A **reservation** is land set aside for American Indians. The commission planned reservations. Some California Indians agreed to give up large areas of land because they believed the reservation lands would be protected from use by others.

Forced to Move

U.S. lawmakers never agreed to the commission's plans because newcomers wanted to take the reservation lands, too. Years later, California Indians were forced to move to reservations that had fewer resources than the reservations the commission planned.

After being forced to move, many California Indians died from disease, starvation, and attacks. From 1848 to 1870, the California Indian population fell from 150,000 to about 30,000.

The Modoc of northern California left the reservations. In 1872, soldiers attacked the Modoc. **Kintpuash** (KHINT poo ahsh) led the Modoc into rugged lava fields.

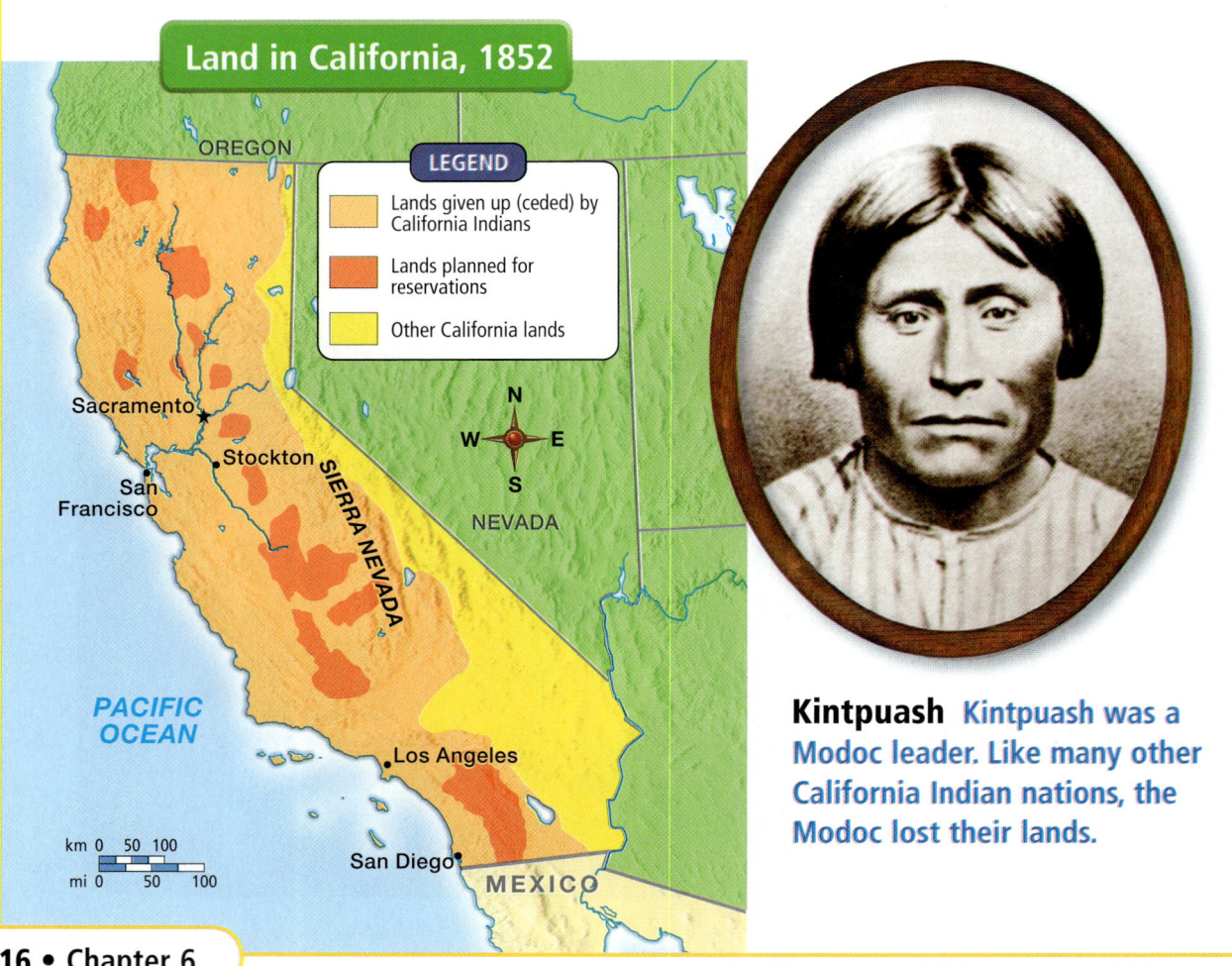

Kintpuash Kintpuash was a Modoc leader. Like many other California Indian nations, the Modoc lost their lands.

Lavabeds National Monument People today visit caves that Modoc people knew well.

Modoc Wars

The Modoc fought for six months. In the end, they were forced to give up their land and move far from their home.

Many decades later, California Indians won protection for their rights. Some also proved their right to lands that had been taken from them.

REVIEW Why did the government move California Indians to reservations?

Lesson Summary

After California became a state, newcomers wanted land. A Land Commission made Californios prove they owned their rancho lands. Newcomers also wanted California Indian Lands. California Indians were forced to move to lands with few resources. Many decades later, California Indians won protection of their rights.

Why It Matters...

California's economy changed after newcomers took rancho and California Indian lands.

Lesson Review

1850 Commission for Indian Reservations
1851 Land Act
1852 Land Commission

❶ **VOCABULARY** Write sentences that explain what **squatters** did in California.

❷ **READING SKILL** Use **details** to write a paragraph that explains why Californios lost their land.

❸ **MAIN IDEA: Economics** Why did many Californios lose their land even though they proved that they owned it?

❹ **MAIN IDEA: History** What did the Commission for Indian Reservations do?

❺ **TIMELINE SKILL** Give the names and dates of two commissions on the timeline.

❻ **CRITICAL THINKING: Analyze** In what ways did treaties affect both Californios and California Indians?

MAP ACTIVITY Choose one of the promised reservation lands on the map. Locate the area on a present-day map and name two towns or cities in that area.

1. HSS 4.4.3 2. HSS 4.4.3 3. HSS 4.4.3 4. HSS 4.4.3 5. HSS 4.4.3 6. HSS 4.4.3 Activity Analysis Skill CST 3

Extend Lesson 4
Readers' Theater

Who Owns This Land?

Ranchos were the center of the Californio world. To new settlers, though, ranchos of 40,000 acres or more were too big. They wanted to start farms and other businesses on smaller pieces of land. Those who came to mine wondered if there was gold on California Indian lands.

To hear what different people thought about who should own land, go back in time to a Sonoma Valley town in 1852.

Characters

William Archer: reporter for *The Californian*

Luz Juarez: ranchera

Pedro Juarez: ranchero

Leah Corey: general store owner from Ohio

Eva Wawona: basketmaker

Grant Sherman: miner from Texas

William Archer: Excuse me. I'm a reporter working on an article about land rights in California. Do you own land around here?

Luz Juarez: Yes, we are ranchers. Our rancho is outside of town.

Pedro Juarez: We have some of the finest cattle in the state.

Luz Juarez: The rancho is our home and work.

William Archer: I've heard that the Land Commission is making Californios prove your property rights or give up your ranchos.

Pedro Juarez: Yes. We had to see a man from the Land Commission last week. He said we must prove that we own our rancho.

Luz Juarez: Why should we have to prove that we own a rancho that has been in my family since before Mexican Independence?

William Archer: Did you show him your ownership papers?

Luz Juarez: Those papers were lost in a fire at the hacienda years ago. The man says we must hire a lawyer to prove our claim.

Pedro Juarez: We came to town to send a message to my cousin in San Francisco. We hope he can help us find a lawyer.

William Archer

Luz Juarez

William Archer: Ma'am, I see you shaking your head. What do you think of this?

Leah Corey: The Juarezes aren't alone. The Wintuan people are in a similar fix. Eva Wawona makes the baskets I sell in my store.

William Archer: Do you think the government has helped here?

Leah Corey: They seem to favor newcomers like me over people who have been here a while.

Eva Wawona: My people have been here for more than "a while," my friend. First the Spanish, then the Mexicans, and now the squatters want our land.

Grant Sherman: Now, wait just a minute. I don't like the word "squatter." I came here from Texas and found a lot of empty land—land folks say they own, but they can't prove it.

Luz Juarez: We Californios have never worried about proving our right to be here, Señor Sherman.

Eva Wawona: Neither have we.

Grant Sherman: Well, all I know is that if you can't prove it in court, you don't own land. Until then, I'm staying put.

Eva Wawona: My sons and I cannot stay put! Nobody in our village can stay put.

Eva Wawona

Pedro Juarez

William Archer: Where are you going?

Eva Wawona: The government tells us to move to a reservation where nothing grows. Even the grasses to make my baskets do not grow there.

Leah Corey: Oh, Eva! That is so unfair! Why, if someone told me I had to give up my store, I don't know what I would do.

William Archer: Will you move to the reservation, ma'am, as the government says?

Eva Wawona: My daughter may be allowed to live on the rancho where she works. My sons and I have little choice.

Luz Juarez: We also have little choice. We must spend money for a lawyer.

Pedro Juarez: The lawyer will take months or years to argue our case. Meanwhile, more and more squatters take over our land.

Grant Sherman: Look, I'm sorry for your troubles. I came out here to help my own family, though. If the government says I can have land, I'll take it.

Eva Wawona: The government gives you land, but many of the rest of us are about to lose our homes, our work, and our way of life.

Luz Juarez: We won't give up easily, Señor Archer. Now, if you will excuse us, we have a message to send.

Activities

1. **TALK ABOUT IT** Name a character and summarize his or her opinion.

2. **WRITE ABOUT IT** Write an article that William Archer might write after he finishes these interviews.

Chapter 6 Review

Visual Summary

1–3. Write a description of each item named below.

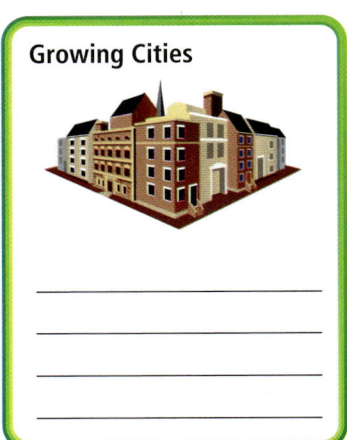

Growing Cities

_____
_____
_____
_____

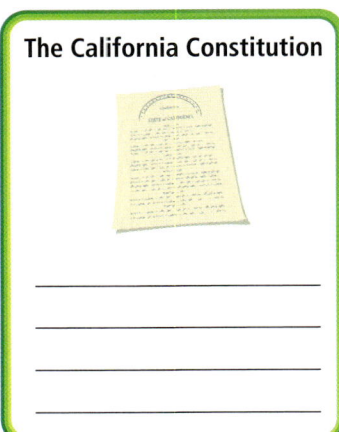

The California Constitution

_____
_____
_____
_____

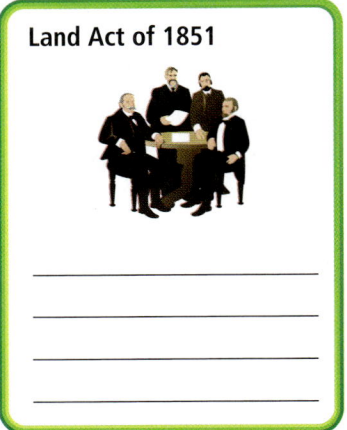

Land Act of 1851

_____
_____
_____
_____

STANDARDS 1. HSS 4.4.2 2. HSS 4.3.5 3. HSS 4.4.3

Facts and Main Ideas

Answer each question below.

4. **Economics** What were the names of two Gold Rush entrepreneurs? What did they do?

5. **Government** Why did delegates meet in Colton Hall in Monterey in 1849?

6. **History** What were two decisions that delegates made at the California constitutional convention?

7. **Economics** What were two reasons Sacramento grew during the Gold Rush?

8. **Geography** Where were the Modoc Wars?

4. HSS 4.4.2 5. HSS 4.3.5 6. HSS 4.3.5 7. HSS 4.4.2 8. HSS 4.4.3

Vocabulary

Choose the correct word from the list to complete each sentence.

consumer, p. 190
delegate, p. 200
commission, p. 215

9. A person chosen to represent others is a _____.

10. A group formed by government to solve a problem is called a _____.

11. Someone who buys goods or services is a _____.

9. HSS 4.3.5 10. HSS 4.4.3 11. HSS 4.4.2

222 • Chapter 6

CHAPTER SUMMARY TIMELINE

- 1849 Constitutional convention
- 1850 California statehood
- 1851 Land Commission
- 1854 Sacramento becomes state capital

Apply Skills

Interpret Historical Images Use what you have learned about interpreting historical images to answer the questions about the image below.

Capitol Building This building was in Benicia, the third state capital. Benicia was California's capital from 1853 to 1854.

12. The picture shows that the capitol building had

    A. one story and a pointed roof
    B. one story and a flat roof
    C. two stories and a flat roof
    D. two stories and a pointed roof

13. What can you learn from the caption?

    A. Benicia was the first state capital of California.
    B. Benicia was the third state capital of California.
    C. California did not have a capital until 1853.
    D. Benicia was the name of the capitol building.

12. Analysis Skill REPV 2 13. Analysis Skill REPV 2

Critical Thinking

Write a short paragraph to answer each question. Use details to support your response.

14. **Synthesize** What was the Compromise of 1850 and how did it affect California?

15. **Apply** What did the United States government do to try to solve conflicts about property rights between Californios and squatters?

Timeline

Use the Chapter Summary Timeline to answer the question.

16. Name two events that happened before the Land Commission.

14. HSS 4.3.5 15. HSS 4.4.3 16. HSS 4.3.5

Activities

Research Activity Do research to find out what the names "Yerba Buena" and "San Francisco" mean.

Writing Activity Think of the individuals you have read about in this chapter. Choose one you admire. Write a personal essay with details that tell why you admire this person.

Activities Analysis Skill CST 3, Analysis Skill HI 2, W 1.2

Technology Get help with your writing at: www.eduplace.com/kids/hmss/

223

Chapter 7 Joining with the Nation

Technology
e • glossary
e • word games
www.eduplace.com/kids/hmss/

Vocabulary Preview

transportation
In the early 1850s, **transportation** between California and the rest of the country was slow. People, mail, and goods traveled by boat or wagon. **page 227**

telegraph
In 1861, **telegraph** wires connected California to Washington, D.C. Electric signals carried messages over the wires. **page 229**

Chapter Timeline

1857 Overland Mail Company

1860 Pony Express

1861 Telegraph wires link California with East

224 • Unit 3

Reading Strategy

Summarize Use this strategy to understand this chapter.

 Take notes as you read. Then highlight the most important information.

transcontinental
The **transcontinental** railroad linked California to places on the other side of the continent.
page 232

investor
Investors spent money to build the transcontinental railroad. They hoped to earn more money if the railroad was successful. **page 233**

1869
Transcontinental railroad complete

1864 — 1866 — 1868 — 1870

225

Core Lesson 1

Linking East and West

1850–1861

VOCABULARY

communication
transportation
telegraph

Vocabulary Strategy

telegraph

The prefix **tele-** means "distance." A **telegraph** message is sent over a distance.

READING SKILL
Problem and Solution
List solutions to problems of communication in California.

STANDARDS
Core: HSS 4.1.4, 4.4, 4.4.1
Extend support: HSS 4.4.1

Build on What You Know Today you can get a message from someone far away in seconds. In 1850, Californians waited months to get messages from other places.

Cut Off in California

Main Idea Because California was far from large cities in the East, news and goods took months to arrive.

In 1850, California was farther away from the nation's capital than any other state. More than 1,200 miles of land separated California from nearly all other states. Mountains and deserts also cut California off from the eastern part of the country. There were no telephones, televisions, or radios. Communication between California and the rest of the country was very slow. **Communication** means sharing information with other people.

Wagon Stuck in Mud Mail and goods were slowed by transportation problems like this.

226 • Chapter 7

Transportation Choices In 1850, no railroads and few roads linked California to the rest of the country. **SKILL** Reading Maps How many major coach and wagon routes reached California?

Slow Transportation

In 1850, the only way people could communicate over long distances was by mail. Mail between California and the rest of the country traveled by ship around the tip of South America. This kind of transportation took about six months. **Transportation** is a way of moving people and goods.

Someone who sent a letter from California to the East might wait more than a year to get an answer. Delays like this caused many problems. State leaders had to wait to find out about decisions made by the national government. Orders for supplies from California businesses took a long time to reach other states.

Waiting for Goods

Slow transportation of goods was another problem. Many goods used in California were made in eastern factories. Railroads in the East didn't run west of the Mississippi. The wagon route added months. Shops waited a long time to get goods they ordered. Some goods never arrived. Goods sent by ship could sink or get stolen.

Business owners paid the costs of losses and delays. They added these costs to what they charged. California goods were more expensive than goods from other states.

REVIEW Why was mail between California and the rest of the United States so slow?

Better Communication

Main Idea Faster mail and the telegraph improved communication.

In 1857, the national government passed a law called the Overland California Mail Act. This law set aside money to create faster mail service to and from California.

The government hired **John Butterfield** to set up this service. Butterfield ran the Overland Mail Company. This company carried mail and passengers in stagecoaches. Stagecoaches were horse-drawn carriages that traveled a certain stage of a route. At the end of each stage, new drivers and horses took over.

The Pony Express

Butterfield's overland mail service carried mail from the East Coast to California in just 25 days. People kept searching for faster ways to get mail to and from California. For a short time, camels carried mail across deserts. Dogsleds also carried it over the snow-covered Sierra Nevada.

In 1860 and 1861, teenaged boys rode swift horses for the Pony Express. They carried mail between California and Missouri at top speed from one point to the next. They changed horses frequently. Sometimes they passed their mailbags to new riders. The Pony Express could cover the route in about 10 days, a record-setting time.

Stagecoach in California Stagecoaches were the fastest way for people as well as mail to travel in the late 1850s.

The Telegraph

In 1844, **Samuel F. B. Morse** sent a telegraph message from Washington, D.C. to Baltimore, a distance of about 40 miles, in only a few minutes. A **telegraph** uses electrical signals to send messages over wires. Telegraph wires went up throughout the eastern United States. In 1861, the Western Union company completed a telegraph line across the country.

The telegraph line joined California to the rest of the United States. The first message sent over these wires was a speech by President **Abraham Lincoln**.

REVIEW What were three ways that communication became faster?

Samuel Morse
He invented a code that made sending and reading messages easier.

Lesson Summary

- Stagecoaches improved communication and transportation.
- The Pony Express and telegraph improved communication.

Why It Matters...

Better communication and transportation connected California to the rest of the nation and increased business opporutnities.

Lesson Review

Timeline:
- 1857 Overland California Mail Act
- 1860 Pony Express
- 1861 Telegraph to California

(1855 — 1860 — 1865)

1 VOCABULARY Fill in the blank.
transportation   telegraph
California was linked with the rest of the country by _____ wires in 1861.

2 READING SKILL Compare two **solutions** to the **problem** of slow communication.

3 MAIN IDEA: Geography In what way did California's location affect communication and transportation with the rest of the United States?

4 MAIN IDEA: History What did the Overland California Mail Act do?

5 TIMELINE SKILL Write sentences about the last two events on the timeline.

6 CRITICAL THINKING: Evaluate What do you think were effects of faster communication in California?

MATH ACTIVITY Draw a graph that compares speeds of communication by ship, by stagecoach, by Pony Express, and by telegraph.

1. HSS 4.4.1 2. HSS 4.4.1 3. HSS 4.4.1 4. HSS 4.4.1 5. HSS 4.4.1 6. HSS 4.4 Activity HSS 4.4.1

Extend Lesson 1
Geography

The PONY EXPRESS

"**Young skinny wiry fellows not over eighteen.**" The Pony Express wanted light riders because extra weight would slow the horses down.

They had to be expert riders who were strong, brave, and tireless and who could cope with any kind of weather. Riders faced vast distances, extreme heat, and bitter cold. Horses could be hard to handle as they galloped over rugged land. Riders and their horses traveled as fast as they could to get mail and news to and from California.

Rugged Land
Rough trails carried riders over deserts, rivers, and mountains.

Harsh Weather
In winter, riders faced blizzards, snow, and freezing cold. Summer brought scorching sun and rainstorms.

230 • Chapter 7

January 8, 1863 On this date, a ceremony was held in Sacramento to celebrate the start of work on the transcontinental railroad.

The Big Four

Theodore Judah was an engineer who planned railroads. An **engineer** designs and builds things. Judah helped build the first railroad in California in 1854. This railroad ran from Sacramento to San Francisco. When it was finished, Judah wanted to build a transcontinental railroad.

In 1861, Judah convinced four California investors that a railroad across the country was a good idea. An **investor** puts money into a business in the hope of earning more money in the future. Investors **Leland Stanford, Charles Crocker, Collis Huntington,** and **Mark Hopkins** became known as the "Big Four."

The Pacific Railway Act

The Big Four started the Central Pacific Railroad Company. They asked lawmakers in Congress to hire their company to build a transcontinental railroad.

In 1862, Congress passed a law called the Pacific Railway Act. This law set aside money for a transcontinental railroad. Part of the money went to the Central Pacific Railroad Company. This company would build track east from California. The other part went to the Union Pacific Railroad Company to build track west from Nebraska.

REVIEW Name the Big Four and tell what they did.

Building the Railroad

Main Idea The transcontinental railroad was difficult to build.

On January 8, 1863, workers for the Central Pacific Railroad Company began to build track stretching east from Sacramento, California. To get tracks across the steep Sierra Nevada, workers had to make a level path for the track.

They cut passes through hills and built tunnels. They filled in low land and built bridges across valleys. They laid track across this rugged land, and then they built sheds to protect the tracks from heavy mountain snow.

Hard Work

There were no bulldozers or dump trucks then to make this work go faster. Workers used picks, shovels, axes, wheelbarrows, and sledgehammers. They used gunpowder to blast away rocks. They worked from sunup to sundown, six days a week.

At first, the Central Pacific hired only about 800 workers. To get the work done as quickly as it needed to be done, however, the company needed at least 4,000 more workers. In 1865, the company began to hire Chinese immigrants. By 1869, nine out of ten Central Pacific workers were Chinese immigrants.

Steep Mountains Workers for both companies had to cross steep mountains and work in harsh weather.

Poor Conditions

By the time the first railroad across the continent was completed, more than 15,000 Chinese immigrants had worked on it. Many came to California for the Gold Rush and worked on the railroads after the Gold Rush ended. Others came from China to earn money doing railroad work.

Chinese workers were paid less than other workers and worked longer hours. In June 1867, two thousand Chinese workers went on strike. A **strike** is when workers stop doing their jobs to protest working conditions or to get higher pay.

A Lasting Contribution

When the workers went on strike, Crocker cut off their supply of food. Workers were forced to end the strike. Although the Big Four did not improve working conditions, they needed the Chinese workers.

> **Without them it would be impossible to complete the western portion of this great national enterprise...**

wrote Leland Stanford in a report to the President of the United States.

REVIEW Why was the transcontinental railroad difficult to build?

Omaha

Union Pacific Workers

Completing the Railroad

Main Idea The transcontinental railroad brought people and businesses to California.

Meanwhile, Union Pacific workers laid tracks westward from Nebraska. Many of these workers came from Ireland. Many were former soldiers, too. For this reason, they were sometimes called "the sledge and shovel army." A sledgehammer was called a sledge.

The government gave companies land and large loans of money for each mile of track they laid. As the two sets of track drew closer together, workers raced to lay more miles of track than workers for the other company.

The Golden Spike

On May 10, 1869, the two lines met near Promontory, Utah. Eight Chinese workers, chosen to honor the work of immigrants, laid the last section of track. Leland Stanford joined the lines by driving a golden spike with a silver hammer. Telegraph lines spread the news across the nation.

The railroad increased trade with Asia and other parts of the United States. Merchants shipped goods by train between California and the eastern United States. They shipped goods by boat from Asia to California and then by train to the rest of the United States.

In the Sierra Nevada This painting by Mian Situ shows railroad workers with sledgehammers. They are getting ready to blast rocks.

Yuba Gap Tunnel Today trains still travel through tunnels like those built for the first transcontinental railroad.

Wealth for Railroad Companies

The owners of the railroads took a big risk, but they earned millions of dollars. Customers paid to travel and to transport goods on trains. Land along the rail lines became very valuable. People bought the land from the companies to build houses, farms, and businesses. The Central Pacific gained great wealth from its land in California.

REVIEW What were two ways that the railroad companies earned money?

Lesson Summary

- The transcontinental railroad was built by the Central Pacific and the Union Pacific companies.
- Most of the workers on the Central Pacific railroad were Chinese immigrants.
- The transcontinental railroad increased business in California.

Why It Matters...

The first transcontinental railroad made California's economy grow.

Lesson Review

1862 Pacific Railway Act
1865 Central Pacific hires Chinese immigrants
1869 Transcontinental Railroad

1860 — 1865 — 1870

1. **VOCABULARY** Fill in the blank. Theodore Judah was a(n) _____ who designed and built railroads.

   engineer   investor   strike

2. **READING SKILL** Use **details** to write a paragraph that describes how the transcontinental railroad was built.

3. **MAIN IDEA: Government** What did the Pacific Railway Act allow?

4. **MAIN IDEA: Economics** How did the transcontinental railroad increase trade?

5. **TIMELINE SKILL** How many years passed between the first and last event shown?

6. **CRITICAL THINKING: Synthesize** What were some costs and benefits for Chinese workers who went on strike?

MAP ACTIVITY Explain what one part of the map on pages 234–235 tells you about the transcontinental railroad.

1. HSS 4.4.1 2. HSS 4.4.1 3. HSS 4.4.1 4. HSS 4.4 5. HSS 4.4.1 6. HSS 4.4.1 Activity HSS 4.4.1

Extend Lesson 2

Economics

THE SLEDGE and SHOVEL ARMY

Central Pacific workers won the race to lay the most miles of track in one day. They also earned more for the Central Pacific company.

The United States government gave land and loans of money to the companies for each mile of track they laid. The more track each company laid, the more land and money they received. After more than six years, Central Pacific and Union Pacific railroad workers laid nearly 1,800 miles of track.

Supplies for 1 Mile of Track
- 25,000 Spikes
- 2,500 Ties
- 350 Rails

The chart shows supplies that were part of the cost of railroad building.

This photograph shows Central Pacific workers in Nevada with some supplies and equipment they used.

telegraph poles

rails

ties

ECONOMICS

Activities

1. **THINK ABOUT IT** Would it be faster to build on flat land or in mountains? Explain your answer.

2. **CALCULATE IT** Use the chart to calculate how many rails and ties you would need to lay ten, twenty, or thirty miles of track.

Skillbuilder

Distinguish Fact from Opinion

> **VOCABULARY**
> fact
> opinion

Careful readers need to be able to tell the difference between a fact and an opinion. An **opinion** is a belief or a feeling. A well-reasoned opinion is supported by facts. A **fact** is information that can be proven. Proof can come from observation, books, artifacts, and other sources.

Learn the Skill

Step 1: Read what the writer wrote.

Step 2: Find words that signal an opinion. Sometimes an opinion contains phrases such as *it seems to me* or *I believe*. An opinion may also include words such as *should, worst, greatest,* or *most important*.

Step 3: Decide what the writer's opinion about the topic seems to be. State the opinion in your own words.

Step 4: Find facts, such as names or dates, that the writer has used. Think about how you would check each fact. Do the facts support the writer's opinion?

Apply Critical Thinking

STANDARDS Analysis Skill REPV 3

Practice the Skill

Read the following statements. Identify each statement as a fact or an opinion. Explain how you made your decision. How would you check any facts in the statements?

1. I believe that building the transcontinental railroad was the best thing anyone ever did for California.

2. Railroad workers had to lay tracks across steep mountains, deep valleys, and hard rock.

3. To make building the railroad easier, railroad companies should have treated workers more fairly.

4. The transcontinental railroad was completed on May 10, 1869.

Apply the Skill

Write a short paragraph that gives your opinion about the transcontinental railroad. Include at least two facts from Lesson 2 to support your opinion.

FACT: It took more than six years to build the transcontinental railroad.

OPINION: I think the railroad was very important for the future of California.

Chapter 7 Review

Visual Summary

1–3. Write a description of each item named below.

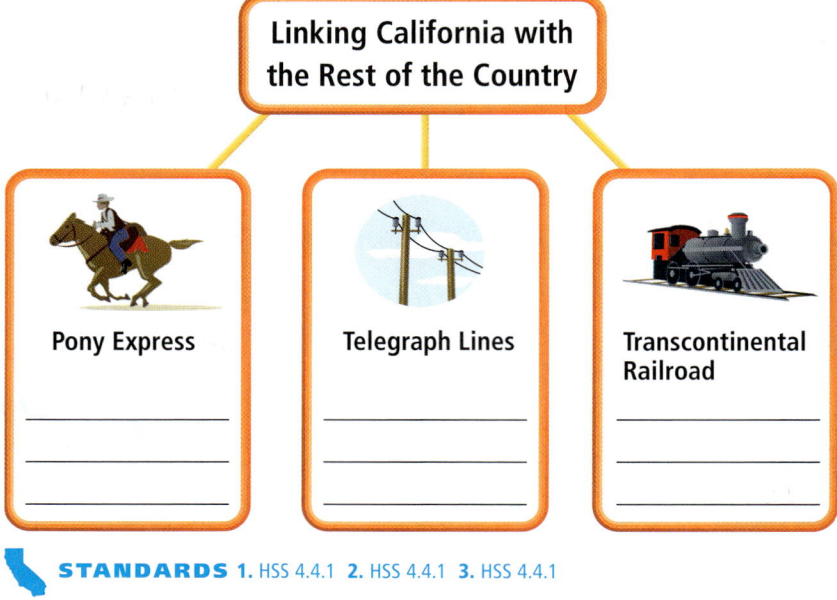

Linking California with the Rest of the Country

- Pony Express
- Telegraph Lines
- Transcontinental Railroad

STANDARDS 1. HSS 4.4.1 2. HSS 4.4.1 3. HSS 4.4.1

Facts and Main Ideas

Answer each question below.

4. **Economics** Why did Californians want faster mail service?

5. **Technology** What was the fastest way to get a message from California to the eastern United States in 1862?

6. **History** What was one thing that Theodore Judah did to help start the transcontinental railroad?

7. **Government** What did the Pacific Railway Act do?

4. HSS 4.4.1 5. HSS 4.4.1 6. HSS 4.4.1 7. HSS 4.4.1

Vocabulary

Choose the correct word from the list below to complete each sentence.

communication, p. 226
telegraph, p. 229
investor, p. 233

8. Someone who is a(n) _____ may decide to put money into a new business.

9. A(n) _____ sends electric signals over wires.

10. Sharing information with other people is _____.

8. HSS 4.4.1 9. HSS 4.4.1 10. HSS 4.4.1

CHAPTER SUMMARY TIMELINE

1857	1860	1861		1869
Overland Mail	Pony Express	Cross-country telegraph message		Transcontinental railroad

1855 — 1860 — 1865 — 1870

Apply Skills

 Fact and Opinion

Read the following paragraph. Then use what you have learned about distinguishing fact and opinion to answer questions about it.

> I believe that horses were the most useful animals for carrying mail overland. In the 1850s, horses pulled wagons or stagecoaches that brought mail. In the 1860s, they carried Pony Express riders. Camels and dogs were not as good as horses for moving mail quickly. Horses are my favorite animal.

11. The paragraph contains
    A. facts and no opinions.
    B. opinions and no facts.
    C. both facts and opinions.
    D. no facts and no opinions.

12. Which of the following words indicate that a statement is an opinion?
    A. I believe
    B. In the 1850s
    C. wagons or stagecoaches
    D. Pony Express riders

11. Analysis Skill REPV 3 12. Analysis Skill REPV 3

Critical Thinking

Write a short paragraph to answer each question below. Use details to support your response.

13. **Apply** What were three ways that people solved the problem of slow communication between California and the East?

14. **Synthesize** Why do you think the Pony Express ended in 1861?

Timeline

Use the Chapter Summary Timeline to answer the question.

15. What were two events that happened after the Pony Express began?

13. HSS 4.4.1 14. HSS 4.4.1 15. HSS 4.4.1

Activities

 Art Activity Draw a picture that could be part of a book about building the transcontinental railroad.

 Writing Activity Write a short essay that describes the achievements of the workers who built the transcontinental railroad.

Activities HSS 4.4.1, HSS 4.4.1, W 1.2

Technology
Writing Process Tips
Get help with your writing at:
www.eduplace.com/kids/hmss/

UNIT 3 Review

Vocabulary and Main Ideas

Write a sentence to answer each question.

1. What **treaty** made California part of the United States?
2. Why did **forty-niners** come to California?
3. What was the document that was written during the 1849 **convention** in Monterey?
4. What was the purpose of the Land **Commission** of 1851?
5. Why was **communication** between California and the rest of the country slow in the early 1850s?
6. What challenges did workers who built the **transcontinental** railroad face?

Critical Thinking

Write a short paragraph to answer each question.

7. **Apply** Write a summary that tells the kinds of business that grew during the first years of the Gold Rush.
8. **Analyze** Describe two solutions to California's problem of slow communication in the 1850s.

Apply Skills

Read the statements below. Then use what you have learned about point of view to answer the questions.

1. "I am an owner of the Central Pacific Railroad Company. I'm proud that our company built the first transcontinental railroad. It's great for our state."

2. "My brother blasted tunnels through mountains. He did dangerous work to build this great railroad. The company didn't pay him enough."

9. What point of view about the transcontinental railroad do both statements share?

   A. The company paid workers well.
   B. The railroad is a great thing.
   C. The work was dangerous.
   D. The owners are proud.

10. Which most clearly describes the point of view in statement #2?

    A. The company paid workers well.
    B. The railroad is a great thing.
    C. The work was dangerous.
    D. The owners are proud.

STANDARDS 1. HSS 4.3.5 2. HSS 4.3.3 3. HSS 4.3.5 4. HSS 4.4.3
5. HSS 4.4.1 6. HSS 4.4.1 7. HSS 4.4.2 8. HSS 4.4.1
9. HSS 4.4.1 10. HSS 4.4.1
Activity HSS 4.4.1, W1.1, W 1.3

Unit Activity

Make a "Before and After" Mural

- Review what you learned about the stagecoach, Pony Express, telegraph, and transcontinental railroad.
- Fold paper in half to sketch before and after scenes for one of these.
- Combine your sketch with others to plan a mural for your school.

At the Library

Learn more by finding books like these at your school or public library.

Bronco Charlie and the Pony Express, by Marlene Targ Brill
Brave adventures of Pony Express rider.

Gold Fever! Tales from the California Gold Rush, by Rosalyn Shanzer
Illustrated writings from Gold Rush diaries, letters, and newspapers.

WEEKLY READER

Current Events

Connect to Today

Find facts about the past and present of a town or city in California.

- Choose a town or city that you read about in this unit. Write a paragraph that summarizes what you learned.
- Locate the town or city on a current map.
- Do research to find facts about the population and economy of the city today.
- Write a paragraph that summarizes your research.

Technology
Weekly Reader online offers social studies articles. Go to:
www.eduplace.com/kids/hmss/

Read About It

Look for these Social Studies Independent Books in your classroom.

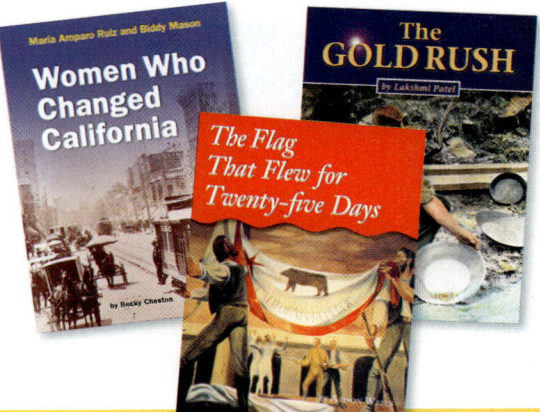

UNIT 4

California Changes

The Big Idea

In what ways do people change places?

"*One of these days... you'll see the loveliest garden in the world in this desert.*"

— William Saroyan, Armenian American writer, 1937

Mary Ellen Pleasant
1812–1904

After she took a streetcar company to court, African Americans were allowed to ride trolley cars in San Francisco. Pleasant's success inspired others. **page 257**

History Makers

George Shima
1865–1926

Shima, a Japanese immigrant, was called the Potato King. He bought irrigated land in the San Joaquin Valley in 1889 and turned it into vast fields of potatoes. **page 249**

Dorothea Lange
1895–1965

She had a keen eye and a longing for justice. Lange's photos of migrant farm families showed the nation the suffering of the poor. Many took action to help those in need. **page 292**

UNIT 4

Almanac

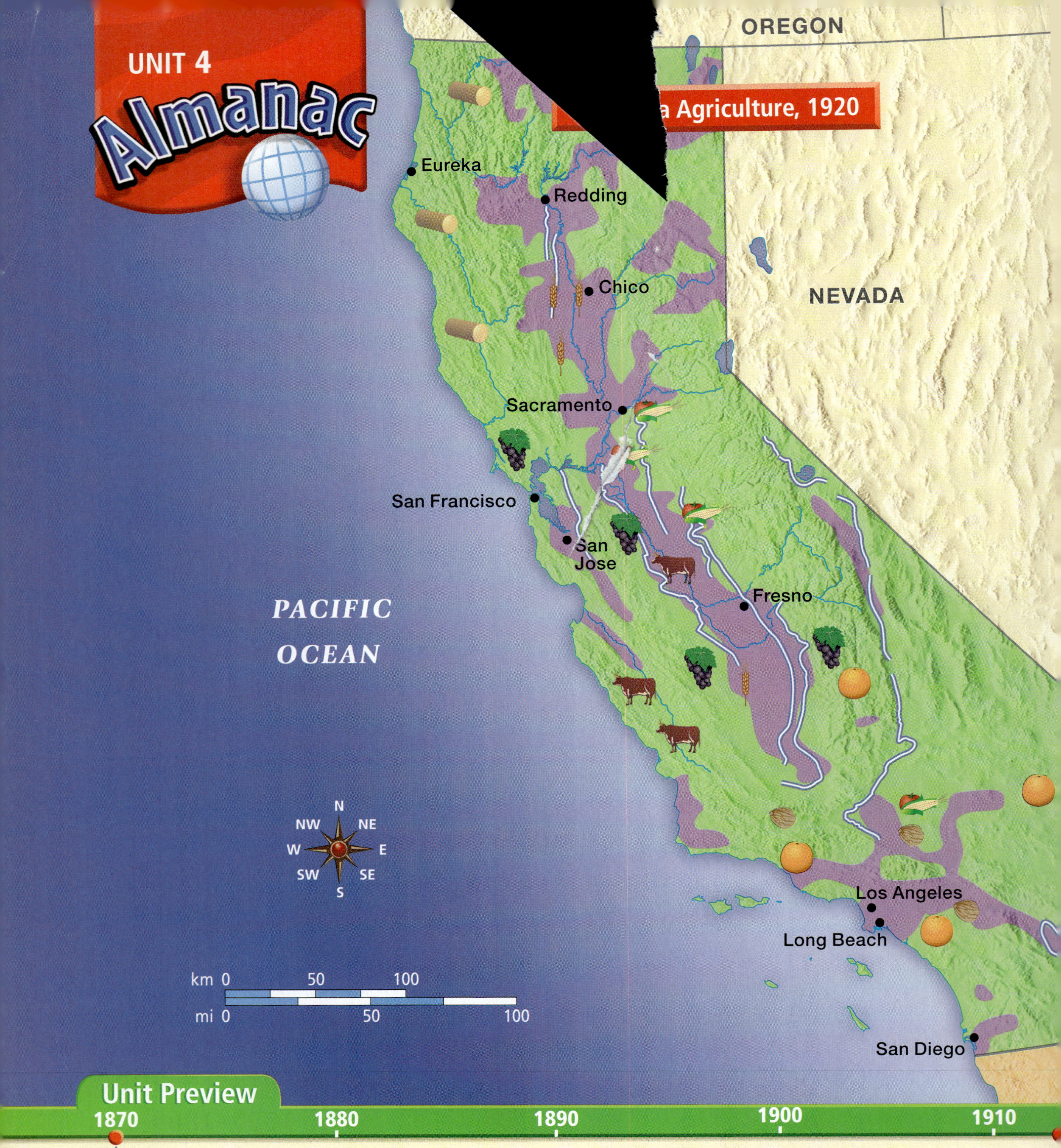

a Agriculture, 1920
OREGON
NEVADA
Eureka
Redding
Chico
Sacramento
San Francisco
San Jose
Fresno
Los Angeles
Long Beach
San Diego
PACIFIC OCEAN
N
NE
E
SE
S
SW
W
NW
km 0 50 100
mi 0 50 100

Unit Preview

1870 · 1880 · 1890 · 1900 · 1910

SWIFT
REFRIGERATOR
LINE

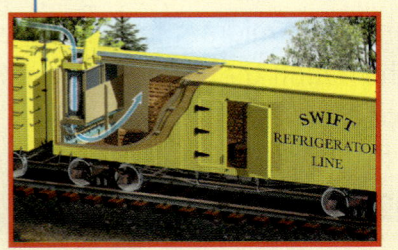

1870
Refrigerated Trains
First ones cross the country
Chapter 8, page 264

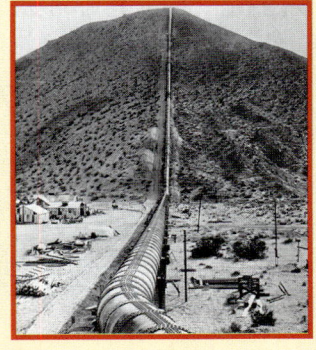

1913
Los Angeles Aqueduct
Water brought to Los Angeles
Chapter 8, page 270

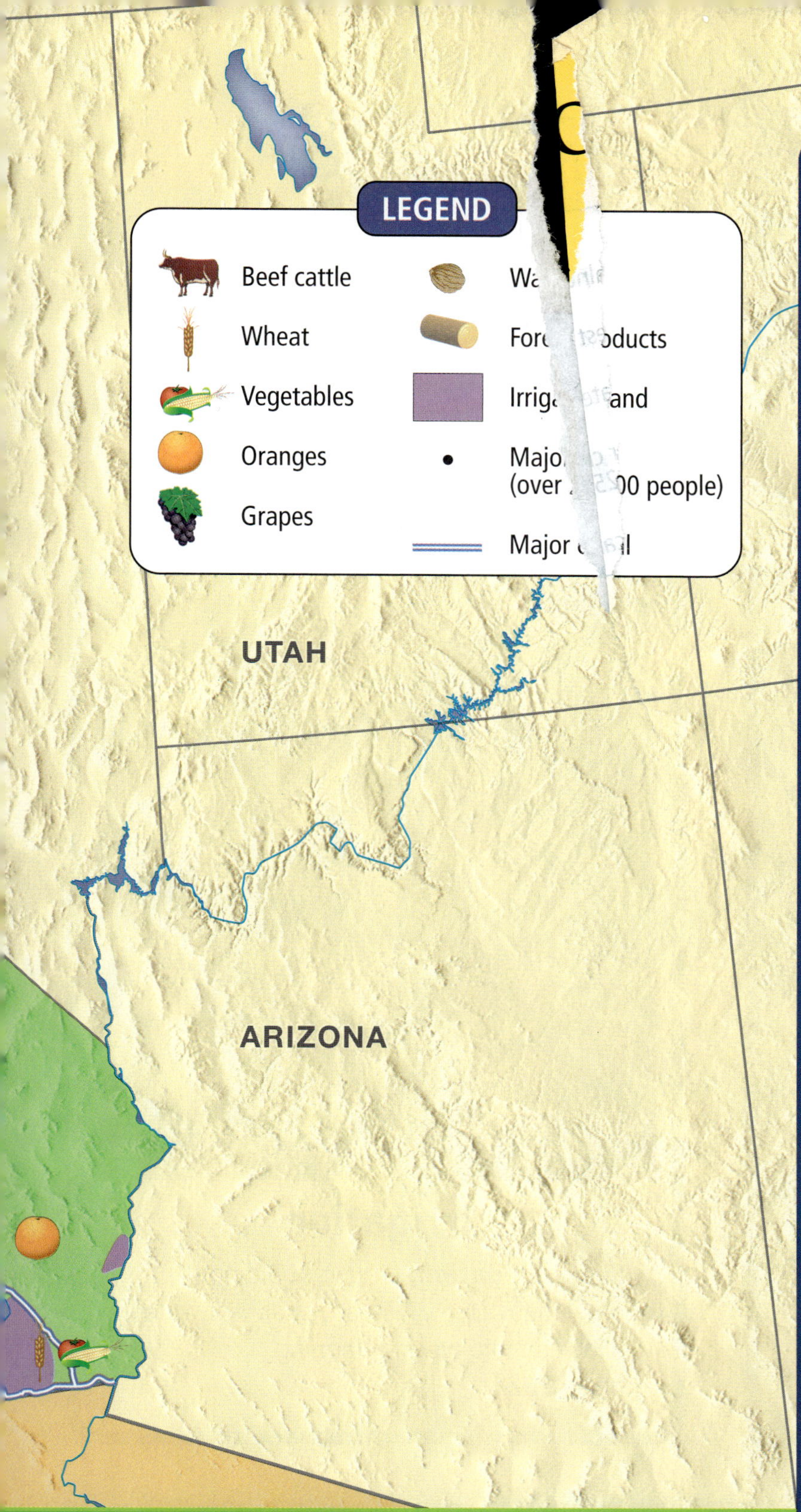

LEGEND

- Beef cattle
- Wheat
- Vegetables
- Oranges
- Grapes
- Wa...
- For... ducts
- Irrig... and
- Majo... (over ... 00 people)
- Major c... l

UTAH

ARIZONA

1920 1930 1940

1927 Movie Industry
First movie with sound
Chapter 9, page 297

1935 The New Deal
Central Valley Project begins
Chapter 9, page 306

Connect to Today

Irrigation, 1919

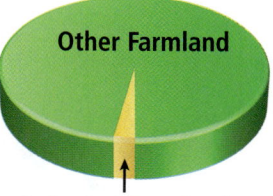

Irrigated Farmland

By 1919, more than 4 million acres of California land had been irrigated.

Irrigation Today

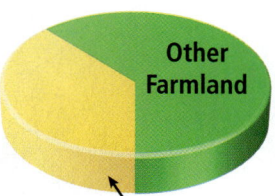

Other Farmland

Irrigated Farmland

With more dams and canals, more land was irrigated. In 2002, close to 9 million acres of land were irrigated.

WEEKLY READER

Current Events

Current events on the web!

For a selection of social studies articles about current events, go to Education Place: www.eduplace.com/kids/hmss/

249

Chapter 8: A Growing State

Vocabulary Preview

Technology
- e • glossary
- e • word games

www.eduplace.com/kids/hmss/

immigration
Immigration rose steadily throughout the 1800s. People moved to California to farm, mine, work in mills, and start their own businesses. **page 252**

irrigation
Before **irrigation**, farmers could not grow many crops. A steady supply of water allowed more types of farming. **page 262**

Chapter Timeline

1870 First refrigerated railroad car crosses the country

1882 Chinese Exclusion Act passed

1860 — 1870 — 1880 — 1890

Reading Strategy

Summarize Use this strategy to focus on important ideas.

 Review the main ideas. Then look for details that support those ideas.

aqueduct
The Los Angeles **Aqueduct** brought water from the Owens Valley to Los Angeles for drinking water and irrigation.
page 270

artists' colony
Artists painted California's beautiful cities and parks. Many lived in **artists' colonies** in San Francisco.
page 279

1906
San Francisco earthquake

1913
Los Angeles Aqueduct completed

1900 — 1910 — 1920

Core Lesson 1

Newcomers in California

VOCABULARY

immigration
exclusion

Vocabulary Strategy

immigration

The prefix **im-** means into. **Immigration** means moving into a new country.

READING SKILL
Compare and Contrast
Compare the experiences of different groups of immigrants who moved to California.

Core: HSS 4.4, 4.4.3, 4.4.4
Extend support: HSS 4.4.3

SKILL Reading Graphs From which countries did more than 30,000 people move to California in 1900?

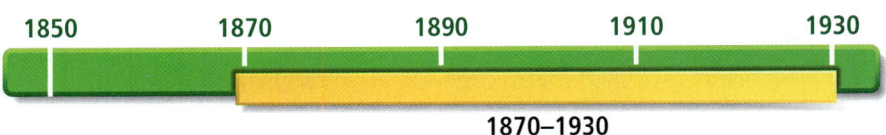

1850   1870   1890   1910   1930

1870–1930

Build on What You Know Who was the first person in your family to come to California? Why did he or she come? Millions of other people probably came to California for the same reasons.

Moving to California

Main Idea People moved to California for jobs and land.

During the late 1800s and early 1900s, immigration to the United States reached a new high point. **Immigration** is the movement of people from one country to another. Millions of people came from countries in Latin America, Europe, and Asia. They left to escape war and crop failures. Many moved to California in search of jobs and land.

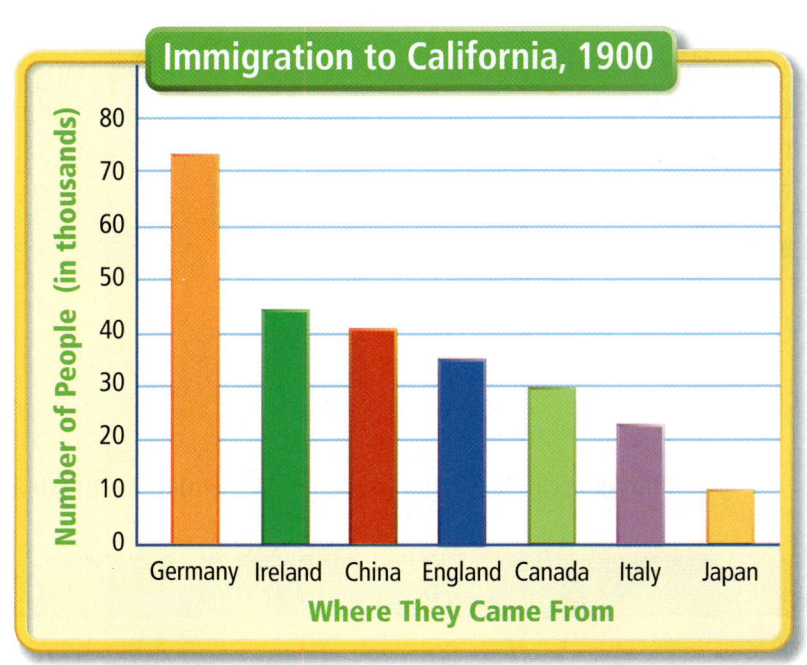

252 • Chapter 8

Arriving by Boat More than 150,000 immigrants came to Angel Island between 1910 and 1940. Most were Chinese.

Chinese Immigration

Between 1848 and 1882, about 300,000 Chinese immigrants came to the United States. Most lived in California. They worked in mines, factories, farms, and railroads. They were often paid less than other workers.

In cities, Chinese immigrants lived in neighborhoods called Chinatowns. By 1870, San Francisco's Chinatown had shops, temples, and restaurants owned and run by Chinese Americans. More than 12,000 Chinese people lived there.

In the late 1870s, the number of jobs in the United States fell. Many workers in California believed that the Chinese had jobs that should be theirs. They wanted to stop Chinese workers from coming to this country.

Members of the United States Congress agreed. In 1882, they passed a new law—the Chinese Exclusion Act. **Exclusion** is the practice of keeping people out. This law said that Chinese workers could no longer move to the United States. Chinese men already in California could not bring over wives or families to join them. However, Chinese students, teachers, merchants, and officials could still come.

To control Asian immigration, the government opened an immigration station on Angel Island in San Francisco Bay. Immigrants could be held there for weeks or even years. Many were turned away. Some years, one in six people returned to China.

REVIEW What work did Chinese immigrants do in California?

Farm Workers from Asia

Main Idea Immigrants from several Asian countries moved to California.

The Chinese Exclusion Act meant there were no longer enough field workers for farms in California. Farm owners began to hire workers from other countries in Asia. One of the largest groups came from Japan.

Many Japanese immigrants bought land and became successful farmers. They grew rice, fruits, and vegetables in valleys near San Francisco. Some brought new ways of farming and new crops, such as strawberries.

By 1920, nearly 75,000 Japanese people lived in the state. They formed communities called Japantowns in cities such as Fresno, Sacramento, and San Francisco.

Immigrants from Korea also moved to California in the early 1900s. Koreans traveled from farm to farm in small groups. Each group did whatever work was needed, from picking fruit to weeding fields. Some Koreans bought farms and businesses. **Kim Hyung-soon** (KIHM HEE uhng soon) owned several orchards. He and his workers created the nectarine.

Sikhs were Asian Indians. They came from the Punjab region of India. From 1908 to 1910, hundreds of Sikhs built and repaired railroad tracks in California. After that, they worked on farms in the Central and Imperial valleys. In summer, they picked grapes, melons, cotton, and wheat. At other times of the year, they built canals and did other farm work.

Farmers from Asia In the early 1900s, nearly half of California's farm workers were Japanese. The 1913 photo card (right) shows this Sikh immigrant is allowed to live and work in California.

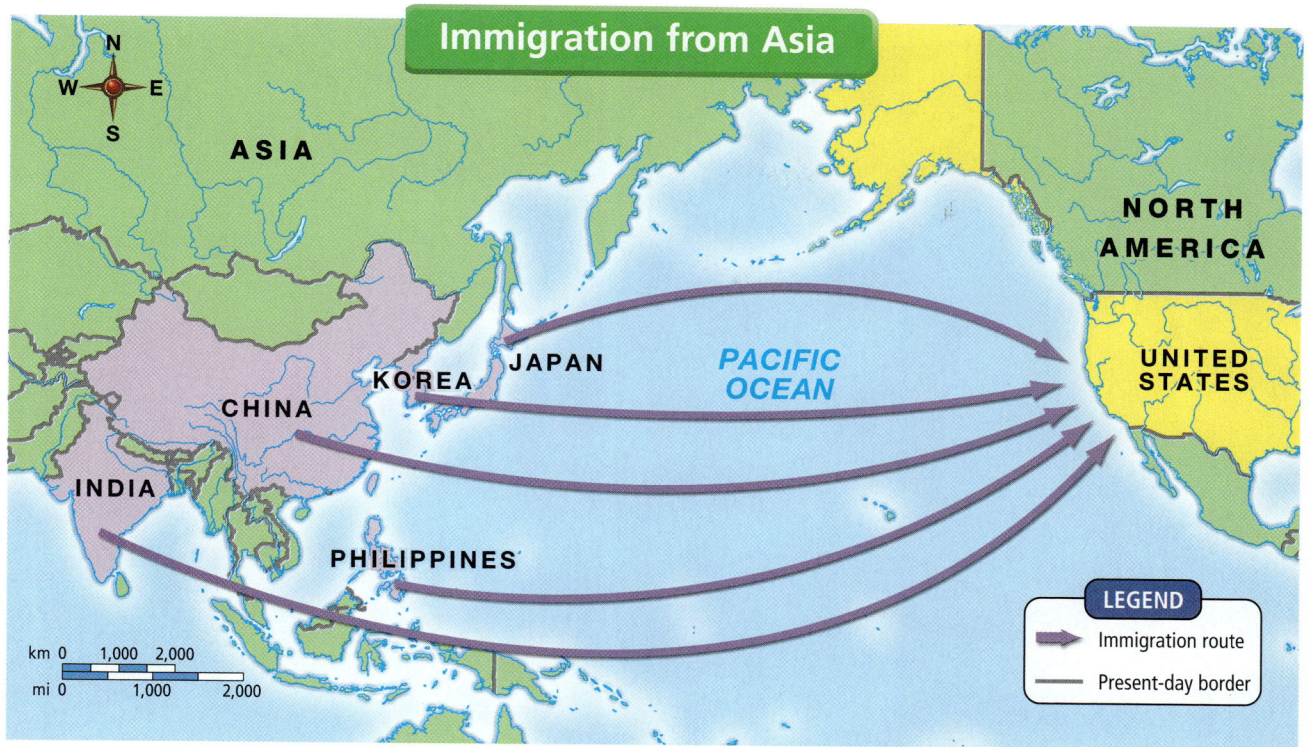

Sailing to California Hundreds of thousands of Asian immigrants made the trip across the Pacific Ocean. **SKILL Reading Maps** Which of the labeled Asian countries is closest to California?

More Immigration Limits

New groups of Asian immigrants faced discrimination, just as the Chinese had. Korean and Japanese children were forced to attend separate schools from other Californians. Restaurant owners sometimes refused to serve Asian customers. At times, immigrants were even attacked.

Laws passed in the early 1900s limited immigration from Asia and kept immigrants from owning land. Then, in 1924, the U.S. Congress passed the Immigration Act. This law limited immigration of people from all countries. Most Japanese, Korean, and Sikh people could no longer move to the United States. Again, landowners looked other places for farm workers.

From the Philippines

In 1898, the United States gained control of the Philippine Islands. After that, Filipinos, or people from the Philippines, became U.S. nationals. This meant they could enjoy some of the rights of U.S. citizens. Unlike some other Asian people, Filipinos could move to the United States.

In the 1920s, more than 30,000 Filipinos came to the United States. Most were young men who settled in Stockton. From there, they moved across California. At different seasons, they worked in asparagus and lettuce fields, fruit orchards, or rice farms.

REVIEW Why could Filipinos move to the United States after laws blocked Asian immigration?

Mexican Americans Some owned businesses like this 1925 grocery store in Los Angeles.

A New Start

Main Idea Immigrants from many places contributed to California's economy.

In the early 1900s, troubles and war in Mexico caused thousands of Mexicans to move to the United States. Those with savings started businesses. Other Mexican immigrants worked in California's booming farm industry.

Many found work in the Imperial Valley, just north of the Mexican border. There they picked cotton, grapes, and melons. As farm workers, they earned from $1 to $3 a day. This was far more than workers could earn in Mexico or in other countries outside the United States. By 1930, nearly one and a half million people from Mexico lived in the United States.

Immigrants also came from Russia. Russians left their country in the early 1900s to escape war. Many were Jewish. They settled in Los Angeles and worked for shipping, lumber, movie, and clothing companies. Jews from Poland and Germany also lived in Los Angeles. To the north, Armenian immigrants started farms in Fresno. Many became successful grape growers.

People from other parts of the United States moved to California, too. People of African heritage had lived in California since the time of the Spanish. By 1900, nearly 8,000 African Americans lived throughout the state. Many moved to California from southern states to work on farms in the Central Valley. African Americans also worked in lumber mills.

Building Communities

Newcomers found discrimination in California. To fight it, Mexican immigrants formed *mutualistas*, or self-help groups. These groups gave money to those in need. They also fought for rights of Mexican workers. People such as **Mary Ellen Pleasant** fought against unfair treatment of African Americans. She sued a San Francisco streetcar company that didn't allow her to ride.

Allen Allensworth also fought discrimination after he moved to Los Angeles. Allensworth started a town in 1908 where African Americans could live free from discrimination. About 300 families moved to the town of Allensworth. They built a school, churches, and businesses there.

REVIEW Why did Mexican immigrants come to the United States in the early 1900s?

Lesson Summary

Between 1860 and 1930, people came to California to find jobs and land. They faced discrimination, but the work of immigrants on California's farms, railroads, and canals added to the state's economy.

Why It Matters...

The hard work and ideas of newcomers helped California's economy grow stronger.

Allen Allensworth The town he founded north of Bakersfield is now an historic park.

Lesson Review

1882 — Chinese Exclusion Act passed
1908 — Allensworth founded

1880 — 1890 — 1900 — 1910 — 1920

1. **VOCABULARY** Use **immigration** in a paragraph about California in the early 1900s.

2. **READING SKILL** Compare and **contrast** the reasons people moved to California from China and the Philippines.

3. **MAIN IDEA: History** Why did Congress pass the Chinese Exclusion Act?

4. **MAIN IDEA: Economics** What work did Japanese immigrants do in California?

5. **TIMELINE SKILL** In what year was Chinese immigration limited?

6. **CRITICAL THINKING: Evaluate** Why did moving to California improve the lives of immigrants in the late 1800s and early 1900s?

WRITING ACTIVITY Write a poem about the experiences of an immigrant who has recently arrived in California. Use sensory details to tell what that person might have seen, heard, and smelled.

1. HSS 4.4.3 2. HSS 4.4.3 3. HSS 4.4.3 4. HSS 4.4.3 5. HSS 4.4.3 6. HSS 4.4.3 Activity HSS 4.4.3

Extend Lesson 1

Primary Source

Chinese Newspapers

中西日報

Reading the News People in San Francisco's Chinatown catch up on the news.

In the early days of San Francisco's Chinatown, people got their news from bulletin boards. Signs were hand-written in Chinese characters and tacked up outside. Crowds gathered around them to read the day's news.

In the 1850s, immigrants wanted new and better ways to stay informed. People began printing newspapers in Chinese. Both *The Chinese Free Press* and Ng Poon Chew's (IHNG poon choo) *Chung Sai Yat Po* told Chinese Americans about events in California, China, and the world. They also printed people's opinions about many subjects, including discrimination toward Chinese immigrants.

Chung Sai Yat Po This newspaper (right) was a special New Year's issue of the first Chinese daily newspaper published in the country. It ran from 1900 to 1951.

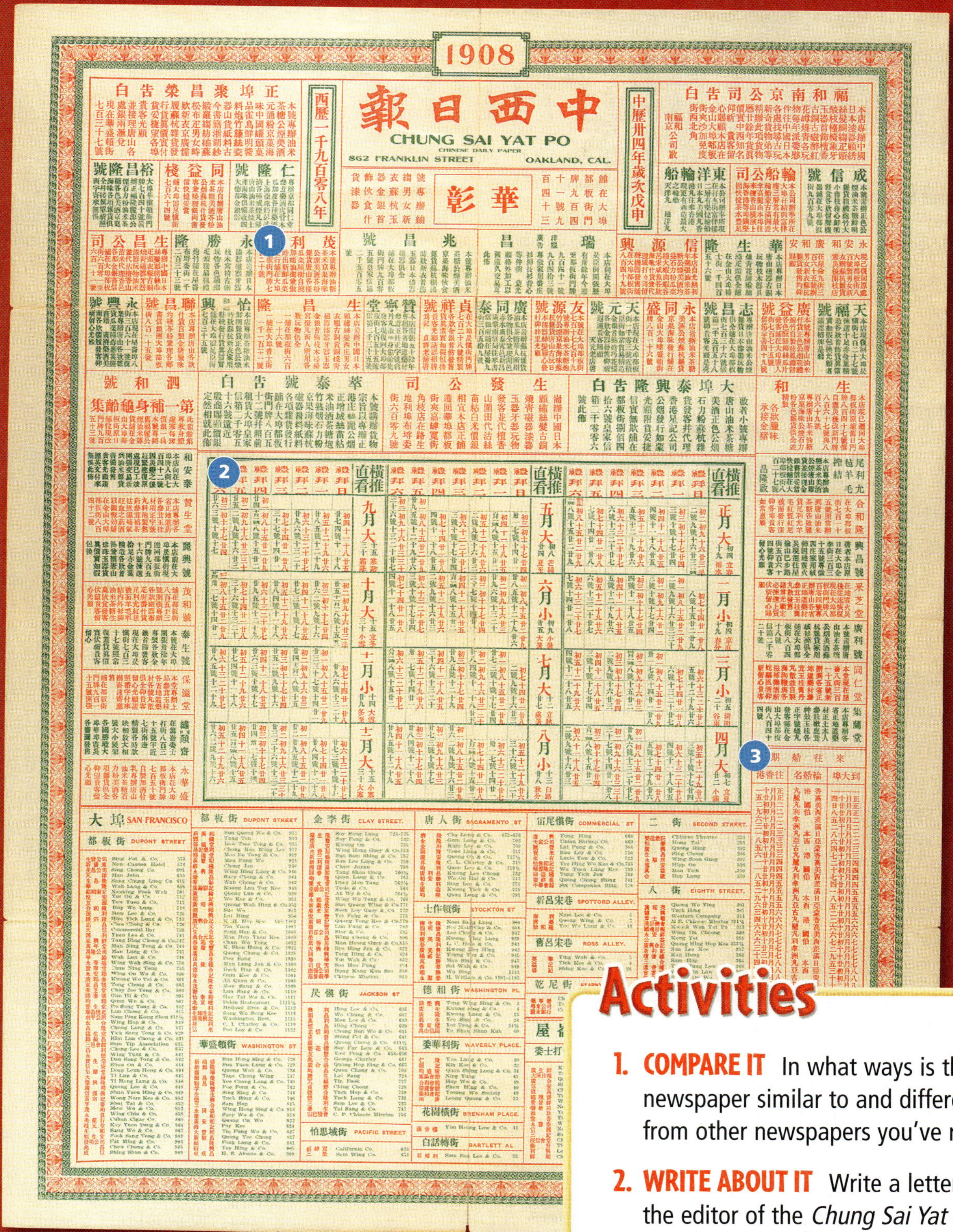
1908

中西日報

CHUNG SAI YAT PO

CHINESE DAILY PAPER

862 FRANKLIN STREET OAKLAND, CAL.

1 Grocery Store Advertisement

2 Yearly Calendar

3 San Francisco-Hong Kong Ferry Schedule

Activities

1. **COMPARE IT** In what ways is this newspaper similar to and different from other newspapers you've read?
2. **WRITE ABOUT IT** Write a letter to the editor of the *Chung Sai Yat Po* about the contributions of Chinese immigrants to California. Include a date, salutation, and closing.

Technology Visit Education Place for more primary sources. www.eduplace.com/kids/hmss/

Core Lesson 2

California Farming

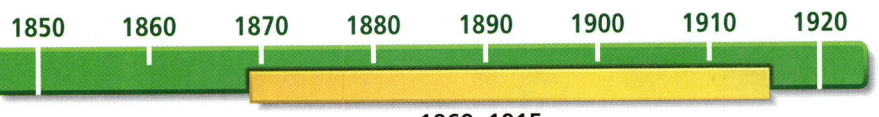
1869–1915

VOCABULARY

irrigation
migrant worker
demand
market

Vocabulary Strategy

<u>migrant</u> worker

A **migrant** is a person who moves. **Migrant workers** move in search of work.

READING SKILL

Cause and Effect As you read, list the causes that led to an increase in California farming.

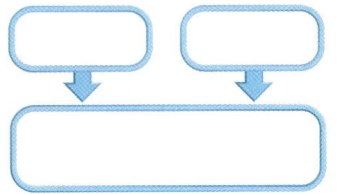

Build on What You Know Many of the fruits and vegetables you see in grocery stores are grown on California farms. California wasn't always a big farming state, but it became one in the late 1800s.

A Good Place to Farm

Main Idea Farming increased in California with the help of new technology and new kinds of crops.

During the Gold Rush, the growing population of miners and workers needed food. Many miners quit looking for gold and became farmers. By 1869, there were more farmers than miners in California. Different types of soil and climates in the state made it possible to grow a wide range of crops.

New Technology In the late 1800s, farmers used large machines like this harvester to farm their land. Production rose quickly as a result.

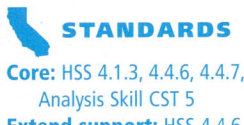 **STANDARDS**
Core: HSS 4.1.3, 4.4.6, 4.4.7, Analysis Skill CST 5
Extend support: HSS 4.4.6

Harvester
Mule Team

260 • Chapter 8

Farming Region The Central Valley has a long growing season and warm weather.

Wheat Farming

In the 1860s, farmers started large farms in the Central Valley. Most farmers raised cattle and grew wheat. Wheat needed little water to grow. It grew well in the dry parts of the Central Valley. By 1875, farmers grew more than 20,000 acres of wheat in the region. Because wheat does not spoil easily, it could be shipped long distances to be sold.

Farmers needed new technology to harvest crops on these large wheat farms. They used gang plows that were pulled by as many as 100 mules. Machines such as the combined harvester cut, threshed, and bagged wheat in one sweep through a field.

New Crops

In other parts of the state, people grew new crops. In 1873, **Eliza** and **Luther Tibbets** planted two orange trees from Brazil on their farm in Riverside. These navel oranges were sweeter and juicier than other oranges grown in California at that time. Soon more California farmers planted navel oranges. By 1914, about 12 million crates of navels and other oranges were sold each year.

In 1875, plant scientist **Luther Burbank** moved to Santa Rosa, California. Over the next 50 years, he developed new types of fruits, vegetables, and flowers. His long-lasting and better-tasting crops are still grown on California farms.

REVIEW Why did wheat farms need new technology?

Luther Burbank One of his most famous creations was the Idaho potato.

Working the Land

Main Idea Irrigation projects and new workers made farms more successful.

By the late 1800s, farmers in the Central Valley were not able to grow as much wheat as they had earlier. When one kind of crop is grown year after year on the same land, the soil becomes less fertile, or rich.

The Central Valley had a long, warm growing season, but many parts lacked enough rain to grow fruits and vegetables. Other parts were too wet to farm, or were often flooded. Farmers who wanted to grow new types of crops had to change the land. Farmers looked for ways to bring water to dry lands, and to take water from wetlands.

Irrigation Projects

In dry areas, farmers turned to irrigation. **Irrigation** is the use of pipes or canals to bring water to dry land. Some farmers also used ditches for irrigation. Ditches carried water from local rivers to farms.

A few Central Valley landowners built large irrigation projects. **Henry Miller**, a wealthy rancher, built a dam to control flooding and to irrigate nearly all the land along the San Joaquin River. Others built canals to carry water from large rivers to dry areas. They also used canals to drain water from wetlands. By 1900, more than 200,000 acres of wetland in the Central Valley had been reclaimed, or made usable for farming.

In the Fields By 1881, a half million orange trees grew near Los Angeles. Farm workers filled shipping crates with oranges.

Farm Workers

In the 1870s, a few farmers and large businesses owned most of the farmland and water in California. Newcomers who couldn't afford to buy their own farms became tenant farmers. A tenant farmer grows crops on land owned by someone else.

Landowners paid tenant farmers a small part of the harvest, but they kept most of it for themselves. By 1900, nearly one-fourth of the farmers in California were tenant farmers.

Landowners also hired migrant workers. A **migrant worker** moves from place to place to find work on farms. Migrant workers are hired to work for only as long as there is work to do. Then they move to another farm.

Migrant workers often had large families. More children meant more workers who could help a family survive. Young children spent long days picking crops beside their parents. At the end of a hard day of work, migrant families often had no shelters in which to sleep.

Farm workers came to California from Mexico, Asia, and Europe. After working for some time, many people saved enough money to buy their own farms. A Japanese immigrant named **George Shima** became very successful. In 1913, about 500 people worked on his 28,000 acre potato farm. Shima was known as the "Potato King."

REVIEW Why did people become tenant farmers in the late 1800s?

Many Farmers In 1910, there were about 88,000 farmers in California. **SKILL** Reading Graphs What portion of farmers owned their land in 1910?

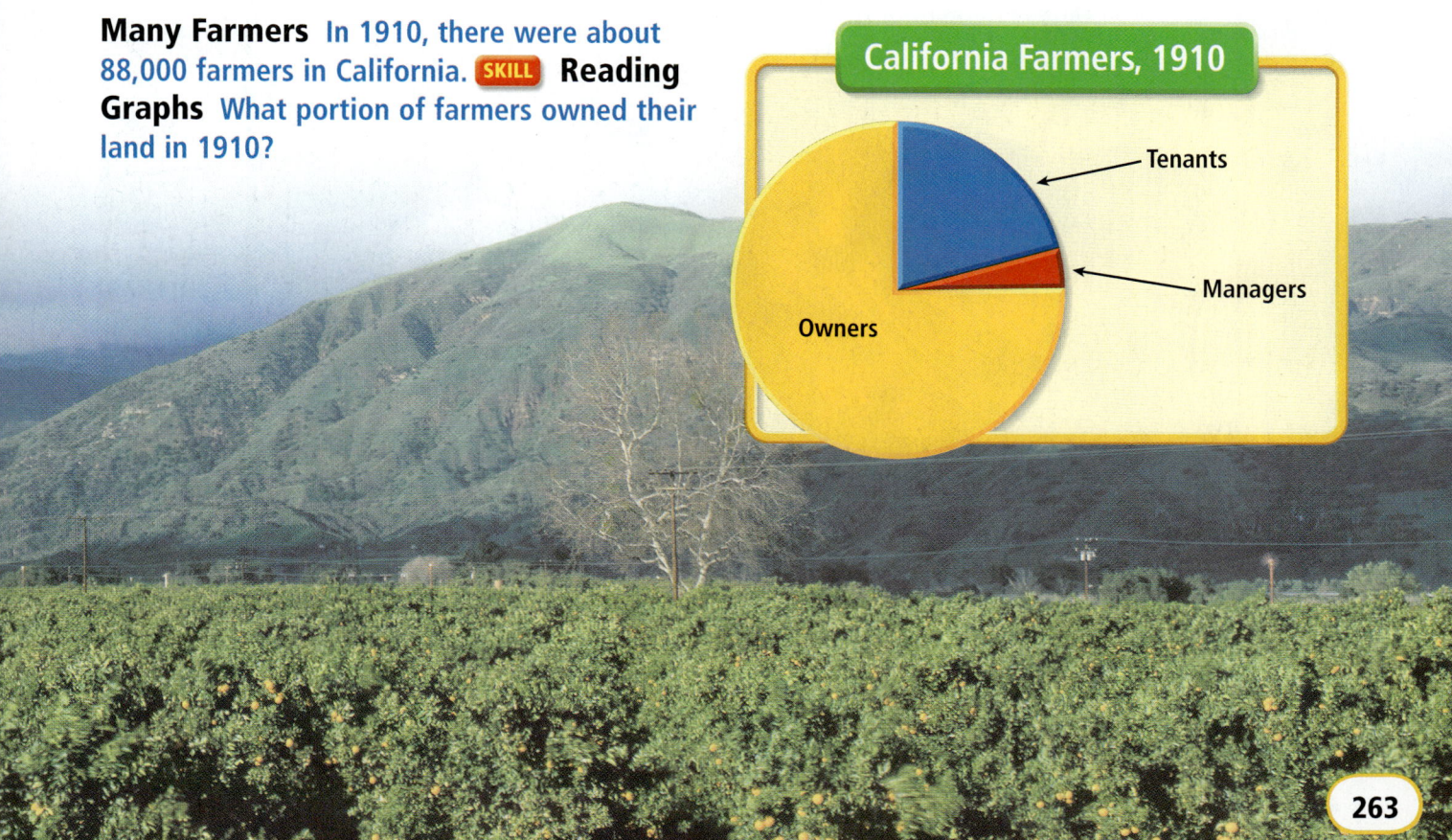

California Farmers, 1910

Owners / Tenants / Managers

263

Railroads and the Market

Main Idea The railroad carried California crops to markets throughout the country.

By 1900, California farms grew more than enough food to feed California's people. Migrant workers harvested huge amounts of navel oranges, grapes, avocados, and dozens of other crops.

People in other states also wanted fresh produce, or fruits and vegetables. For much of the year, the only produce many city people ate came from cans. There was a growing demand for fresh fruits and vegetables from California. **Demand** is the amount of a good or service that consumers want to buy at different prices.

Partly to meet this demand, companies built more railroads. Trains carried crops to distant markets. A **market** is a setting where goods and services are exchanged.

Railroad companies wanted land to build tracks. They competed with farmers for land. Sometimes, farmers were told to move off the land the railroads wanted. Many refused, but they were often forced off.

Though new railroads connected California to eastern markets, shipping goods was still slow and expensive. Because trains had to travel across great distances, the produce could rot before it reached the East Coast. People experimented with new technology to keep produce cold so it wouldn't spoil.

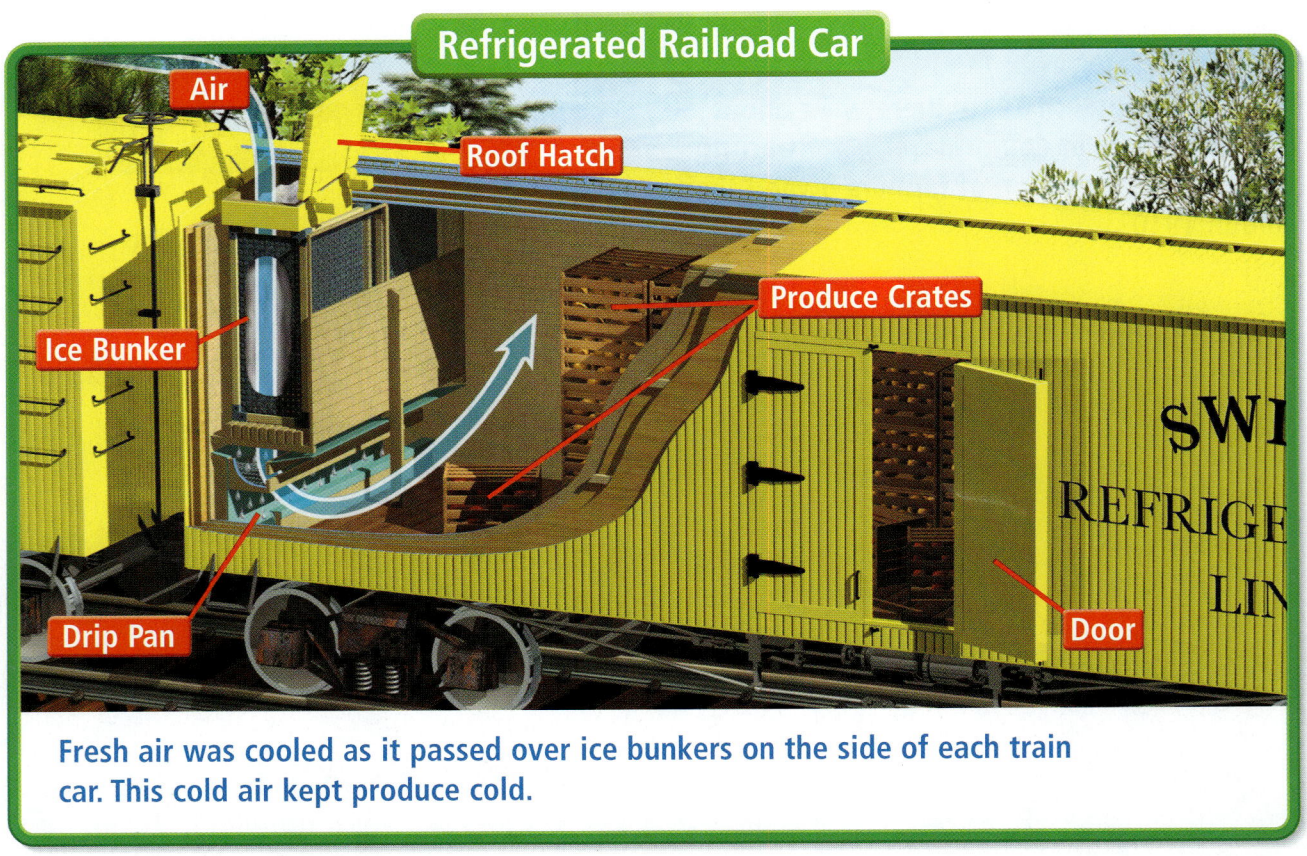

Refrigerated Railroad Car

Fresh air was cooled as it passed over ice bunkers on the side of each train car. This cold air kept produce cold.

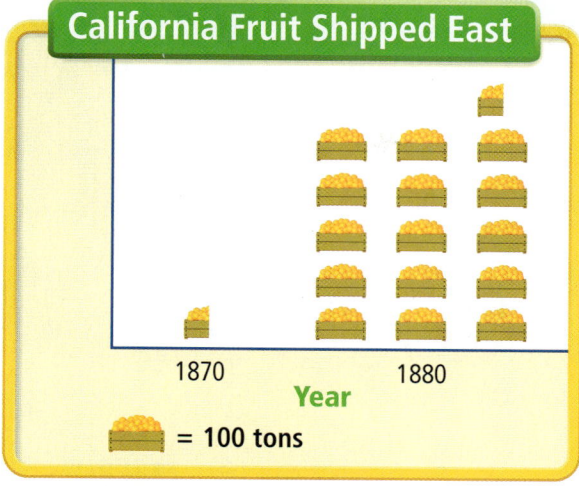

California Fruit Shipped East

1870   1880
Year

= 100 tons

SKILL Reading Graphs About how many tons of fruit were shipped east in 1880?

In 1870, the first refrigerated, or cooled, railroad cars traveled from California to the East. They carried 70 tons of apples, grapes, pears, and plums. Thousands of pounds of ice kept the fruit cold. As technology improved, the state's farms shipped even more produce at lower prices.

The refrigerated railroad car made California a major source of farm produce. People in other parts of the United States could now enjoy fresh vegetables and fruits year round, just as people in California did.

REVIEW Why did farming grow after the invention of the refrigerated railroad car?

Lesson Summary

- After the Gold Rush, many miners became farmers.
- Technology and irrigation projects helped Californians grow new crops.
- Railroads and refrigeration let farmers ship their goods to markets.

Why It Matters...

California's irrigated farmland grows each year, allowing more parts of the state to produce and sell crops.

Lesson Review

1869 More farmers than miners in California
1870 First refrigerated train crosses the country

1860 1865 1870 1875 1880

1 VOCABULARY Write two sentences that describe the differences between **migrant workers** and tenant farmers.

2 READING SKILL In what way did the Tibbetses and Luther Burbank **cause** farming to increase?

3 MAIN IDEA: Geography Why did Central Valley farmers use irrigation?

4 MAIN IDEA: Economics Why was there a demand for California produce on the East Coast?

5 TIMELINE SKILL When did the first refrigerated railroad car travel to the East?

6 CRITICAL THINKING: Synthesize Contrast the ways railroads helped and hurt California farmers.

MAP ACTIVITY Draw a product map of California to show where five crops are grown. Create a symbol for each crop and draw it in its correct place on your map. Use information from the lesson and other resources.

1. HSS 4.4 2. HSS 4.4.6 3. HSS 4.4.7 4. HSS 4.4 5. HSS 4.4 6. HSS 4.4 Activity HSS 4.1.3

Extend Lesson 2
History

The Imperial Valley

Who would try to farm a hot, dry desert called the Valley of the Dead? Charles Rockwood and George Chaffey, that's who. These irrigation engineers knew the soil was rich and was good for crops. All they needed was water.

Workers built a 70-mile-long canal from the Colorado River. In 1901, the canal opened. Within a year, 2,000 people moved to the valley to work on new farms. They came from India, Korea, Greece, and other countries. Rockwood renamed these 100,000 acres of former desert the Imperial Valley.

Sikh Farmers Sikh immigrants from the Punjab region of India worked on farms in the Imperial Valley. The region's land and climate reminded them of their homeland.

Colorado Desert
Western part of Sonoran Desert

Salton Sea
Formed during 1905 floods

Irrigated Farmlands
Crops include cotton, melons, and lettuce

Activities

1. **THINK ABOUT IT** Why did Rockwood and Chaffey think the Valley of the Dead could become good farmland?

2. **CONTRAST IT** Look at the upper and lower parts of the picture to compare and contrast land before and after the canal was built. Make a chart of differences.

Core Lesson 3

Los Angeles

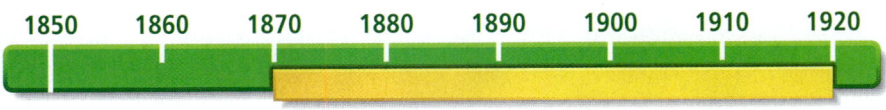
1870–1920

Build on What You Know Think of all the ways you use water every day. In the early 1900s, people in Los Angeles did not have enough water.

History of the City

Main Idea Los Angeles grew quickly because of new railroads and the growth of the port of San Pedro.

The Spanish founded Los Angeles in 1781 as a farming community. Fewer than 50 people lived in the small village. These first settlers included California Indians and farmers with Spanish, African, and Mexican ancestors. They grew food for the nearby presidios.

Los Angeles, 1850 About 1,600 people lived in this small town.

VOCABULARY

aqueduct
reservoir
hydroelectric power

Vocabulary Strategy

aqueduct

The prefix **aqua-** means water. An **aqueduct** is a duct, or channel, that carries water.

READING SKILL
Main Idea and Details List details that support the first main idea.

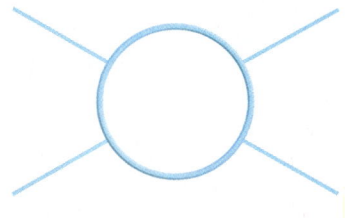

 STANDARDS

Core: HSS 4.1.4, 4.1.5, 4.4.4, 4.4.7, Analysis Skill CST 3
Extend support: HSS 4.1

268 • Chapter 8

Growing City Thousands of families moved to Los Angeles. This Japanese American family was photographed in Los Angeles about 1900.
SKILL Reading Graphs About how many people lived in the city in 1900?

Better Transportation

Los Angeles was hard to reach from the rest of the country. Deserts and mountains surrounded the city. It was near the ocean, but had no natural harbor. In 1872, the Southern Pacific Railroad linked Los Angeles to the transcontinental railroad in the north. In 1885, the Santa Fe Railway built a direct line to the city from the East.

Railroad companies convinced people to ride trains to California. Advertisements told about California's sunshine and natural beauty. An advertisement tells about a product or business. Thousands of visitors came to Los Angeles. Many stayed. They built houses and hotels. By 1920, southern California had as many people as northern California.

Port of San Pedro

The growing population of Los Angeles needed supplies. Ships carried lumber and food into the port of San Pedro, a town 20 miles south of Los Angeles. As Los Angeles grew, so did San Pedro. Workers dug out the port to make it deeper and built a huge breakwater, or long wall, to protect ships. A railroad linked the port to Los Angeles. In 1907, San Pedro became the official port of Los Angeles.

The port continued to grow after the Panama Canal was built in 1914. This canal connected the Atlantic and Pacific oceans. It made shipping to California from Europe and the East Coast faster and less expensive.

REVIEW Why did Los Angeles's location make growth difficult in its early years?

Los Angeles Aqueduct

When it was finished, the aqueduct crossed hundreds of miles of land, including parts of the Sierra Nevada and Mojave Desert.

Water for Los Angeles

Main Idea Los Angeles also grew because it was able to get water from the Owens River.

Many newcomers to Los Angeles started farms. They used water from the Los Angeles River for their crops.

By the early 1900s, the Los Angeles River did not have enough water for the growing city. **William Mulholland** was the head engineer of Los Angeles's water department. He decided to take water from the Owens River, about 200 miles northeast of Los Angeles.

Mulholland and others convinced people who lived along the river in the Owens Valley to sell their water rights. Water rights allow people to control the use of a body of water.

Farmers in Owens Valley believed that their land would still be irrigated, but Mulholland tricked them. Instead of irrigating Owens Valley, he built a huge aqueduct. An **aqueduct** is a pipe or channel that moves water across great distances.

The Los Angeles Aqueduct took five years, thousands of workers, and millions of dollars to complete. It carried water up and down hills, through more than 200 miles of tunnels and channels. Along the way, water from the Owens River flowed through a network of dams and reservoirs. A **reservoir** is a tank or lake for storing large amounts of water. On November 5, 1913, Owens River water reached Los Angeles for the first time.

Lasting Effects

The aqueduct took most of the water from Owens Valley. By the 1920s, ranchers and farmers didn't have enough water to grow crops or raise animals. What was once a rich farming region became very dry.

In Los Angeles, however, the aqueduct provided hydroelectric power as well as water for people and farms. **Hydroelectric power** is electricity created by using the power of moving water.

Aqueducts still bring water and power to Los Angeles. Because fresh water is a limited resource, water conservation is very important. People save water by running only full loads of laundry. Others fix leaky pipes, water their lawns less often, or conserve water in other helpful ways.

REVIEW Why did people in Los Angeles want more water in the early 1900s?

Conservation This girl turns off the water while brushing her teeth.

Lesson Summary

- Increased railroad service helped Los Angeles grow.
- The port of San Pedro grew so more goods could be shipped into the city.
- The Los Angeles Aqueduct created a new water supply for the city.

Why It Matters...

Better transportation and the Los Angeles Aqueduct helped Los Angeles become one of the world's great cities.

Lesson Review

1885 Railroad links Los Angeles to East

1913 Los Angeles Aqueduct completed

1880 — 1890 — 1900 — 1910 — 1920

❶ **VOCABULARY** Explain the way that **reservoirs** helped Los Angeles get water.

❷ **READING SKILL** Use **details** to tell how new railroads helped Los Angeles grow.

❸ **MAIN IDEA: History** What are two things that made the port of San Pedro grow?

❹ **MAIN IDEA: Technology** What did Los Angeles use to transport water from the Owens Valley to the city?

❺ **TIMELINE SKILL** In what year was it first possible to ship goods from Los Angeles and the East by railroad?

❻ **CRITICAL THINKING: Apply** What effect did Mulholland's actions have on the environment in southern California?

HANDS ON MATH ACTIVITY Find out how much water people in your town or city use. Chart the number of gallons people use each day. List things they could do to conserve water.

1. HSS 4.4.7 2. HSS 4.4.4 3. HSS 4.4.4 4. HSS 4.4.7 5. HSS 4.4.4 6. Analysis Skill CST 3 **Activity** HSS 4.1.5

271

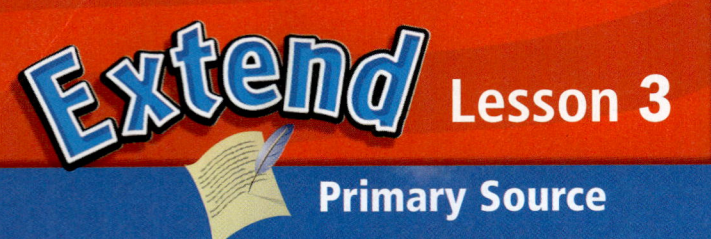

Extend Lesson 3
Primary Source

California's Song

Music rang from the deck of the first ship to pass through the Panama Canal in 1914. This new canal helped the ports of Los Angeles and other California cities grow. It's no wonder that the song playing was "I Love You, California." In 1951, Californians made it their state's official song.

"I Love You, California" is just one of many songs written about California. The state's vast farms, sunny beaches, and crowded cities have inspired songwriters for decades. How many songs can you think of that sing about California?

I Love You, California

Words by Frank Silverwood
Music by Alfred Frankenstein

I love you, Cal-i-forn-ia, you're the great-est state of all. I love you in the win-ter, sum-mer, spring, and in the fall. I love your fer-tile val-leys; your dear moun-tains I a-dore. I love your grand old o-cean and I love her rug-ged shore. Where the

Activities

1. **FIND IT** What features and places in California does this song tell about? Find the words and phrases that mention them.

2. **WRITE ABOUT IT** Create your own verse for "I Love You, California" that describes the region in which you live. Use descriptive and rhyming words.

Skillbuilder

Summarize

VOCABULARY
summarize

When you **summarize** something you've read, you tell the most important points in your own words. Summarizing can help you organize information and understand what you read. The steps below will help you summarize this paragraph about Los Angeles from Lesson 3.

> Because fresh water is a limited resource, water conservation is very important. People save water by running only full loads of laundry. Others fix leaky pipes, water their lawns less often, or conserve water in other helpful ways.

Learn the Skill

Step 1: Find the subject of the passage. The subject is what the passage is about. Write the subject in the top box of the diagram.

Step 2: Find the main points. These are ideas or examples that explain the subject. Place each main point in a box.

Step 3: Use your own words to write a summary of the subject and main ideas. Combine the information in the boxes into one or two sentences.

276 • Chapter 8

Practice the Skill

STANDARDS Analysis Skill HI 1

Write a summary of the following paragraph. Make a diagram like the one on page 276 to help you identify the main points.

> In 1908, the building of the Los Angeles Aqueduct began. Workers from Mexico, Greece, Switzerland, and many other countries moved to California to help build the aqueduct. They set up work camps in the Mojave Desert. The work was difficult in the harsh desert weather, but the jobs paid well. Because of their hard work, the Los Angeles Aqueduct was completed 20 months ahead of schedule.

Apply the Skill

Read the two paragraphs on page 269 in Lesson 3 about how railroads helped Los Angeles grow. Fill out a diagram like the one on the opposite page. Then write a summary of the information.

Core Lesson 4

San Francisco

1850 1860 1870 1880 1890 1900 1910 1920

1870–1910

Build on What You Know What kinds of public transportation have you used? Many cities have buses and trains. After the Gold Rush, San Franciscans rode on cable cars.

A Growing City

Main Idea Transportation and new technology helped San Francisco grow after the Gold Rush.

Thousands of people who moved to California during the Gold Rush went to San Francisco. It was the largest port near the goldfields. Bankers, lawyers, builders, and workers moved there to earn money and find new opportunities. Very quickly, San Francisco changed from a small town to a big city.

New Transportation Horse-drawn streetcars were soon replaced by cable cars in San Francisco.

VOCABULARY

artists' colony
construction

Vocabulary Strategy

construct*ion*

To **construct** means to build. Think of other words that have the word part struct, such as structure.

READING SKILL

Predict Outcomes Note details about how San Francisco grew. Then predict how you think San Francisco will change after the 1906 earthquake.

STANDARDS
Core: HSS 4.1.4, 4.4, 4.4.2, 4.4.4
Extend support: HSS 4.1.3

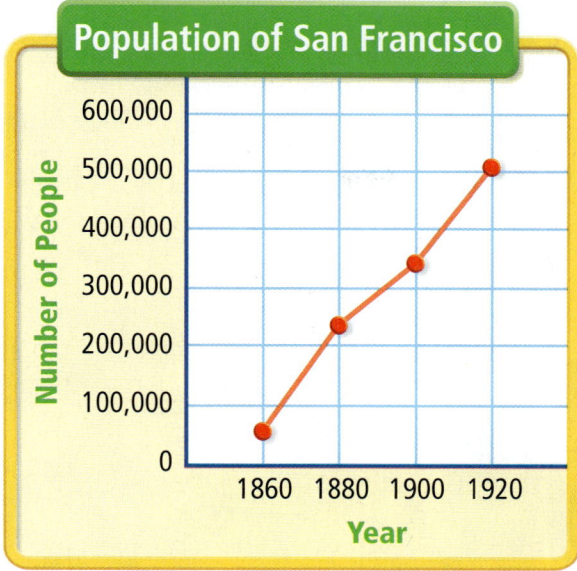

Traveling to San Francisco The *Ocean Express* sailed to the city from New York.

SKILL Reading Graphs About how many more people lived in San Francisco in 1920 than in 1900?

Ships and Railroads

San Francisco Bay has one of the largest natural harbors in the world. This harbor made the city a major center of trade in the late 1800s.

Ships carried goods to people in Asia and other places who wanted products from northern California. Products like flour and lumber were made in factories using nearby resources, such as wheat and redwood trees. Ships returned with goods from Asia, such as silk and furniture.

In 1869, the transcontinental railroad reached Oakland, a city across the bay from San Francisco. This railroad allowed people and goods to travel easily between the San Francisco Bay area and other parts of the country.

City Life

Some people made fortunes during or after the Gold Rush. They built huge houses in a neighborhood called Nob Hill. Artists such as **William Smith Jewett** came to sell paintings to these wealthy people. Many settled in artists' colonies. An **artists' colony** is a community where artists live, work, and learn together.

Visitors came to enjoy restaurants, theaters, and new technology. For example, San Francisco had the first cable car line in the country. It was built in 1873. The city also had the tallest building on the West Coast. It was sixteen stories high.

REVIEW Why was San Francisco's harbor important to the city?

After the Earthquake Fires started when the earthquake caused gas pipes to break. A total of 514 city blocks burned.

The Earthquake

Main Idea The earthquake and fires of 1906 caused terrible damage to San Francisco.

Early on the morning of April 18, 1906, San Francisco began to shake. The first jolt lasted just a few seconds. It was followed by a longer jolt. For almost a full minute, the city shook. A major earthquake had hit the coast.

Many buildings collapsed immediately. Others were damaged beyond repair. Dozens of people lay trapped in the fallen buildings.

The earthquake broke the city's gas pipes. As natural gas escaped into the air, small sparks started fires. Within minutes, the city was on fire.

Fires Spread

For three days, more than fifty fires burned. About 28,000 buildings were destroyed. More than half of the city's population lost their homes.

Many people thought poor planning made the damage worse. The earthquake broke water pipes. Fire fighters had no water to put out the fires. Poorly made buildings fell down.

The earthquake brought San Franciscans together, however. Rich and poor people faced some of the same problems. They stood in the same lines for water. They slept in the same tents as they rebuilt their homes. They worked together with a new spirit, "the spirit of San Francisco."

Starting Over

Five days after the earthquake, the governor of California told newspapers that "the work of rebuilding" had begun. Architects and engineers studied the buildings that still stood. They saw which kinds of construction survived the earthquake. **Construction** is the way something is built. San Franciscans began building a safer city.

The earthquake also showed people that automobiles could be useful. In 1906, people used horse-drawn carriages and cable cars to move around the city. During the fires, the few cars in the city carried people to safety when horses and cable cars could not.

REVIEW Why did fires start after the 1906 earthquake hit San Francisco?

Lesson Summary

San Francisco's port and nearby railroads brought people and businesses to the city.

In 1906, a huge earthquake struck the city, resulting in fires.

San Franciscans learned from the earthquake and worked to rebuild their city.

Why It Matters...

After the 1906 earthquake, San Franciscans learned ways to better protect buildings from fire and earthquakes.

Lesson Review

1873 — First cable car line
1906 — San Francisco earthquake
1870 | 1880 | 1890 | 1900 | 1910

❶ **VOCABULARY** Write a sentence using the term **artists' colony** to describe San Francisco.

❷ **READING SKILL** Check your **prediction**. How did the earthquake affect San Francisco?

❸ **MAIN IDEA: Culture** List two kinds of new technology used in San Francisco in the late 1800s.

❹ **MAIN IDEA: History** What did people learn from studying earthquake damage?

❺ **TIMELINE SKILL** In what year was the first cable car line built?

❻ **CRITICAL THINKING: Synthesize** What could have been done to prevent so much damage from the 1906 earthquake?

WRITING ACTIVITY Write a short newspaper article describing what happened on the day of the San Francisco earthquake. Include a headline, and answer the questions Who?, What?, Where?, When?, and Why?

1. HSS 4.4.2 2. HSS 4.4.4 3. HSS 4.4.4 4. HSS 4.1.3 5. HSS 4.4.4 6. HSS 4.1.3 Activity Analysis Skill HI 1

281

Extend Lesson 4
Geography

Earthquake Safety

Furniture sways. Lights flicker. When pieces of Earth's crust grind against each other, they cause an earthquake.

Scientists have found ways to keep people safe during earthquakes. By studying areas that have had earthquakes in the past, they can tell where they might happen in the future, so people can prepare for them.

Scientists and engineers have also found better forms of construction. Government and businesses in San Francisco have spent billions of dollars to strengthen freeways, bridges, and public buildings. For example, some buildings will sway back and forth during an earthquake. These buildings are more likely to stay standing when the ground beneath them shakes.

San Andreas Fault The edges of two pieces of Earth's crust meet in western California. These large pieces of crust are called tectonic plates.

Better Buildings The slanted rails on the Oakland Coliseum will help keep this building standing during an earthquake.

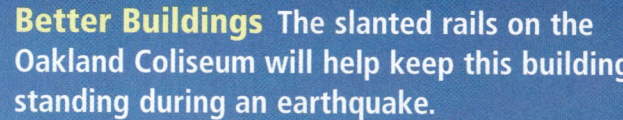

GEOGRAPHY

Hiroo Kanamori He is a scientist in Pasadena who studies ways to improve building safety.

Activities

1. **CONNECT IT** Write a paragraph about how the three pictures on this page are connected to the main idea of earthquakes.

2. **DRAW IT** Make your own design for a building or structure that could sway without breaking during an earthquake.

283

Skillbuilder

Identify Primary and Secondary Sources

▶ **VOCABULARY**

primary source
secondary source

You can learn more about the San Francisco earthquake by reading primary and secondary sources. A **primary source** is written by someone who was present at an event. Letters, diaries, and newspaper reports are primary sources. A **secondary source** is written by someone who did not see the event. Secondary sources may give an overview of an event or summarize what happened. History books, biographies, and encyclopedias are secondary sources.

Source A

On April 18, 1906, shortly after 5:00 A.M., a great earthquake struck San Francisco and a long narrow band of towns, villages, and countryside. Many buildings were wrecked; hundreds of people were killed; electric power lines and gas mains [pipes] were broken. Fires broke out and burned wildly for days because of severed [broken] water mains.

Source B

I just held on to [the] side of the bed to keep from falling out and ducked my head in the pillow, for I was so scared I couldn't even yell. When the shaking had somewhat subsided [lessened] I jumped up and ran into my mother's room where my father and mother and my small sister slept.

Apply Critical Thinking

STANDARDS Analysis Skill REPV 1

Learn the Skill

Step 1: Read the source.

Step 2: Look for clue words such as *I* and *my*. These words are sometimes used in primary sources.

Step 3: Decide whether the passage is a primary source or a secondary source. Ask yourself questions such as, *Who wrote the passage? Was the writer at the event?*

Practice the Skill

Read the sources on page 284 to answer these questions.

1. What is the subject of Sources A and B?
2. Which is a primary source? What clues tell you so?
3. Which is a secondary source? What clues tell you so?
4. What is a major difference between the primary source and the secondary source?

Apply the Skill

Find a newspaper or magazine article that is an example of a primary source. Then find an article that is an example of a secondary source. In a paragraph, explain how you identified each type of source.

Chapter 8 Review

Visual Summary

1–4. Write a description for each item named below.

Immigration

Farming

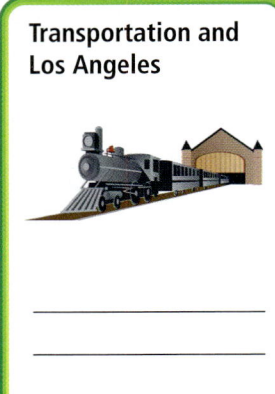
Transportation and Los Angeles

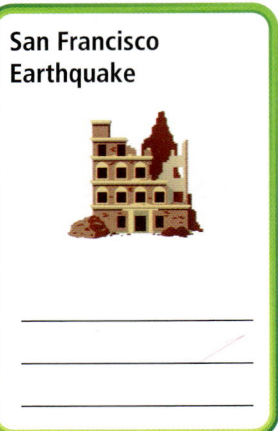
San Francisco Earthquake

STANDARDS 1. HSS 4.4.3 2. HSS 4.4 3. HSS 4.4.4 4. HSS 4.4.4

Facts and Main Ideas

Answer each question below.

5. **History** In what way did the Chinese Exclusion Act in 1882 affect people who wanted to immigrate from China?

6. **Economics** What invention helped farmers meet the growing demand for California produce in the East?

7. **History** What was the purpose of the Los Angeles Aqueduct?

8. **Geography** Why did San Francisco's location help it grow in the late 1800s?

5. HSS 4.4.3 6. HSS 4.4 7. HSS 4.4.7 8. HSS 4.4.4

Vocabulary

Choose the correct word from the list below to complete each sentence.

immigration, p. 252
migrant worker, p. 263
aqueduct, p. 270

9. A(n) _____ is one who moves from one farm to another to harvest crops.

10. A(n) _____ is used to move water from one place to another.

11. _____ increased in the 1900s as more people moved to the United States.

9. HSS 4.4 10. HSS 4.4.7 11. HSS 4.4.3

CHAPTER SUMMARY TIMELINE

- **1869** More farmers than miners in California
- **1882** Chinese Exclusion Act
- **1906** San Francisco earthquake
- **1913** Los Angeles Aqueduct

1860 — 1870 — 1880 — 1890 — 1900 — 1910 — 1920

Apply Skills

Study Skill Apply what you know about primary and secondary sources. Use the quotations to answer each question.

> During the early 1900s, more than 150,000 immigrants passed through Angel Island. Most came from China. They waited weeks or longer to find out if they could enter the country.

> My family and I arrived at Angel Island in April. We waited in a crowded shelter for two weeks. We did not know if we would be allowed into the United States, but we hoped to start our new lives quickly.
> — Sing Lum, Chinese immigrant

12. What clue tells you that the first passage is a secondary source?
    A. the use of "I" and "we"
    B. the use of "during"
    C. the writer summarized the event
    D. the writer had been at Angel Island

13. The second passage is an example of
    A. a report
    B. an encyclopedia entry
    C. a primary source
    D. a secondary source

12. Analysis Skill REPV 1   13. Analysis Skill REPV 1

Critical Thinking

Write a short paragraph to answer each question.

14. **Synthesize** In what ways did new forms of transportation affect life in the early to mid-1900s? Discuss railroads, ships, and automobiles in your answer.

15. **Infer** The phrase, "the spirit of San Francisco," was used after the 1906 earthquake. What did it mean?

Timeline

Use the Chapter Summary Timeline above to answer the question.

16. When did people in Los Angeles begin receiving water from Owens Valley?

14. HSS 4.4.6   15. HSS 4.4.4   16. HSS 4.4.4

Activities

Art Activity Find out which crops grow in different regions of California. Draw a map or illustrated chart that shows what and where they grow.

Writing Activity Write an announcement for the opening of the Los Angeles Aqueduct. Give the date, time, and purpose of the event. Tell why the event is important.

Activities HSS 4.4.6, HSS 4.4.7, W 1.1

Technology
Writing Process Tips
Get help with your writing at
www.eduplace.com/kids/hmss/

Chapter 9 A Stronger California

Vocabulary Preview

Technology
e • glossary
e • word games
www.eduplace.com/kids/hmss/

reform

Citizens worked for **reform** in the early 1900s. One change many wanted government to make was to guarantee women's right to vote. **page 291**

industry

Companies that build airplanes are just one part of California's airplane **industry**. Other businesses supply parts for airplanes and fly them. **page 297**

Chapter Timeline

1911 Women gain the vote in California

1914 World War I begins

1900 — 1905 — 1910 — 1915 — 1920

Reading Strategy

Predict and Infer Use this strategy before you read.

 **Quick Tip** Look at the pictures in a lesson to predict what it will be about.

tourism

Railroads and automobiles helped build **tourism** in California. When tourists visit California, they spend money and help the economy. **page 299**

depression

During the 1930s, a **depression** hit the country. Thousands of Californians lost their jobs as businesses closed.
page 304

1932
Roosevelt elected President

1935
Central Valley Project Act

1925 — 1930 — 1935 — 1940

Core Lesson 1

VOCABULARY

bribe
reform
suffrage

Vocabulary Strategy

form

The prefix **re-** means again. A **reform** is an action to form something again to make it better.

READING SKILL

Cause and Effect Note the causes that led people to work for reform.

Core: HSS 4.4
Extend support: HSS 4.4

Time of Reform

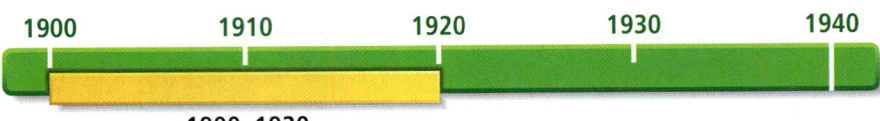

1900–1920

Build on What You Know Think of a time you tried to change rules that were unfair in a game. Some California citizens worked to change unjust laws that gave some people more power than others.

Cleaning Up State Government

Main Idea Californians changed dishonest relationships between government and some businesses.

In the early 1900s, California's government was in trouble. San Francisco's mayor was arrested for taking bribes in 1906. A **bribe** is money paid to do something illegal or dishonest. The mayor and other leaders took bribes from water, electric, and railroad companies. In exchange, they passed laws to help those businesses make money.

Californians were angered by this and wanted the bribes to end. **Hiram Johnson,** a lawyer, was a leader in the effort to make government more honest.

Hiram Johnson The political button (left) is from 1912, when he ran for Vice President of the United States.

The Progressives

Citizens called progressives worked to improve government through reforms. A **reform** is an action that tries to make something better. Progressives wanted to end the power of railroad companies in California government.

By the early 1900s, the Big Four ran all of the railroads in California. These men had invested in the first transcontinental railroad in the 1860s. Now they controlled much of California's trade and shipping. They had a great deal of power and wealth, and they used it dishonestly. They bribed officials and controlled government in Los Angeles and elsewhere.

Hiram Johnson promised to bring reforms to politics and limit the power of the Southern Pacific and other railroads. In 1910, voters elected him governor of California. During his first year in office, Johnson helped pass several laws to change California's government. These laws brought reforms that gave the government more control of railroad companies.

Changes to the state constitution also gave California voters more power. They were able to vote on new laws. They also gained the power to remove elected officials from their positions at any time.

REVIEW Why did some businesses bribe city leaders?

Railroad Cartoon This political cartoon compared the Big Four to an octopus squeezing other businesses.

SKILL Reading Visuals Which businesses in this cartoon are being squeezed?

291

Women Work for Change

Main Idea Progressives fought for the rights of consumers, workers, and women.

Katherine Philips Edson was another progressive who worked for change. After learning that babies were being harmed by unclean milk, she led the 1909 fight for "pure milk." She convinced the government of Los Angeles to make sure that only clean milk was sold to consumers.

Edson and other progressives also fought for the rights of workers. Women and children earned less money than European American men. They often worked long 12-hour days in unsafe and unhealthy factories.

A Minimum Wage

In 1911, progressives convinced lawmakers to shorten working hours for women to eight hours a day. The next year Governor Johnson hired Edson to study laws affecting pay for women workers. Edson fought for better working conditions and a minimum wage for women and children. A minimum wage law says that workers must be paid not less than a certain amount per hour.

In 1913, the state government set a minimum wage. New laws also created better working conditions. Employers were made to pay the medical bills for people injured at work.

Factory Work Katherine Philips Edson (left) helped improve conditions in California workplaces such as this fruit canning factory.

The Right to Vote

In the early 1900s, some laws did not protect the rights of women. Women such as Katherine Edson and **Grace Simons** started groups that worked for suffrage. **Suffrage** is the right to vote. Members of groups that worked for reform wrote letters, made speeches, and led marches.

In October 1911, California became the sixth state to guarantee women the right to vote in state elections. In 1920, women won the right to vote in national elections.

REVIEW What were two changes for which progressives fought?

Lesson Summary

- In the early 1900s, railroad companies controlled government in California.
- Hiram Johnson put limits on the power of railroad companies and increased the rights of voters.
- Women fought for consumers' and workers' rights and for suffrage.

Why It Matters...

The reforms that progressives worked for in the early 1900s still protect Californians today.

Mae Ella Nolan In 1922, she became the first California woman elected to the U.S. House of Representatives.

Lesson Review

Timeline: 1906 — 1908 — 1910 (Johnson elected governor) — 1911 (Women gain suffrage in California) — 1912 — 1914

① **VOCABULARY** Explain why women fought for **suffrage**.

② **READING SKILL** What **effect** did Johnson's election have on California voters?

③ **MAIN IDEA: Government** What did Hiram Johnson do to limit the power of railroad companies?

④ **MAIN IDEA: History** In what ways did Katherine Philips Edson help workers?

⑤ **TIMELINE SKILL** In what year did women gain the right to vote in California?

⑥ **CRITICAL THINKING: Evaluate** Why do you think progressives wanted to work for change in California?

SPEAKING ACTIVITY Progressives such as Katherine Philips Edson made speeches to share their views with a large audience. Prepare a speech Edson might have given about a reform she wanted.

1. HSS 4.4 2. HSS 4.4 3. HSS 4.4 4. HSS 4.4 5. HSS 4.4 6. HSS 4.4 Activity HSS 4.4

Extend Lesson 1
Citizenship

THE RIGHT TO VOTE

Voting is a basic right of adult citizens in the United States. People did not always think so, however. When California became a state in 1850, only Californios and other Americans who were white males over the age of 21 could vote. African Americans, California Indians, Chinese Americans, women, and others were left out.

Over the next several decades, people worked long and hard to gain full and equal protection of voting rights. Some held suffrage parades and marches. Others gave speeches and passed out flyers to educate people about injustice. Today, nearly every United States citizen over the age of 18 is guaranteed the right to vote.

1911
Women's Suffrage in California
California is the sixth state to guarantee women's right to vote.

1943
Chinese Exclusion Act Ends
Chinese Americans can become U.S. citizens.

1850 — 1900 — 1950

1870
Fifteenth Amendment
African American men are guaranteed suffrage.

1920
Nineteenth Amendment
All U.S. women are guaranteed suffrage.

Oakland March, 1908
About 300 members of the California Equal Suffrage Association marched for women's rights.

1971
Twenty-Sixth Amendment
Voting age lowered from 21 to 18 in every state.

2000

1975
Voting Rights Act
Protects voting rights of American Indians.

Activities

1. **TALK ABOUT IT** Why do you think the voting age was lowered in 1971? Should it be lowered again? Talk over your ideas with a partner.

2. **RESEARCH IT** Use more than one source of information to find out about a voting reform people are working for today. Write a report to explain this reform and tell why people want it.

Core Lesson 2

A Growing Economy

VOCABULARY

industry
tourism

Vocabulary Strategy

tou**r**ism

Find **tour** in **tourism**. The business of tourism helps people who tour, or visit, a new place.

READING SKILL
Main Idea and Details
Chart details that support the main idea on page 298.

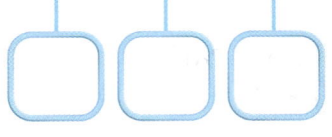

STANDARDS
Core: HSS 4.1, 4.4.6, 4.4.9
Extend support: HSS 4.4.6

California Soldiers Soldiers from Camp Kearney near San Diego prepare for war.

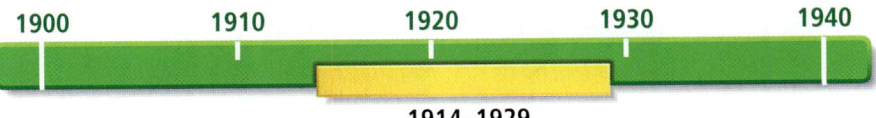

1914–1929

Build on What You Know What do you own that is made from cotton? During World War I, California farms grew cotton used to make soldiers' uniforms.

Effects of World War I

Main Idea During World War I, California companies made supplies for the military.

In 1914, World War I started in Europe. Many nations in Europe and other parts of the world fought against each other. In 1917, the United States joined the war on the side of Britain and France.

The United States military sent hundreds of thousands of soldiers to Europe to fight in World War I. California alone sent 150,000 soldiers overseas. The war brought hardship and loss to people all over the world. It also changed the economy of California.

296 • Chapter 9

Airplane Industry A worker at an Oakland factory (right) builds parts for aircraft used in World War I.

California's Contributions

Soldiers needed food and clothing. Many of these supplies were produced in California. Farmers grew more food to feed soldiers in Europe. In the San Joaquin Valley, people grew more cotton. This cotton was used to make millions of uniforms for soldiers.

California's airplane industry also grew during the war. An **industry** is made up of businesses that sell certain products and services. In 1916, **Allan** and **Malcolm Loughead** built a factory in Santa Barbara, starting the company that became Lockheed Aircraft.

After the war, California factories built other types of planes. In 1927, **Charles Lindbergh** flew from New York City to Paris, France, in a plane built in San Diego.

The movie industry grew during the war as well. Motion pictures had recently been invented, and millions of people went to the movies to try to forget the bad news of the war.

Most of the first movies were made on the East Coast. In the early 1900s, filmmakers began moving to a part of Los Angeles called Hollywood. The warm, sunny climate made filming outdoors easier than in the East. **Louis B. Mayer**, a theater owner from the East, moved to Hollywood in 1918 to make movies. He helped start a movie studio called Metro-Goldwyn-Mayer. It became one of the most successful studios in Hollywood history.

REVIEW Why did farm production increase during World War I?

The 1920s

Main Idea Economic growth continued in California after World War I ended.

By the end of World War I, movie-making was the fifth-largest industry in the country. During the 1920s, movies became even more popular. Movie palaces, or very fancy movie theaters, opened in big cities. In 1927, the first "talkie," or movie with sound, played in theaters across the country.

The agriculture and airplane industries were growing, and yet another industry was bringing jobs to California in the 1920s. Oil companies had found huge pools of petroleum, or oil, under the ground near Los Angeles in the early 1900s.

Long Beach Oil Boom After oil was found here, derricks used for drilling oil were built among the houses.

SKILL Reading Graphs About how much oil did California produce in 1910?

A Leading Oil Producer

By 1924, California produced more oil than any other state in the country. California oil was shipped all over the world. The port of Los Angeles became the biggest on the West Coast.

Demand for oil increased as people bought more cars. Cars used gasoline made from oil. Car sales rose partly because **Henry Ford** found a way to build cars that cost much less than earlier automobiles. People all over the United States, and especially in California, bought cars for the first time.

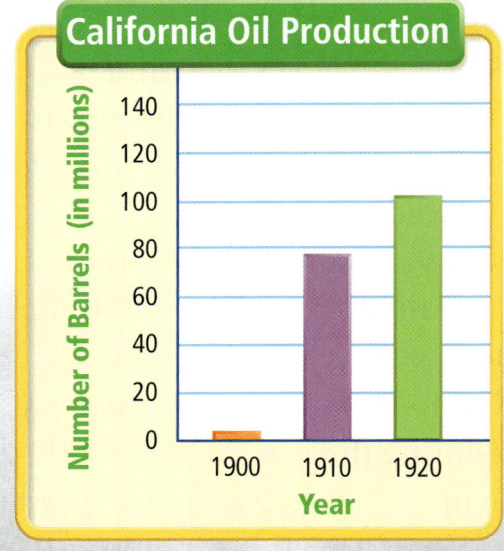

California Oil Production

Cars Change California

By 1929, there were more than 23 million cars in the United States. Close to two million of these were in California. The state built bridges, tunnels, and hundreds of miles of roads. Because people could drive places, they lived farther from work, schools, and shops than ever before.

Gas stations, restaurants, and motels lined California's new roads. Tourism grew. **Tourism** is the business of providing goods and services to people who visit places for pleasure. Tourists drove to California to see the dramatic scenery of areas such as Yosemite Valley and Palm Springs.

REVIEW What California industries grew because of increased automobile use?

Lesson Summary

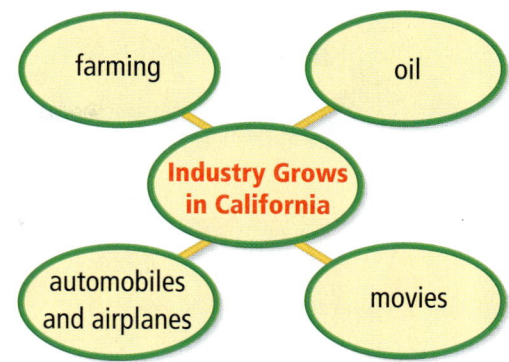

Why It Matters...

California's airplane, movie, and tourism industries are still important in California today.

New Cars Californians drove cars such as this 1928 Chevrolet.

Lesson Review

1914 — World War I
1924 — California leads U.S. oil production
1929 — About 2 million cars in California

1914 — 1918 — 1922 — 1926 — 1930

1. **VOCABULARY** Use **industry** and **tourism** in a few sentences about California's economy in the 1920s.

2. **READING SKILL** Which industries grew in the 1920s? Use **details** from the lesson in your answer.

3. **MAIN IDEA: Culture** Why did many filmmakers move to Hollywood?

4. **MAIN IDEA: Economics** Why did demand for oil increase in the 1920s?

5. **TIMELINE SKILL** By what year were there two million cars in California?

6. **CRITICAL THINKING: Analyze** Which industry in this lesson do you think has had the greatest impact on California? Explain your answer.

WRITING ACTIVITY Write an information report about the early movie industry in California. Collect information from two reference sources. Include facts and details in your report.

1. HSS 4.4.6 2. HSS 4.4.6 3. HSS 4.4.6 4. HSS 4.4.6 5. HSS 4.4.6 6. HSS 4.4.6 Activity HSS 4.4.6

Extend Lesson 2
Economics

MAKING MOVIES

How many people does it take to make a movie? In the early 1900s, as today, it took many types of talented workers. Movies needed writers, directors, set designers, and film crews. They also needed actors, of course. Mary Pickford was one of the first major movie stars. In 1916, this young woman became the highest-paid performer of her time, earning a million dollars in two years.

Movies filmed in California were shown all over the country and the world. Demand for movies rose so high that, by 1917, movie-making was the country's fifth-largest industry. California, especially Los Angeles, was at the center of it all.

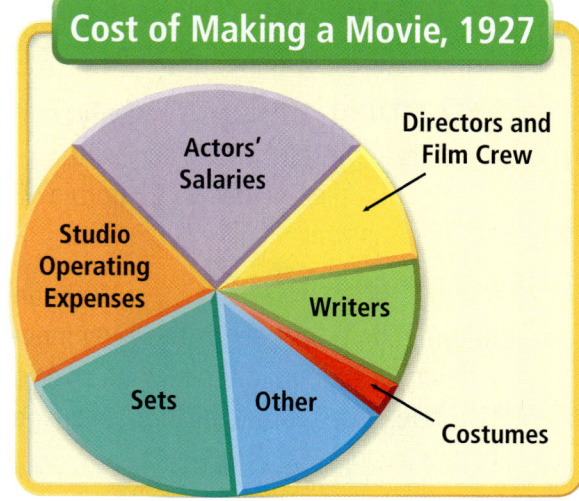

Cost of Making a Movie, 1927

ECONOMICS

Directors and camera operators film an action-packed scene in 1929.

Activities

1. **THINK ABOUT IT** Look at the chart. What was the most expensive part of making a movie in 1927? What was the least expensive part?

2. **WRITE ABOUT IT** Put yourself in the scene of this photograph. What do you see and hear? Write a description of what it might have been like to work on this set.

Skillbuilder

Read a Circle Graph

VOCABULARY
circle graph

Circle graphs are a way to make some types of information easier to understand. A **circle graph** is a chart that shows how pieces of information are part of a whole. A circle graph is also called a pie chart because it looks like a pie cut into pieces. The circle graph on the next page shows different types of work that people in California did in 1920.

Learn the Skill

Step 1: Read the title to find out what the graph is about. This graph gives information about jobs in California in 1920. The whole circle represents the total number of jobs in California.

Step 2: Read the labels for each section of the graph. Each section of this graph stands for the number of people who work in a certain kind of job.

Step 3: Compare the sizes of the different sections. In this graph, a larger section means that more people work in that kind of job. A smaller section means that fewer people work in that kind of job.

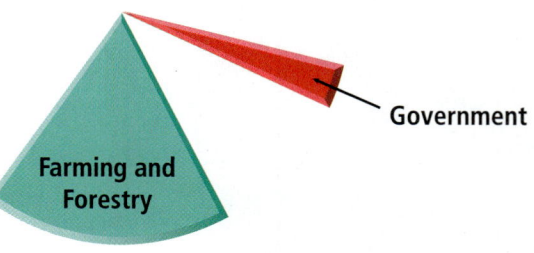

302 • Chapter 9

STANDARDS HSS 4.6.6

Jobs in California, 1920

Practice the Skill

Use the circle graph to answer these questions.

1. List the categories of jobs shown on this graph.
2. Which job category had the most workers?
3. Which job category had the fewest workers?
4. Did more Californians work in farming and forestry or in transportation? How do you know?

Apply the Skill

Create a circle graph to show how you spend your time during a typical school day. First draw a circle that stands for a whole day. Then divide it into sections to show all of your activities and the time you spend on them.

303

Core Lesson 3

The Great Depression

VOCABULARY

depression
unemployment
drought

Vocabulary Strategy

unemployment

The prefix **un-** means not. Employment means having a job. **Unemployment** is not having a job.

READING SKILL
Problem and Solution
List problems Californians faced during the Great Depression. Then note ways people solved them.

Problem	Solution

STANDARDS
Core: HSS 4.4.5, 4.4.9
Extend support: HSS 4.4.5

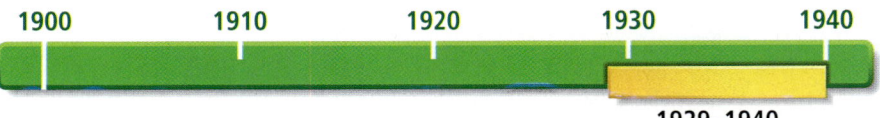

1900   1910   1920   1930   1940

1929–1940

Build on What You Know No one can do everything alone, especially in times of trouble. Californians asked the state and federal government for help during the hard years of the 1930s.

The Depression Years

Main Idea During the Great Depression, many Americans lost their jobs and homes.

During much of the 1920s, business and industry grew quickly in California and the United States. However, hard times were ahead. In the late 1920s, businesses and factories began to close. People who lost their jobs did not earn money to buy things. Stores went out of business.

Over the next few years, this economic depression spread across the country and the world. A **depression** is a time when businesses fail and jobs are hard to find. This period in the 1930s became known as the Great Depression.

Moving West As farms failed in Kansas, Nebraska, Oklahoma, and Texas, people traveled west.

Losing Jobs

In California, the Great Depression affected many industries. Banks closed. Oil companies lost money. Tourism decreased because people had little income to spend on tourist attractions. In 1932, farms earned half as much money as they had just three years earlier. Many farmers lost land because they couldn't pay their bills.

As banks and businesses closed, unemployment rose. **Unemployment** is the number of people who are looking for a job but can't find one. By 1932, more than one-fourth of California workers were unemployed. Without jobs, people could not pay for a place to live. Many families lost their homes.

The Dust Bowl

A severe drought caused even more problems in parts of the United States. A **drought** is a long, dry period when there is little or no rain. By 1934, the country was suffering from its worst drought in history. Farmland was ruined. Soil dried up and blew away. Terrible dust storms turned the sky black and covered houses in dirt. This region in the middle of the country became known as the Dust Bowl.

As farms in the Dust Bowl failed, tens of thousands of people headed to California to look for jobs. They hoped to make a new beginning.

REVIEW Why did some people move to California during the Great Depression?

New Deal Murals WPA artists were paid by the government to paint murals, or large paintings on walls. This one is in a post office in Selma.

The New Deal

Main Idea The government took action to help people during the Great Depression.

Many Dust Bowl migrants were disappointed when they reached California. Work was hard, pay was low, and jobs were hard to find.

Artists told about the suffering of these migrant farmers. **John Steinbeck** wrote about an Oklahoma farm family that moves to California in *The Grapes of Wrath*. **Dorothea Lange's** pictures of poor migrant families showed the hardships they went through.

The movie industry grew during the Depression, however. The singing and dancing of stars such as **Shirley Temple** helped people forget the hard times.

Back to Work

In 1932, voters chose **Franklin D. Roosevelt** for President. He promised to do whatever he could to help the United States recover from the Great Depression.

Roosevelt convinced lawmakers to pass laws that were part of a plan called the New Deal. The laws kept banks from closing and protected people's savings. They also created jobs. Many of these jobs were for the government.

The Works Progress Administration (WPA) gave jobs to millions of people. WPA workers built bridges, schools, dams, and roads. In California, workers built hiking trails in national parks such as Yosemite. WPA writers wrote guidebooks about California.

The Central Valley Project

In 1935, the Central Valley Project Act created one of the biggest New Deal programs in California. Over several decades, workers built a network of dams and canals to control water for Central Valley farmers.

The largest dam, called the Shasta Dam, stretched across the Sacramento River. It stored water, protected against flooding, and produced hydroelectric power. While the dam helped turn the Central Valley into a rich farming area, it destroyed important wetlands. Birds and fish lost their natural habitats.

Voters re-elected Roosevelt in 1936, 1940, and 1944. Many Californians believed that his ideas would bring them a better future.

REVIEW What was the Works Progress Administration?

Lesson Summary

During the Great Depression of the 1930s, millions of people lost their jobs. Drought ruined farms in the Dust Bowl. Migrants came to California, but few found jobs. President Roosevelt's New Deal employed millions of Americans.

Why It Matters...

Roosevelt's New Deal gave the government a more active role in the nation's economy for the first time.

Shasta Dam This dam helped irrigate dry areas in central California.

Lesson Review

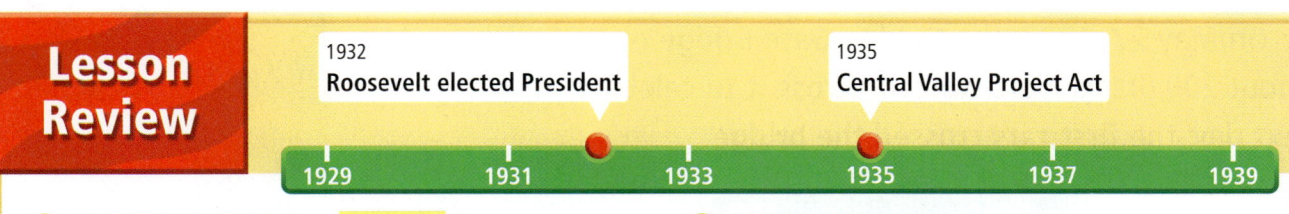

1932 — Roosevelt elected President
1935 — Central Valley Project Act

1. **VOCABULARY** Use **drought** in a sentence about the effects of the Dust Bowl on California.

2. **READING SKILL** Make an outline of programs President Roosevelt used to help **solve problems** during the Depression.

3. **MAIN IDEA: Economics** Why did unemployment rise in the 1930s?

4. **MAIN IDEA: Government** In what ways did the Shasta Dam help Californians?

5. **TIMELINE SKILL** In what year was Franklin D. Roosevelt first elected President?

6. **CRITICAL THINKING: Evaluate** Explain why you think Americans chose to re-elect Franklin D. Roosevelt three more times.

WRITING ACTIVITY Write five questions you might ask someone who lived through the Great Depression. Then write two paragraphs telling how that person might have replied. Include facts, details, and explanations.

1. HSS 4.4.5 2. HSS 4.4.5 3. HSS 4.4.5 4. HSS 4.4.5 5. HSS 4.4.5 6. HSS 4.4.5 Activity HSS 4.4.5

Extend Lesson 3
History

The Golden Gate Bridge

People said it was impossible, but engineer Joseph B. Strauss did it. He designed a bridge to cross the Golden Gate Strait. It would connect San Francisco to land north of the city.

It took four years to build the Golden Gate Bridge. At a time when <mark>unemployment</mark> was high, hundreds of workers found jobs building the bridge. When it was finished, it was the world's longest suspension bridge. On this kind of bridge, the road is suspended, or hung, from cables attached to the frame.

On May 27, 1937, the Golden Gate Bridge opened. About 200,000 people walked across it to celebrate. The next day, the first cars crossed the bridge.

North Tower
In Marin County

Bridge Building The bridge is made of 83,000 tons of steel and 80,000 miles of wire. It soars 220 feet above the water.

Catwalk
Connects the towers

HISTORY

Activities

1. **DISCUSS IT** What are the workers in the picture wearing to keep safe?

2. **COMPUTE IT** Use a map to estimate how many miles people traveled from San Rafael to San Francisco before the Golden Gate and other San Francisco Bay bridges were built. Then explain why these bridges are important.

Chapter 9 Review

Visual Summary

1–4. Write a description of each item named below.

Progressives
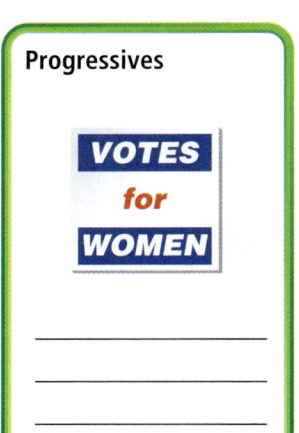
_____
_____
_____

Oil Industry

_____
_____
_____

Dust Bowl

_____
_____
_____

New Deal

_____
_____
_____

STANDARDS 1. HSS 4.4 2. HSS 4.4.6 3. HSS 4.4.5 4. HSS 4.4.5

Facts and Main Ideas

Answer the questions below.

5. **History** What did Hiram Johnson want to do as governor of California?

6. **Economics** What effect did the discovery of oil have on Los Angeles?

7. **Geography** Why did parts of the country become known as the Dust Bowl in the 1930s?

8. **Government** What was the purpose of the New Deal?

5. HSS 4.4 6. HSS 4.4.6 7. HSS 4.4.5 8. HSS 4.4.5

Vocabulary

Choose the correct word from the list below to complete each sentence.

reform, p. 291
industry, p. 297
unemployment, p. 305

9. Factories in the airplane _____ produced planes for the war.

10. _____ goes up when people lose their jobs.

11. People working for _____ fought to make government better.

9. HSS 4.4.6 10. HSS 4.4.5 11. HSS 4.4

310 • Chapter 9

CHAPTER SUMMARY TIMELINE

1911 California women win the vote
1917 U.S. joins World War I
1927 First movie with sound
1932 Roosevelt elected President

1900 — 1910 — 1920 — 1930 — 1940

Apply Skills

Read a Circle Graph Use what you have learned about circle graphs to answer each question.

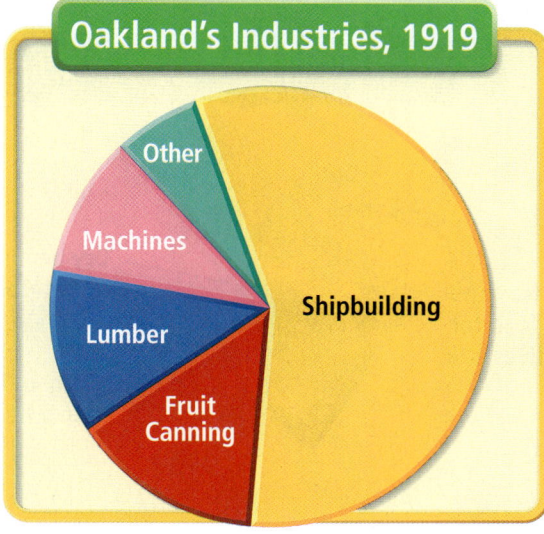
Oakland's Industries, 1919 (Other, Machines, Lumber, Shipbuilding, Fruit Canning)

12. What was Oakland's largest industry in 1919?
    A. shipbuilding
    B. fruit canning
    C. lumber
    D. machines

13. Which two industries made up about a quarter of Oakland's 1919 industries?
    A. shipbuilding and fruit canning
    B. shipbuilding and machines
    C. shipbuilding and lumber
    D. fruit canning and lumber

12. HSS 4.4.6   13. HSS 4.4.6

Critical Thinking

Write a short paragraph to answer each question.

14. **Cause and Effect** Describe the effects of the Central Valley Project on the land and people of central California.

15. **Compare and Contrast** Contrast California's economy during World War I with California's economy during the Great Depression.

Timeline

Use the Chapter Summary Timeline above to answer the question.

16. In what year did the first "talkie" play in theaters?

14. HSS 4.4.5   15. HSS 4.4.6   16. HSS 4.4.9

Activities

Speaking Activity Find out more about an industry discussed in this chapter. Prepare an oral report describing its contributions to California.

Writing Activity Write a narrative about the experiences of migrant families who moved to California from the Dust Bowl. Use sensory details.

Technology
Writing Process Tips
Get help with your writing at www.eduplace.com/kids/hmss/

Activities HSS 4.4.6, HSS 4.4.5, W 2.1

UNIT 4 Review

Vocabulary and Main Ideas

Write a sentence to answer each question.

1. In what way did the Chinese **Exclusion** Act change **immigration**?
2. Why was there a **demand** for fresh California produce in other states in the late 1800s?
3. What problem did the city of Los Angeles try to solve by building an **aqueduct**?
4. What was one **reform** that Californians wanted to make in government during the early 1900s?
5. Why did the airplane **industry** grow in California during World War I?
6. In what way does a **depression** affect businesses?

Critical Thinking

Write a short paragraph to answer each question.

7. **Summarize** Tell why immigrants left their home countries and moved to California.
8. **Cause and Effect** What caused tourists to visit California in the late 1800s and early 1900s?

Apply Skills

Read a Circle Graph Use what you know about reading circle graphs to answer each question below.

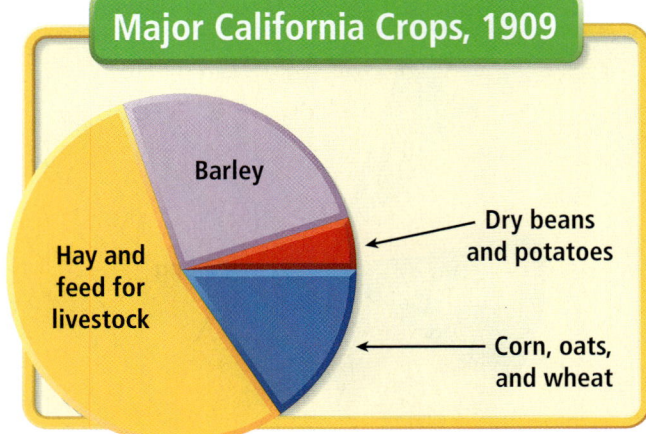

Major California Crops, 1909

9. What type of crop did California farms grow the most of in 1909?

   A. Corn, oats, and wheat
   B. Hay and feed for livestock
   C. Barley
   D. Dry beans and potatoes

10. What type of crop did California farms grow the least of in 1909?

    A. Corn, oats, and wheat
    B. Hay and feed for livestock
    C. Barley
    D. Dry beans and potatoes

STANDARDS 1. HSS 4.4.3 2. HSS 4.4.6 3. HSS 4.4.4 4. HSS 4.4
5. HSS 4.4.6 6. HSS 4.4.5 7. HSS 4.4.3 8. HSS 4.4.4
9. HSS 4.4.6 10. HSS 4.4.6
Activity Analysis Skill HI 2, W1.1

Unit Activity

Design a Cover of a Magazine

- Look back at Unit 4. Choose a person who helped change California.
- Do research to find out about ways the person changed California.
- Design a magazine cover to feature the person you chose. Find ways to combine words and pictures on the cover.

At the Library

You may find these books at your school or public library.

Shannon: A Chinatown Adventure: San Francisco, 1880 by Kathleen Kudlinski
Shannon, an Irish immigrant new to San Francisco, meets Mi Ling, a frightened Chinese girl whom she befriends.

Earthquake by Seymour Simon
Color photos enhance Simon's clear explanations of earthquakes, fault lines, sand boils, and much more.

WEEKLY READER
Current Events

Connect to Today

Create a poster about farming in California.

- Look for information about farming in a region of California today, such as the Central Valley or the Imperial Valley.
- Write a description of the region. Explain where it is and what kinds of crops are farmed there.
- Find pictures of farms and farmers. Create a poster with this information.

 Technology
Weekly Reader online offers social studies articles. Go to:
www.eduplace.com/kids/hmss/

Read About It

Look in your classroom for these Social Studies Independent Books.

313

UNIT 5

Modern California

The Big Idea

What part will you play in California's future?

"I . . . learned early in life to . . . speak up for what I thought was right."

—from an interview with Miriam Matthews

Dianne Feinstein
1933–

Who was the first California woman elected to the U.S. Senate? Dianne Feinstein, who was also the first woman mayor of San Francisco.
Page 349

History Makers

Rueben Martinez
1940–

This barber gave out books along with haircuts. So many visitors came for the books, Martinez opened two bookstores.
Page 409

Ellen Ochoa
1958–

This Californian has seen the whole world. She became the first Hispanic woman astronaut in 1990. Since then, she has made several trips into space. **Page 366**

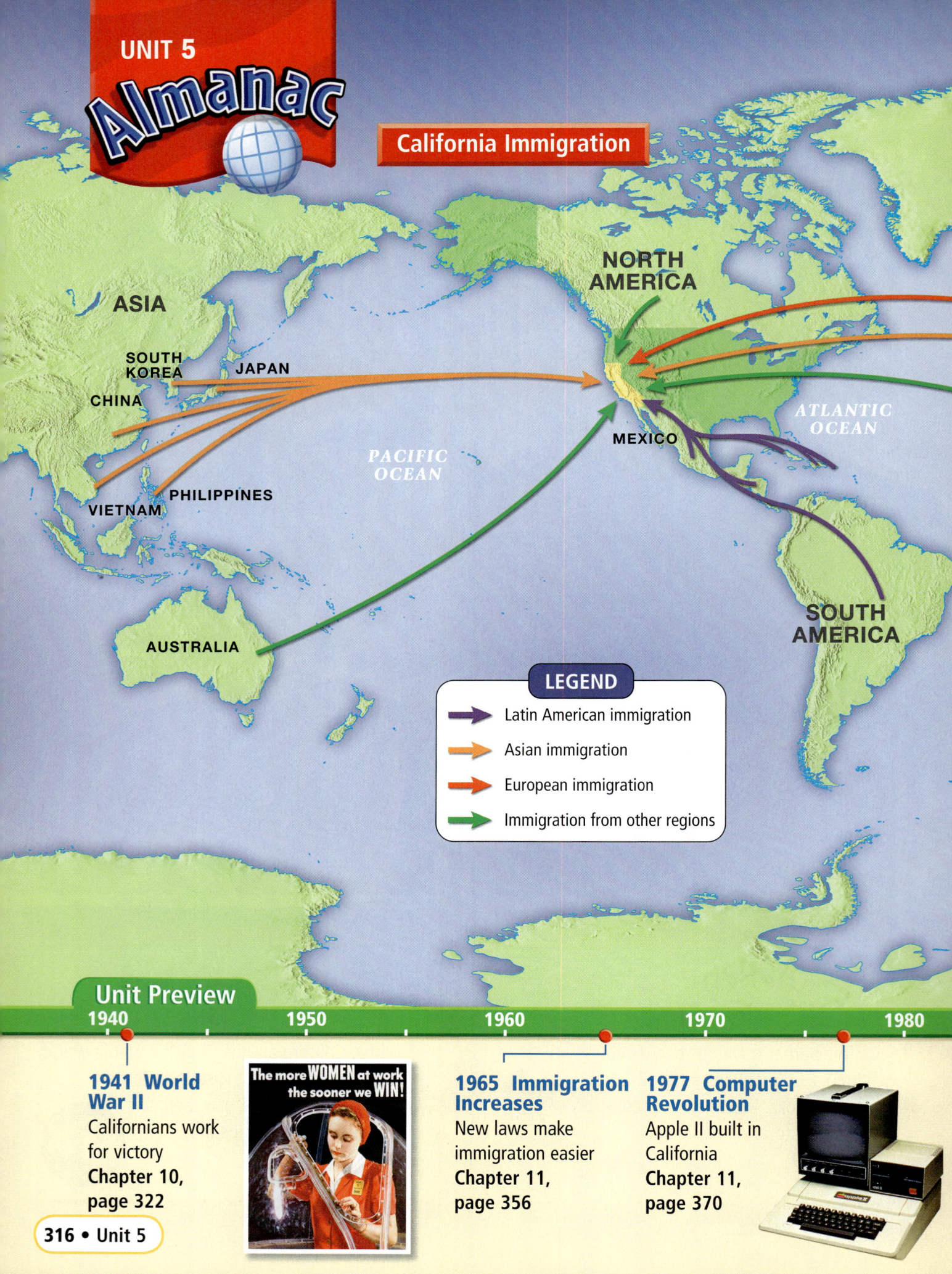

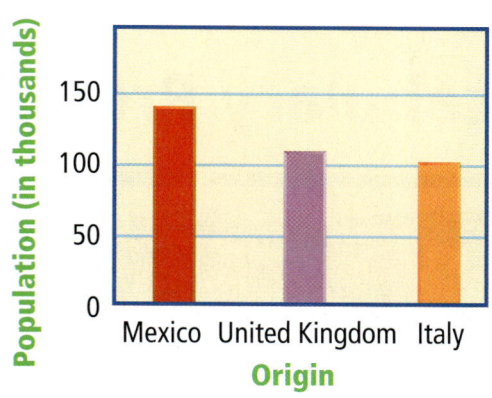

Connect to Today

Californians Born in Other Nations, 1940 and 2002

1940
In 1940, the top countries of origin included European nations.

2002
In 2002, more Californians had come from Asia than Europe.

WEEKLY READER Current Events

Current events on the Web!

For a selection of social studies articles, go to Education Place.
www.eduplace.com/kids/hmss/

1992 NAFTA
California's exports to Mexico and Canada rise
Chapter 11, page 372

2002 Alameda Corridor
Rail link speeds trade
Chapter 11, page 373

317

Chapter 10: World War II to the Seventies

e • glossary
e • word games
www.eduplace.com/kids/hmss/

Vocabulary Preview

manufacturing
During World War II, California women took jobs in **manufacturing** plants. They built planes, tanks, and ships in factories.
page 322

aerospace industry
California's **aerospace industry** began building rockets and spacecraft for space exploration in the 1960s.
page 333

Chapter Timeline

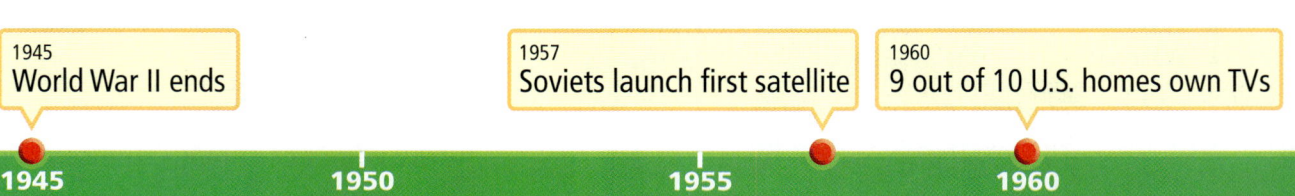

1945 — World War II ends
1957 — Soviets launch first satellite
1960 — 9 out of 10 U.S. homes own TVs

Reading Strategy

Monitor and Clarify Use this strategy to check your understanding of the text in this chapter.

 Quick Tip If you are confused about what is in a lesson, reread or read ahead.

barrio
Today, East Los Angeles has the nation's largest Mexican American **barrio**, or neighborhood of Spanish-speaking people. **page 339**

nonviolent protest
Cesar Chavez led Mexican American farm workers in **nonviolent protest.** They fought for change without using violence. **page 345**

1970
Delano grape strike ends

1970 — 1975 — 1980

Core Lesson 1

California and World War II

VOCABULARY

internment camp
manufacturing
defense industry
civilian

Vocabulary Strategy

civilian

The word **civil** means of society. A civilian is someone who is part of society, not the military.

READING SKILL
Cause and Effect
Note the effects that the war had on Californians.

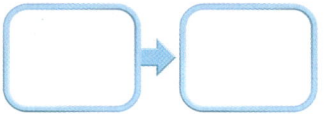

Core: HSS 4.4, 4.4.5, 4.4.6
Extend support: HSS 4.4.5

Pearl Harbor The attack damaged hundreds of U.S. Navy ships and airplanes.

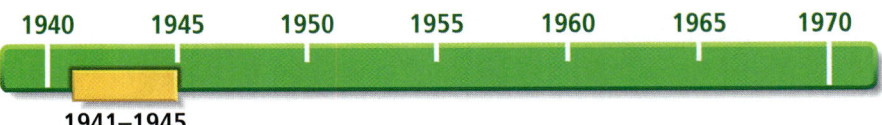

1941–1945

Build on What You Know When have you worked on a team to do something? During World War II, Californians of all ages helped win the war.

Wartime California

Main Idea World War II caused many changes in the lives of Californians.

In September 1939, war started in Europe. The fighting spread to other places. Germany, Italy, and Japan fought on one side. Great Britain, France, Russia, and other countries fought against them. This war became known as World War II.

On December 7, 1941, Japan bombed Pearl Harbor, Hawaii. The surprise attack killed more than 2,000 people, most of them sailors. The next day, the United States entered the war.

320 • Chapter 10

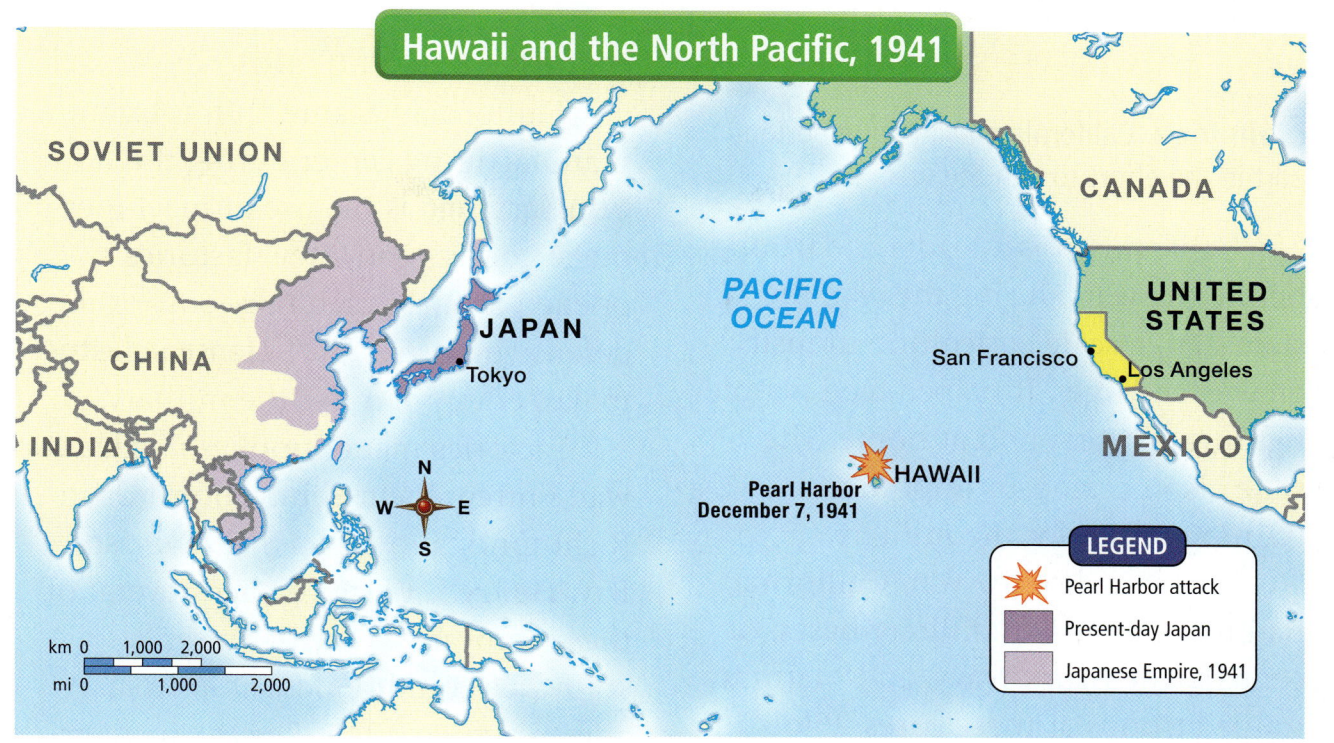

In the Pacific The Pearl Harbor naval base is on the island of Oahu, Hawaii. **SKILL** Reading Maps In which direction would you go to travel from California to Pearl Harbor?

Internment Camps

The United States fought with Great Britain against Germany, Italy, and Japan. Many people worried that Japanese Americans would help Japan attack California. They had no proof that this would happen.

In February 1942, **President Roosevelt** ordered Japanese Americans in California, Washington, Oregon, and southern Arizona to leave their homes. The government moved them to internment camps where they could be watched. An **internment camp** is a place where a person is held captive.

About 110,000 Japanese Americans moved to camps in California and other states. Half of them were children and teenagers. They left businesses, farms, and homes behind.

Though they were treated unjustly, Japanese Americans helped the United States in the war. In factories inside internment camps, they made nets used by the Army to hide equipment. They rolled bandages and painted posters urging people to join the Navy.

Japanese American men could leave the camps to join an army unit of Japanese American soldiers. This unit, the 442nd regiment, earned more medals than any other unit of its size.

In 1990, President **George Bush** sent letters of apology on behalf of the country to people who had been in camps during the war. The nation also paid people who had been in camps for part of the property they lost.

REVIEW Why were Japanese Americans sent to internment camps?

War Industries

Main Idea California played an important part in the effort to win the war.

California was a leader in farming before the war. During the war, the state's large-scale agriculture industry grew even larger. It helped feed people fighting overseas and at home. The state also became an important training center for the military.

By the end of the war, California had more than 140 military bases, or centers. The Army, Navy, and Marines trained troops at these bases. Pilots learned to fly in California's clear skies. Soldiers learned to fight on mountains and beaches and in deserts. Thousands of troops sailed from California ports to fight in the Pacific.

Factories and Shipyards

California became an important manufacturing center during the war. **Manufacturing** is the use of machines to make goods. Many new factories opened to manufacture goods for the defense industry. The **defense industry** makes equipment for the military.

Factories made supplies needed for war. Entrepreneurs built shipyards in Richmond, a town on San Francisco Bay. **Henry J. Kaiser** owned several of these shipyards. One of Kaiser's shipyards could build a ship in just a few days. By 1945, Kaiser's workers had built nearly 1,500 ships.

Other California factories made weapons, steel, and parts for airplanes. More airplanes were built in California than in any other state in the country.

CALIFORNIA AND THE WAR EFFORT

Richmond Shipyards The *Robert E. Peary* was built in 1942 in a record four days. As more shipyards opened, Richmond's population grew.

Industry Workers

Compared to other types of work, factory jobs paid well. However, before the war, factories hired few workers who were not white men. The war changed that. As men joined the armed forces, new workers were needed.

California shipyards and factories hired thousands of women. By the end of the war, almost half the workers in these factories were women. African Americans were also hired to build ships and airplanes. Nearly 500,000 African Americans moved to California to work during the war.

Mexican Americans, too, went to work on California farms and in steel and aircraft factories. Many worked at the Douglas Aircraft factory in Long Beach.

Californians in the War

Mexican Americans also fought in the war. **Guy Louis Gabaldon** (GEE loo EE gah bahl DOHN) came from East Los Angeles. His neighbors were from Armenia, Russia, and Japan.

Gabaldon learned Japanese from his neighbors. He used this knowledge during the war to capture hundreds of Japanese soldiers. He won a medal for his bravery.

Over a million Californians served in the armed forces. The costs of the war were high. Many people were injured or lost their lives. Resources that might have been used in other ways were used to fight the war.

REVIEW What new industries started or grew in California during the war?

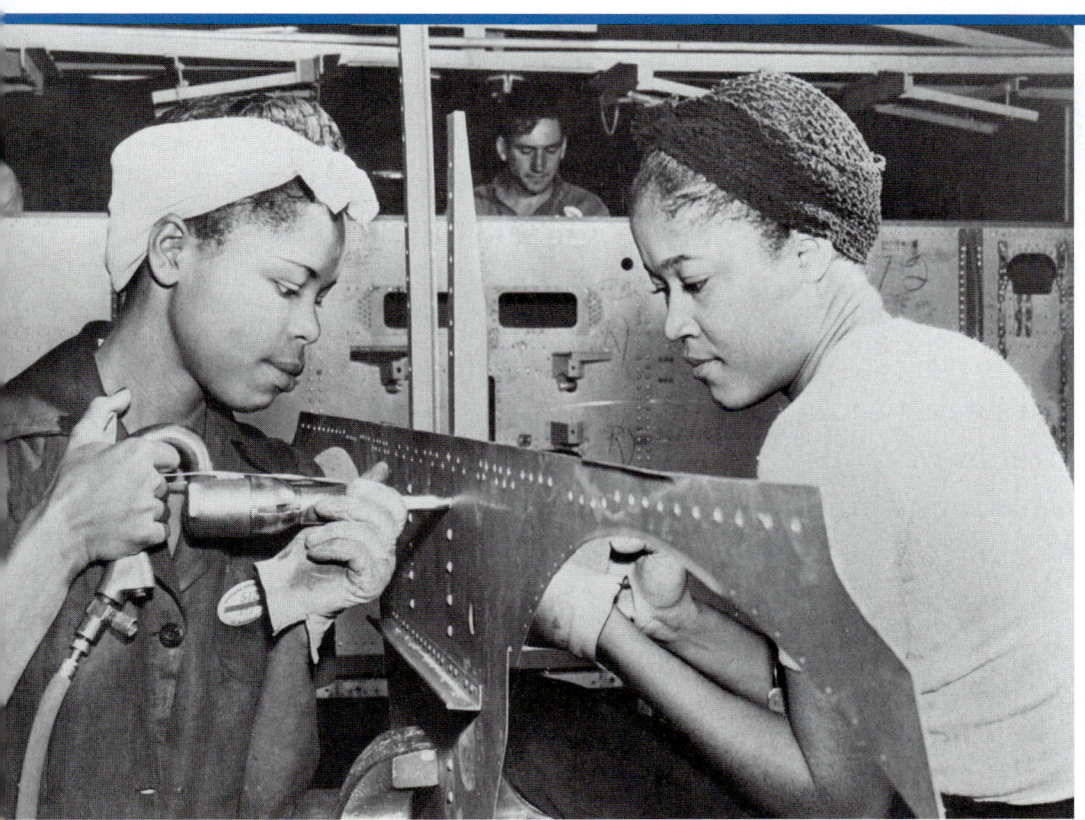

Women in the Workforce Workers at Douglas Aircraft in Long Beach work on an airplane part.

On the Home Front Children collect old bed frames and other scrap metal to be made into equipment for the war.

Pitching In

Main Idea Citizens, including children, helped the United States win the war.

Americans who were too young or too old to work in a factory or fight wanted to help win the war. The work civilians did on the home front shortened the war. A **civilian** is a person who is not in the armed forces.

People saved everything that could be turned into equipment or weapons for the war. They collected rubber tires to be recycled into new parts. Metal cans and toothpaste tubes were gathered and melted down. People even saved bacon grease, which was used in cannon shells.

Children helped collect these resources. They gathered metal, rubber, and paper from neighbors. By June 1942, Boy Scouts all over the country had collected 150,000 tons of waste paper. It was used to make packing cartons and other supplies.

People in California's movie industry also helped in the war. Famous movie stars, such as **John Wayne** and **Judy Garland**, raised money for the military. They put on shows to entertain men and women overseas. Directors made movies to show people why the war was important. Cartoons showed civilians ways they could help win the war.

Victory Gardens

As the military used more food, the United States government gave out booklets to citizens that told them how to raise food. Vegetable gardens bloomed in backyards, city lots, and even in zoos. People called these gardens victory gardens. By 1943, a third of all the vegetables Americans ate came from victory gardens.

The hard work on the home front and overseas paid off. The war ended in 1945. The United States and the countries on its side won.

REVIEW What did civilians do to help the United States during World War II?

Lesson Summary

The United States entered World War II after the attack on Pearl Harbor. California's defense industry produced equipment and supplies that helped win the war. California's people helped in the armed forces and at home.

Why It Matters...

California's economy might be very different today if World War II had not taken place.

Growing Gardens Posters showed U.S. citizens how they could help win the war at home.

Lesson Review

1941 Pearl Harbor attacked
1945 World War II ends
1940 | 1941 | 1942 | 1943 | 1944 | 1945

❶ **VOCABULARY** Write a paragraph using **manufacturing** and **defense industry** that tells what California industries produced for the war.

❷ **READING SKILL** What **caused** men to leave their factory jobs? What was one **effect** of this?

❸ **MAIN IDEA: History** What jobs did women have during the war?

❹ **MAIN IDEA: Citizenship** Why did civilians grow victory gardens?

❺ **TIMELINE SKILL** When was Pearl Harbor attacked?

❻ **CRITICAL THINKING: Evaluate** Why do you think Japanese Americans chose to help their country during the war despite being treated unjustly?

CHART ACTIVITY Research items that were collected by civilians during the war. Create a two-column chart showing which items were collected, and for what the military used each item.

1. HSS 4.4.6 2. HSS 4.4.5 3. HSS 4.4.5 4. HSS 4.4.5 5. HSS 4.4.5 6. HSS 4.4.5 Activity HSS 4.4.5

Extend Lesson 1
Literature

Journey to Topaz

from a book by Yoshiko Uchida

The Sakane family is adjusting to a new life. Eleven-year-old Yuki, her brother, Ken, and their mother have been forced to pack up their home in Berkeley and move to an **internment camp.** They have just arrived at a horse racetrack in San Bruno where they will wait for months before moving to a camp in Utah. As they look for the place where they will live, they meet many old friends.

Crowded along the rail around the racetrack, watching for arriving friends, were hundreds of Japanese who had been evacuated earlier from the Bay Area. The first familiar face Yuki saw was Mr. Toda. She waved eagerly and he waved back in an awkward sort of salute. Yuki waved again and again, feeling better just at the sight of someone she knew.

As they got off the bus, they were directed to an area roped off beneath the grandstand where each family registered, filled out forms, and went through a brief medical inspection. The baggage they carried was inspected for contraband and then they were assigned living quarters.

326 • Chapter 10

"Barrack 16, Apartment 40," Ken read from the slip handed to him.

"Golly," Yuki said impressed, "we get an apartment!" She had never lived in an apartment and found the prospect intriguing. She moved eagerly now, keeping close to Ken.

"Hey, Ken!" It was Ken's classmate Jim Hirai.

"Hey, Jim!" Ken shouted back, and they pounded each other on the back as though they hadn't seen each other for ten years.

"I'll help you find your quarters," Jim offered.

But now Mother was surrounded by her church friends who had arrived two days earlier. She was bowing and greeting them as though they were meeting on the sunny walk outside their church in Oakland. They quickly exchanged barrack numbers and Mr. Toda and the minister promised to come visit them later.

"I am in the Bachelors' Quarters here," Mr. Toda said rather dismally. "I must share a room with five other men. It is a strange new life," he added, and he did not look happy.

Yuki was anxious to see where they would be living. "Come on, Mama," she urged, and they quickly followed Ken and Jim down the racetrack.

It had rained the night before and the track was muddy and pocked with puddles. Yuki's new saddle shoes were soon covered with mud and Mother's blue kid shoes were oozing with it. "I'm glad I packed rubber boots for us," she remarked, and she held on to Yuki's arm to keep from slipping.

As they walked along, Yuki saw that wherever there was room tar-papered army barracks had been put up for the eight thousand Japanese who would soon be living there. Barrack 16, however, was not among them. Now Ken and Jim were leaving the northern end of the track and disappearing beyond a cluster of eucalyptus trees. When Yuki and Mother caught up with them, they were going up the wide ramp of a stable that stood about a foot above the ground. There was a sign tacked to a corner of the stable that read "Barrack 16."

"This isn't a barrack at all," Yuki said, disappointed. "It's just a dirty old stable."

They followed Ken and Jim along the narrow walk that took them past a dozen stalls, each marked with a number, and then stopped in front of the one marked "40."

"Well, this is it," Jim said, nudging the door open.

The stall was narrow and dark, with two small windows high up on either side of the door. It measured about ten by twenty feet and was empty except for three army cots that lay folded on the floor. There were no mattresses or bedding of any kind. Dust and dirt and woodshavings still littered the linoleum.

Yuki looked around the stall feeling as though she'd been handed an empty ice cream cone. "This is an apartment?" she asked, dismayed.

Even Mother, who usually found something cheerful to say about most difficulties, seemed at a loss for words. "Well," she said at last, "the first thing we need to do is sweep out this place. Can you help us find a broom, Jim?"

Activities

1. **LIST IT** How does Yuki feel as she adjusts to life in the internment camp? Make a list of the emotions she expresses in this passage.

2. **WRITE ABOUT IT** Write a letter that Yuki or Ken might have written to one of their school friends about their experiences.

Skillbuilder

Use a Special Purpose Map

VOCABULARY

special purpose map

Some maps have a special purpose. A **special purpose map** uses symbols to tell about the different features of a place. The map below uses symbols to show army, air force, and naval bases in California during World War II.

World War II Military Bases

LEGEND
- Navy base
- Air Force base
- Army base

Learn the Skill

STANDARDS Analysis Skill CST 4

Step 1: Read the map title to find out what the map shows.

Step 2: Study the map legend. Notice what each symbol represents.

Step 3: Note where the symbols appear on the map.

Practice the Skill

Use the map on page 330 to answer these questions.

1. Look at the map legend. What is the symbol for an air force base?
2. Which army base was located the farthest north?
3. Why do you think the San Francisco area had so many naval bases?

Apply the Skill

Study the special purpose map on page 330. Then write a paragraph that summarizes the information shown on the map.

331

Core Lesson 2

Peacetime Industries

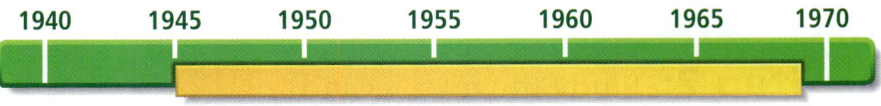
1945–1969

VOCABULARY

space race
aerospace industry
bracero

Vocabulary Strategy

aero**space** industry

Find **space** in **aerospace industry**. This industry makes equipment for space flight.

READING SKILL
Main Idea and Details Find details to support the main idea that the aircraft industry changed after the war ended.

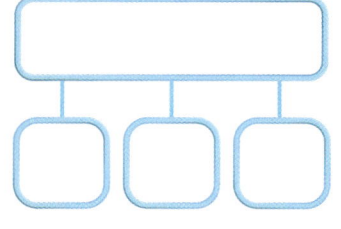

Core: HSS 4.4.5, 4.4.6
Extend support: HSS 4.4.6

Build on What You Know What does it take to build a spacecraft that will reach the moon? New ideas? Inventions? Engineers and skilled workers from California helped make space exploration possible.

Defense and Space Industries

Main Idea The defense and aircraft industries continued to grow in California in the 1950s and 1960s.

After World War II ended, people in the United States worried about a different problem. The Soviet Union had taken over several smaller nations. It was making powerful weapons. Many in the United States feared the Soviets would use those weapons.

This threat was one reason the defense industry continued to grow in California. Factories developed missiles, or weapons with engines that make them fly. Companies such as Hughes Aircraft produced faster airplanes and more powerful aircraft.

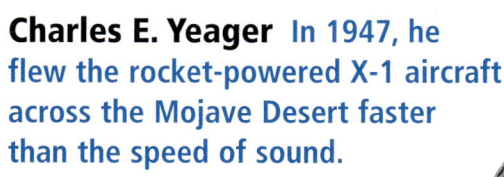

Charles E. Yeager In 1947, he flew the rocket-powered X-1 aircraft across the Mojave Desert faster than the speed of sound.

The Space Race

In 1957, the Soviet Union sent the first satellite into space. A satellite is an object that orbits, or circles, the Earth. This started a space race. The **space race** was the competition between the United States and the Soviet Union to be the leader in space exploration.

Scientists at the California Institute of Technology and the Jet Propulsion Laboratory in Pasadena researched ways to reach space. Aircraft factories in southern California built equipment for the space program. By 1965, about 500,000 Californians worked in the aerospace industry. The **aerospace industry** is all the businesses that design and make rockets and spacecraft.

Workers at Hughes Aircraft in Culver City made satellites and the first spacecraft to land safely on the moon. Hughes and Douglas Aircraft engineers designed parts of the Saturn V rocket. In 1969, this rocket boosted American astronauts to the moon. The United States had finally won the space race.

REVIEW Why did the defense industry continue to grow after World War II ended?

Saturn V Rocket Over 360 feet tall, this was the largest rocket ever launched. It carried spacecraft that landed on the moon.

The Leading Farm State

Main Idea New technology let California farms grow more food.

Just as California's manufacturing industries grew after the war, so did agriculture. In 1947, California became the nation's leading farm state. It grew more crops than any other state.

Large companies owned much of California's farmland. These vast farms had thousands of acres of land. Most large-scale farms grew only one or two crops. However, farms in the state produced about 300 different kinds of fruits, vegetables, and other foods. The nation's almonds, figs, artichokes, and olives were grown in California. The state's farmers also grew one-third of the country's fruit.

Increased Productivity This bean picker harvested and bagged crops more quickly than people could by hand.

SKILL Reading Graphs About how big was the average farm in 1960?

Agricultural Research

Farm owners wanted to increase productivity. Productivity is the amount of goods produced by a worker in an hour. One way to increase productivity was with new machines.

Researchers at the University of California at Davis invented a tomato picker to harvest tomatoes without breaking them. A nut harvester shook nuts from trees.

Because productivity increased, farmers hired fewer workers. However, some plants were too fragile to be picked by machines. Grape and lettuce growers still needed many workers at harvest time.

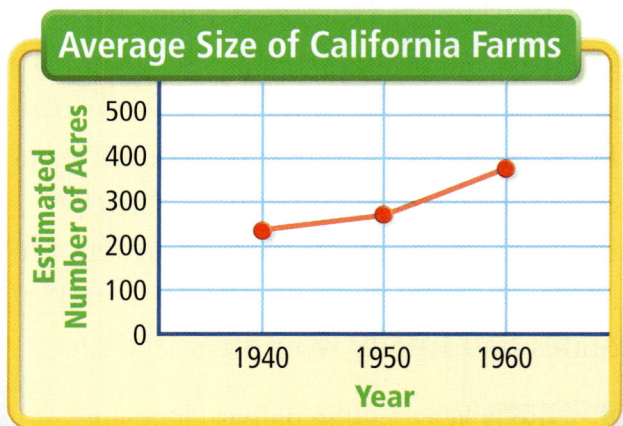

Average Size of California Farms

The Bracero Program

During World War II, farms needed workers to replace those who had gone to war. The United States made an agreement with Mexico to hire Mexican workers, or braceros. In Spanish, a **bracero** is a person with strong arms.

Farmers paid braceros and gave them food and shelter. Although the work was hard and living conditions were poor, braceros still came. Workers earned much more in the United States than they could earn in Mexico. By 1957, nearly 200,000 braceros worked on California farms. The bracero program continued until 1964.

REVIEW In what ways did new machines help California farms?

Mexican Workers This bracero picks lettuce on a farm in Salinas.

Lesson Summary

- California's aerospace industry helped the United States land astronauts on the moon.
- Large farms harvested more crops using new machines.
- Many Mexican farm workers worked on California farms as braceros.

Why It Matters...

The space race marked the beginning of the aerospace industry in California.

Lesson Review

1947 — Chuck Yeager flies X-1
1957 — Soviets launch first satellite

1945 — 1950 — 1955 — 1960

1. **VOCABULARY** Write a sentence to explain the purpose of the **bracero** program.

2. **READING SKILL** Use **details** from the lesson to write a paragraph showing how the aircraft industry changed after the war.

3. **MAIN IDEA: History** Which countries competed in the space race?

4. **MAIN IDEA: Economics** Name one way California farms increased productivity after World War II.

5. **TIMELINE SKILL** In what year did the Soviet Union launch the first satellite?

6. **CRITICAL THINKING: Apply** What caused California to become the leading farm state after World War II?

ART ACTIVITY Design a stamp that honors the 1969 moon landing. Include pictures and words to show how California's aerospace industry helped make it happen.

1. HSS 4.4.6 2. HSS 4.4.6 3. HSS 4.4.5 4. HSS 4.4.6 5. HSS 4.4.6 6. HSS 4.4.6 Activity HSS 4.4.6

Extend Lesson 2
Technology

The Space Race

California was the perfect place for the aerospace industry. The wide-open spaces and dry climate of the Mojave Desert were ideal for testing spacecraft. Scientists from California's universities did the research. At the height of the space race, half a million people in California worked in factories and businesses that were part of the aerospace industry. They made aircraft, electronic equipment, missiles, and other equipment for space exploration. California companies such as Hughes Aircraft made parts of the spacecraft shown in the timeline below.

This badge honors the Apollo 11 mission. The name of the spacecraft that landed on the Moon was "Eagle."

Major Achievements

1961–1963
Mercury Missions
John Glenn becomes first American to orbit Earth.

1966–1968
Lunar Surveyors
First American spacecraft land successfully on the Moon.

1968–1974
Apollo Missions
In 1969, Neil Armstrong becomes first person to set foot on the Moon.

2003–
Mars Rover
The Jet Propulsion Laboratory in Pasadena built it to explore the geography of Mars.

TECHNOLOGY

Activities

1. **TALK ABOUT IT** Tell a partner why California became a center for space research.

2. **CONNECT IT** Find out what the aerospace industry builds today. Write a paragraph to compare it to what was built in the 1960s.

Core Lesson 3

Building New Communities

1950–1960

Build on What You Know What community do you live in? Is it in a city or near one? In the 1950s, many new communities formed near California cities.

Life in the 1950s

Main Idea New communities formed as people continued to move to California after World War II.

In 1950, California had the second-highest population of any state. Hundreds of thousands of veterans returned to California after World War II ended. Veterans are people who have served in the military. These veterans wanted to start new lives.

Congress passed a law near the end of the war to help veterans. This law, called the GI Bill, helped veterans pay for college and career training. It also gave them loans to buy houses.

VOCABULARY

barrio
suburb
pollution
smog

Vocabulary Strategy

smog

Smog combines the first two letters of *smoke* and the last two letters of *fog*.

READING SKILL
Compare and Contrast As you read, think about what California was like before and after the 1950s.

Before	After

STANDARDS
Core: HSS 4.1.5, 4.4.9
Extend support: HSS 4.4.9

Housing Boom In the 1950s, about 100 new houses were built each day in Los Angeles County.

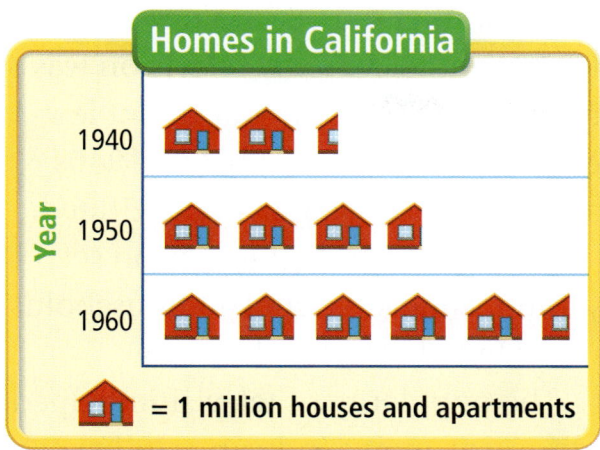

Buying Homes Veterans and other Californians bought homes in suburbs.

SKILL Reading Graphs About how many houses and apartments existed in 1960?

Barrios and Suburbs

Along with veterans, many other people came to California. Immigrants arrived from Mexico and other countries south of the United States. Others came from Asian nations such as Japan, Korea, and the Philippines.

Newcomers found jobs on farms and in cities. They worked in the oil, aviation, and movie industries. Some started small businesses.

Spanish-speaking immigrants in some cities settled in barrios. **Barrio** means neighborhood in Spanish. Many other immigrants also settled near family and friends. They taught their children the customs, traditions, and religious beliefs of their culture.

Not everyone had much choice about where to live. People sometimes refused to sell or rent property to people of different racial and ethnic groups. Many fought against this injustice, but discrimination continued for years.

As the number of people in California grew, they needed more places to live. Builders bought land near large cities. They plowed over orchards and fields to make suburbs. A **suburb** is a community built near a city.

Many people who bought houses had never been able to afford a home before. Houses in new suburbs such as Westchester and Lakewood were inexpensive. Developers built them all the same to keep the cost low.

REVIEW Why did suburbs develop in the 1950s?

Transportation and Entertainment

Main Idea During the 1950s, Californians created freeways and new entertainment.

Suburbs had many houses, but few businesses. California built freeways so people could drive from their homes to their jobs.

As freeways made driving easier, more Californians bought cars. Gas and chemicals from cars and factories caused air pollution. **Pollution** is any substance in the air, water, or soil that harms the environment.

The mountains around Los Angeles trapped smog. **Smog** is a mixture of smoke and fog. People kept buying cars in record numbers, though, and the automobile industry grew.

Television

As families settled into new homes, they bought televisions. Television was invented before World War II, but few people owned a set. In the late 1940s and 1950s, most people in the United States bought their first television set. By 1960, almost 9 out of 10 households in the United States had TV sets.

The popularity of television helped California's movie industry. Hollywood movie studios made short movies and shows for television. Hollywood and the nearby city of Burbank became centers of the television industry on the West Coast. Californians such as actress **Lucille Ball** appeared on their own shows and became famous. Ball also ran a company that made television programs.

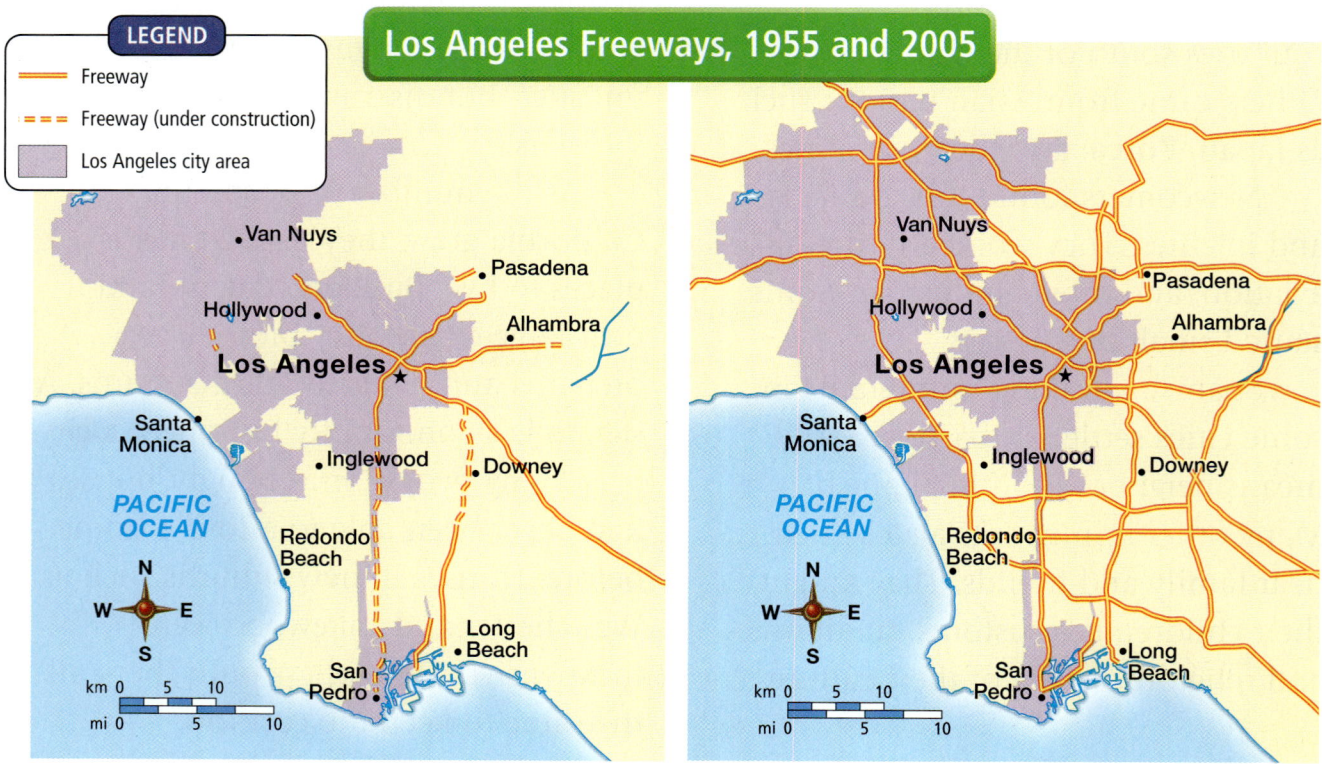

Los Angeles Freeways, 1955 and 2005

LEGEND
— Freeway
=== Freeway (under construction)
▓ Los Angeles city area

New Roads Today, Los Angeles County has 533 miles of freeways.

SKILL Reading Maps About how far is Pasadena from San Pedro?

Cartoons and Theme Parks

Cartoonist **Walt Disney** was one of the first people in the film industry to make cartoons for television. In 1954, *The Wonderful World of Disney* aired on television for the first time. Many families spent Sunday evenings watching this series.

In 1955, Disney opened a theme park based on his cartoons. The Disneyland theme park in Anaheim became California's most popular tourist attraction. Today, millions of people visit Disneyland and other theme parks in California each year.

REVIEW What new forms of entertainment became popular in the 1950s?

Lesson Summary

- People moved to California barrios and suburbs in the 1950s.
- Freeways made driving between cities and suburbs easier.
- Californians enjoyed new forms of entertainment, such as television and theme parks.

Why It Matters . . .

Freeways changed the California landscape in the 1950s.

Disneyland At this theme park, children can visit well-known cartoon characters.

Lesson Review

1950 California has second-highest population in U.S.

1955 Disneyland opens

1950 — 1951 — 1952 — 1953 — 1954 — 1955

1. **VOCABULARY** Write a few sentences to explain how **smog** and **pollution** are related.

2. **READING SKILL** **Contrast** the movie industry before and after the 1950s.

3. **MAIN IDEA: Culture** What language did people who settled in California barrios speak?

4. **MAIN IDEA: History** Why did Californians build freeways?

5. **Timeline Skill** In what year did Walt Disney's theme park open?

6. **Critical Thinking: Analyze** What were the positive and negative effects of freeways on the people and land of California? List two of each.

WRITING ACTIVITY Write a description of the community where you live. Discuss the kinds of transportation and entertainment it offers. Use concrete sensory details in your description.

1. HSS 4.4 2. HSS 4.4.9 3. HSS 4.4 4. HSS 4.4 5. HSS 4.4.9 6. HSS 4.4 Activity HSS 4.1.5

Extend Lesson 3
History

Car Culture

In the 1950s, it seemed that Californians were crazy for cars. Some loved their cars so much that they looked for ways to spend more time in them. At drive-in restaurants, waiters hooked trays of food to parked cars so people could eat without leaving their cars. Drive-in movie theaters let people watch movies outdoors on giant screens while sitting in their cars. By 1959, the United States had more than 4,000 drive-in theaters.

Speedy Service At drive-in restaurants, food servers were called carhops. Why do you think they were given that name?

HISTORY

Drive-in Restaurant At a diner in California, food is carried to parked cars on conveyor belts.

Activities

1. **STEP INTO IT** Put yourself in the picture on this page. Talk about what it might be like to work or eat at this restaurant.

2. **CHART IT** Make one list of how cars make life better. Make another list of the problems caused by cars. Create a chart showing your findings.

343

Core Lesson 4

A Call for Equality

VOCABULARY

segregation
civil rights
nonviolent protest
boycott

Vocabulary Strategy

nonviolent protest

The prefix **non-** means not. **Nonviolent protest** is a way of bringing change that does not use violence.

READING SKILL
Problem and Solution
List problems faced by Californians in their struggles for equal rights. Then note their solutions.

Core: HSS 4.4
Extend support: HSS 4.4

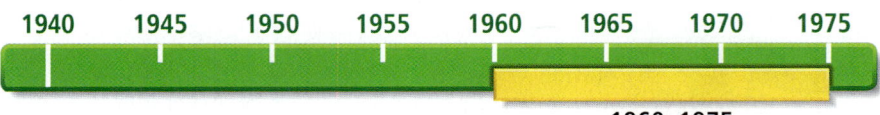
1940 1945 1950 1955 1960 1965 1970 1975

1960–1975

Build on What You Know What have you done to make things happen that were important to you? In the 1960s and 1970s, Californians worked to gain equal rights for diverse groups of people.

Civil Rights

Main Idea Californians took part in the struggle for civil rights for African Americans.

African American veterans had fought bravely during World War II. Yet when they came home, they still faced discrimination. Segregation was one form of discrimination. **Segregation** is the practice of keeping different groups of people separate.

In southern states, laws forced African Americans to attend separate schools, eat in separate restaurants, and go to separate parks and theaters. Many people in California also refused to respect the rights of African Americans and citizens of other racial groups.

Tom Bradley In 1973, he became the first African American mayor of Los Angeles.

344 • Chapter 10

San Francisco Protest
Martin Luther King Jr. inspired thousands of Californians to join the fight for civil rights.

Martin Luther King Jr.

The Reverend **Martin Luther King Jr.**, a minister from Georgia, was a leader in the fight for civil rights. **Civil rights** are the rights that countries guarantee their citizens. In the United States, the Constitution lists these rights. They include the right to vote and to be treated equally by law.

Martin Luther King Jr. urged people to use nonviolent protest to work against segregation. **Nonviolent protest** is a way to bring change without using violence. People marched in large groups, or refused to spend money in places that practiced discrimination. These protests led the federal government to pass the Civil Rights Act in 1964. This act made discrimination illegal in public places. California's government also passed laws against discrimination.

Discrimination in California

In 1963, lawmakers said it was illegal to refuse to sell or rent a house to a person because of race. However, many Californians did not agree with this law. The following year, citizens voted to overrule it.

This event and other acts of discrimination angered many people. In 1965, riots broke out in Watts, a mostly African American community in Los Angeles. Living conditions in Watts were poor. It was crowded and many residents did not have jobs.

After six days, the riots ended. Local leaders worked to rebuild Watts. They built new hospitals, libraries, and bus lines. In 1970, Los Angeles schools were ordered to end segregation.

REVIEW What did California lawmakers do to try to end housing discrimination?

United Farm Workers

Main Idea Cesar Chavez helped farm workers by forming a labor union.

Other groups in California, such as farm workers, also faced unequal treatment. Unlike workers in trucking, railroad, and shipping industries, farm workers did not have a labor union. A labor union is an organization of workers who work together for good pay and working conditions.

Cesar Chavez, a director of a group that helped Mexican Americans, knew how hard life was for farm workers. When Chavez was a child, he picked crops on farms in the Imperial Valley with his family. Chavez met **Dolores Huerta** at his work. They both saw the need to start a labor union.

Building the Union

In 1962, Chavez and Huerta left their jobs to form a union. They hoped the union would increase pay and improve living conditions for farm workers in California.

Chavez and Huerta traveled throughout the state asking Mexican American workers to join them. At that time, a union of Filipino farm workers was starting a strike for better wages and safer working conditions. Mexican and Filipino farm workers decided to work together. They formed a union that would later become the United Farm Workers, or UFW.

In 1965, union members went on strike against more than 30 grape growers in Delano. The strikers refused to work.

Delano Grape Strike Union members carried signs reading, "Viva la Huelga," which means "Long Live the Strike."

Winning at Last

For the next five years, UFW members held nonviolent protests against grape growers. People all over California supported the UFW. They sent food and money to the strikers and their families so they could survive while refusing to work.

Chavez asked people across the United States to stop buying grapes or products made from grapes grown on California farms. Millions of people joined the boycott, and sales of California grapes fell. A **boycott** is a refusal to buy, sell, or use certain goods. It is used to force a change. Because of the boycott, grape growers lost money. Some feared their business might fail.

When the strike ended in 1970, nearly all of the Delano grape growers agreed to meet with the UFW. Union leaders made agreements with grape growers that gave farm workers more money and better working conditions.

Chavez and Huerta went on to lead strikes and boycotts against lettuce growers and other agricultural businesses. Chavez gave speeches across the country to educate the public about the hardships facing farm workers. Through the UFW's work, farm workers received some of the things given to other workers, such as health care and retirement programs.

REVIEW Why did Chavez and Huerta want to form a farm workers union?

A Call for Help Chavez showed people across the country the suffering of farm workers. Many joined in his fight.

Equal Rights for All

Main Idea Other groups also fought against discrimination in the 1960s.

Cesar Chavez inspired Mexican Americans who were not farm workers as well. Mexican Americans and other Spanish-speaking people in California cities worked for equal rights.

For example, in 1968, Hispanic students held protests in several East Los Angeles high schools. They wanted to receive the same education as students in wealthy parts of the city. The protests caused school officials to make reforms. These included adding classes about Mexican American studies and hiring more Hispanic teachers and principals.

Struggle for Alcatraz

American Indians suffered from some of the worst conditions in California. They had the highest rate of unemployment in the state. Close to half of all California Indians had not gone to school past the eighth grade. Many were forced to leave their land and give up their traditions.

In 1969, American Indians from many nations took over Alcatraz Island in San Francisco Bay. The protesters wanted to make others aware of the poor conditions on reservations. They also wished to turn the island into an educational center. Newspapers printed stories about the protest. People across the country learned about problems facing American Indians.

Alcatraz Island American Indians took over empty buildings on this island, once a federal prison. The protest lasted 19 months.

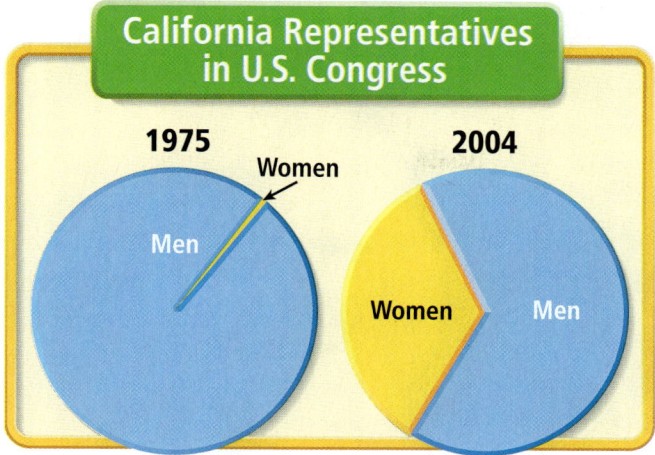

Women Make Laws California has elected more women to Congress than any state.

Women's Rights

Women also spoke out against unequal treatment in the 1960s. They protested discrimination in business and government. They demanded the same rights as men and equal pay for the same jobs. Like other groups, they used nonviolent protests to call attention to their cause.

Their fight led Californians to elect more women to the national, state, and local government. In 1978, **Dianne Feinstein** became the first woman mayor of San Francisco. In 1992, she was elected senator of California.

REVIEW What was one result of California women's fight for equal rights in the 1960s?

Lesson Summary

In the 1960s and 1970s, African Americans, Mexican Americans, American Indians, and women fought for equal rights. Martin Luther King Jr. led African Americans to fight against segregation. Cesar Chavez helped farm workers form a labor union.

Why It Matters . . .

The fight for equal rights gave many Californians better lives and greater opportunities.

Lesson Review

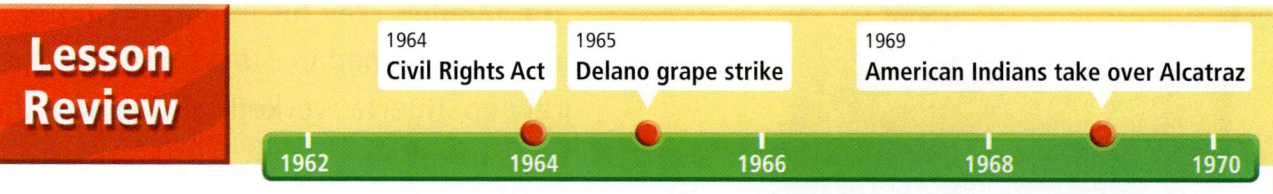

1. **VOCABULARY** Write a paragraph about the struggle for civil rights in the 1960s.

2. **READING SKILL** Give three examples of nonviolent protest that Californians used to solve problems.

3. **MAIN IDEA: Economics** Why did the Delano grape strike lead to changes for farm workers?

4. **MAIN IDEA: Citizenship** Why did American Indians take over Alcatraz?

5. **TIMELINE SKILL** In what year was the Civil Rights Act passed?

6. **CRITICAL THINKING: Synthesize** Why do you think so many different groups of people fought for equal rights at the same time?

WRITING ACTIVITY Write newspaper headlines telling about three nonviolent protests in California during the 1960s. Tell when, where, and why they took place.

Extend Lesson 4

Biographies

Farm Union Leaders

Can two people make a difference? Yes. In the 1960s, Dolores Huerta and Cesar Chavez led the way to improve the lives of California farm workers.

Posters like this one told people about boycotts that supported the farm workers' union.

Dolores Huerta *1930–*

Dolores Huerta learned to help others at a young age. Her mother let farm families stay for free at the hotel her family owned in Stockton. When she grew up, Huerta worked full-time for the rights of others.

She spoke out against segregation and worked for laws that allowed Spanish-speaking citizens to vote in Spanish. As a union leader, Huerta convinced landowners to give farm workers health plans and to stop using chemicals that harmed farm workers and the environment. In 1993, Huerta became a member of the National Women's Hall of Fame.

CHARACTER TRAIT: Fairness

Cesar Chavez 1927–1993

"My motivation to change these injustices came from . . . watching what my mother and father went through when I was growing up; from what we experienced as migrant farm workers in California."

—Cesar Chavez

Picking beans and pulling beets was hard work for young Cesar Chavez. His family moved so often to find farm work, that he missed a lot of school. He learned from his parents to be kind and to stand up for others.

In 1948, Chavez met a priest who inspired him to work for better treatment of farm workers. Chavez read about unions and about Mahatma Gandhi, a leader of nonviolent protests in Africa and Asia. He used what he learned to make the lives of farm workers better. Each year, people in California celebrate Chavez's birthday, March 31, with a state holiday.

Activities

1. **TALK ABOUT IT** In what way did Huerta and Chavez work for **fairness** for farm workers?

2. **DRAW IT** Create a book jacket for a biography about either Cesar Chavez or Dolores Huerta.

 Technology Visit Education Place for more biographies. www.eduplace.com/kids/hmss/

Chapter 10 Review

Visual Summary

1–4. Write a description of each item named below.

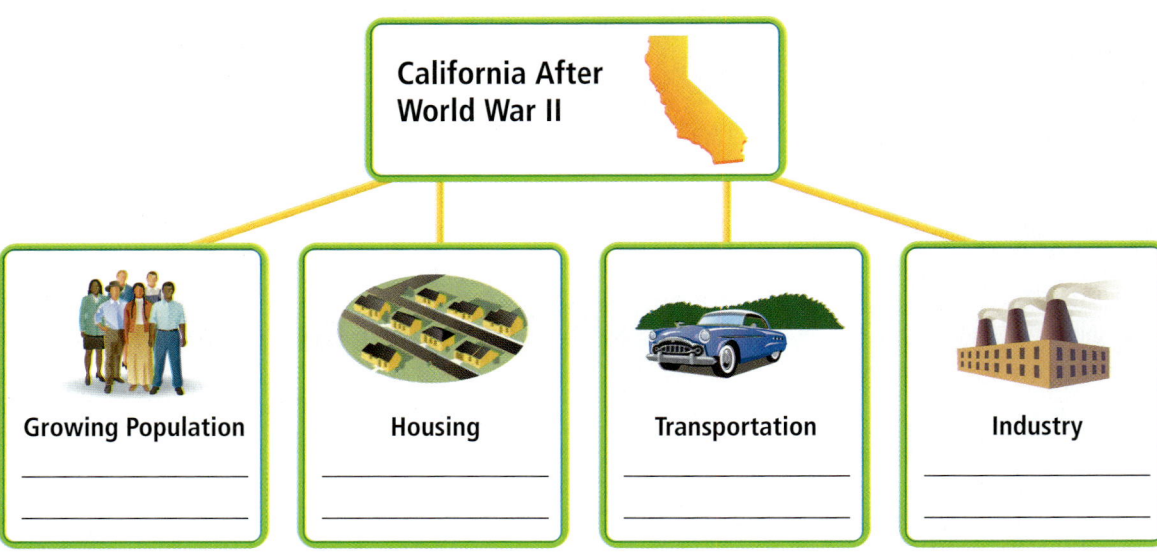

STANDARDS 1. HSS 4.4 2. HSS 4.1 3. HSS 4.1 4. HSS 4.4.6

Facts and Main Ideas

Answer each question with information from the chapter.

5. **History** What did Japanese Americans do to help the United States win World War II?

6. **Economics** What kinds of work did Californians do in the aerospace industry?

7. **Geography** What effect did more cars have on the environment in California?

8. **Government** What was the 1964 Civil Rights Act?

5. HSS 4.4.5 6. HSS 4.4.6 7. HSS 4.4.6 8. HSS 4.5

Vocabulary

Choose the correct word from the list below to complete each sentence.

defense industry, p. 322
aerospace industry, p. 333
boycott, p. 347

9. Cesar Chavez led a(n) _____ to protest against grape growers in California.

10. During World War II, people in the _____ made supplies for the military.

11. Companies that make parts for spacecraft are part of the _____.

9. HSS 4.4.6 10. HSS 4.4.6 11. HSS 4.4.6

352 • Chapter 10

CHAPTER SUMMARY TIMELINE

- 1941 Pearl Harbor attacked
- 1947 Chuck Yeager flies X-1
- 1955 Disneyland opens
- 1965 Delano grape strike begins

Apply Skills

Map Skill Study the map of a part of Yosemite National Park below. Then use your map skills to answer each question.

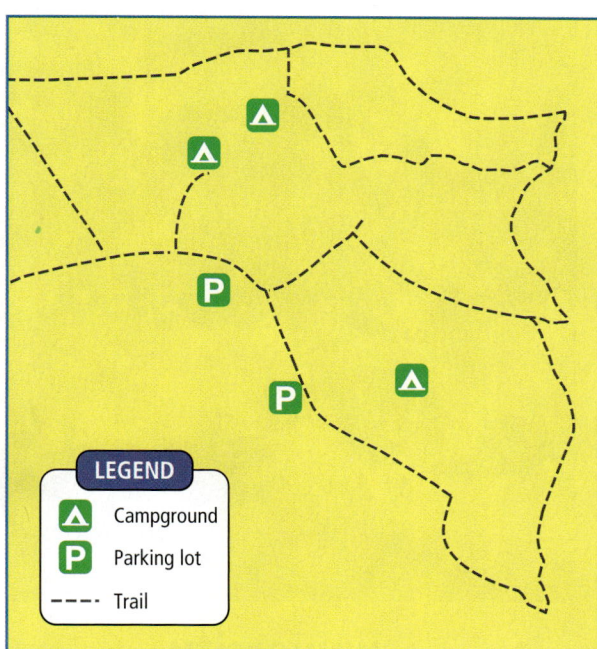

12. What is the purpose of this map?
    A. to provide a guide for visitors
    B. to identify plants and animals
    C. to show where hiking is difficult
    D. to show the hours the park is open

13. How many places for people to camp does the map show?
    A. one
    B. two
    C. three
    D. four

12. Analysis Skill CST 4   13. Analysis Skill CST 4

Critical Thinking

Write a short paragraph to answer each question.

14. **Cause and Effect** What caused California's population to grow during and after World War II?

15. **Draw Conclusions** Why did pay and working conditions improve for farm workers after they formed a union?

Timeline

Use the Chapter Summary Timeline above to answer the question.

16. In what year did the United Farm Workers begin its strike against grape growers?

14. HSS 4.4   15. HSS 4.4   16. HSS 4.4.6

Activities

Drama Activity Prepare a dialogue between two people discussing plans for a new freeway in the 1950s. What might be their reasons for or against it?

Writing Activity Write a personal essay to explain why you think Martin Luther King Jr. and Cesar Chavez used nonviolent protests to fight for rights.

Activities HSS 4.4.6, 4.4, W 1.2

Technology
Writing Process Tips
Get help with your writing at
www.eduplace.com/kids/hmss/

Chapter 11 New Steps Forward

Vocabulary Preview

Technology
e • glossary
e • word games
www.eduplace.com/kids/hmss/

naturalized citizen
An immigrant can take a test and apply to become a **naturalized citizen.**
page 360

university
After high school, a student may want to go to a **university** to study in a certain subject area.
page 366

Chapter Timeline

1965 New laws allow more immigration to the U.S.

1977 Apple II computer is introduced

1965 — 1970 — 1975 — 1980 — 1985

Reading Strategy

Summarize Use the summarize strategy to focus your reading.

 Note the most important information. Put it into your own words.

high-tech

Some people in **high-tech** industries design computers. Others create new types of medical equipment.
page 371

trend

The skateboarding **trend** started in California. Then people all over the country began skateboarding, too.
page 377

1992
NAFTA signed

1990 — 1995 — 2000 — 2005

Core Lesson 1

New Neighbors Arrive

VOCABULARY

professional
refugee
naturalized citizen

Vocabulary Strategy

refugee

A synonym for **refuge** is protection. A **refugee** seeks protection.

READING SKILL
Main Idea and Details
As you read, note ways new laws changed immigration to California.

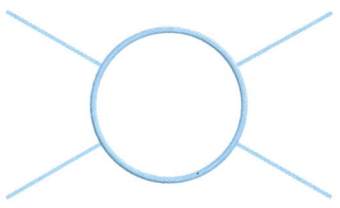

Core: HSS 4.4
Extend support: HSS 4.4

Build on What You Know You know that California was once a part of Mexico. Today, Mexican immigrants continue to move to California.

From Around the World

Main Idea Laws passed in 1965 gave people more opportunities to immigrate to California.

In the 1960s, the economy of the United States was growing. Businesses in California and other states wanted more workers than they could find. Employers wanted to be able to hire people from other countries. They asked the United States government to make it easier for certain groups of people to move to the United States. The 1965 Immigration and Naturalization Act did this.

Skilled Professionals Many Mexican Americans were born in California. Others immigrated to the United States from Mexico.

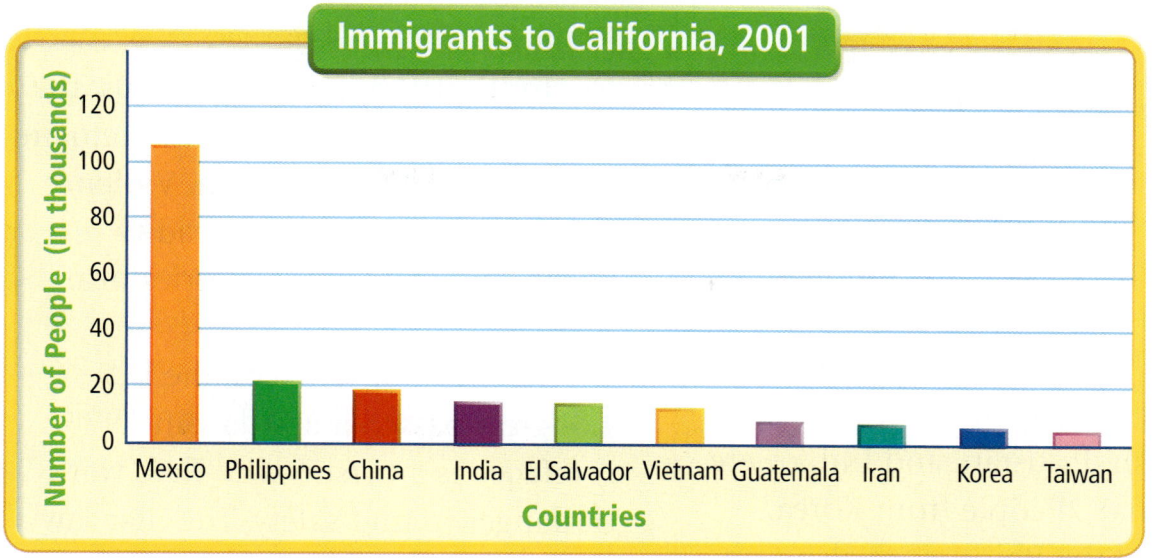

Immigration: The Top Ten Nations Immigration gives California one of the most diverse populations in the world.

SKILL Reading Graphs Which nation did more immigrants come from in 2001, Korea or Guatemala?

Easier Immigration

The Immigration Act of 1965 removed barriers that had blocked some immigrants from coming to the United States. People with relatives in this country could join them more easily. Skilled workers and professionals could also come more easily. A **professional** is a person with special knowledge and training. Doctors, nurses, engineers, artists, and scientists were especially needed.

This law caused changes in California. Between 1930 and 1960, most people who moved to California came from other states. By 1970, most came from other countries. From 1970 to 1980, almost half of California's newcomers came from Mexico.

Coming from Mexico

Larger numbers of Mexicans came to California after 1965 for three main reasons. First, farms and businesses needed workers. California's economy was creating jobs very quickly. Second, California is next to Mexico. Finally, Mexican Americans living in California had started groups to help Mexicans who moved to the United States.

Most Mexican immigrants before 1965 were men who worked on farms. After 1965, women as well as men immigrated. Many Mexicans worked on farms, but many others worked in factories, restaurants, stores, and on construction sites.

REVIEW What reasons did Mexicans have for coming to California?

357

Coming from Asia

Main Idea After 1965, Asian immigration to California increased.

The 1965 Immigration and Naturalization Act made immigration from Asia easier, too. Between 1970 and 1980, about one-third of Asian immigrants from Sri Lanka, Bangladesh, Pakistan, and India were professionals. People from Korea, China, and the Philippines also came to the United States in larger numbers in the 1960s and 1970s.

Many of these immigrants were well educated and highly trained. Some came because there were few jobs for professionals in their homelands. Others came to escape unjust governments.

From Southeast Asia

In the 1960s and early 1970s, the United States fought a war in Vietnam, a country in southeast Asia. Violence from the Vietnam War spread to Cambodia and Laos, countries near Vietnam.

To help war refugees, the U.S. Congress passed a new law in 1975. A **refugee** is a person who flees war or danger to find safety. The new law allowed more refugees into the United States.

In Vietnam and Laos, the U.S. government helped many war refugees leave their countries. Many others, including Cambodians, faced great danger to find safety. Many refugees who came to the United States settled in California.

Vietnamese Immigration Immigrants from Vietnam arrive in California in 1979.

From Asia to California
The land, climate, and traditions of Southeast Asia are different from those of California.

SKILL Reading Maps
Which country is larger in area, Vietnam or Cambodia?

From Vietnam

Before 1964, there were only about 600 Vietnamese people in the United States. After the Vietnam War, millions came to live in the United States.

Like immigrants of earlier times, many Vietnamese people settled near relatives. Westminster, California, has many Vietnamese American businesses in an area called Little Saigon. Many Vietnamese have started businesses in San Francisco, San Jose, and Santa Ana, as well. Almost four out of ten stores in downtown San Jose are owned by people from Vietnam or their families.

Today, Vietnamese Americans are in state and national government. **Tony Lam**, of Westminster, was the first Vietnamese American to serve in an elected office. **Viet Dinh,** who was born in Saigon, served the United States as Assistant Attorney General.

From Cambodia and Laos

Refugees from Cambodia and Laos also came to California. In the 1980s, **Bun Tek Ngoy** (BUHN TEK nyoy) started a chain of doughnut shops in California. Many Cambodians found jobs in his shops and learned the business. Working with others who shared their language and customs helped many Cambodians start new lives. Today, Cambodian families own many of California's doughnut shops.

Some Mien and Hmong refugees from Laos struggled to start new lives. It was hard for them to find jobs, partly because farms in Laos were very different from those in California. Children of Laotian immigrants are adapting through education, however.

REVIEW What is the difference between refugees and other immigrants?

Entrepreneurs Some immigrants build businesses. This doughnut shop in Long Beach is one example.

Life in the United States

Main Idea Immigrants contribute to the culture and economy of California.

Today, California attracts more immigrants than any other state. Almost half are from Latin America. In 2002, about four out of ten came from Asia. The largest number of Asian immigrants came from the Philippines. Between 1970 and 1990, nearly 900,000 Filipinos came to the United States. More than half settled in California. Most Filipino immigrants speak English, and about two-thirds are professionals.

Immigrants who do not speak English when they arrive often live near others from the same country. Los Angeles has the largest population of Korean people outside Korea. More Cambodians live in Long Beach than any place outside Cambodia.

Naturalized Citizens

Many immigrants become naturalized citizens. A **naturalized citizen** is someone who was not born a United States citizen but becomes one. Many people in California became naturalized citizens by taking a test and making a promise to be loyal to the United States.

Although laws have changed to allow more immigration, not everyone who wants to immigrate can do so. Some people enter the United States illegally. Many illegal immigrants want to work.

Some farm and business owners hire illegal immigrants when it is hard to find local workers. Also, they can pay illegal immigrants less. Illegal immigrants and those who hire them are breaking laws and can be punished.

A Stronger Economy

Immigrants come to the United States today for the same reasons they have come for centuries. They are looking for new opportunities and a chance to live in freedom and safety.

Immigrants bring labor, skills, and new ideas to California's economy. They start new businesses, publish newspapers, work in offices and factories, and start schools. Their ideas influence fashion, films, and music.

Immigrants also build connections between the United States and other countries. California has become a center for trade with countries of the Pacific Basin, as well as Central America and South America.

REVIEW Why is immigration important to California's economy?

Lesson Summary

- The Immigration and Naturalization Act of 1965 opened the way for many professionals and other workers to immigrate to the United States.
- Between 1970 and 1980, about half of California's newcomers were Mexicans.
- Refugees from southeast Asia came to California after the Vietnam War.

Why It Matters...

California is home to many immigrants seeking opportunities and safety. Immigrants contribute work and new ideas to California's economy.

Special Skills Many California immigrants have advanced skills, like this electronics expert.

Lesson Review

1. **VOCABULARY** Use **refugee** in a paragraph to tell why someone might want to come to the United States.

2. **READING SKILL** Use **details** to write a paragraph about how the Immigration Act of 1965 changed California.

3. **MAIN IDEA: Government** What is a naturalized citizen?

4. **MAIN IDEA: Culture** What do immigrants contribute to the culture of California?

5. **CRITICAL THINKING: Analyze** Contrast reasons different immigrant groups came to the United States after 1965.

WRITING ACTIVITY Write a summary of the last two pages of this lesson. Include the main ideas and most important details in your summary.

1. HSS 4.4 2. HSS 4.4 3. HSS 4.4 4. HSS 4.4 5. HSS 4.4 Activity Analysis Skill HI 1

Extend Lesson 1
Citizenship

The WATTS TOWERS

Sabato Rodia

These towers are a love letter made of stone and steel. Sabato Rodia, an immigrant who came to California as a teenager, wanted to show his love for the United States. In 1921, he bought a piece of land in Los Angeles' Watts neighborhood. Over the next 25 years, he built these towers of steel and cement.

Rodia's love for the United States was a form of patriotism, or love of country. Today, the Watts Towers remind visitors how much one patriot can do to show love for this country.

The Materials Rodia used many kinds of materials to decorate the towers. They include pieces of glass, pottery, seashells, and even spouts from teapots.

CHARACTER TRAIT: Patriotism

The Towers The towers' highest point reaches 99 feet above the ground.

CITIZENSHIP

Activities

1. **TALK ABOUT IT** Think of another patriotic monument you have seen. What does it have in common with the Watts Towers?

2. **WRITE ABOUT IT** Using library resources, find out more about the towers. Write a short report about them based on what you learn.

Core Lesson 2

Education in California

VOCABULARY

public
tax
school district
university

Vocabulary Strategy

university

The prefix **uni-** means one. A university is one place of higher learning that includes several colleges.

READING SKILL

Categorize As you read, list the different categories of schools in California and facts about them.

 STANDARDS

Core: HSS 4.4, 4.4.8
Extend support: HSS 4.4.8

Build on What You Know Does your school have many students or just a few? No matter how large or small a school is, California makes sure that all children get the chance to learn.

Education for All

Main Idea Many Californians worked to create a public school system for the state.

When California's leaders wrote the state's first constitution in 1849, they talked about public schools. **Public** means for the people. They knew that people need to be educated to make good decisions about their government.

Most citizens wanted schools for everyone. Yet many communities did not have enough money to pay for schools. In 1863, John Swett became the head of the state's public schools. He thought taxes could pay the costs of building and running schools. A **tax** is money people pay the government for services it provides. Taxes are still used to pay for schools in California today.

William Leidesdorff
Leidesdorff helped start the first public school in what is now San Francisco.

364 • Chapter 11

Education in the Past

Before John Swett, all schools in California did not offer the same subjects. Sometimes, if a teacher left, the school closed. San Francisco's first town school shut down after the teacher ran off to hunt for gold.

Schools in the past were very different from today's schools. Many were just a single room. Students of all grades sat in the room together. One teacher taught all the students, no matter how old they were.

Students often recited their lessons, or did their schoolwork on small chalkboards called slates. They learned the basics: reading, spelling, writing, and arithmetic.

Education Today

More than six million students attend public school in California. It is the largest school system in the country. To make running these schools easier, the state's schools are part of districts. A **school district** builds and runs public schools for students in a certain area. Los Angeles Unified is the largest school district in the state. In 2003, it had over 750,000 students. Alpine County is the smallest school district. It had two students in 2003.

Sometimes, people disagree about how to run schools or what subjects should be taught. Still, Californians agree that all children have the right and responsibility to get an education.

REVIEW How does California pay for its public schools?

One-room School In some towns, students of all ages studied in the same room.

University of California System

School	Students	School	Students
University of California at Berkeley	32,814	University of California at Riverside	17,105
University of California at Davis	30,065	University of California at San Diego	23,045
University of California at Irvine	23,290	University of California at San Francisco	2,800
University of California at Los Angeles	38,598	University of California at Santa Barbara	19,799
University of California at Merced	a new university	University of California at Santa Cruz	14,984

The University of California System Around 188,000 students attend one of the University of California's schools each year.

SKILL Reading Charts Which of the universities has the greatest number of students?

The University System

Main Idea Graduates of California's colleges and universities contribute to the state and the nation.

California has the largest system of public colleges, universities, and community colleges in the United States. A **university** is made up of different colleges that offer programs in many subjects.

The University of California at Berkeley was the state's first public university. It started in 1868. New branches were added as California's population grew. The newest university in the system is at Merced.

California's universities and colleges prepare students for many different jobs. College graduates are needed in government, factories, and research labs. High-tech businesses depend on trained workers.

Teachers and students at colleges and universities do important research. They find new medicines and ways to solve problems. **Ellen Ochoa** studied at San Diego State University before she became an astronaut. She says,

"I always liked school and being an astronaut allows you to learn continuously, like you do in school."

Affording College

California has several grant programs for California residents. A grant is money to pay for education. For example, grants can help students whose families cannot pay for college. Students who want to be teachers can get grants. Students who get high grades in high school may be able to get scholarships to cover some of their costs. Students who work hard can usually get help with college costs.

REVIEW Why are colleges and universities important to California's businesses?

Lesson Summary

California's early leaders knew public education was important. More than six million students attend public schools. The state's public colleges and universities educate citizens and workers for government and business.

Why It Matters...

California needs educated citizens to participate in government and business.

Happy Graduates These students have just earned their diplomas. Data shows that college graduates have more job opportunities than high school graduates.

Lesson Review

1. **VOCABULARY** Use **public** and **university** in a paragraph about California's schools.

2. **READING SKILL** Write sentences describing each category of California public school.

3. **MAIN IDEA: Citizenship** What is the purpose of California's school districts?

4. **MAIN IDEA: Economics** In what way does education help the economy?

5. **CRITICAL THINKING: Infer** Why do you think California offers so many kinds of colleges?

WRITING ACTIVITY Write a paragraph that explains when your school was built and how it got its name.

STANDARDS 1. HSS 4.4.8 2. HSS 4.4.8 3. HSS 4.4.8 4. HSS 4.4 5. HSS 4.4.8 Activity HSS 4.4.8

Extend Lesson 2
Primary Sources

SCHOOL in 1900

Are you ready for school? Put on your apron or bow tie. Pick up your slate and chalk. Walk a mile to the one-room building. Step into a chilly classroom and hope that there's enough wood for the stove to warm the room. Say a polite "Good morning, ma'am," to the teacher. That's how students at this Alameda, California, school may have started the day.

The writing on the chalkboard tells you about what these students learned. For example, they studied math, just like students today. California has always planned for the future in education. The state now has one of the largest public education systems in the world.

Pencil Box Students used pencils for much of their writing around 1900. Computers would not be invented for decades.

Textbooks Schools used textbooks around 1900, just as they do today.

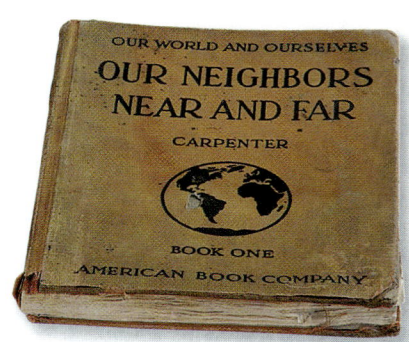

Lunch Pail Students used lunch pails like this one early in the 1900s.

Activities

1. **THINK ABOUT IT** Think of ways the classroom above is similar to your own classroom.

2. **DRAW IT** If you were designing a new school, what would it look like? Draw a picture of a future school.

Core Lesson 3

Technology and Trade

VOCABULARY

high-tech
international trade

Vocabulary Strategy

international trade

The prefix **inter-** means **between** or **among**. International trade is trade between or among nations.

READING SKILL

Draw Conclusions List facts and details to help you decide whether high-tech industries are important to California.

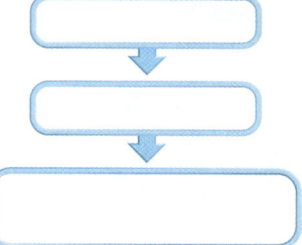

STANDARDS
Core: HSS 4.1.4, 4.4, 4.4.6
Extend support: HSS 4.4.6

Build on What You Know Anytime you punch in a phone number or use an electronic keyboard you use computer technology. California led the way in making computers as useful and common as they are today.

Leading the Computer Industry

Main Idea California has been a leader in computer technology.

The first computers were big and hard to use. Many people thought that only governments and very big companies would ever be able to use them.

Steven Jobs and Stephen Wozniak had a different idea. They thought that people who could not afford big computers might want small ones. In 1977, they formed a company in California and began to produce a small computer called the Apple II. It was one of the first personal computers and one of the easiest to use.

Steve Wozniak This Californian was elected to the Inventors Hall of Fame in 2000.

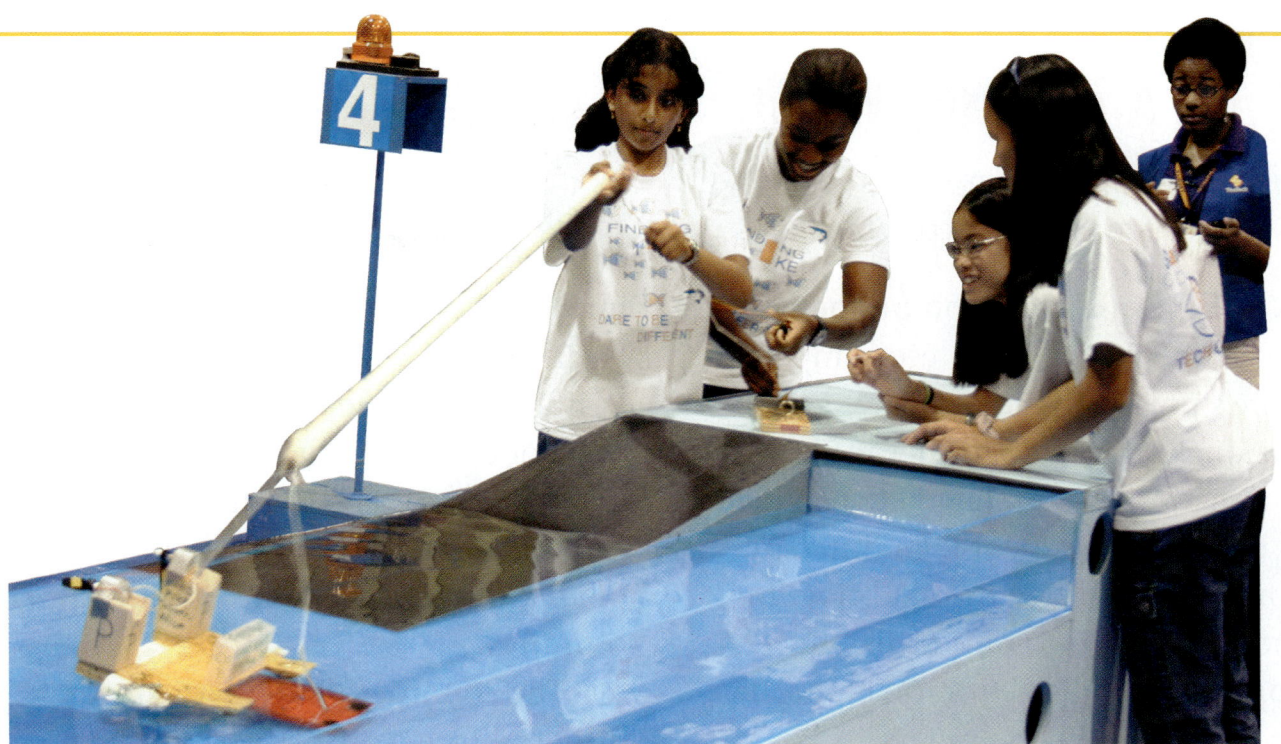

High-Tech Challenge In Silicon Valley, students take part in an annual competition to build high-tech machines.

Silicon Valley

Cupertino, the city where Wozniak and Jobs grew up, is in a part of California now called Silicon Valley. The valley got its name from the tiny silicon chips that made personal computers possible. Silicon Valley is the home of many high-tech companies. **High-tech** is technology that is very advanced.

Silicon Valley grew up around Stanford University. In the 1950s, **Frederick Terman**, a professor at Stanford, started a research park. A research park is a place where scientists from businesses, government, and universities can work together. By the 1960s, nearly all the companies that made computer chips were in Silicon Valley.

In 1959, about 18,000 people worked in high-tech and electronics in Silicon Valley. By 2000, that number had reached half a million. It is home to computer companies, software developers, and Internet businesses.

Silicon Valley is one of California's high-tech areas. The Tech Coast stretches from Santa Barbara to San Diego. It is a center for medical research. The technology industry around Sacramento is growing, too.

All together, California's high-tech companies produce more than $150 billion in goods and services each year. High-tech industries strengthen California's economy. About one-fifth of all the nation's high-tech exports come from California.

REVIEW What made Silicon Valley grow?

Trade Around the World

Main Idea Trade with Pacific Basin nations is important to the state's economy.

California's location on the Pacific Ocean helps the state's economy. The state's ports and airports have grown, making California a leader in international trade. **International trade** is trade between people in different countries. The exports that bring the most income into California are computers and electronics. Electronics use tiny built-in computers.

The Port of Los Angeles in San Pedro is one of the biggest ports in the nation. About 3,000 ships arrive there every year. They carry containers of manufactured goods such as cars.

The Pacific Basin

During one month in 2004, ships brought more than 350,000 containers of imports into the port. Many of the imports they carried came from the Pacific Basin. The Pacific Basin, or Pacific Rim, includes nations along the coast of the Pacific Ocean, such as Canada, Korea, Japan, China, and Chile. California has important trade links with these and other Pacific Rim countries.

The countries that buy the most from California are Canada, Mexico, and Japan. The United States joined Canada and Mexico in the North American Free Trade Agreement (NAFTA) in 1992. This agreement makes trade in North America easier.

The Port of Long Beach About eight cargo ships arrive in the port every day. The containers are lifted off the ship by cranes and placed on trucks and trains for quick transportation

Alameda Corridor This series of bridges, underpasses, and overpasses keeps trains away from traffic so they can go faster.

The Alameda Corridor

California government and businesses are always looking for ways to make trade faster and cheaper. In 2002, the state opened a 20-mile-long, high-speed railroad track called the Alameda Corridor. This railroad line links the ports of Los Angeles and Long Beach to train yards in Los Angeles. Goods from the ports can be quickly carried all over the country by rail, truck, or plane.

REVIEW What is the purpose of the North American Free Trade Agreement?

Lesson Summary

- California is a leader in high-tech industries.
- Many new high-tech industries started in Silicon Valley.
- California has important international trade links with Pacific Rim and NAFTA nations.

Why It Matters...

Technologies developed in California have had a huge impact on the way businesses are run.

Lesson Review

1 VOCABULARY Write three sentences about why California is a center of the **high-tech** industry in the United States.

2 READING SKILL: Draw Conclusions Write a paragraph explaining your conclusions about the importance of high-tech industry to California.

3 MAIN IDEA: Technology Why did Steven Jobs and Stephen Wozniak form a computer company?

4 MAIN IDEA: Geography In what way does California's location help trade with countries in Asia?

5 CRITICAL THINKING: Apply What effect does having big ports have on California's computer industry?

WRITING ACTIVITY Write a summary of the section "Trade Around the World." Be sure to include supporting details.

STANDARDS 1. HSS 4.4.6 2. HSS 4.4.6 3. HSS 4.4.6 4. HSS 4.1.4 5. HSS 4.1.4 **Activity** Analysis Skill HI 1

Extend Lesson 3
Economics

The PACIFIC RIM

Where would you go to find some of the strongest economies in the world? Take a look at the Pacific Rim, or Pacific Basin. The states and nations that border the Pacific Ocean have some of the world's fastest-growing economies.

Trade helps these economies grow. Ships and planes filled with goods cross the Pacific in a constant stream. Many leave from or arrive in California. California is the nation's leading state for international trade. Much of that trade is with countries around the Pacific Basin.

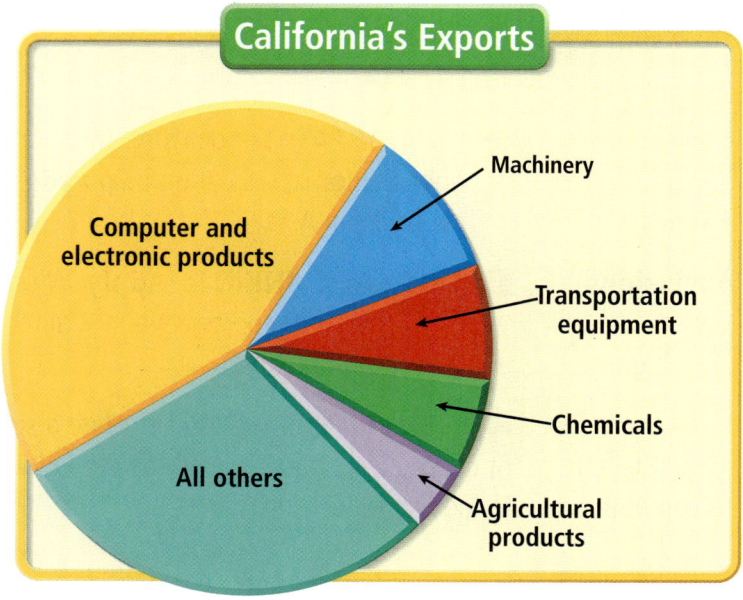

California's Exports: Computer and electronic products, Machinery, Transportation equipment, Chemicals, Agricultural products, All others

Exports to Other Countries, 2003

Country	Value of California Exports
1. Mexico	$18.8 billion
2. Japan	$11.7 billion
3. Canada	$11.2 billion
4. China	$5.4 billion
5. South Korea	$4.8 billion

Activities

1. **THINK ABOUT IT** Think about why growing economies in Asia help California's economy.

2. **GRAPH IT** What do you think California's biggest imports are? Write down your prediction. Then research the correct answer and create a graph or chart that shows the results.

ECONOMICS

375

Core Lesson 4

California's Art and Culture

VOCABULARY

trend
festival

Vocabulary Strategy

festival

The word **festival** is related to the word feast. Eating is a part of many California festivals.

READING SKILL

Categorize As you read, list different categories of festivals in California.

1	
2	
3	
4	

STANDARDS
Core: HSS 4.4, 4.4.9
Extend support: HSS 4.4.9

Build on What You Know Would you rather go to the movies or ride a skateboard? Either way, you would be enjoying something that first became popular in California.

Artists and Trends

Main Idea Californians have contributed to the arts and culture of the United States in many ways.

One of California's biggest industries is the movie industry. Every year, people around the world see films made in California. Some of the world's most important directors, writers, producers, and actors have come to California to work in its movie industry.

George Lucas is a film director and producer who was born in Modesto. He uses computers to create amazing special effects. His *Star Wars* films are some of the most popular movies ever made.

George Lucas People around the world have enjoyed this Californian's movies.

The Getty Museum Around 1 million people visit this art museum each year. Many people consider the building itself a piece of art.

Artists and Museums

California artists make all kinds of art. **Isamu Noguchi** (i SOM oo no GOO chi) built sculpture gardens and playgrounds. Architect **Julia Morgan** was an engineer and an artist. The Julia Morgan Engineering Program at the University of California at Berkeley is named for her.

Today, **Julie Rodriguez Jones** combines art and science in paintings of outer space. **Rosie Lee Tompkins** uses African American traditions in colorful, suprising quilts.

Museums in California show paintings, sculpture, and other art forms. The Crocker Art Museum in Sacramento was California's first art museum. The Getty Museum in Los Angeles and the de Young Museum in San Francisco are also art museums.

California Trends

Many trends start in California. A trend is a style or activity that spreads quickly. During the 1950s and 1960s, movies and magazines showed the rest of the United States pictures of California surfers. **Brian Wilson**, from Hawthorne, was part of a California band called the Beach Boys. He wrote many popular songs about surfing.

California's athletes create new sports and new records. Windsurfing and mountain biking began in California. Skateboarding started in California, too. **Tony Hawk**, a champion skateboarder, is from Carlsbad. Another California champion is skater **Michelle Kwan**, of Torrance.

REVIEW Name two Californians who have contributed to the arts.

Many Celebrations

Main Idea Californians celebrate the state's history and people in many ways.

Some California holidays honor important people. **Martin Luther King, Jr.** Day honors the civil rights leader each January. **Cesar Chavez** Day is March 31. Chavez led efforts to win justice for farm workers. Both days are state holidays.

Other holidays celebrate traditions of California's people. On May 5, many celebrate Cinco de Mayo, which recalls a day of victory for Mexican soldiers.

In late winter, many Californians celebrate the Chinese New Year with parades and dancing. San Francisco's celebration is California's largest.

California Festivals

Many California festivals honor customs of the past. A **festival** is a day or period of time set aside for celebration. Old Spanish Days Fiesta takes place every year in Santa Barbara. For more than eighty years, visitors have come to this event to learn about the area's early settlers. Visitors can see how rancheros once lived.

People from Denmark built the town of Solvang almost a hundred years ago. Many buildings in the town look like houses in Denmark. Stores and restaurants sell Danish foods and crafts. Every year the town holds the Danish Days Festival. During the three-day event, thousands of tourists come to Solvang to watch folk dancers and learn about Danish traditions.

Old Spanish Days Santa Barbara is one of many California cities that honors its Spanish heritage.

California's Farms

Other festivals celebrate California farms. In Oxnard, crowds gather to listen to music and eat ripe berries at the Strawberry Festival. Visitors try treats like strawberry pizzas. Other festivals feature artichokes, raisins, and dates.

Agricultural Fairs Many young Californians take part in agricultural fairs.

The annual California State Fair is a week-long agricultural festival. The week is highlighted by horse shows, livestock competitions, and farming demonstrations. It is one of the largest fairs in the country. More than one million visitors attended in 2001.

REVIEW Which two state holidays honor United States citizens?

Lesson Summary

Why It Matters...

Artists and festivals express the culture and history of California.

Lesson Review

1 VOCABULARY Use **trend** in a description of California today.

2 READING SKILL Write an explanation for why you chose your categories for California's holidays and festivals.

3 MAIN IDEA: Culture What are three types of art made by Californians?

4 MAIN IDEA: Citizenship What can festivals teach people about history?

5 CRITICAL THINKING: Analyze What do different art forms, such as movies and sculpture, have in common?

WRITING ACTIVITY Find out about a California artist, filmmaker, or musician. Write a report on what you learn. Use facts and details to support a main idea.

1. HSS 4.4.9 2. HSS 4.4 3. HSS 4.4.9 4. HSS 4.4 5. HSS 4.4.9 Activity HSS 4.4.9

Extend Lesson 4
Biographies

California Creativity

Creative people are everywhere in California. Some of the nation's best-loved actors, writers, and dancers come from California. Even the state's entrepreneurs have won awards for their creative work.

Evelyn Cisneros
Dancer (Born 1958)

Evelyn Cisneros fell in love with dancing at age 7. When she was 16, she moved to San Francisco to dance with the San Francisco Ballet Company. She was the first Hispanic woman to be a lead dancer of a major American ballet company.

John Steinbeck
Writer (1902–1968)

John Steinbeck set many of his books in the area around Salinas, where he was born. His books told about California workers on farms and in factories.

CHARACTER TRAIT: **Courage**

John Wayne
Actor (1907–1979)

As a college student, John Wayne had a summer job at a movie studio. While working there, he got his first role in a movie. Wayne became one of Hollywood's top stars. His career lasted over 40 years.

Synthia Saint James
Artist (Born 1949)

Born in Los Angeles, Synthia Saint James is creative in many ways. She is best-known for her bright, colorful paintings, but she also writes books and even songs. She is creative in the way she manages her business, too, and has won awards as both an artist and an entrepreneur.

Amy Tan
Writer (Born 1952)

Amy Tan was born in Oakland, the daughter of Chinese immigrants. Tan bases many of her books on stories her mother told her about China. She also writes about her own experiences growing up Chinese American in California.

Activities

1. **TALK ABOUT IT** Talk with a partner about the ways the people on this page show **courage**.

2. **WRITE ABOUT IT** Research the life of Shirley Temple Black or some other creative Californian. Write a summary of the person's career.

 Technology
Writing Process Tips
Get help with your writing at:
www.eduplace.com/kids/hmss/

BIOGRAPHIES

Skillbuilder

Make a Decision

You make decisions every day. When you make a choice about what to do or say, you are making a decision. It is important to think about the costs and benefits of different actions before you make a decision. A <mark>cost</mark> is a loss or sacrifice. A <mark>benefit</mark> is a gain or an advantage. The chart and the steps below will help you learn how to make a decision.

> **VOCABULARY**
> cost
> benefit

Learn the Skill

Step 1: Identify the decision you want to make.

Step 2: Think of the possible actions you could take to solve the problem.

Step 3: Consider the costs and benefits of each action.

Step 4: Choose the action with the fewest costs and the most benefits for the most people.

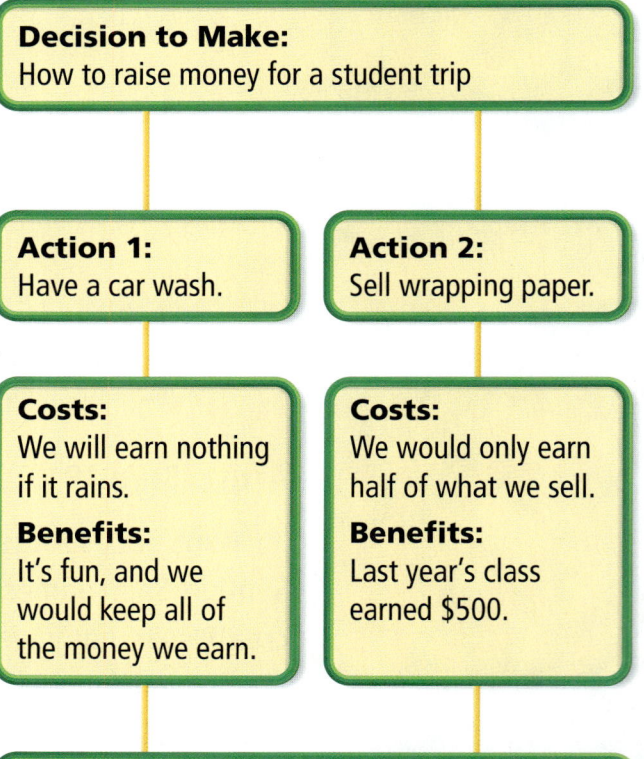

382 • Chapter 11

Apply Critical Thinking

Practice the Skill

Sometimes making a decision means choosing between two things you want. Reread the section of Lesson 4 on California's celebrations that begins on page 378. Suppose you wanted to go to the Strawberry Festival and the Danish Days Festival, but they were on the same day. Use a chart like the one on page 382 to help you make a decision about which one to attend.

Apply the Skill

Choose a topic that people in California or in your community must make a decision about. For example, people could be trying to find ways to celebrate an event, or looking for a place to build a new museum. Fill out a chart like the one on page 382. Then write a paragraph explaining what you would decide and why.

Chapter 11 Review

Visual Summary

1–3. Write a description of each item named below.

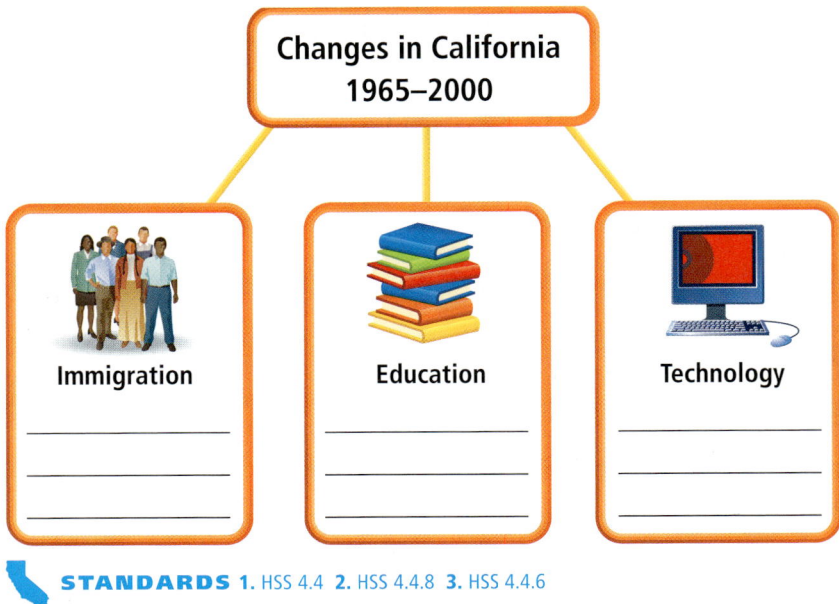

Changes in California 1965–2000
- Immigration
- Education
- Technology

STANDARDS 1. HSS 4.4 2. HSS 4.4.8 3. HSS 4.4.6

Facts and Main Ideas

Answer each question below.

4. **Citizenship** What effect did the Immigration Act of 1965 have?

5. **Citizenship** What can a person who immigrates to California do to become a citizen?

6. **Government** Why is public education important in California?

7. **Economics** Which three nations are California's biggest trade partners?

8. **Culture** What are two types of art you can see in museums such as the Getty or de Young museums?

4. HSS 4.4 5. HSS 4.4 6. HSS 4.4.8 7. HSS 4.4.6 8. HSS 4.4.9

Vocabulary

Choose the correct word from the list below to complete each sentence.

school district, p. 365
trend, p. 377
festival, p. 378

9. Los Angeles Unified is the largest _____ in California.

10. Skateboarding is a _____ that started in California.

11. Santa Barbara holds a _____ every year to celebrate its history and culture.

9. HSS 4.4.8 10. HSS 4.4.9 11. HSS 4.4.9

384 • Chapter 11

CHAPTER SUMMARY TIMELINE

- **1965** New immigration laws
- **1977** Apple II is introduced
- **1992** NAFTA signed

1965 — 1970 — 1975 — 1980 — 1985 — 1990 — 1995 — 2000 — 2005

Apply Skills

Make Decisions Read the passage. Then use what you have learned about making decisions to answer each question.

> Ana is planning to go to college. She would like to go to one of California's state universities. The closest one is just a few miles away. However, it does not offer all the classes she would like to take. Another state university has all the classes she wants, but it is in another city. Ana would have to move to go to school there. Moving is difficult, but Ana decides to go to the university with all the classes she wants.

12. What decision did Ana face?
    - A. where to work
    - B. which university to go to
    - C. what her favorite subject is
    - D. whether to go to college

13. What is one consequence of her decision?
    - A. She will not take the classes she wants.
    - B. She will stay in the same city.
    - C. She will have to move.
    - D. She will take more science classes.

12. Analysis Skill HI 4   13. Analysis Skill HI 4

Critical Thinking

Write a short paragraph to answer each of the questions below.

14. **Synthesize** Explain how Silicon Valley's high-tech industries helped California's economy.

15. **Evaluate** What do the many cultural festivals celebrated in California tell you about its people?

Timeline

Use the chapter summary timeline above to answer the question.

16. Which event took place in the 1970s?

14. HSS 4.4.6   15. HSS 4.4.9   16. HSS 4.4.6

Activities

Art Activity Draw a new piece of clothing that could start a fashion trend. It could be something that people wear while skateboarding or mountain biking.

Writing Activity Write a summary of the contributions California has made to technology.

Activities Analysis Skill HI 2, HSS 4.4.6, W 2.4

Technology
Writing Process Tips
Get help with your writing at:
www.eduplace.com/kids/hmss/

385

Chapter 12 The Twenty-First Century

Vocabulary Preview

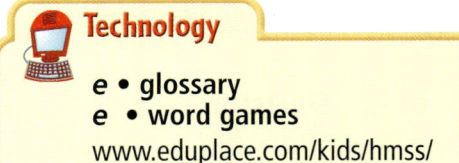

Technology
e • glossary
e • word games
www.eduplace.com/kids/hmss/

legislative branch
The governments of the United States and California each have a **legislative branch.** Members of this branch make laws. **page 389**

city manager
Some cities have a **city manager** who is hired to handle the daily operations of the city. **page 402**

Reading Strategy

Monitor/Clarify Use this strategy to check your understanding.

 **Quick Tip** If you are confused, reread or read ahead.

population density

Some places in California have many people in a small area. Others, like Markleeville in Alpine County, have a low **population density.** page 406

landfill

What happens when something gets thrown away and not recycled? It may end up in a **landfill** like this one. page 414

Core Lesson 1

United States Government

VOCABULARY

legislative branch
executive branch
judicial branch
democracy

Vocabulary Strategy

legislative branch

Like a branch on a tree, the **legislative branch** of the government is separate from other branches, but part of the same system.

READING SKILL
Main Idea and Details
Note details about the national government's powers.

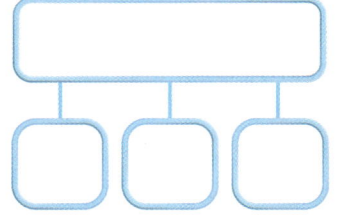

STANDARDS
Core: HSS 4.5, 4.5.1
Extend support: HSS 4.5

Build on What You Know You have seen the President on television and in newspapers. The President leads the government of the United States.

The United States Constitution

Main Idea The Constitution sets out the structure and rules of our national government.

More than 200 years ago, leaders of our new nation wrote the Constitution of the United States. This written document is the basic law of the United States. It tells the structure and purpose of the United States government. It describes how the national government, the states, and local governments share power. The Constitution protects the safety, liberty, and rights of citizens.

To protect our rights, the Constitution divides the national government into three branches, or parts. Each branch has different powers and duties.

The Constitution The Preamble to, or beginning of, the Constitution reminds readers that the power of the government comes from all the people.

Ronald Reagan This former California governor was the 40th President of the United States. Californians Herbert Hoover and Richard Nixon were also United States Presidents.

The Three Branches

The United States Congress is the legislative branch of government. The **legislative branch** legislates, or makes laws. It includes the Senate and the House of Representatives. Voters from each state elect two senators to represent them in the Senate.

The House of Representatives has more members. The larger a state's population, the more representatives its citizens elect. California has 53 representatives. This is more than any other state. Each representative from California serves a different district, or area, of the state.

The President is elected by the nation's citizens to lead the executive branch. The **executive branch** carries out the nation's laws. This branch includes many departments that help run the government.

In the judicial branch, the United States Supreme Court is the highest court. The **judicial branch** decides when laws have been broken and settles disagreements about laws. The Supreme Court decides what laws passed by Congress mean and whether they agree with the Constitution.

Each branch has limits on its power. For example, the President commands the military. However, Congress alone can declare war. The judicial branch limits the powers of the other branches. It can decide whether Congress or the President has acted against the Constitution. Also, the federal government leaves many powers and duties to the states. California's state government operates highways, parks, and other programs.

REVIEW What are the three branches of the national government?

389

Rights and Duties

Main Idea American citizens have both rights and responsibilities.

The United States is a democracy. A **democracy** is a form of government in which the authority to govern comes from the people. Our country is also a republic in which representatives elected by the people make the laws. If citizens think their representatives are doing a poor job, they can choose new representatives at the next election.

The rights of citizens are protected by the Constitution of the United States. Voting is one right. Many other rights, such as freedom of speech and freedom of religion, are protected by a special section of the Constitution called the Bill of Rights.

Responsibilities

Along with their rights, American citizens have responsibilities, or duties. For example, all citizens should obey the law. If laws are unjust, they can work to change them. Adult citizens have more responsibilities. They pay taxes and serve on juries. Many citizens join the armed forces to help protect our nation. Others take part in local government to make their city or town a better place to live.

Voting is both a right and a duty for citizens over 18. It gives citizens real power in government. However, citizens may vote for a person who does not win. Responsible citizens agree to be governed by the person who receives the most votes, even if they voted for someone else.

Young Citizens These students are speaking out in favor of a clean environment.

Food Drive The food gathered at this event will go to people who need it.

A Role for You

Californians who are too young to vote still take part in government. Young people must obey the laws just like adults. Many students also take part in community groups. They might help people in need or work to clean up their neighborhood. These actions make the community a better place for everyone.

REVIEW What responsibilities do citizens have?

Lesson Summary

The Constitution is the plan for the government of the United States. It spreads power among three branches. Each branch plays a role in making, carrying out, or deciding the meaning of laws. The Bill of Rights protects citizens' rights. Citizens also have a duty to take part in government.

Why It Matters...

By acting on their rights and responsibilities, citizens protect democracy in the United States.

Lesson Review

1. **VOCABULARY** Write a few sentences about the national government using **legislative branch.**

2. **READING SKILL** Choose one **detail** from your chart and write a paragraph explaining its importance.

3. **MAIN IDEA: Government** Which branch has the power to decide if Congress's laws agree with the Constitution?

4. **MAIN IDEA: Citizenship** Name three rights of citizens protected by the Constitution.

5. **CRITICAL THINKING: Synthesize** Why is it important in a democracy for voters to agree to be governed by whoever wins an election?

WRITING ACTIVITY Write an information report about a senator or representative from your district. Include facts and details about what the person has done since he or she was elected.

1. HSS 4.5 2. HSS 4.5 3. HSS 4.5 4. HSS 4.5.1 5. HSS 4.5 Activity HSS 4.5

Extend Lesson 1
Readers' Theater

Voting Day

Antonio has just turned 18 and is getting ready to vote in his first California election. Maria and David are curious about how it works. In this story, they find out about how people vote in California.

Characters:

Narrator

David Alarcón: 4th grader, Maria's twin brother

Maria Alarcón: 4th grader, David's twin sister

Antonio Alarcón: Maria and David's older brother

Aunt Laura: aunt

Mrs. Alarcón: mother

CHARACTER TRAIT: Responsibility

Narrator: David and Maria are at home with their aunt and their brother, Antonio. Their mother comes in from work.

Mrs. Alarcón: Hey guys, how was school?

Maria: We voted for the student council.

David: The fifth graders running for president gave speeches. I voted for Lucy Ruiz because she's on my soccer team.

Maria: I voted for Ian Willis. I liked his posters about a new school logo.

Antonio: That reminds me. I need to register to vote for the elections in November.

Maria: What do you mean register to vote? We didn't register! We just folded a paper ballot and dropped it in a box.

Mrs. Alarcón: States make people register so that only people who are supposed to vote actually do vote. They also have to make sure that people only vote once. Where are you going to register, Antonio?

Antonio: I'll go to the Board of Elections website and fill out a voter registration form.

Aunt Laura: You can also pick up a form at the library, or at the post office.

Maria: I want to register, too.

Mrs. Alarcón: You'll have to wait until you turn 18. You can come with me on voting day, though.

Narrator: Because Antonio is 18, a U.S. citizen, and California resident, he can register to vote. After filling out a registration form, Antonio gets information in the mail about when and where to vote. He also gets information about some of the propositions, or plans, that will be on the ballot.

Now, it is Election Day. Antonio and his family are outside the polling place, or the place where people vote.

Maria: How do you know how to vote?

Mrs. Alarcón: I read the newspaper. Other people listen to the radio, or watch TV.

Aunt Laura: It's a lot like your school elections. You learn about the candidates and vote for ones you agree with. We vote on propositions, too.

David: Propositions? What are those?

CHARACTER TRAIT: Responsibility

Mrs. Alarcón: A proposition is a plan or proposal. There are a couple of propositions to vote on today.

David: So voting isn't just something you do on a certain day.

Antonio: That's right. I also talk to my friends to find out what they think. You really need to prepare. Look at this Proposition 43, for example. It's a plan for a city park. I don't think we need one, myself.

Mrs. Alarcón: I'm against it, too. We should fix up the park we have.

Aunt Laura: The other park is very nice for walks or picnics, but this park will have a swimming pool, a baseball field, and tennis courts.

David: Did you say a baseball field? A new field would give a huge boost to the school team. Mom, Antonio, you've got to vote for Proposition 43!

Antonio: Hearing you talk about it makes me change my mind about how to vote.

Narrator: After the polls close, the votes are counted. Later that evening, the election results are announced on radio and television stations.

David: Did you hear? Proposition 43 passed by more than 2,000 votes!

Aunt Laura: You'd better get to bed, David, so you'll have plenty of energy to hit the ball out of the new park.

Activities

1. **TALK ABOUT IT** As citizens, how do Mrs. Alarcón and Antonio show their sense of responsibility?

2. **CHART IT** Find out more about how propositions are put on the ballot. Make a flow chart that shows the process.

Skillbuilder

Draw Conclusions

VOCABULARY
conclusion

To draw a conclusion, readers use what they already know and think, as well as what they are learning. A **conclusion** is a judgment or decision based on facts, ideas, and opinions. When you draw a conclusion, you use your own experience and knowledge to decide how facts and opinions are connected.

Learn the Skill

Step 1: Carefully read the facts and ideas that the writer presents.

Step 2: Think about what you already know about the topic. Look for connections between the facts and ideas presented and what you already know.

Step 3: Draw a conclusion. Your conclusion should state your opinion about what the facts and ideas mean.

| What I Know: California is a state. | + | Facts I Read: Each state has two senators. | = | Conclusion: California must have two senators. |

Apply Critical Thinking

Practice the Skill

Read the paragraph about the writing of the United States Constitution. Then answer the questions.

> At first, delegates to the Constitutional Convention could not agree on how many representatives each state should have in Congress. States with more people wanted the number to be based upon each state's population. States with fewer people disagreed. They wanted every state to have the same number of representatives. People agreed to divide the Congress into two parts. In one part, the Senate, each state would have two representatives. In the other part, the House of Representatives, each state would send a number of representatives based on the state's population.

1. What can you conclude about why larger states would want representation based on their population?
2. What conclusion could you draw about why smaller states disagreed with the larger states? Why would their suggestion help small states?

Apply the Skill

Use information from Lesson 1 to draw conclusions about why the federal government has three branches. Use details to support your conclusion.

Core Lesson 2

State and Local Government

VOCABULARY

city manager
county
rancheria

Vocabulary Strategy

city **manage**r

The term **city manager** includes the word **manage**. A city manager manages a city's government.

READING SKILL
Compare and Contrast List ways that the California and United States governments are alike and different.

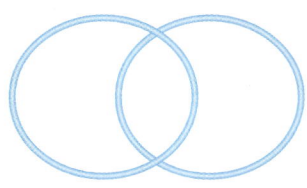

STANDARDS
Core: HSS 4.5.2, 4.5.3, 4.5.4, 4.5.5
Extend support: HSS 4.5.4

Build on What You Know What does the government do in your community? Every time you enter your school, hear a fire truck, or play in a public park, state or local government is at work.

State Government

Main Idea California's government protects people and provides services.

The national government is not the only type of government Californians have. The national government shares power with state and local governments. National, state, and local governments are separate from each other and have different responsibilities.

Like the national government, California has a
written constitution. The state's first constitution was written in 1849. A new constitution was written in
1879, and it is still in effect today. However, it has been amended, or changed, many times since 1879.

The State Capitol The state capitol is located in Sacramento, home of the state government.

398 • Chapter 12

Two Constitutions California's constitution is similar to the United States Constitution in important ways. **SKILL** Reading Visuals What do the two constitutions have in common?

State and National Constitutions

California's constitution is like the national Constitution in many ways. Both are based on the consent, or agreement, of the people. People show their consent in many ways. For example, they obey laws and take part in elections.

The rule of law is central to both levels of government. It means that no one, not even the government, can ignore the laws. It also means that laws treat all people as equals.

California's constitution and the national Constitution are different from each other in some ways. California's government cannot make laws for other states or the whole nation. For example, the state cannot control the nation's military. California's laws must follow the United States Constitution.

Services of State Government

California's state government provides many services. State workers repair state highways and bridges. The state also makes rules about who can have a driver's license. State officials make sure businesses obey health and safety laws. The state school board decides the length of the school year.

State leaders make rules about state and local elections. They decide when to hold elections and who can vote. Their rules must follow laws in the state and national constitutions.

California collects taxes to pay for these services. People pay sales taxes when they buy certain goods. The state also collects an income tax on the money people earn.

REVIEW What is one similarity between the California and national constitutions?

399

The Three Branches

Main Idea California's state government has three branches.

Like the national government, California's state government is divided into three branches. Each branch has its own responsibilities and powers.

The legislative branch, or legislature, is responsible for making laws. The members are elected by voters. California's legislature has two houses, or parts. These are the Senate and the Assembly. The Senate has 40 members. The Assembly has 80 members.

California's senators and members of the Assembly make laws to solve problems and meet future challenges. For example, California lawmakers worried about the environment of the state's coastal waters. In 1999 they passed a law to protect some areas from pollution and overfishing. Over 80 areas along the coast are now protected.

The Executive and Judicial Branches

California's governor heads the executive branch. This branch is responsible for carrying out laws. The governor's role is like the President's role at the national level. The governor can approve or turn down laws passed by the legislature. He or she is elected by voters in the state.

The executive branch has departments that handle different jobs. The Department of Education is part of the executive branch, for example. This department runs California's schools.

The third branch of California's government is the judicial branch. The California Supreme Court is the highest court. It has seven judges. They decide whether laws made by the legislature are allowed under the state constitution. Many other courts are part of the state court system.

REVIEW What are the three branches of California's government?

Frederick Roberts In 1918, he became the first African American elected to the State Assembly.

California State Government

Executive Branch

Governor

Responsibilities

Make sure state's laws are carried out

Approve or disapprove laws passed by legislature

Appoint members of the judicial branch

Governor Arnold Schwarzenegger led the executive branch after his election.

Legislative Branch

Legislator

Responsibilities

Write and vote on laws

Accept or reject some executive appointments

Remove members of other branches for wrongdoing

Gloria Molina was the first Hispanic woman elected to the State Assembly, which is part of the legislative branch.

Judicial Branch

Chief Justice

Responsibilities

Make sure state laws are carried out fairly

Decide whether state laws agree with the state constitution

Chief Justice Ronald George became the leader of the State Supreme Court in 1996.

Local Government

Main Idea: California communities have governments that serve the public.

Californians also have local governments. Local governments provide services such as fire and police protection, trash collection, and street repair. Local governments provide parks, schools, and libraries, too.

As with state and national government, California's local governments are based on the consent of the governed and the rule of law. In some communities, voters elect city councils.

Councils are groups of citizens who make local laws. A mayor often works with the city council. In large cities such as San Francisco, people vote for the mayor. In some places, someone elected to the city council is chosen as mayor by the council. Some city councils hire a city manager to run the city. A **city manager** takes care of the daily business of running the city.

California is divided into 58 counties. A **county** is a section of a state that has its own government. Voters elect county boards of supervisors. This group makes decisions about county property.

City Leadership The city manager (left) and mayor (right) of Burbank, California, work together in the city government. The city manager is hired, while the mayor is an elected official.

402 • Chapter 12

Districts and Rancherias

California has almost 5,000 special districts. These areas may include several cities or counties. Some are for fire protection or insect control. Water districts are special districts. State lawmakers may also create special districts for recycling and getting rid of waste.

California Indians have their own local governments on reservations and rancherias. A **rancheria** is land protected for California Indians. People of reservation and rancheria communities elect their council governments.

REVIEW What are some services provided by local governments in cities?

Lesson Summary

California's state government has three branches.

Every city, town, and county in California has some type of government.

State, local, and county governments provide many services.

Why It Matters...

State and local governments affect the daily lives of Californians.

Counties County government provides services such as fire protection.

Lesson Review

1. **VOCABULARY** Write two sentences explaining the role of a **city manager** in local government.

2. **READING SKILL Compare** the California state government and the national government. What are two ways they are alike?

3. **MAIN IDEA: Economics** In what ways does state government pay for the services it provides?

4. **MAIN IDEA: Government** What are some reasons for special districts in California?

5. **CRITICAL THINKING: Apply** Why do cities need governments?

WRITING ACTIVITY Research the job of your governor, mayor, or city manager. Write a paragraph describing what you think would be the hardest part of the job and the best part. Give reasons for your opinion.

1. HSS 4.5 2. HSS 4.5.2 3. HSS 4.5.3 4. HSS 4.5.1 5. HSS 4.5.3 Activity HSS 4.5.4

Extend Lesson 2
Citizenship

CALIFORNIA FIRSTS

"Everybody in favor, say 'Yes!'" When you say 'Yes,' you give your consent, or agreement. California's government is based on the consent of its citizens. People show their consent by participating in the government. They vote and hold public office. People who serve in government today represent all of California's people. Here are some pioneer public officials from the Golden State.

Yvonne Braithwaite Burke

She held two California firsts. In 1966, Burke became the first African American woman elected to the State Assembly. Then in 1972, she became the first African American woman elected to the United States Congress from California.

Rose Ann Vuich

In 1976, she became the first woman elected to California's Senate. Senators represent larger areas than members of the Assembly and serve longer terms.

CHARACTER TRAIT: Civic Virtue

March Fong Eu

When she became California's Secretary of State in 1994, Eu was the first Asian American woman to be elected to a position by the whole state. One of her duties was to make sure elections in our state are fair and lawful.

Cruz Reynoso

He was the first Hispanic to serve on California's State Supreme Court. This is the state's highest court. Its judges review decisions of lower courts to see if they agree with state law.

Activities

1. **TALK ABOUT IT** Serving in government can be hard work. In what way does it show **civic virtue**?

2. **WRITE IT** Find a copy of California's state constitution and review the Preamble. In your own words, write the purpose of the constitution.

CITIZENSHIP

Core Lesson 3

Californians Today

VOCABULARY

population density
metropolitan area
population distribution
service industry

Vocabulary Strategy

service **industry**

Remember that **industry** means work. People in the **service industry** do work that serves the needs of others.

READING SKILL
Main Idea and Details
List details that support the second main idea in the lesson.

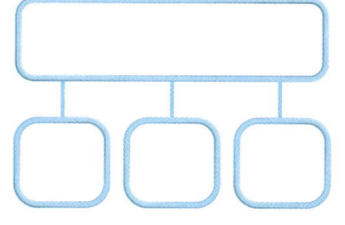

Core: HSS 4.1.4, 4.4.6
Extend support: HSS 4.1.5

San Jose Large cities such as San Jose are surrounded by suburbs. Many who work in the city live in these suburbs.

Build on What You Know How many different cities have you seen? What were they like? Most people in California live in one of its big cities.

Where Californians Live

Main Idea Knowing how many people there are in California, and where they live, is important for the future.

Over 34 million people live in California. It has the largest population of any state in the nation. The population density is very different in different parts of the state, however. **Population density** is the average number of people in a measured area.

For example, Trinity County in northwestern California has about 2 people per square mile, while San Francisco has over 16,000 people per square mile.

California's 10 Largest Cities, 2003

Name	Population	National Rank
Los Angeles	3,819,951	2
San Diego	1,266,753	7
San Jose	898,349	11
San Francisco	751,682	14
Long Beach	475,460	32
Fresno	451,455	36
Sacramento	445,335	37
Oakland	398,844	43
Santa Ana	342,510	51
Anaheim	332,361	53

California's Cities The national rank shows that California has some of the nation's largest cities.

SKILL Reading Charts Is San Francisco closer in population to Los Angeles or Sacramento?

Cities and Towns

California has 24 of the 100 biggest cities in the nation. Some of California's largest cities are clustered in metropolitan areas. A **metropolitan area** is an area that includes one or more big cities and their suburbs. The state's largest metropolitan areas are around Los Angeles and San Francisco.

Cities are centers of business, government, and culture. Many people move to cities such as Sacramento or San Jose, or to their suburbs, to be near jobs.

Other parts of California have fewer cities, jobs, and people. The way population is spread around the state is called population distribution. **Population distribution** is the pattern of where people live.

When Population Changes

People have moved to California from other places throughout its history. People move from place to place within California, too.

California's leaders want to know how the state's population distribution is changing. This helps them plan for the future. For example, Riverside's population grew by almost 25,000 between 2000 and 2003. As the city grows, residents need more services such as traffic control.

Many families with young children live in Stockton. In 2000, almost one-third of the people in Stockton were under age 18. This area will need more schools. In other areas, the number of people over the age of 65 is rising. These areas may need changing health services in the future.

REVIEW Why do many people settle near San Jose and Sacramento?

On Top of San Francisco People with special talents can find almost any kind of job in California. Many Californians work in construction jobs.

Californians at Work

Main Idea Californians have many different job choices.

Californians work in many industries. One of the most famous is the entertainment industry. It employs more than 100,000 people, including actors, makeup artists, and electricians.

Entertainment is part of the service industry. The **service industry** includes businesses that provide services, such as banks, hospitals, and restaurants. Almost half of Californians over age 16 work in businesses like these.

Trade and transportation is another big industry in California. People who work in this industry sell and deliver everything from food to furniture to flowers.

Communications and Electronics

About one in ten Californians works in manufacturing. This industry makes goods such as auto parts and airplanes. Other California workers have jobs in the mining, agriculture, or construction industries.

Companies in California's communications and electronics industries hire people to design, make, and sell products such as handheld and wireless networking devices. California companies create new electronic and communication tools. As technologies change, the jobs of workers change as well. For example, the growth of the Internet has created jobs that did not exist 20 years ago, such as designing web pages and managing Internet businesses.

Different Jobs for Different People

More than 22 million people in California have jobs. Workers need skills to do different jobs. Some people learn their skills as they work. Others go to college or other schools to learn. Whatever their skills, most people look for work they enjoy.

Reading is a skill that is needed in most jobs. **Rueben Martinez** knows the importance of reading. He has won an award for encouraging young people to read. He says,

"*Reading is a ladder to a better future.*"

REVIEW What do workers in the manufacturing industry do?

Lesson Summary

- California has many large cities.
- Californians can choose from jobs in different industries.
- As technologies change, the jobs workers do change as well.

Why It Matters...

Where people choose to live and the work people choose to do are among the most important decisions they make.

Agriculture in California Thousands of Californians work in agriculture. These workers are raising flowers to sell.

Lesson Review

1. **VOCABULARY** Write a sentence using **population distribution** that explains where Californians live.

2. **READING SKILL** What **details** from the lesson tell you that many people choose to work in the service industry?

3. **MAIN IDEA: Geography** Why do California's leaders need to know about the state's population distribution?

4. **MAIN IDEA: Economy** What are three industries that employ many workers in California?

5. **CRITICAL THINKING: Evaluate** Why do you think people choose to live in certain cities, such as Los Angeles?

MATH ACTIVITY Use information from the table of California's largest cities to create a bar graph.

1. HSS 4.1.5 2. HSS 4.4.6 3. HSS 4.1.5 4. HSS 4.4.6 5. HSS 4.1.5 Activity HSS 4.4.5

Extend Lesson 3
Economics

Public Servants

Who would rush into a burning building in the middle of the night? Firefighters, that's who. They are public servants who fight fires for you and other members of the public.

You may never have seen a firefighter at work, but you have seen many public servants. Public servants are people who are paid by local, state, or national governments. That means they are paid by the public to do work the public wants done. Governments use tax money to hire teachers, firefighters, police officers, health workers, park rangers, and others. Even the governor of California is a public servant!

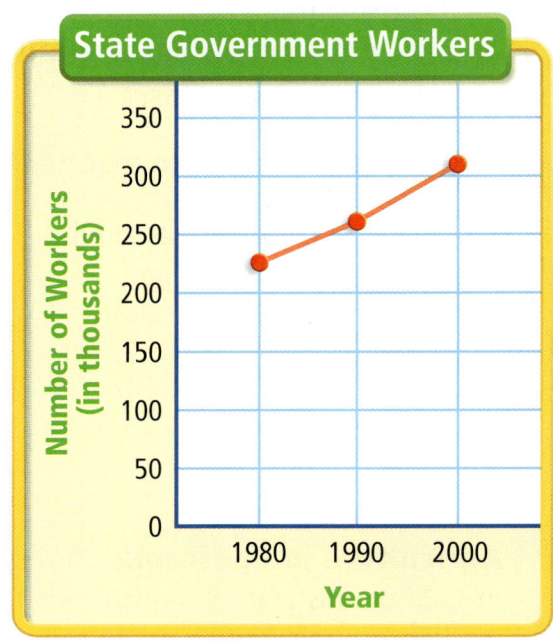

Police Officers

Police Police do one of the most important of all government jobs. They keep people safe and make sure laws are obeyed.

410 • Chapter 12

California Condor Tracker

Protecting Wildlife This worker is keeping track of California Condors. Californians work hard to protect the state's wildlife and environment.

Firefighters

Safety First Fighting fires is one way public servants protect people. This firefighter is practicing with a high-power hose.

Activities

1. **TALK ABOUT IT** With a partner, talk about the jobs these workers have and which ones sound interesting to you.

2. **MAP IT** List the types of public servants you know about. Draw a map of your town or city, showing places where these public servants might be found.

ECONOMICS

Core Lesson 4

The Challenge of the Future

VOCABULARY

recycle
landfill
watershed

Vocabulary Strategy

landfill

The **land** in landfill is a clue to the word's meaning. Land covers trash at landfills.

 READING SKILL
Problem and Solution As you read, list problems California may face in the future. Then list possible solutions.

Problem	Solution

 **STANDARDS**
Core: HSS 4.1, 4.1.3, 4.4.6, 4.4.7
Extend support: HSS 4.4.7

Build on What You Know When you wake up in the morning, you may think about your plans for the day. California's leaders must also look ahead and make plans.

A Great State

Main Idea Californians learn from the past to meet current challenges.

California leads the United States in many areas. It has more people than any other state. It attracts more immigrants than any other state and has the most diverse population in the country.

California is the leading state in agriculture and industry. It has some of the best colleges and universities in the world. Some plants and animals that live in California live nowhere else. From beautiful beaches, to rich farmlands, to stunning mountains, Californians have a lot to be proud of!

Giant Sequoia The giant sequoia grows only in California. It is the largest tree in the world.

412 • Chapter 12

New Technologies As technology improves, electric cars such as this one may become more common.

Learning from the Past

Thinking about past successes helps people in California solve the problems of today. For example, in the 1970s, southern California had a problem with air pollution. One cause of the pollution was exhaust, or smoke, from car and truck engines. Exhaust includes harmful chemicals that mix with the air.

Californians wanted to solve this problem, but they had to be careful. The state depends on transportation. How could California reduce pollution without hurting its economy?

California lawmakers passed new laws. They said that cars in California had to use a type of gasoline that produces less exhaust.

Less exhaust from cars made the air in southern California cleaner. Other states noticed California's new laws. They passed new rules about cleaner gasoline, too. California's example led to cleaner air all over the country.

People in California today are finding new ways to reduce air pollution. Some Californians drive cars that produce no exhaust at all. Others drive cars that run partly on electricity, which is very clean. California still leads the country when it comes to protecting the air.

REVIEW In what way did new laws make air cleaner in southern California?

Today's Challenges

Main Idea As California grows, its people learn to solve new problems.

California is one of the nation's fastest-growing states. The state's growing population needs food, water, homes, transportation, and electricity. Leaders in business and government must find ways to provide these while protecting the environment.

One thing California communities do to meet this challenge is recycle paper, glass, plastic, and metals. To **recycle** means to reuse materials to make new goods. Recycling saves resources. It also keeps trash out of landfills. A **landfill** is a site where trash is buried in the ground. Since 1990, more than 200 million tons of trash have been recycled instead of being put in California's landfills.

Protecting water resources is one of California's biggest challenges. Parts of the state receive lots of rain and snow, but much of California does not. To get water to the homes, farms, and businesses that need it, the state has built a network of dams, aqueducts, and reservoirs.

These projects have changed the environment. Damming wild rivers can harm plants and animals in the watershed. A **watershed** is a region that drains into a river. If people use too much water, not enough sinks into the soil to fill underground water sources. These sources can dry up over time.

People in California try to use water carefully. New technology helps farmers use less water for irrigation. Recycling programs help save water. Individuals are also finding ways to use less water for their daily needs.

California's Water System

A Water System Dams, canals, and other structures bring water to California's people and farms.

Looking Beyond Today

People of all ages can take part in building a better future in California. For example, residents can elect leaders they think will protect the environment. Students who are too young to vote can recycle trash, save water, and write to leaders to express their views.

By learning from the past and taking action today, Californians are preparing for a better tomorrow. A student reading this book today may need to make decisions about how to protect California's environment and how to care for its people. That student might be you!

REVIEW What problems are created by damming rivers?

Lesson Summary

California faces challenges as its population grows. These problems include air pollution and a growing need for water. Citizens are learning from the past to find ways to solve these and other problems.

Why It Matters...

The things you do at home, at school, and in your community can help protect California's environment.

Young Volunteers These Californians are working for a cleaner environment.

Lesson Review

1. **VOCABULARY** Write two sentences that tell ways in which **landfills** are affected by recycling in California.

2. **READING SKILL** Write a paragraph to summarize **solutions** people are using to solve problems facing California. Then include a solution of your own.

3. **MAIN IDEA: Citizenship** In what way did California set an example by reducing its air pollution problem?

4. **MAIN IDEA: Technology** In what ways do Californians conserve water?

5. **CRITICAL THINKING: Apply** Why does a growing population cause a trash problem?

ART ACTIVITY Think of a product that could be made of recycled materials. Draw a picture or make a model of it. Add captions to explain what the product is made of.

1. HSS 4.1.3 2. Analysis Skill HI 1 3. HSS 4.1.3 4. HSS 4.4.7 5. HSS 4.1.3 Activity Analysis Skill HI 4

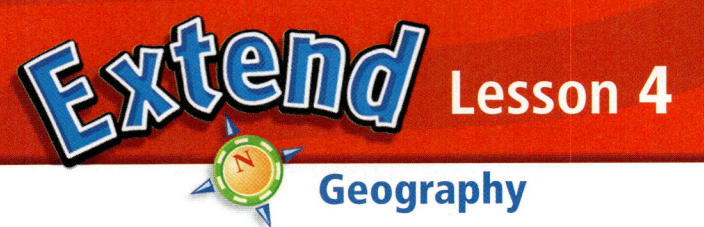

Extend Lesson 4
Geography

Water: A Resource for All

No resource has been more important to California than water. The state's farms, businesses, and cities all needed water to grow. Water is also important to California's wildlife. Fish such as salmon and steelhead need clean, free-flowing rivers to survive.

There are fewer salmon and steelhead in California's rivers today than there were 100 years ago. Pollution has hurt the fish in some places. Dams also block them from swimming upstream. Some Californians are trying to help. Dams have been taken down, and new laws protect the Central Valley watershed. Californians know that water is one resource that all of California depends on.

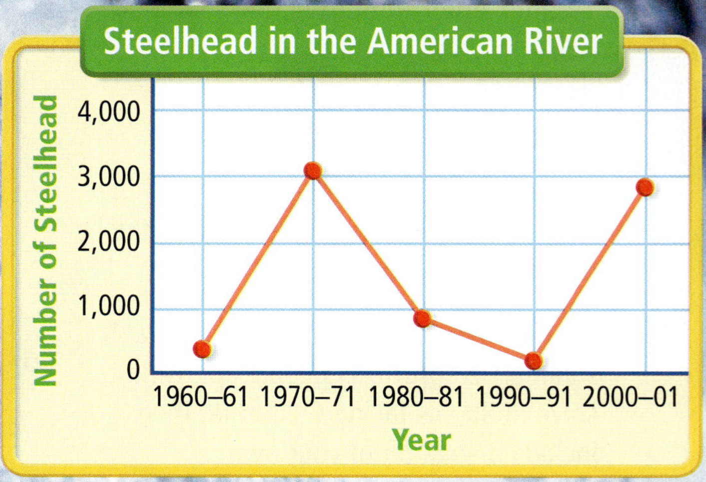

Counting Fish Scientists count the number of steelhead and salmon in the American River to better protect the fish.

GEOGRAPHY

Releasing Fish Volunteers release young steelhead into the American River.

Activities

1. **THINK ABOUT IT** What is the river nearest your home? Think of the times you have seen it and the ways people use it.

2. **WRITE ABOUT IT** What can you do to help protect the environment? Write a short essay about actions that young people could take to improve the environment where you live.

417

Skillbuilder

Resolve Conflicts

When people or groups want different things, they may have a conflict. A **conflict** is a disagreement. To resolve, or settle, a conflict, people need to listen to what each side wants. Sometimes a compromise can resolve a conflict. A **compromise** is a plan that everyone agrees on.

VOCABULARY
conflict
compromise

Learn the Skill

Step 1: Describe the conflict. For example, your class wants to give the school a gift, but you cannot agree on what to give.

Step 2: Allow each group to explain what they want. For example, one group may want to donate musical instruments. Another group may want to buy art supplies for the school.

Step 3: Brainstorm solutions. Look for ways to make the most people happy. For example, the class could give both art supplies and instruments, but less of each.

1) Buy both, but less of each.
2) Ask the principal what the school needs most.
3) Join with another class to give both.

Step 4: Agree on a solution that resolves the conflict. Understand that both sides may have to give something up to reach a compromise.

Apply Critical Thinking

Practice the Skill

Read this passage about a conflict in California. Then answer the questions.

> California redwood forests are home to many plant and animal species. People in California need food, jobs, and places to live. Some people want to cut down redwood forests to build houses, create farmland, and sell timber. Others want to protect the redwood forests.

1. What differences create the conflicts about redwood forests?
2. What are the goals of the people on each side of the conflict?
3. Brainstorm ways that people in both groups can work together to resolve the conflict.

Apply the Skill

Find out about a conflict in your community. Use the steps in Learn the Skill to identify the conflict and the goals of each side. Then suggest possible solutions to the conflict.

Chapter 12 Review

Visual Summary

1–3. Explain what each branch of government does.

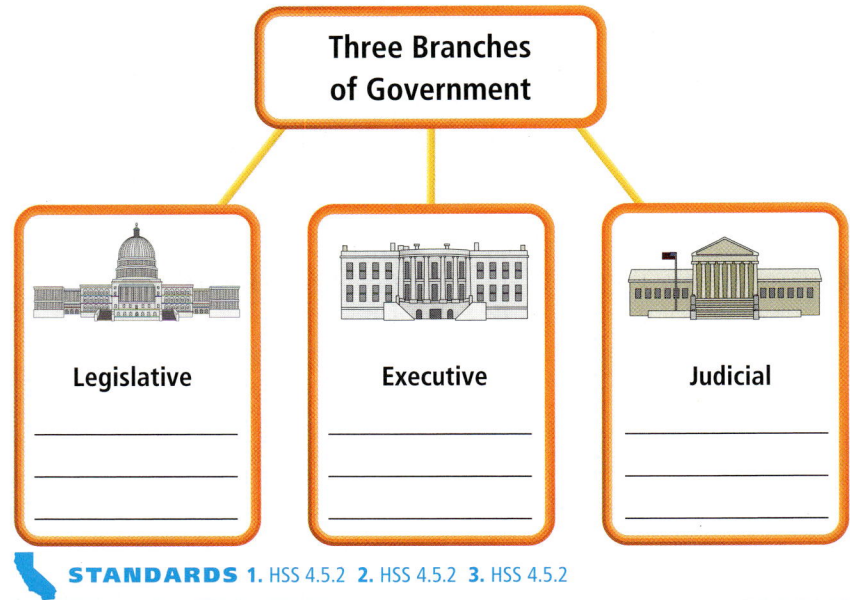

STANDARDS 1. HSS 4.5.2 2. HSS 4.5.2 3. HSS 4.5.2

Facts and Main Ideas

Answer each question below.

4. **Government** What is the written document that describes the structure of the United States government?

5. **Citizenship** Who is the leader of the executive branch of California's government?

6. **Government** In what ways do state and local government help residents?

7. **Geography** What city in California has the highest population density?

8. **Citizenship** What is one way that Californians protect the environment?

4. HSS 4.5.1 5. HSS 4.5.4 6. HSS 4.5.3 7. HSS 4.1.5 8. HSS 4.1.5

Vocabulary

Choose the correct word from the list below to complete each sentence.

democracy, p. 390
rancheria, p. 403
metropolitan area, p. 407

9. A government based on the power of the people is a _____.

10. Los Angeles is part of a large _____.

11. A _____ is land protected for California Indians.

9. HSS 4.5.3 10. HSS 4.1.5 11. HSS 4.5.5

420 • Chapter 12

Apply Skills

Citizenship Skill Read the paragraph below and use what you have learned about resolving conflicts to answer each question.

> The city council may allow a wind farm to be built near our town. A wind farm can supply energy at low cost. Wind farms are clean. They do not cause pollution. Some people do not like the way the windmills look, though. Others worry that the windmills will hurt birds as they migrate. The city council invites residents to a meeting to discuss whether to allow a wind farm in our community.

12. Which is a reason cited for setting up a wind farm?

    A. It can supply energy at low cost.

    B. Everyone likes wind farms.

    C. Wind farms might harm birds.

    D. Wind farms are pretty.

13. What is the city council doing to resolve the wind farm conflict?

    A. It has decided against the wind farm.

    B. It is taking no action at this time.

    C. It is asking other city councils about wind farms.

    D. It is inviting residents to discuss the issue in a meeting.

Critical Thinking

Write a short paragraph to answer the questions below.

14. **Evaluate** What might happen if California's government was not divided into branches with different powers?

15. **Synthesize** Tell how the growing population of California has affected the state's water resources.

16. **Analyze** If California's tourist industry continues to grow, how might it affect the number of service jobs in the state?

12. HSS 4.1.3   13. HSS 4.4.5   14. HSS 4.5.3   15. HSS 4.4.7
16. HSS 4.4.6

Activities

 Art Activity Make a display showing some services that state, local, or county governments provide for the residents of your community.

Writing Activity Describe a job you would like to do when you're older. Tell what industry the job is part of.

Activities HSS 4.5.4, 4.4.6, W 1.2.C

 **Technology**
Writing Process Tips
Get help with your writing at
www.eduplace.com/kids/hmss/

421

UNIT 5 Review

Vocabulary and Main Ideas

✓ Write a sentence to answer each question.

1. Where does money for **public** education come from?
2. In what ways did the **aerospace industry** change after 1957?
3. Why are California's ports important to **international trade**?
4. What is the difference between a **metropolitan area** and a city?

Critical Thinking

✓ Write a short answer for each question. Use details to support your answer.

5. **Apply** What are some ways in which California in the 1950s was different from the way it is today?
6. **Evaluate** In what ways might California's growing population affect Californians in the future?

Apply Skills

✓ **Reading and Thinking Skill** Read the paragraph below and answer the questions.

> Soldiers needed ships and airplanes to win the war. California's shipyards built many ships. One California shipyard could build a ship in just 10 days. California's factories also made airplanes. More airplanes were built in California than in any other state.

7. What can you conclude about California during World War II?

   A. Ships and airplanes built in California were used in the war.
   B. Californians sailed ships and flew airplanes during the war.
   C. There were not enough ships and airplanes in California.
   D. Californians built more ships than airplanes during the war.

8. What conclusion could you draw about California's workers?

   A. There were too many workers.
   B. California workers went to other states for jobs.
   C. Many workers made ships and airplanes.
   D. California was the only state where airplanes were built.

422 • Unit 5

STANDARDS 1. HSS 4.4.8 2. HSS 4.4.6 3. HSS 4.4.6
4. HSS 4.4.4 5. HSS 4.4.4 6. HSS 4.4.4
7. HSS 4.4.5 8. HSS 4.4.5 Activity
Analysis Skill HI 2, W 1.1

Unit Activity

Have a Role Model Round Table

- Choose a person discussed in this unit who would be a good role model.
- Use the form below to write reasons he or she is inspiring.
- In a small group, talk about your choices and the reasons you made them.

> I want to be like Cesar Chavez because:
>
> 1. He fought for what he believed in.
> 2.
> 3.

WEEKLY READER
Current Events

Connect to Today

Create a book about California's arts, culture, government, or environment today.

- Find information from several sources about the area you chose.
- Summarize your information from each source.
- Collect the summaries into a book. Illustrate it with drawings.

Technology
Weekly Reader online offers social studies articles. Go to:
www.eduplace.com/kids/hmss/

At the Library

You may find these books at your school or public library.

Harvesting Hope: The Story of Cesar Chavez by Kathleen Krull

Chavez, an advocate for migrant workers, led marches during the California grape-pickers strike.

Bottle Houses: The Creative World of Grandma Prisbrey by Melissa Eskridge Slaymaker

The author tells the true story of Grandma Prisbrey, who created Bottle Village.

Read About It

Look for these Social Studies Independent Books in your classroom.

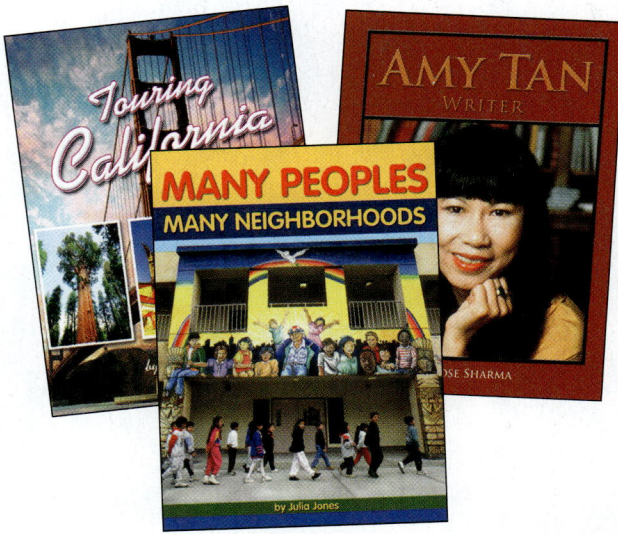

423

References

Citizenship Handbook

Pledge of Allegiance R2
English, Spanish, Tagalog, Russian, Arabic, Chinese

Character Traits R4

California Databank R6

California Immigration R8

California Governors R10

California Counties R12

History Makers—Biographical Dictionary R15

Resources

Geographic Terms R22

Atlas R24

Gazetteer R44

Glossary R50

Index R58

Primary Source References R67

Acknowledgments R71

R1

Pledge of Allegiance

*I pledge allegiance to the flag
of the United States of America
and to the Republic for which it stands,
one Nation under God, indivisible,
with liberty and justice for all.*

Spanish

Prometo lealtad a la bandera de los Estados Unidos de América, y a la república que representa, una nación bajo Diós, indivisible, con libertad y justicia para todos.

Russian

Я даю клятву верности флагу Соединённых Штатов Америки и стране, символом которой он является, народу, единому перед Богом, свободному и равноправному.

Tagalog

Ako ay nanunumpa ng katapatan sa bandila ng Estados Unidos ng Amerika, at sa Republikang kanyang kinakatawan, isang Bansang pumapailalim sa isang Maykapal hindi nahahati, may kalayaan at katarungan para sa lahat.

Arabic

ادين بالولاء لعلم الولايات المتحده الامريكيه والى الجمهوريه التي تمثلها دولة واحدة تؤمن باللة متحدة تمنح الحرية والعدالة للجميع

Chinese

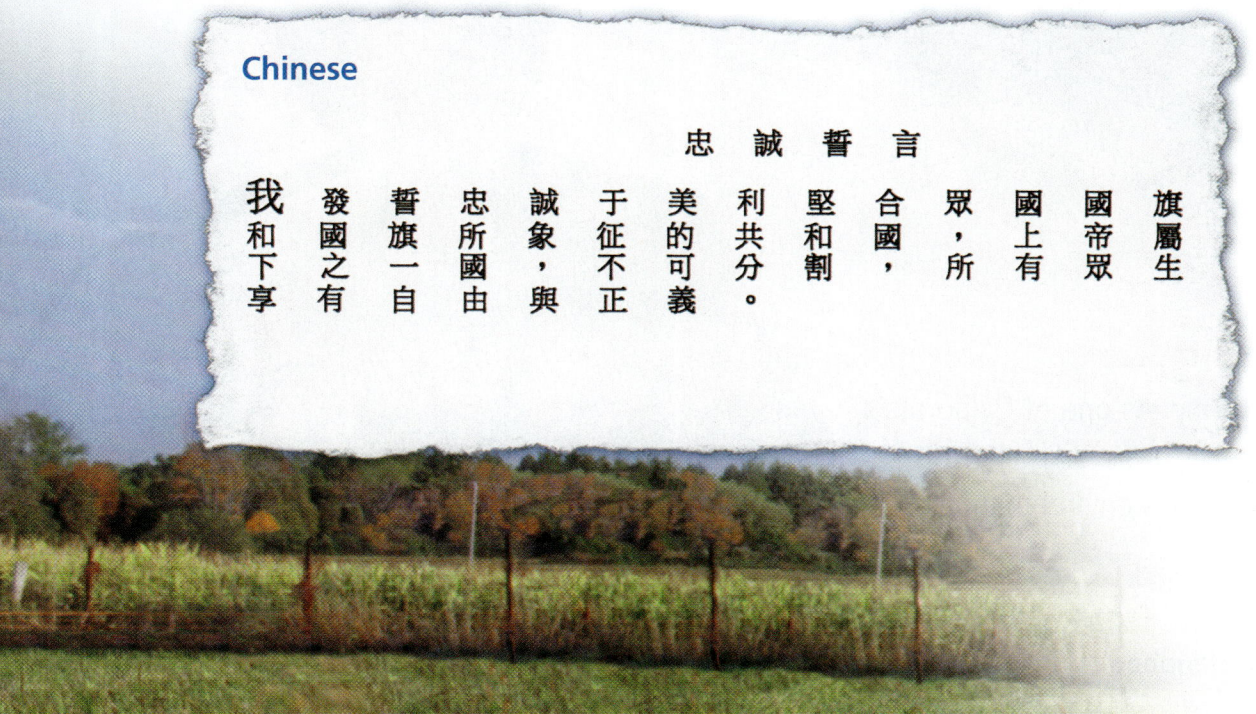

Character Traits

Character includes feelings, thoughts, and behaviors. A character trait is something people show by the way they act. To act bravely shows courage. Courage is one of several character traits.

Positive character traits, such as honesty, caring, and courage, lead to positive actions. Character traits are also called "life skills." Life skills can help you do your best, and doing your best leads to reaching your goals.

Ng Poon Chew
Fairness Chew traveled the United States to tell about unjust treatment of Chinese immigrants.

Barbara Boxer
Responsibility As one of California's senators, Boxer has worked hard to protect the state's environment.

Courage means acting bravely. Doing what you believe to be good and right, and telling the truth, requires courage.

Responsibility is taking care of work that needs to be done. Responsible people are reliable and trustworthy, which means they can be counted on.

Fairness means working to make things fair for everyone. Often one needs to try again and again to achieve fairness. This is diligence, or not giving up.

Caring means noticing what others need and helping them get what they need. Feeling concern or compassion is another way to define caring.

Patriotism means working for the goals of your country. When you show national pride, you are being patriotic.

Respect means paying attention to what other people want and believe. The "golden rule," or treating others as you would like to be treated, shows thoughtfulness and respect.

Civic virtue is good citizenship. It means doing things, such as cooperating and solving problems, to help communities live and work well together.

Character Traits

California Databank

State motto — EUREKA
31 stars for the 31st state
Minerva, goddess of wisdom
California grizzly bear
Miner

California Facts	
Population, 2000	13,871,648
Total Area	163,707 square miles
Economy	**Leading Crops:** Milk, grapes, vegetables, cotton, almonds, hay, tomatoes, beef, cattle, greenhouse and nursery plants **Leading Industries:** Electronic equipment and computers, entertainment, aviation, petroleum, natural gas, mining
Song	"I Love You, California" by F.B. Silverwood
State Nicknames	The Golden State (official), The Land of Milk and Honey, The Grape State, The El Dorado State

California Symbols

State Flower
Golden poppy These flowers grow wild throughout California. They were a source of food for California Indians.

State Animal
California grizzly bear Though none are left today, these animals once lived in many parts of California.

State Fish
Golden trout Once found only in the Kern River, they now live in streams and rivers throughout large areas of the Sierra Nevada.

State Tree
California redwood The tallest trees in the world grow along California's Pacific coast and in the Yosemite Valley.

State Mineral
Gold After it was found at Sutter's Mill in 1848, thousands of people rushed to California. Most hoped to make a quick fortune.

State Gemstone
Benitoite These blue stones are also known as "blue diamonds." They are named for California's San Benito River, where the first one was found.

California Immigration

For thousands of years, California Indians were the only people in California. That changed in 1769, when Spain started a colony in California. Ever since then, people have been moving to California from all over the world.

1769–1840

When Spain started the colony of Alta California in 1769, people from Spain and New Spain, or Mexico, settled along the coast. They brought plants and animals from Spain and from present-day Mexico. Many people who lived in Spanish settlements had ancestors who were American Indian and African as well as Spanish.

1841–1850

Until the late 1840s, California was part of Mexico. Trappers and traders from the United States came to find furs. In 1848, at about the time California became part of the United States, gold was discovered. Thousands of people rushed to California from Europe, Australia, Latin America, China, and the rest of the United States to look for gold.

1851–1900

Many Chinese came to California to build railroads and to work on farms and in factories. After 1890, thousands of people came from Japan and other Asian countries. Europeans came during this period, as well. For example, people from Portugal came and worked in the fishing and dairy industries.

1901–1950

In the early 1900s, Sikhs, Filipinos, Koreans, and Armenians came to California. Italians moved to California's cities, and Russians came to get away from war. In the 1920s, about 300,000 Mexican immigrants came to work on California's farms. In the 1930s, farm families from the midwestern United States moved to California to escape the Dust Bowl.

1951–Today

Since 1965, many skilled workers have immigrated to California to find better jobs. Refugees have come to flee war and violence. Most immigrants today come from Mexico, the Philippines, China, India, El Salvador, Vietnam, Guatemala, Iran, South Korea, and Taiwan. Europeans and people from other parts of the United States continue to come as well.

California Governors

Spanish Governors

Gaspar de Portolá
Term: 1767–1770

Matías de Armona
Term: 1769–1770

Pedro Fages
Term: 1770–1774

Felipe de Barri
Term: 1771–1774

Fernando Rivera y Moncada
Term: 1774–1777

Felipe de Neve
Term: 1775–1782

Pedro Fages
Term: 1782–1791

José Antonio Roméu
Term: 1791–1792

José Joaquín de Arrillaga
Term: 1792–1794

Diego de Borica
Term: 1794–1800

José Joaquín de Arrillaga
Term: 1800–1814

José Darío Argüello
Term: 1814–1815

Pablo Vicente de Solá
Term: 1815–1822

Mexican Governors

Luís Antonio Argüello
Term: 1822–1825

José María Echeandía
Term: 1825–1831

Manuel Victoria
Term: 1831

Pío Pico
Term: 1832

José María Echeandía
Term: 1832–1833

Agustín Juan Vicente Zamorano
Term: 1832–1833

José Figueroa
Term: 1833–1835

Mexican Governors (cont.)

José Castro
Term: 1835–1836

Nicolás Gutiérrez
Term: 1836

Mariano Chico
Term: 1836

Nicolás Gutiérrez
Term: 1836

José Castro
Term: 1836

Juan Bautista Alvarado
Term: 1836–1842

Manuel Micheltorena
Term: 1842–1845

Pío Pico
Term: 1845–1846

José María Flores
Term: 1846–1847

Andrés Pico
Term: 1847

U.S. Military Governors

John Drake Sloat
Term: 1846

Robert Field Stockton
Term: 1846–1847

John Charles Frémont
Term: 1847

Stephen Watts Kearny
Term: 1847

Richard Barnes Mason
Term: 1847–1849

Persifor Frazer Smith
Term: 1849

Bennett Riley
Term: 1849

U.S. State Governors

Peter Hardeman Burnett
Term: 1849–1851
Lifespan: 1807–1895
Birthplace: Nashville, Tennessee

John McDougal
Term: 1851–1852
Lifespan: 1818–1866
Birthplace: Ross County, Ohio

John Bigler
Term: 1852–1856
Lifespan: 1805–1871
Birthplace: Carlisle, Pennsylvania

John Neeley Johnson
Term: 1856–1858
Lifespan: 1825–1872
Birthplace: Johnson Township, Indiana

John B. Weller
Term: 1858–1860
Lifespan: 1812–1875
Birthplace: Montgomery, Ohio

Milton Slocum Latham
Term: 1860
Lifespan: 1827–1882
Birthplace: Columbus, Ohio

John Gately Downey
Term: 1860–1862
Lifespan: 1827–1894
Birthplace: Roscommon County, Ireland

Leland Stanford
Term: 1862–1863
Lifespan: 1824–1893
Birthplace: Watervliet, New York

Frederick Ferdinand Low
Term: 1863–1867
Lifespan: 1828–1894
Birthplace: Frankfort, Maine

Henry Huntley Haight
Term: 1867–1871
Lifespan: 1825–1878
Birthplace: Rochester, New York

Newton Booth
Term: 1871–1875
Lifespan: 1825–1892
Birthplace: Salem, Indiana

U.S. State Governors (cont.)

Romualdo Pacheco
Term: 1875
Lifespan: 1831–1899
Birthplace: Santa Barbara, California

William Irwin
Term: 1875–1880
Lifespan: 1827–1886
Birthplace: Butler County, Ohio

George Clement Perkins
Term: 1880–1883
Lifespan: 1839–1923
Birthplace: Kennebunkport, Maine

George Stoneman
Term: 1883–1887
Lifespan: 1822–1894
Birthplace: Busti, New York

Washington Bartlett
Term: 1887
Lifespan: 1824–1887
Birthplace: Savannah, Georgia

Robert Whitney Waterman
Term: 1887–1891
Lifespan: 1826–1891
Birthplace: Fairfield, New York

Henry Harrison Markham
Term: 1891–1895
Lifespan: 1840–1923
Birthplace: Wilmington, New York

James Herbert Budd
Term: 1895–1899
Lifespan: 1851–1908
Birthplace: Janesville, Wisconsin

Henry Tifft Gage
Term: 1899–1903
Lifespan: 1852–1924
Birthplace: Geneva, New York

George Cooper Pardee
Term: 1903–1907
Lifespan: 1857–1941
Birthplace: San Francisco, California

James Norris Gillett
Term: 1907–1911
Lifespan: 1860–1937
Birthplace: Viroqua, Wisconsin

Hiram Warren Johnson
Term: 1911–1917
Lifespan: 1866–1945
Birthplace: Sacramento, California

William Dennison Stephens
Term: 1917–1923
Lifespan: 1859–1944
Birthplace: Eaton, Ohio

Friend William Richardson
Term: 1923–1927
Lifespan: 1865–1943
Birthplace: Friends Colony, Michigan

Clement Calhoun "C.C." Young
Term: 1927–1931
Lifespan: 1869–1947
Birthplace: Lisbon, New Hampshire

James Rolph, Jr.
Term: 1931–1934
Lifespan: 1869–1934
Birthplace: San Francisco, California

Frank Finley Merriam
Term: 1934–1939
Lifespan: 1865–1955
Birthplace: Hopkinton, Iowa

Culburt Levy Olson
Term: 1939–1943
Lifespan: 1876–1962
Birthplace: Fillmore, Utah

Earl Warren
Term: 1943–1953
Lifespan: 1891–1974
Birthplace: Los Angeles, California

Goodwin Jess Knight
Term: 1953–1959
Lifespan: 1896–1970
Birthplace: Provo, Utah

Edmund Gerald "Pat" Brown, Sr.
Term: 1959–1967
Lifespan: 1905–1996
Birthplace: San Francisco, California

Ronald Wilson Reagan
Term: 1967–1975
Lifespan: 1911–2004
Birthplace: Tampico, Illinois

Edmund Gerald "Jerry" Brown, Jr.
Term: 1975–1983
Lifespan: 1938–
Birthplace: San Francisco, California

George Deukmejian
Term: 1983–1991
Lifespan: 1928–
Birthplace: Menands, New York

Pete Wilson
Term: 1991–1999
Lifespan: 1933–
Birthplace: Lake Forest, Illinois

Joseph Graham "Gray" Davis, Jr.
Term: 1999–2003
Lifespan: 1942–
Birthplace: New York, New York

Arnold Alois Schwarzenegger
Term: 2003–
Lifespan: 1947–
Birthplace: Thal bei Graz, Austria

California Governors

California Counties

County	County Seat	Year Organized	Population	Origin of Name
Alameda	Oakland	1853	1,443,741	from Spanish word meaning "place where trees grow"
Alpine	Markleeville	1864	1,208	origin unknown; may refer to county's mountainous terrain
Amador	Jackson	1854	35,100	Jose Maria Amador started a mining town here in 1848
Butte	Oroville	1850	203,171	for the Marysville or Sutter Buttes
Calaveras	San Andreas	1850	40,554	for the Calaveras River
Colusa	Colusa	1850	18,804	for a California Indian tribe that lived in the area
Contra Costa	Martinez	1850	948,816	for its location across the bay from San Francisco; "contra costa" means "opposite coast" in Spanish
Del Norte	Crescent City	1857	27,507	from Spanish word meaning "north"
El Dorado	Placerville	1850	156,299	for a legendary region of gold and other riches
Fresno	Fresno	1856	799,407	for the ash trees in the area; "fresno" means "ash tree" in Spanish
Glenn	Willows	1891	26,453	for Dr. Hugh J. Glenn, an important California wheat farmer
Humboldt	Eureka	1853	126,518	for explorer Baron Alexander von Humboldt
Imperial	El Centro	1907	142,361	for the Imperial Land Company
Inyo	Independence	1866	17,945	from California Indian word meaning "dwelling place of the great spirit"
Kern	Bakersfield	1866	661,645	for topographer Edward Kern
Kings	Hanford	1893	129,461	for Kings River
Lake	Lakeport	1861	58,309	for the county's many lakes
Lassen	Susanville	1864	33,828	for Mount Lassen, named for Peter Lassen, guide and trapper
Los Angeles	Los Angeles	1850	9,519,338	for the city of Los Angeles; "los angeles" means "the angels" in Spanish

R12 • Citizenship Handbook

County	County Seat	Year Organized	Population	Origin of Name
Madera	Madera	1893	123,109	from Spanish word meaning "timber"
Marin	San Rafael	1850	247,289	may be for Chief Marin of the Licatiut tribe
Mariposa	Mariposa	1850	17,130	from Spanish word meaning "butterfly"
Mendocino	Ukiah	1850	86,265	for the family Mendoza
Merced	Merced	1855	210,554	for the Merced River
Modoc	Alturas	1874	9,449	for the Modoc nation, which was located along the Pit River
Mono	Bridgeport	1861	12,853	for Mono Lake, named for the nearby Monachie nation
Monterey	Salinas	1850	401,762	from a Spanish phrase meaning "king of the forest"
Napa	Napa	1850	124,279	origin unknown; may come from Patwin word meaning "house"
Nevada	Nevada City	1851	92,033	for the mining town of Nevada City
Orange	Santa Ana	1889	2,846,289	for the area's many orange groves
Placer	Auburn	1851	248,399	for placer mining, a method of gold mining
Plumas	Quincy	1854	20,824	for the Feather River; "plumas" means "feathers" in Spanish
Riverside	Riverside	1893	1,545,387	for the city of Riverside
Sacramento	Sacramento	1850	1,223,499	for the Sacramento River
San Benito	Hollister	1874	53,234	for the Catholic saint
San Bernardino	San Bernardino	1853	1,709,434	for the Catholic saint
San Diego	San Diego	1850	2,813,833	for the Catholic saint
San Francisco	San Francisco	1850	776,733	for the Catholic saint
San Joaquin	Stockton	1850	563,598	for the Catholic saint
San Luis Obispo	San Luis Obispo	1850	246,681	for the Catholic saint
San Mateo	Redwood City	1856	707,161	for the Catholic saint
Santa Barbara	Santa Barbara	1850	399,347	for the Catholic saint
Santa Clara	San Jose	1850	1,682,585	for the Catholic saint

California Counties

California Counties

County	County Seat	Year Organized	Population	Origin of Name
Santa Cruz	Santa Cruz	1850	255,602	from Spanish phrase meaning "Holy Cross"
Shasta	Redding	1850	163,256	for the Shasta nation
Sierra	Downieville	1852	3,555	for the Sierra Nevada
Siskiyou	Yreka	1852	44,301	for the Siskiyou Mountain Range
Solano	Fairfield	1850	394,542	for Chief Solano, whose people lived in the area
Sonoma	Santa Rosa	1850	458,614	from a Chocuyen name meaning "valley of the moon"
Stanislaus	Modesto	1854	446,997	for the Stanislaus River
Sutter	Yuba City	1850	78,930	for John Sutter, who received a large land grant from Mexico
Tehama	Red Bluff	1856	56,039	for the city of Tehama
Trinity	Weaverville	1850	13,022	for the Trinity River
Tulare	Visalia	1852	368,021	for the tule plants that grow here
Tuolumne	Sonora	1850	54,501	origin unknown; may mean "many stone houses," "land of mountain lions," or "very steep"
Ventura	Ventura	1872	753,197	for Mission San Buenaventura, shortened to Ventura
Yolo	Woodland	1850	168,660	origin unknown; may refer to the Yo-loy tribe, Chief Yodo, or the village Yodoi
Yuba	Marysville	1850	60,219	for Spanish word meaning "grape"

Biographical Dictionary

The page number after each entry refers to the place where the person is first mentioned. For more complete references to people, see the Index.

A

Adams, Ansel 1902–1984, photographer known for his pictures of Yosemite (page 17).

Allen, Jane Bushton 19th c., forty-niner who came from England and ran a boarding house in Monterey (page 193).

Allensworth, Allen 1842–1914, founder of Allensworth, a town settled by African Americans (page 257).

Anza, Juan Bautista de 1736–1788, Spanish soldier who led soldiers and settlers overland to Alta California (page 108).

Argüello, Luís Antonio 1784–1830, first leader of California under Mexican rule, 1822–1825 (page 127).

Argüello, Maria de la Concepción 1791–1857, Californio woman known for her work for the poor (page 131).

Armstrong, Neil 1930–, astronaut who became the first person to set foot on the moon (page 337).

Austin, Mary 1868–1934, author of many books about the West and Southwest.

B

Baker, Lily Maidu basket weaver (page 61).

Ball, Lucille 1911–1989, star of the popular television series, "I Love Lucy" (page 340).

Ballou, Mary 19th c., keeper of a boarding house in a mining town during the Gold Rush (page 154).

Bandini-Stearns-deBaker, Arcadia 1825?–1912, wealthy Californio landowner who helped build Los Angeles (page 160).

Bartleson, John 19th c., pioneer who helped lead one of the first groups of settlers from the United States overland to California (page 140).

Bass, Charlotta 1880?–1969, civil rights activist who edited and published the *California Eagle* newspaper.

Beckwourth, James 1798–1867, trapper and trader who found the lowest pass through the Sierra Nevada (page 139).

Beechey, Frederick William 1796–1852, explorer of the North Pacific who visited San Francisco in 1826 (page 130).

James Beckwourth

Bering, Vitus 1681–1741, Danish explorer for Russia who was among the first Europeans to sail to Alaska (page 90).

Bidwell, John 1819–1900, pioneer who led one of the first groups of settlers from the United States overland to California (page 140).

Black, Shirley Temple *See* Temple, Shirley.

Boxer, Barbara 1940–, one of California's United States senators.

Bradley, Tom 1917–1998, first African American mayor of Los Angeles, who was elected to the office five times (page 344).

Brannan, Sam 1819–1889, pioneer who helped found San Francisco (page 173).

Briones de Miranda, Juana 1802–1889, landowner and ranchera in San Francisco and Palo Alto.

Burbank, Luther 1849–1926, scientist who created over 800 new types of plants (page 261).

Burke, Yvonne Braithwaite 1932–, first African American woman elected to the Calfornia State Assembly (page 404).

Bush, George H. W. 1924–, 41st President of the United States, 1989–1993 (page 321).

Luther Burbank

Butterfield, John 1801–1869, creator of the Overland Mail Company (page 228).

R15

Cabrillo, Juan Rodriguez

Cabrillo, Juan Rodríguez 1500?–1543, Spanish explorer who led the first European expedition to Alta California (page 82).

Chaffey, George 1848–1932, engineer and investor who built canals in the Imperial Valley (page 266).

Chavez, Cesar 1927–1993, labor leader who worked to improve conditions for migrant farm workers (page 346).

Chew, Ng Poon 1866–1931, Chinese immigrant and newspaper publisher who fought against prejudice toward Chinese Americans (page 258).

Cisneros, Evelyn 1959–, first Hispanic woman to become lead dancer at a major American ballet company (page 380).

Clapp, Louise 1819–1906, author of *The Shirley Letters*, which describes life in California mining towns (page 181).

Clemens, Samuel Langhorne (Mark Twain) 1835–1910, author of many books and stories, including *The Celebrated Jumping Frog of Calaveras County*.

Columbus, Christopher 1451–1506, European explorer who reached the Americas in 1492 (page 80).

Cook, James 1728–1779, British explorer who mapped the northern Pacific coast of North America (page 91).

Cortés, Hernán 1485–1547, conquistador who claimed Mexico and Baja California for Spain (page 81).

Crespi, Juan 1721–1782, missionary who recorded the events of Gaspar de Portolá's expedition in his diary (page 92).

Crocker, Charles 1822–1888, an owner of the Central Pacific Railroad Company that helped build the first transcontinental railroad (page 233).

Crowley, Patrick 19th c., chief of police in San Francisco from 1866 to 1897 (page 209).

Dana, Richard Henry, Jr. 1815–1882, sailor who wrote about his visit to California in *Two Years Before the Mast* (page 138).

Davis, Gray 1942–, governor of California, 1999–2003.

DeMille, Cecil B. 1881–1959, early film director who co-founded Paramount Pictures.

Dinh, Viet 1968–, Vietnamese immmigrant to Fullerton who became Assistant Attorney General (page 359).

Disney, Walt 1901–1966, creator of popular cartoon characters who built Disneyland theme park in Anaheim (page 341).

Dixon, Lafayette Maynard 1875–1946, artist who created large landscapes of the Southwest.

Dominguez, Manuel 1803–1882, delegate to California's Constitutional Convention (page 200).

Donner, George 1784–1847, brother of Jacob Donner and organizer of the Donner Party.

Donner, Jacob 1781?–1846, brother of George Donner and organizer of the Donner Party.

Drake, Francis 1540?–1596, English sailor who landed in California after attacking Spanish ships for treasure (page 83).

Echeandía, José María ?–1871?, governor of Mexican California, 1825–1831 and 1831–1833.

Edson, Katherine Philips 1870–1933, Los Angeles suffragist leader and activist for labor rights (page 292).

Elizabeth I 1533–1603, queen of England when Francis Drake landed in California (page 83).

Eu, March Fong 1922–, first Asian American elected to the California State Assembly (page 405).

Katherine Philips Edson

Jackson, Ida Louise

Feinstein, Dianne 1933–, former mayor of San Francisco and the first woman elected to the United States Senate from California (page 314).

Ford, Henry 1863–1947, engineer who designed the first mass-produced automobile, the Model T Ford (page 298).

Francisco, John Bond 1863–1931, co-founder and conductor of the Los Angeles Symphony Orchestra.

Frémont, Jesse Benton 1813–1890, author and civic leader who wrote and spoke about events in California's history; wife of John Frémont (page 165).

Frémont, John Charles 1813–1890, explorer who helped lead the Bear Flag Revolt; military governor of California; husband of Jesse Frémont (page 139).

John C. Frémont

Gabaldón, Guy Louis 1927–, World War II hero from Los Angeles (page 323).

Gálvez, José de 1720–1787, official in New Spain who planned Gaspar de Portolá's expedition to Alta California (page 91).

Gandhi, Mahatma 1869–1948, leader of nonviolent protests in Asia and Africa (page 351).

Garland, Judy 1928–1969, movie actress and singer best known for her role in *The Wizard of Oz* (page 324).

Geisel, Theodore S. 1904–1991, children's book author better known as Dr. Seuss.

George, Ronald M. 1940–, Chief Justice of the Supreme Court of California, 1996– (page 401).

Ghirardelli, Domenico "Domingo" 1817–1894, immigrant entrepreneur who became successful by starting a chocolate company in San Francisco (page 192).

Gibbs, Mifflin Wistar 1823–1915, entrepreneur and African American community leader in San Francisco (page 208).

Glenn, John 1921–, astronaut who became the first American to orbit the Earth and later became a United States senator (page 336).

Graves, Mary 1826–1891, member of the Donner party who survived (page 141).

Guerrero, Vicente 1782–1831, rebel leader in the Mexican War for Independence (page 119).

Hawk, Tony 1968–, world champion skateboarder from San Diego (page 377).

Hearst, Phoebe Apperson 1842–1919, founder of the first public (free) kindergarten in the United States.

Hidalgo y Costilla, Miguel 1753–1811, Mexican priest known as the father of Mexican independence (page 119).

Hoover, Herbert 1874–1964, 31st President of the United States, 1929–1933, founder of the Hoover Institution at Stanford University (page 389).

Hopkins, Mark 1813–1878, treasurer of the Central Pacific Railroad Company (page 233).

Huerta, Dolores 1930–, labor leader and co-founder of the United Farm Workers (page 346).

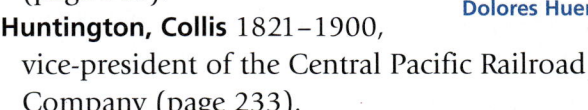
Dolores Huerta

Huntington, Collis 1821–1900, vice-president of the Central Pacific Railroad Company (page 233).

Hyung-soon, Kim Korean immigrant who owned orchards in California (page 254).

Iturbide, Agustín de 1783–1824, officer during the Mexican War for Independence and Emperor of Mexico (page 120).

Jackson, Helen Hunt 1830–1885, author of *Ramona*, a novel about injustice toward California Indians (page 204).

Jackson, Ida Louise 1902–1996, first African American public school teacher in Oakland.

Jeffers, Robinson 1887–1962, poet who lived in Carmel.
Jewett, William Smith 1789–1874, San Francisco artist who painted many wealthy and well-known people (page 161).
Jobs, Steven 1955–, co-founder of Apple Computers, Inc. (page 370).
Johnson, Eliza Steen 1824–1899, Gold Rush entrepreneur who ran a clothing shop in San Francisco (page 192).
Johnson, Hiram 1866–1945, governor of California, 1911–1917; United States senator, 1917–1945 (page 290).

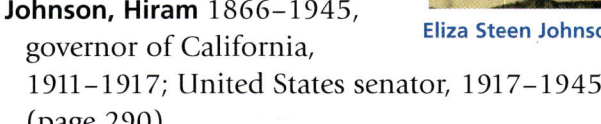

Eliza Steen Johnson

Jones, Julie Rodriguez artist who worked in science for many years and now creates images of outer space, as well as other subjects. (page 377).
Judah, Theodore 1826–1863, engineer who planned the first transcontinental railroad (page 233).

Kaiser, Henry J. 1882–1967, California shipyard owner (page 322).
Kanamori, Hiroo 1936–, earthquake scientist who helps improve building safety (page 282).
Kearny, Stephen W. 1794–1848, United States Army general who led battles in California during the Mexican-American War (page 168).
King, Martin Luther, Jr. 1929–1968, civil rights leader who practiced nonviolent protest (page 345).
Kintpuash 1837?–1873, Modoc leader who fought against the United States Army after the Modoc were forced to leave their land (page 216).
Kwan, Michelle 1980–, Olympic champion figure skater from Torrance (page 377).

Lam, Tony city councilman in Westminster who was the first Vietnamese American to be elected to office in the United States (page 359).

Lange, Dorothea 1895–1965, photographer known for pictures of workers and farmers during the Great Depression (page 306).
Leidesdorff, William 1818–1848, African American businessman and early supporter of public education in California (page 364).
Lester, Peter 1824?–?, co-owner of the Pioneer Boot and Shoe Emporium in San Francisco in the early 1850s (page 208).
Lincoln, Abraham 1809–1865, 16th President of the United States, 1861–1865 (page 229)
Lindbergh, Charles 1902–1974, first pilot to fly alone non-stop from New York City to Paris (page 297).
London, Jack 1876–1916, San Francisco-born author of stories such as *The Call of the Wild* and *White Fang*.
Loughead, Allan 1889–1969, co-founder of airplane manufacturing company later called Lockheed Aircraft (page 297).
Loughead, Malcolm 1887–1958, co-founder of airplane manufacturing company later called Lockheed Aircraft (page 297).
Lucas, George 1944–, film director who wrote and directed the Star Wars trilogy (page 376).

Marshall, James 1810–1885, lead carpenter at Sutter's Mill when gold was discovered (page 172).
Martinez, Rueben 1940–, owner of Spanish language bookstores who promotes literacy in California; winner of a MacArthur Fellowship (page 315).
Mason, Bridget "Biddy" 1818–1891, one of the first African American women to own property in Los Angeles (page 202).
Matthews, Miriam 1905–2003, first African American librarian in the Los Angeles Public Library system (page 314).
Mayer, Louis B. 1885?–1957, head of MGM studios for 24 years (page 297).
Megquier, Mary Jane 1813–1899, forty-niner who ran a boarding house in San Francisco and wrote about events of the period.

R18 • Citizenship Handbook

Merritt, Ezekiel 19th c., trapper and settler who helped lead the Bear Flag Revolt (page 162).

Miller, Henry 1827–1916, landowner who irrigated thousands of acres of land along the San Joaquin River (page 262).

Molina, Gloria 1948–, first Hispanic woman elected to the California State Assembly (page 400).

Morelos, José María 1765–1815, rebel leader in the Mexican War for Independence (page 119).

Morgan, Julia 1872–1957, San Francisco architect who designed hundreds of buildings (page 377).

Morse, Samuel F. B. 1791–1872, inventor of the telegraph and Morse Code (page 229).

Muir, John 1838–1914, conservationist who founded the Sierra Club (page 17).

Mulholland, William 1855–1935, chief engineer of the Los Angeles Aqueduct (page 270).

Narjot, Ernest 1826–1898, French artist who painted landscapes, portraits, and murals in California.

Neve, Felipe de 1728–1784, governor of Alta California who founded the first pueblos there (page 110).

Ngoy, Bun Tek Cambodian immigrant and businessman (page 359).

Nixon, Richard 1913–1994, 37th President of the United States, born in Yorba Linda, California (page 389).

Noguchi, Isamu 1904–1988, artist from Los Angeles famous for sculptures, playgrounds, and parks (page 377).

Nolan, Mae Ella 1886–1973, first California woman elected to the United States House of Representatives (page 293).

Norris, Frank 1870–1902, San Francisco author who wrote *The Octopus*.

Ochoa, Ellen 1958–, first Hispanic woman astronaut (page 315).

Ontiveros, Juan and Martina Californio ranchers who owned Rancho San Juan Cajon de Santa Ana (page 215).

Owings, Margaret 1913–1999, California environmentalist (page 17).

Philip II 1527–1598, king of Spain who ordered exploration of North America (page 83).

Pickford, Mary 1892–1979, movie star and producer in the early 1900s (page 300).

Pico, Andrés 1810–1876, Mexican army general during the Mexican-American War in California; Californio leader and state senator (page 168).

Pico, Pío 1801–1894, Californio ranchero and governor of Mexican California 1845–1846 (page 143).

Pleasant, Mary Ellen 1814?–1904, activist who fought for equal rights for African Americans in San Francisco (page 246).

Pío Pico

Polk, James K. 1795–1849, 11th President of the United States, 1845–1849, during the Mexican-American War and start of the Gold Rush (page 161).

Pollar, Odette African American entrepreneur.

Portolá, Gaspar de 1723?–1784?, Spanish soldier who led an expedition to settle Alta California; first governor of California 1767–1770 (page 92).

Reagan, Ronald 1911–2004, California governor and 40th President of the United States (page 389).

Reynoso, Cruz 1931–, first Hispanic to serve on California's State Supreme Court (page 405).

Rezanov, Count Nikolai 1764–1807, Russian trader who brought Alaskan furs to Spanish California (page 131).

Riley, Bennett 1787–1853, military governor of California who organized 1849 constitutional convention that planned a state government (page 199).

Risling, David 1921–, co-founder of the Native American Rights Fund, a legal service (page 69).

Roberts, Frederick 1880–1952, first African American elected to the California State Assembly (page 399).

Robles, Mitchell E. 1955–, Chumash painter from Santa Barbara (page 68).

Rockwood, Charles 1860–1922, engineer who designed the Imperial Valley's first canal (page 266).

Rodia, Sabato 1879–1965, Italian immigrant who created the Watts Towers (page 362).

Roosevelt, Franklin D. 1882–1945, 32nd President of the United States, 1933–1945, creator of the New Deal (page 306).

Roosevelt, Theodore 1858–1919, 26th President of the United States, 1901–1909, who started national park system (page 19).

Royce, Sarah 1819–1891, forty-niner who published her memories of Gold Rush life.

Ruef, Abraham 1864–1936, San Francisco political leader who was sent to jail for taking bribes.

Ruiz de Burton, María Amparo 1832–1895, first Hispanic author to publish a novel in English in the United States (page 215).

Ruiz de Rodriguez, Bernarda 1802–1880, peacemaker who helped write the treaty that ended fighting in California during the Mexican-American War (page 168).

Saint James, Synthia 1949–, artist and author who has written or illustrated many books (page 381).

Saroyan, William 1908–1981, Armenian American writer who grew up in Fresno (page 246).

Saubel, Katherine Siva 1920–, Cahuilla scholar and teacher who works to preserve Cahuilla language and culture (page 69).

Katherine Siva Saubel

Schmitz, Eugene 1864?–1928, mayor of San Francisco, 1902–1907, who was sent to jail for taking bribes.

Schwarzenegger, Arnold 1947–, actor and governor of California, 2003– (page 401).

Semple, Robert 1807?–1854, leader at first constitutional convention in California and founder of the state's first newspaper (page 200).

Serra, Junípero 1713–1784, Spanish missionary who started nine missions in California (page 92).

Shan, Hwui 5th c., Buddhist monk who sailed east from China in 458 C.E. and returned with stories of lands across the Pacific.

Shima, George 1864–1926, Japanese immigrant who created new farming methods and became known as "the Potato King" (page 263).

Simons, Grace 20th c., Los Angeles suffragist leader (page 293).

George Shima

Situ, Mian 1953–, Chinese artist who paints historical scenes of life in the western United States (page 236).

Sloat, John D. 1781–1867, leader in the United States Navy who claimed California for the United States on July 7, 1846 (page 167).

Smith, Anna Deveare 1950–, San Francisco playwright and actress; winner of a MacArthur Fellowship.

Smith, Jedediah Strong 1799–1831, explorer and trapper who was the first American to reach California by land and cross the Sierra Nevada (page 139).

Stanford, Leland 1824–1893, president of the Central Pacific Railroad Company; governor of California, 1862–1863; United States senator, 1885–1893 (page 233).

Stearns, Abel 1798–1871, merchant and ranchero who took part in the state constitutional convention of 1849 (page 160).

Steinbeck, John 1902–1968, author from Salinas who wrote *The Grapes of Wrath* (page 306).

Stockton, Robert 1795–1866, military governor of California, 1846–1847; United States senator, 1851–1853 (page 167).

Strauss, Joseph B. 1870–1938, chief engineer of the Golden Gate Bridge (page 308).

Strauss, Levi 1829–1902, San Francisco business owner who created denim blue jeans (page 192).

Sutter, John Augustus 1803–1880, pioneer who founded New Helvetia, where gold was later found (page 142).

Swett, John 1830–1913, educator who founded California's system of free public education (page 364).

Tan, Amy 1952–, Chinese American author, creator of the television show *Sagwa* (page 381).

Temple, Shirley 1928–, child actress from Santa Monica who later became a United States ambassador (page 306).

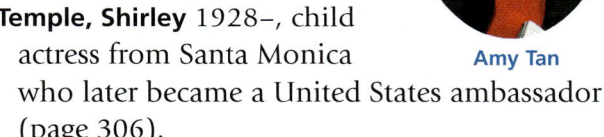
Amy Tan

Terman, Frederick 1900–1982, head of Stanford University; started a research park that led to the creation of Silicon Valley (page 371).

Tibbets, Eliza and Luther Calvin 1825–1898 and 1820–1902, grew some of the first navel orange trees in California (page 261).

Tompkins, Rosie Lee 1936–, African American artist who makes quilts (page 377).

Toypurina 1761?–?, Tongva woman who planned a revolt against Mission San Gabriel (page 102).

Ulloa, Francisco de ?–1540, Spanish explorer of Mexico's Pacific coast (page 88).

Vallejo, Mariano Guadalupe 1808–1890, Mexican officer, ranchero, and Californio civic leader (page 133).

Mariano Vallejo

Vizcaíno, Sebastián 1550?–1628?, Spanish explorer who mapped the California coast and found Monterey Bay (page 84).

Vuich, Rose A. 1927?–2001, first female California State Senator, 1976–1991 (page 404).

Wakefield, Lucy Stoddard 19th c., Gold Rush entrepreneur who baked and sold pies (page 192).

Walker, Joseph 1798–1876, trapper and trader who explored California and found Walker Pass (page 148).

Wayne, John 1907–1979, actor from southern California who is best known for roles in Western films (page 324).

Weber, Charles 1814–1881, German immigrant who founded the town of Stockton in 1849 (page 207).

Wiggin, Kate Douglas 1856–1923, author and educator who opened the first free kindergarten in the western United States.

Wilson, Brian 1942–, California composer, producer, and singer in the Beach Boys, a 1960s rock and roll group (page 377).

Wilson, Luzena Stanley 1820?–?, entrepreneur who opened a hotel in the gold mining town of Nevada City (page 193).

Woods, Daniel B. 19th c., forty-niner and teacher from Pennsylvania who published his diary of life during the Gold Rush (page 185).

Woods, Eldrick "Tiger" 1975–, golfer from Cypress who became the first person to hold all four major golfing championships at the same time.

Wozniak, Stephen 1950–, computer designer and co-founder of Apple Computers, Inc. (page 370).

Yeager, Charles E. "Chuck" 1923–, United States Air Force pilot who was the first person to fly faster than the speed of sound (page 332).

Yorba, Maria de los Delores Ontiveros 1833–1894, ranchera from the area of present-day Santa Ana (page 133).

Geographic Terms

basin
a round area surrounded by higher land

bay
part of a lake or ocean that is partially enclosed by land

canyon
a valley with steep cliffs shaped by erosion

cape
a piece of land that points out into a body of water

coast
the land next to a sea or ocean

coastal plain
a flat area of land near an ocean

delta
land that is formed by soil deposited near the mouth of a river

desert
a dry region with little vegetation

fault
a break or crack in the earth's surface

glacier
a large mass of ice that slowly moves down a mountain or over land

hill
a raised area of land, smaller than a mountain

island
an area of land surrounded by water

isthmus
a narrow piece of land connecting two larger land areas

lake
a large body of water surrounded by land

mountain
a raised mass of land with steep slopes

mountain pass
a gap or low place between mountains

ocean
a large body of salt water that covers much of the earth's surface

peninsula
a strip of land surrounded by water on three sides

plain
a large area of flat or nearly flat land

plateau
a high, flat area of land surrounded by lower land

port
a sheltered part of a lake or ocean where ships can dock

prairie
a flat area of grassland with few trees

river
a body of water that flows from a high area to a lower area

river basin
an area that is drained by a river

strait
a channel that connects two larger bodies of water

tributary
a river or stream that flows into another river

valley
a low area of land between hills or mountains

volcano
an opening in the earth's surface through which melted rock and gases escape

wetland
an area that is soaked with water, such as a marsh or a swamp

R23

Atlas

The World: Political

ALB.	—Albania
AZER.	—Azerbaijan
BOS. & HERZ.	—Boznia & Herzegovina
CEN. AFR. REP.	—Central African Republic
DEM. REP. OF CONGO	—Democratic Republic of Congo
FR.	—France
IT.	—Italy
LIECH.	—Liechtenstein
LUX.	—Luxembourg
NETH.	—Netherlands
N.Z.	—New Zealand
REP. OF CONGO	—Republic of Congo
SERB. & MONT.	—Serbia & Montenegro
SLOV.	—Slovenia
SWITZ.	—Switzerland
U.A.E.	—United Arab Emirates
U.K.	—United Kingdom
U.S.	—United States

R24 • Resources

The World: Physical

ARCTIC OCEAN
Barents Sea
Arctic Circle
Iceland
EUROPE
North Sea
Central Siberian Plateau
Yenisey River
Ob River
Volga River
Danube River
Alps
Pyrenees
ASIA
Lake Baikal
Amur River
Sea of Okhotsk
Kamchatka Peninsula
Gobi Desert
Aral Sea
Caspian Sea
Mt. Elbrus 18,510 ft.
Black Sea
Caucasus Mountains
Sea of Japan
Huang He
Strait of Gibraltar
Atlas Mtns.
Mediterranean Sea
Plateau of Tibet
Himalaya Mountains
Mt. Everest 29,035 ft.
Chang Jiang
East China Sea
PACIFIC OCEAN
Tropic of Cancer
SAHARA
Red Sea
Ganges River
SAHEL
Nile River
Niger River
Arabian Sea
Bay of Bengal
South China Sea
Philippine Islands
Micronesia
AFRICA
Congo River
Lake Victoria
Mt. Kilimanjaro 19,340 ft.
Great Rift Valley
Sumatra
Borneo
Equator
Melanesia
New Guinea
Java
Strait of Sunda
Prime Meridian
INDIAN OCEAN
Coral Sea
Madagascar
Great Sandy Desert
Kalahari Desert
Tropic of Capricorn
AUSTRALIA
ATLANTIC OCEAN
Nullarbor Plain
Darling River
Tasman Sea
Cape of Good Hope
Mt. Kosciusko 7,310 ft.
North Island
South Island
SOUTHERN OCEAN
Antarctic Circle
ANTARCTICA
0
20E
40E
60E
80E
100E
120E
140E
160E
80N
60N
40N
20N
0
20S
60S

SOUTHERN OCEAN
Antarctic Circle
Antarctic Peninsula
Waddell Sea
Prime Meridian
ANTARCTICA
Vinson Massif 16,067 ft.
South Pole
Transantarctic Mountains
Ross Sea
SOUTHERN OCEAN
30W
30E
60W
60E
90W
90E
120W
120E
150W
150E
180
80S
70S
60S
km 0 300 600
mi 0 300 600

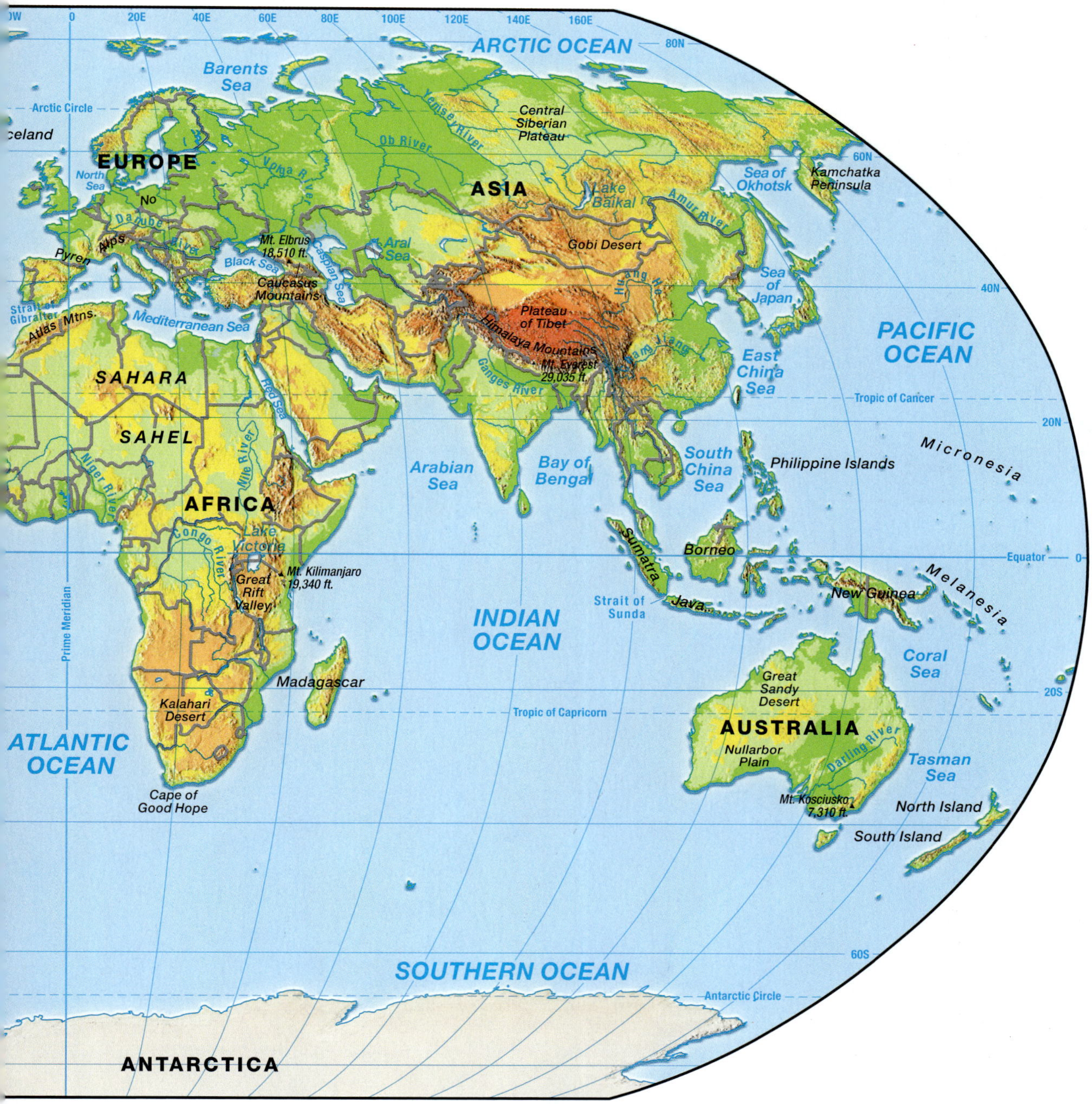

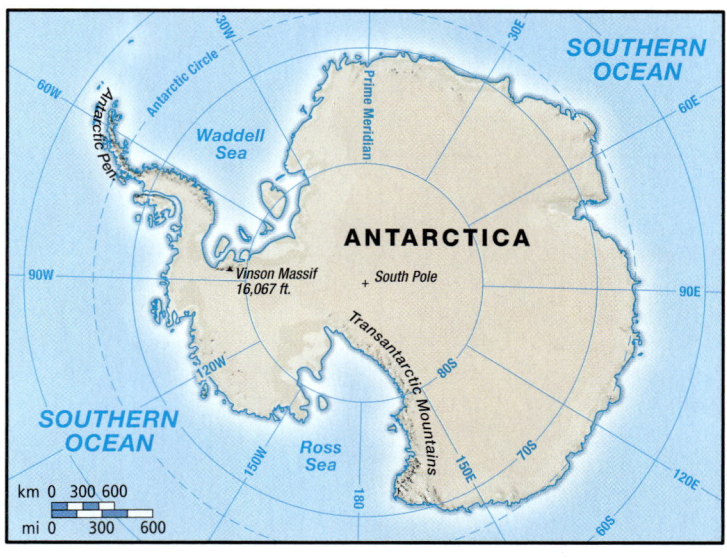

United States: Political

Atlas

Alaska inset
- ARCTIC OCEAN
- RUSSIA
- ALASKA
- Yukon River
- Fairbanks
- CANADA
- Anchorage
- Juneau
- Aleutian Islands
- PACIFIC OCEAN
- km 0 250 500
- mi 0 250 500

Legend
- ⊛ National capital
- ★ State capital
- • Major city
- ── National boundary
- ── State boundary

Main map labels
- Seattle
- Olympia ★
- WASHINGTON
- Portland
- Columbia R.
- ★ Salem
- OREGON
- Helena ★
- MONTANA
- Billings
- IDAHO
- ★ Boise
- Pocatello
- Snake River
- WYOMING
- Casper
- Cheyenne ★
- Sacramento ★
- San Francisco
- Reno
- Carson City ★
- NEVADA
- Salt Lake City ★
- Provo
- UTAH
- COLORADO
- Denver ★
- Colorado Springs
- Pueblo
- CALIFORNIA
- Las Vegas
- Colorado River
- Los Angeles
- San Diego
- ARIZONA
- ★ Phoenix
- Tucson
- Santa Fe ★
- Albuquerque
- NEW MEXICO
- El Paso
- Rio Grande
- PACIFIC OCEAN
- Gulf of California
- MEXICO

Hawaii inset
- HAWAII
- Kauai
- Niihau
- Oahu
- Kailua
- Honolulu
- Molokai
- Lanai
- Maui
- Kahoolawe
- Hilo
- Hawaii
- PACIFIC OCEAN
- km 0 50 100
- mi 0 50 100

R28 • Resources

R29

United States: Physical

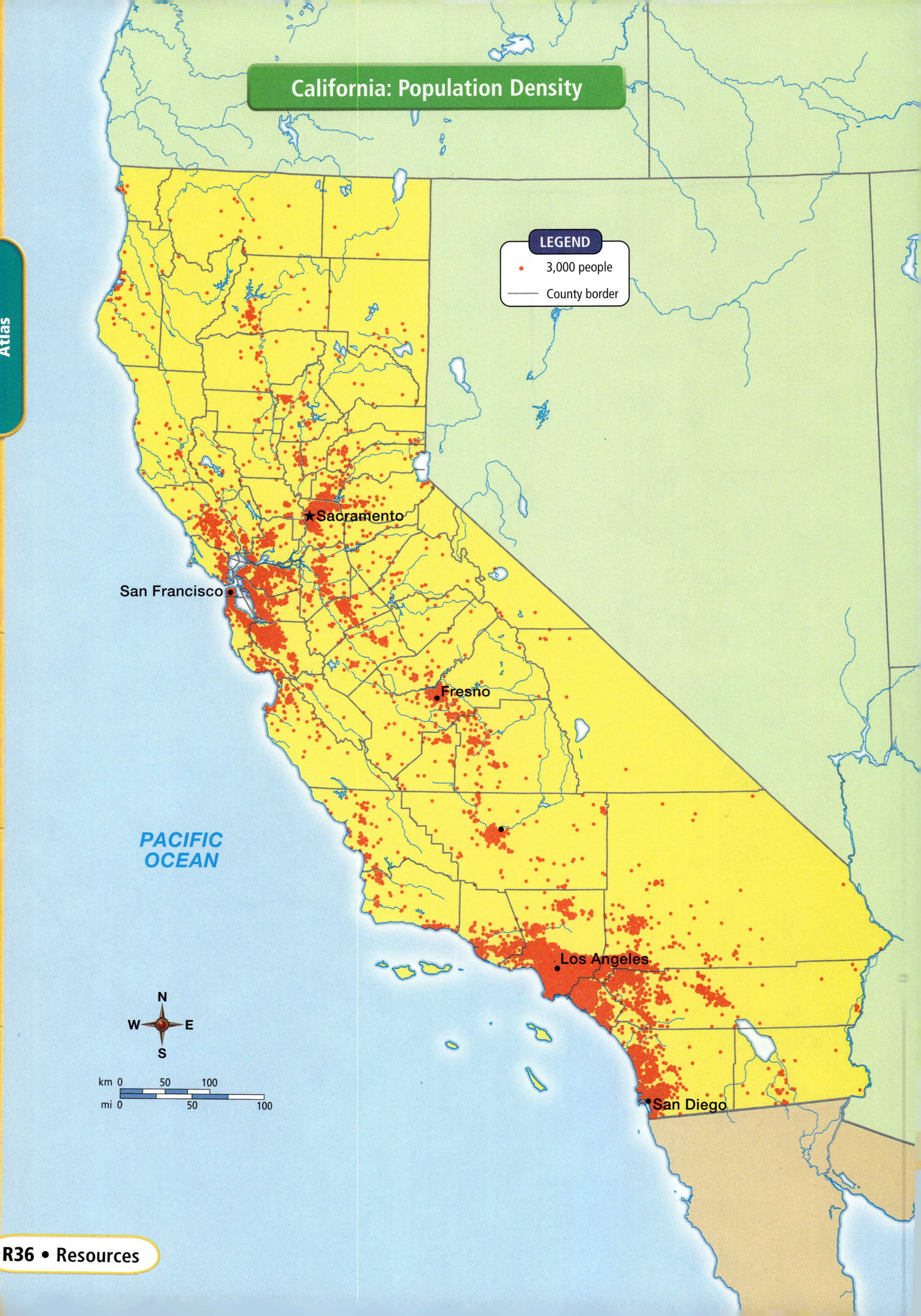

California: Population Density
LEGEND
3,000 people
County border
Sacramento
San Francisco
Fresno
Los Angeles
San Diego
PACIFIC OCEAN
N
S
W
E
km 0 50 100
mi 0 50 100

Atlas

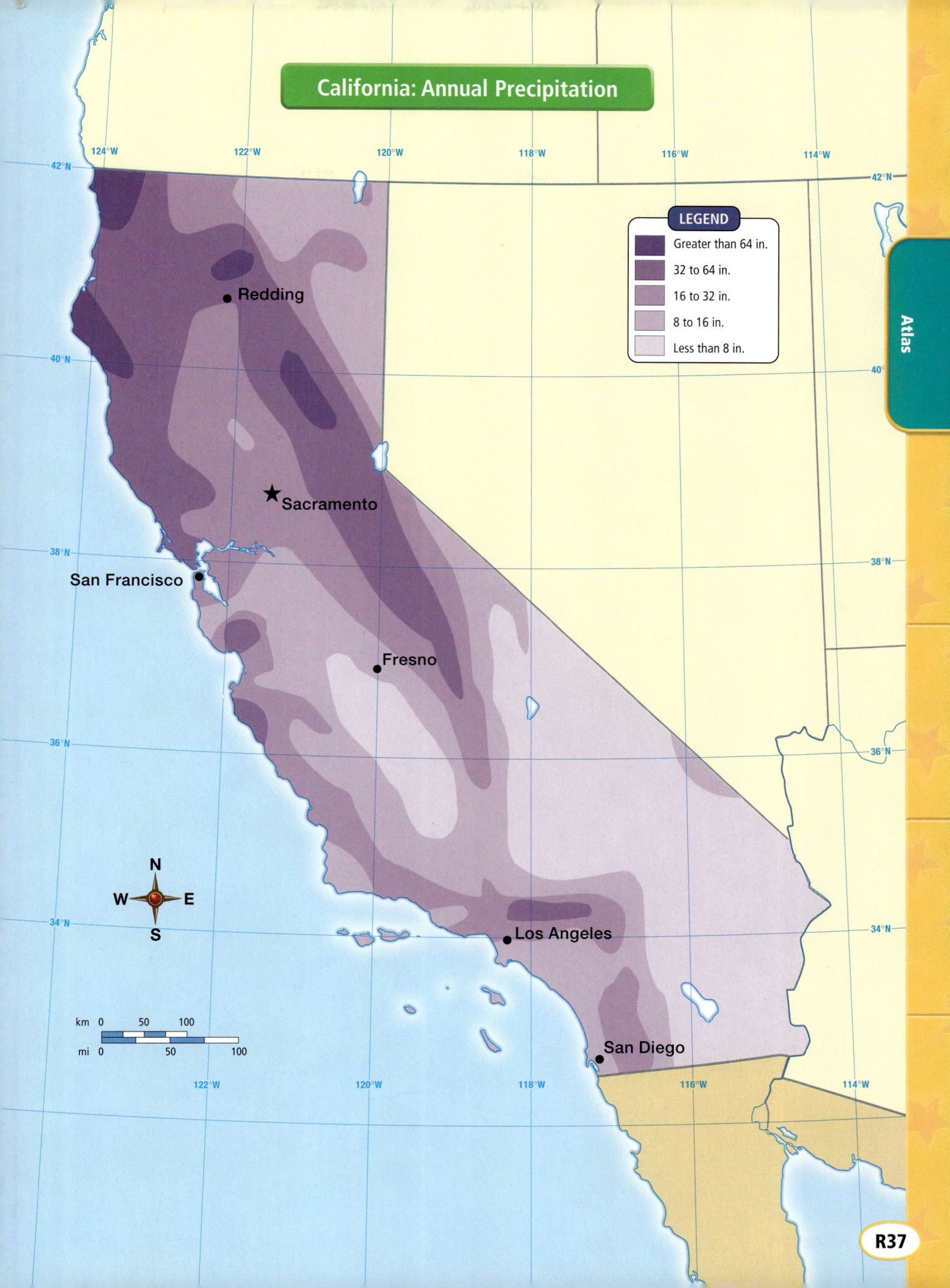

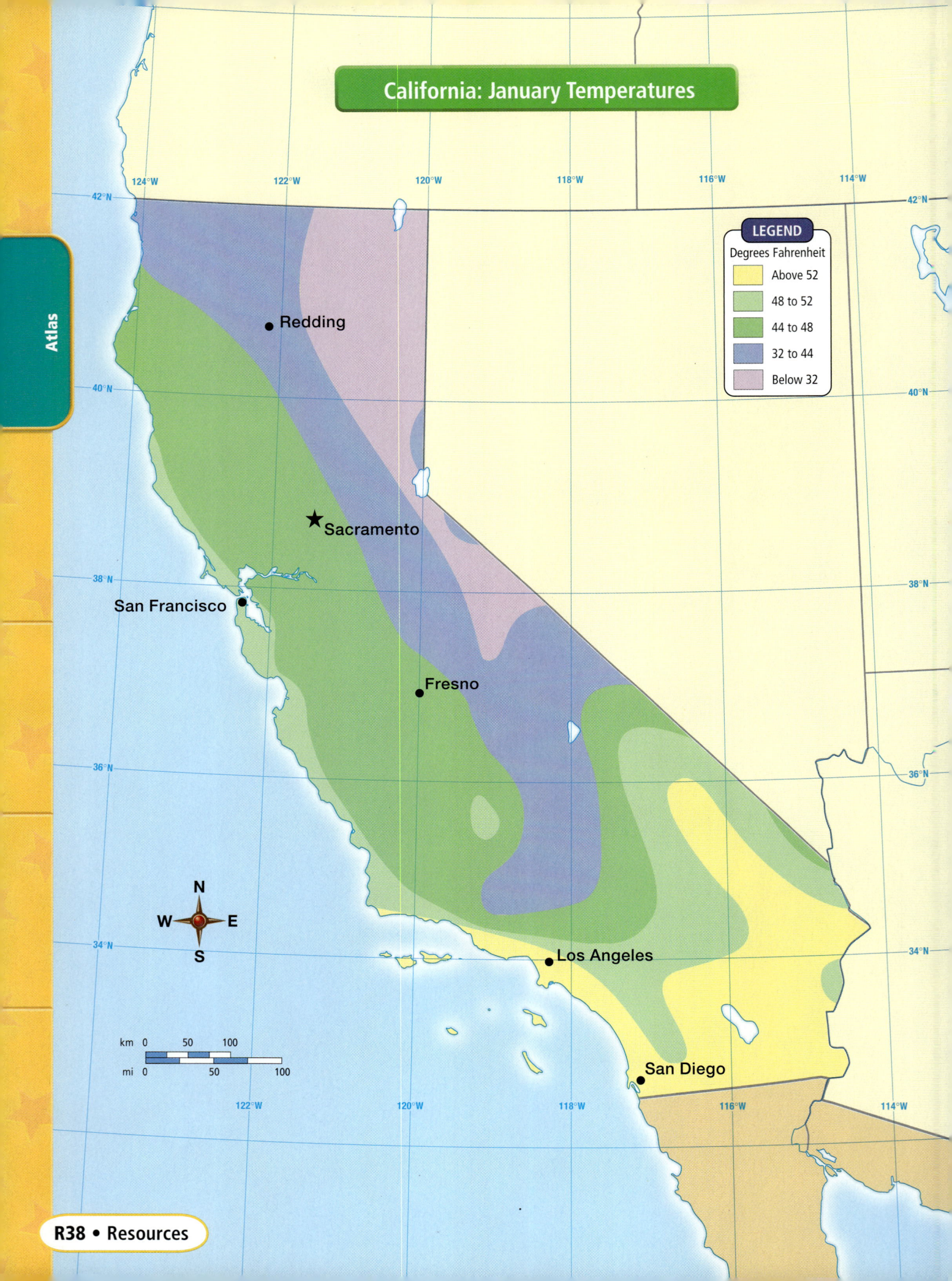

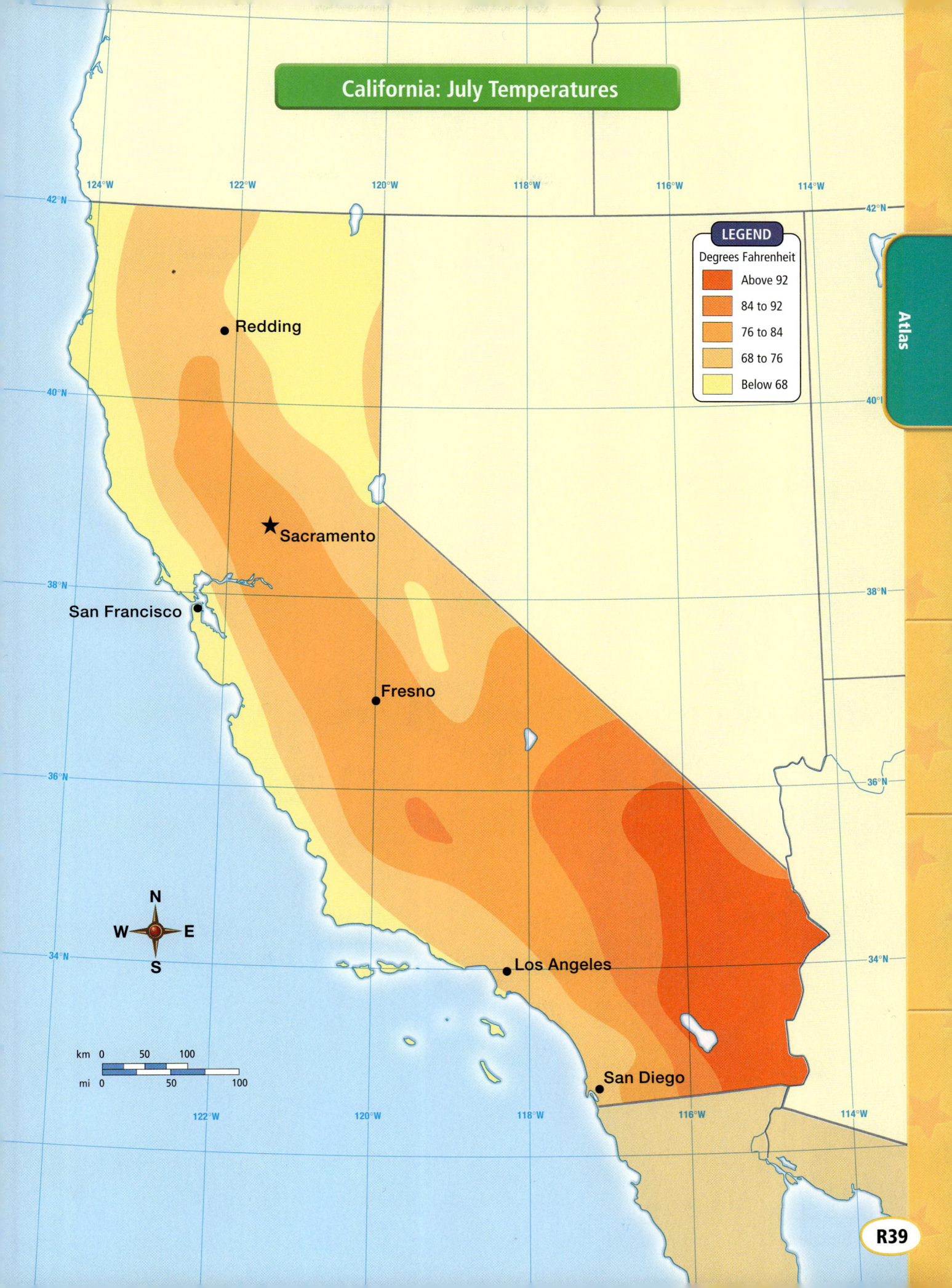

Atlas

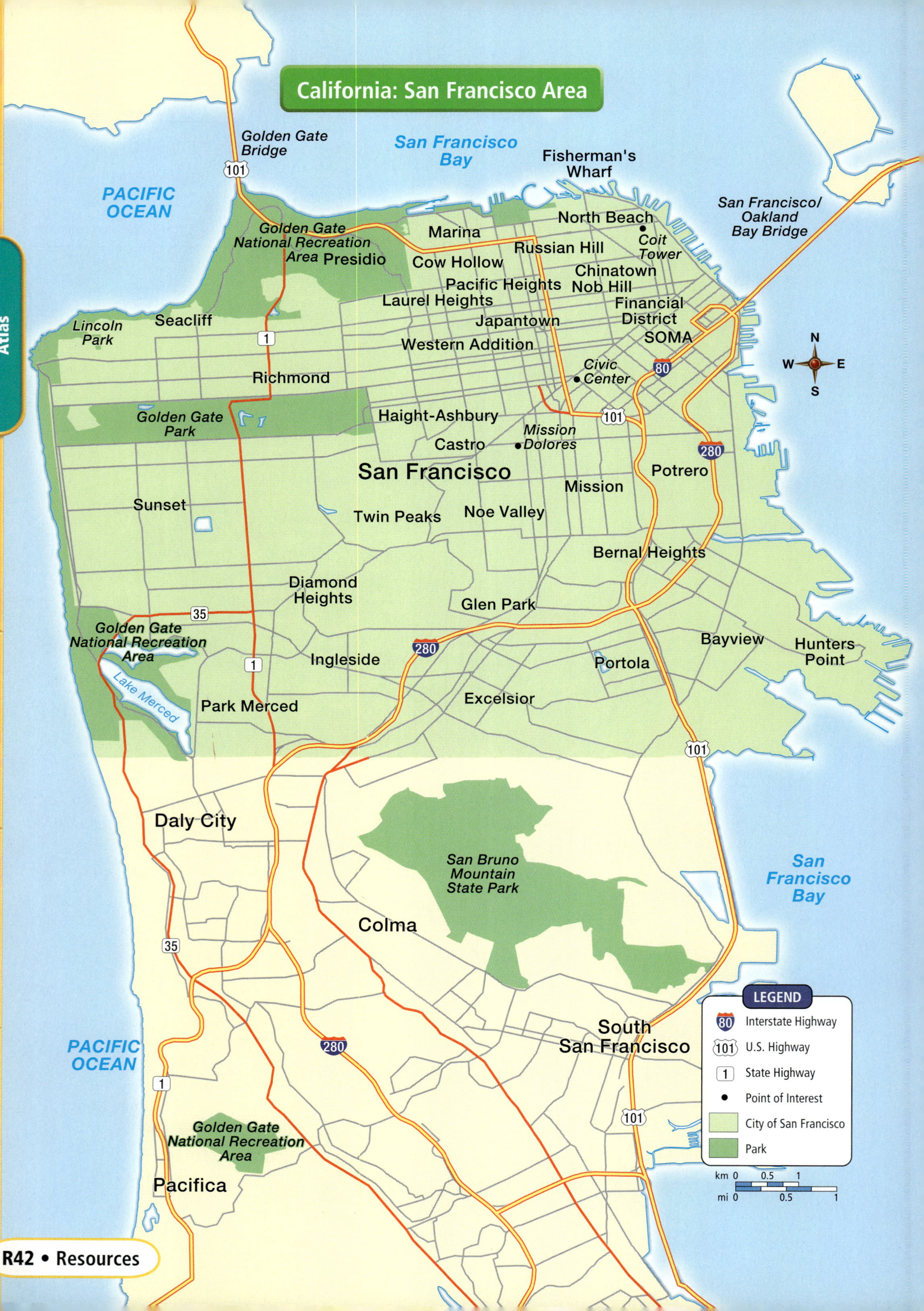
California: San Francisco Area
Golden Gate Bridge
San Francisco Bay
Fisherman's Wharf
PACIFIC OCEAN
San Francisco/ Oakland Bay Bridge
North Beach
Coit Tower
Golden Gate National Recreation Area
Presidio
Marina
Russian Hill
Cow Hollow
Chinatown
Nob Hill
Pacific Heights
Laurel Heights
Financial District
Lincoln Park
Seacliff
Japantown
SOMA
Western Addition
Civic Center
Richmond
Golden Gate Park
Haight-Ashbury
Mission Dolores
Castro
San Francisco
Potrero
Mission
Sunset
Twin Peaks
Noe Valley
Bernal Heights
Diamond Heights
Glen Park
Golden Gate National Recreation Area
Bayview
Hunters Point
Ingleside
Portola
Lake Merced
Park Merced
Excelsior
Daly City
San Bruno Mountain State Park
San Francisco Bay
Colma
PACIFIC OCEAN
South San Francisco
Golden Gate National Recreation Area
Pacifica
N
S
E
W
LEGEND
80 Interstate Highway
101 U.S. Highway
1 State Highway
Point of Interest
City of San Francisco
Park
km 0 0.5 1
mi 0 0.5 1

Gazetteer

Acapulco City in Mexico (16°N, 99°W) p. 84
Africa 2nd largest continent (10°N, 22°E) p. 7
Alabama 22nd state; capital: Montgomery (33°N, 88°W) p. 157
Alameda Town in California (37°N, 122°W) p. 368
Alaska 49th state; capital: Juneau (64°N, 150°W) p. 90
Alcatraz Island Island in San Francisco Bay (37°N, 122°W) p. 348
Alhambra City in southern California (34°N, 118°W) p. 340
Allensworth First African American town in California (35°N, 119°W) p. 257
Alpine County California county with the smallest population (38°N, 119°W) p. 365
American River River in northern California (38°N, 121°W) p. 172
Anaheim City in southern California (34°N, 117°W) p. 341
Angel Island Immigration station in San Francisco Bay (38°N, 122°W) p. 253
Antelope Valley Valley in California (39°N, 122°W) p. 6
Arctic Ocean Smallest ocean; north of North America (71°N, 153°W) p. 7
Arizona 48th state; capital: Phoenix (34°N, 113°W) p. 8
Arkansas 25th state; capital: Little Rock (34°N, 92°W) p. 157
Arkansas River River that runs into the Mississippi River (33°N, 91°W) p. 156
Armenia Country in central Asia (40°N, 45°E) p. 256
Asia Largest continent in the world (50°N, 100°E) p. 7
Atlantic Ocean Extends from Arctic to Antarctic, east of the United States (5°S, 25°W) p. 80
Australia Smallest continent (30°S, 151°E) p. 7

Baja California Peninsula in Mexico (30°N, 117°W) p. 81
Bakersfield City in the Central Valley of California (35°N, 119°W) p. 12
Bangladesh Country in southern Asia (24°N, 90°E) p. 358
Beckwourth Pass Lowest pass through the Sierra Nevada (39°N, 120°W) p. 139
Benicia City in California; former state capital (38°N, 122°W) p. 203
Bering Strait Waterway connecting Arctic Ocean and Bering Sea (65°N, 170°W) p. 90
Big Sur Rugged region of California between Carmel and Monterey (36°N, 121°W) p. 17
Bodega Bay Harbor north of San Francisco (38°N, 123°W) p. 122
Boston Capital of Massachusetts (42°N, 71°W) p. 29
Buffalo City in northern New York (42°N, 78°W) p. 29
Burbank City in southern California (34°N, 118°W) p. 340

Cajon Pass Mountain pass on Old Spanish Trail from Sante Fe to Los Angeles (34°N, 117°W) p. 156
California 31st state; capital: Sacramento (38°N, 121°W) p. 6
Cambodia Country in Southeast Asia (13°N, 105°E) p. 358
Campo de Cahuenga Part of Los Angeles where treaty was signed in January, 1846 (13°N, 105°E) p. 170
Canada Country north of the United States (50°N, 100°W) p. 7
Cape Mendocino Cape in California (40°N, 124°W) p. 86
Carlsbad Town in California (33°N, 117°W) p. 377
Carson City Capital of Nevada, on Pony Express route (39°N, 119°W) p. 230

R4 • Resources

Goose Lake

Cascade Range Mountain range that extends from western Canada into northern California (43°N, 122°W) p. 23

Central America Region of southern North America extending from Guatemala to Panama (11°N, 87°W) p. 174

Central Valley Major farming region of California (40°N, 122°W) p. 11

Channel Islands Islands off the coast of California (33°N, 119°W) p. 50

Charleston City in South Carolina (32°N, 79°W) p. 174

Chicago City in Illinois (41°N, 87°W) p. 29

Chile Country in South America (35°S, 72°W) p. 372

China Country in eastern Asia (37°N, 93°E) p. 175

Clair Engle Lake Lake in Trinity National Park, California (40°N, 122°W) p. 12

Coachella Valley Valley in California (33°N, 116°W) p. 30

Coast Ranges Mountain system in western North America that extends from southern Alaska to Baja California (40°N, 121°W) p. 14

Coloma Town near Sutter's Mill in northern California (38°N, 120°W) p. 172

Colorado Desert Desert in southeastern California (33°N, 115°W) p. 267

Colorado River River that forms border between California and Arizona (34°N, 114°W) p. 16

Columbia River River that runs through Oregon (46°N, 124°W) p. 156

Culver City City in California (34°N, 118°W) p. 333

Cupertino City in Silicon Valley (37°N, 127°W) p. 371

Death Valley Lowest point in North America (36°N, 116°W) p. 25

Delano Town in the Central Valley of California (35°N, 119°W) p. 345

Denver Capital of Colorado (40°N, 105°W) p. 29

Detroit City in Michigan (42°N, 85°W) p. 29

Dolores Town in Mexico where the Mexican Revolution began (21°N, 100°W) p. 119

Donner Pass Mountain pass in the Sierra Nevada (39°N, 120°W) p. 156

Drakes Bay Bay in California near San Francisco (37°N, 122°W) p. 83

East Los Angeles City in California near Los Angeles (34°N, 118°W) p. 323

El Salvador Country in Central America (13°N, 88°W) p. 357

England Country in western Europe; part of the United Kingdom (52°N, 2°W) p. 83

Eureka City in California (40°N, 124°W) p. 22

Europe 2nd smallest continent (50°N, 15°E) p. 7

Feather River River in northern California (39°N, 120°W) p. 12

Florida 27th state; capital: Tallahassee (31°N, 85°W) p. 120

Fort Bridger Settlement in Utah, on Oregon Trail and Pony Express route (41°N, 110°W) p. 156

Fort Churchill Settlement in Nevada, on Pony Express route (39°N, 119°W) p. 230

Fort Laramie Settlement in Wyoming, on Oregon Trail and Pony Express route (42°N, 104°W) p. 156

Fort Ross Trading post in California started by Russians; now a state park (38°N, 123°W) p. 122

France Country in western Europe (47°N, 1°E) p. 143

Fresno City in California (38°N, 120°W) p. 21

Germany Country in western Europe (51°N, 10°E) p. 256

Gila River River in New Mexico and Arizona (33°N, 108°W) p. 156

Golden Gate Strait Body of water connecting San Francisco Bay and the Pacific Ocean (38°N, 122°W) p. 308

Goose Lake Lake partly in California and partly in Oregon (41°N, 120°W) p. 12

Great Britain

Great Britain Island in Europe containing England, Scotland, and Wales (55°N, 5°W) p.169

Great Salt Lake Lake in Utah (41°N, 113°W) p.156

Greece Country in southeastern Europe (39°N, 22°E) p. 266

Guatemala Country in Central America (16°N, 92°W) p. 357

Gulf of California Gulf between Baja California and the rest of Mexico (25°N, 110°W) p. 88

Gulf of Mexico Body of water along southern United States and Mexico (25°N, 94°W) p. 157

Hawaii 50th state; capital: Honolulu (20°N, 158°W) p. 320

Hawthorne Town in California (34°N, 118°W) p. 377

Hollywood Area of Los Angeles; center of the American movie industry (34°N, 118°W) p. 297

Houston City in Texas (29°N, 95°W) p. 29

Humboldt Bay Bay in northern California (40°N, 124°W) p. 84

Imperial Valley Valley in California; rich farming area (33°N, 116°W) p. 31

India Country in southern Asia (23°N, 78°E) p. 254

Indiana 19th state; capital: Indianapolis (40°N, 87°E) p. 157

Independence Town in Missouri, origin of early trails and routes to California (39°N, 94°W) p. 157

Indian Ocean Ocean south of Asia (2°N, 48°E) p. 7

Ingelwood City in southern California (34°N, 118°W) p. 340

Iran Country in central Asia (32°N, 53°E) p. 357

Ireland Country in Europe (53°N, 6°W) p. 192

Isthmus of Panama Part of land in Central America connecting North and South America (9°N, 80°W) p. 174

Israel Country in the Middle East (31°N, 34°E) p. 377

Italy Country in southern Europe (44°N, 11°E) p. 192

Japan Island country in eastern Asia (37°N, 134°E) p. 254

Kansas 34th state; capital: Topeka (39°N, 100°W) p.304

Kentucky 15th state; capital: Frankfort (38°N, 88°W) p.157

Kings Canyon National Park National park in California (37°N, 119°W) p. 18

Klamath Mountains Mountains in northern California; part of the Coast Ranges (41°N, 123°W) p. 23

Klamath River River in northern California (41°N, 122°W) p. 12

La Paz City in Mexico (24°N, 110°W) p. 88

Lake Superior Lake in the United States; largest of the Great Lakes (47°N, 88°W) p. 157

Lake Tahoe Lake and resort on California-Nevada border (39°N, 120°W) p. 16

Lakewood City in southern California (34°N, 118°W) p. 339

Laos Country in southeast Asia (18°N, 105°E) p. 358

Lassen Peak Mountain in California (40°N, 121°W) p. 15

Las Vegas City in Nevada (36°N, 115°W) p. 29

Lava Beds National Monument Land where Modoc Indians lived in northern California (41°N, 121°W) p. 217

Louisiana 18th state; capital: Baton Rouge (31°N, 93°W) p. 157

Long Beach City in southern California (34°N, 118°W) p. 31

Los Angeles Largest city in California (34°N, 118°W) p. 22

Manila Capital of the Philippines (14°N, 120°E) p. 83

Massachusetts 6th state; capital: Boston (42°N, 73°W) p. 160

Memphis City in Tennessee (35°N, 90°W) p. 29

Merced River River in central California (37°N, 120°W) p. 12

Mexico Country south of the United States (24°N, 104°W) p. 7

Mexico City Capital of Mexico (19°N, 99°W) p. 92

Miami City in Florida (25°N, 80°W) p. 29

Minneapolis City in Minnesota (45°N, 93°W) p. 29

Mississippi River Principal river of the United States and North America (32°N, 92°W) p. 157

Missouri 24th state; capital: Jefferson City (38°N, 94°W) p. 140

Missouri River River that runs into the Mississippi River (41°N, 96°W) p. 156

Mobile City in Alabama (30°N, 88°W) p. 157

Modesto City in California (38°N, 120°W) p. 376

Mojave Desert Desert in southeastern California (35°N, 117°W) p. 25

Mokelumne River River in northern California (38°N, 120°W) p. 172

Monterey City in California (37°N, 122°W) p. 8

Monterey Bay Bay in California (37°N, 122°W) p. 82

Mono Lake Lake in California (38°N, 119°W) p. 16

Mount Shasta A volcanic mountain in northern California (41°N, 122°W) p. 15

Mount Whitney Highest mountain in the lower 48 states, in east-central California (36°N, 118°W) p. 3

Navidad City on the Pacific coast of Mexico (20°N, 104°W) p. 83

Nebraska 37th state; capital: Lincoln (42°N, 102°W) p. 233

Nevada 36th state; capital: Carson City (40°N, 117°W) p. 8

Nevada City Town in California (39°N, 121°W) p. 193

New Jersey 3rd state; capital: Trenton (41°N, 75°W) p. 205

New Mexico 47th state; capital: Santa Fe (35°N, 107°W) p. 169

New Orleans City in Louisiana (30°N, 90°W) p. 29

New York City City in New York; largest city in the United States (41°N, 74°W) p. 192

North America Northern continent of Western Hemisphere (45°N, 100°W) p. 7

North Pole Northern end of Earth's axis of rotation, in the Arctic (90°N) p. 7

Northern Hemisphere Half of Earth that is north of the equator p. 7

Oakland City in California (37°N, 122°W) p. 279

Ohio 17th state; capital: Columbus (41°N, 83°W) p. 157

Ohio River River flowing from Pennsylvania to the Mississippi River (37°N, 88°W) p. 157

Oklahoma 46th state; capital: Oklahoma City (36°N, 98°W) p. 304

Oregon 33rd state; capital: Salem (44°N, 122°W) p. 8

Owens River River in California (37°N, 119°W) p. 270

Owens Valley Valley in California (37°N, 119°W) p. 270

Oxnard City in California (34°N, 119°W) p. 379

P

Pacific Ocean Largest ocean; west of the United States (0°N, 170°W) p. 7
Pakistan Country in central Asia (30°N, 70°E) p. 254
Palm Springs City in southern California (34°N, 116°W) p. 30
Panama Country in Central America, site of the Isthmus of Panama (9°N, 80°W) p. 174
Paris Capital of France (48°N, 2°E) p. 297
Pasadena City in California near Los Angeles (34°N, 118°W) p. 333
Pearl Harbor Harbor in Hawaii (21°N, 158°W) p. 320
Philippines Island country in eastern Asia (14°N, 125°E) p. 83
Placerville Town in northern California goldfields (38°N, 120°W) p. 191
Platte River River that runs through Nebraska (41°N, 94°W) p. 156
Poland Country in eastern Europe (52°N, 21°E) p. 256
Portland Settlement in Oregon Territory; later became city in Oregon state (46°N, 123°W) p. 156
Promontory Place in Utah where tracks of the two parts of the first transcontinental railroad met in 1869 (41°N, 112°W) p. 236

R

Red River River along the northern border of Texas (32°N, 99°W) p.157
Redding City in California (40°N, 122°W) p. 34
Richmond City in California (38°N, 122°W) p. 322
Rio Grande River along the border between Mexico and Texas (26°N, 97°W) p. 156
Riverside City in California (34°N, 117°W) p. 261
Rocky Mountains Mountain range in western North America that stretches from Alaska to the Mexican border (50°N, 114°W) p. 161
Russia Country in eastern Europe and northern Asia (61°N, 60°E) p. 90

S

Sacramento Capital of California (39°N, 122°W) p. 142
Sacramento Valley Valley region in northern California (39°N, 122°W) p. 182
Sacramento River River in northern California (40°N, 123°W) p. 16
Saigon City in Vietnam, officially named Ho Chi Minh City (10°N, 106°E) p. 359
St. Joseph Town in Missouri on Pony Express route (39°N, 95°W) p. 230
St. Louis City in Missouri on the Mississippi River (39°N, 90°W) p.157
Salton Sea Lake in southern California (33°N, 116°W) p. 267
San Diego City in southern California (32°N, 117°W) p. 82
San Francisco City in California (38°N, 122°W) p. 22
San Francisco Bay Bay in California (38°N, 122°W) p. 16
San Gabriel City in California near Los Angeles (34°N, 118°W) p. 93
San Joaquin River River in California (37°N, 120°W) p. 16
San Joaquin Valley Valley region in central California (34°N, 118°W) p. 140
San Jose City in California south of San Francisco, former state capital (37°N, 122°W) p. 110
San Juan Capital of Puerto Rico (18°N, 66°W) p. 92
San Luis Obispo City in California (35°N, 121°W) p. 31
San Pedro Neighborhood of Los Angeles (34°N, 116°W) p. 269
Santa Ana City in southern California (34°N, 118°W) p. 359
Santa Barbara City in southern California (34°N, 120°W) p. 31
Santa Catalina Island Island off the coast of southern California; one of the Channel Islands (33°N, 118°W) p. 50
Santa Cruz City in California (37°N, 122°W) p. 28

Santa Rosa City in California (38°N, 123°W) p. 261

Seattle City in Washington State (47°N, 122°W) p. 29

Sequoia National Park National park in the Sierra Nevada (36°N, 118°W) p. 18

Salt Lake City Capital of Utah (41°N, 112°W) p. 230

Sierra Nevada Mountain range mainly in eastern California (39°N, 120°W) p. 14

Solvang City in California (34°N, 116°W) p. 378

Sonoma Town in California (38°N, 122°W) p. 162

Sonoma Valley Valley north of San Francisco (38°N, 122°W) p. 133

Sonoran Desert Large desert in southeastern California and southwestern Arizona (32°N, 114°W) p. 83

South America Southern continent of Western Hemisphere (10°S, 60°W) p. 7

South Korea Country in eastern Asia on Korean peninsula (37°N, 127°W) p. 254

South Pole Southern end of Earth's axis of rotation, in Antarctica (90°S) p. 7

Southern Hemisphere Half of Earth that is south of the equator p. 7

Soviet Union Large Communist country in northern Asia and eastern Europe that split into separate republics in 1991, the largest one being Russia (61°N, 64°E) p. 332

Spain Country in southwestern Europe (40°N, 5°W) p. 80

Sri Lanka Island country in the Indian Ocean, south of India (7°N, 81°E) p. 358

Stanislaus River River in central California (38°N, 119°W) p. 12

Stockton City in the Central Valley of California (34°N, 116°W) p. 207

Switzerland Country in central Europe (47°N, 8°E) p. 277

Taiwan Island country in Asia, southeast of China (23°N, 121°E) p. 157

Tennessee 16th state; capital: Nashville (36°N, 88°W) p. 157

Texas 28th state; capital: Austin (31°N, 101°W) p. 169

Topeka Capital of Kansas (39°N, 95°W) p. 29

Torrance City in southern California (34°N, 118°W) p. 377

Transverse Ranges Mountain range that runs from Santa Barbara coast to the Mojave Desert, dividing central and southern California (34°N, 188°W) p. 23

Trinity County County in California (40°N, 123°W) p. 406

United States Country in central and northwest North America (38°N, 110°W) p. 7

Utah 45th state; capital: Salt Lake City (40°N, 112°W) p. 169

Vallejo City in California; former state capital (38°N, 122°W) p. 203

Van Nuys Neighborhood of Los Angeles (34°N, 118°W) p. 340

Veracruz City in Mexico (19°N, 96°W) p. 92

Vietnam Country in southeast Asia (18°N, 107°E) p. 357

Washington 42nd state; capital: Olympia (48°N, 121°W) p. 321

Washington, D.C. Capital of the United States (38°N, 77°W) p. 167

Westchester Neighborhood of Los Angeles (34°N, 118°W) p. 339

Westminster City in southern California (34°N, 118°W) p. 359

White Mountains Mountain range that runs along the east side of the Owens Valley in California (38°N, 118°W) p. 23

Yosemite National Park National park in California (38°N, 119°W) p. 18

Yosemite Valley Valley in California (38°N, 119°W) p. 17

Yuba River River in California (39°N, 120°W) p. 12

Glossary

A

adapt (uh DAPT) to change in order to live in a new environment. (p. 42)

adobe (uh DOH bee) a brick made of dried clay and straw. (p. 99)

advertisement (ad vur TIZE muhnt) a public notice, often appearing in a newspaper or on television, that tells people about a product or business. (p. 269)

aerospace industry (AYR oh spays IHN duh stree) businesses that provide goods and services related to space travel. (p. 333)

agriculture (AG rih kul chur) farming. (p. 65)

alcalde (ahl KAHL day) the mayor and judge in a Spanish pueblo. (p. 110)

amend (uh MEHND) to change or add to a law or document. (p. 398)

ancestor (AN sehs tur) a relative who was born a long time ago. (p. 60)

aqueduct (AWK wuh duhkt) a large channel or pipe that carries water across great distances. (p. 270)

armed forces (ahrmd FAWR sehz) groups of people organized to protect a country. (p. 166)

artists' colony (AR tihsts kawl uh nee) a community where groups of artists live, work, and learn together. (p. 279)

assembly (uh SEHM blee) a group of people who gather together to make laws for a place. (p. 127)

atlas (AT luhs) a book or collection of maps. (p. 55)

B

barrio (BAHR ee oh) a neighborhood where Spanish-speaking people live in the United States. (p. 339)

barter (BAHR tur) the trade of one good or service for another without using money. (p. 51)

base (bays) a center or headquarters for military activities. (p. 322)

basin (BAY sihn) a low bowl-shaped area of land. (p. 22)

bay (bay) a body of water that is partly surrounded by land and has a wide opening to the sea. (p. 16)

benefit (BEHN uh fiht) a gain or an advantage. (p. 382)

boom (boom) a time when businesses succeed and grow quickly. (p. 190)

boycott (BOY kaht) a protest in which people refuse to buy, sell, or use certain goods. (p. 347)

bracero (bruh SAYR oh) a Mexican farm worker hired to work in the United States for a limited time. (p. 335)

branch (branch) one part of something larger, such as a government. (p. 388)

breakwater (BRAYK waw tur) a wall that protects an area of the shore from waves. (p. 269)

bribe (bryb) money or gifts given to a person to encourage him or her to do something illegal or dishonest. (p. 290)

business (BIHZ nihs) a small or large organization that sells goods or services to earn a profit. (p. 190)

C

Californio (KAL ih FOUR nee oh) a native-born Californian from a Spanish family. (p. 122)

capital (KAP ih tl) the city where a state or national government is located. (p. 203)

capitol (KAP ih tl) the main government building in a capital city. (p. 207)

century (SEHN chuh ree) a period of 100 years. (p. 96)

ceremony (SEHR uh moh nee) a formal act that honors an event or occasion as part of a custom. (p. 59)

R50 • Resources

circle graph (SUR kuhl graf) a graph that divides a whole into wedges. (p. 302)

citizen (SIHT ih zuhn) a loyal member of a city, state, or nation. (p. 127)

city council (SIHT ee KOWN suhl) a group of citizens who make local laws. (p. 402)

city manager (SIHT ee MAN uh juhr) a person who takes care of the daily business of running a city. (p. 402)

civil rights (SIHV uhl rytz) the rights that all citizens of a country are guaranteed, including the right to be treated equally under the law. (p. 345)

civilian (sih VIHL yuhn) a person who is not a member of the armed forces. (p. 324)

claim (klaym) a piece of land a person claims to own. (p. 180)

clan (klan) a large group of people who share an ancestor. (p. 67)

climate (KLY miht) the usual weather of a place over time. (p. 20)

colony (KAHL uh nee) a settlement or region ruled by another country. (p. 91)

commission (kuh MIHSH uhn) a group of people assigned to carry out certain tasks. (p. 215)

communication (kuh myoo nih KAY shuhn) the sharing of information through words, pictures, or code. (p. 226)

communication industry (kuh myoo nih KAY shuhn IHN duh stree) businesses that produce the technology and products people use to communicate. (p. 408)

community (kuh MYOO nih tee) a group of people who live in the same area under the same laws. (p. 42)

compass rose (KUHM puhs rohz) a symbol on a map that shows directions. (p. 13)

compromise (KAHM pruh myz) an agreement reached by two sides that gives something to each. (p. 202)

conclusion (kuhn KLOO zhuhn) a judgment or decision based on facts, ideas, and opinions that is made after thinking carefully. (p. 396)

conflict (KAHN flihkt) a disagreement between groups of people or individuals. (p. 418)

congress (KAHN gris) a formal meeting of people who make laws for a country. (p. 120)

conquistador (kahn KEES tuh dawr) a Spanish conqueror of Mexico, Central America, or Peru. (p. 81)

consent (kuhn SEHNT) agreement or acceptance. (p. 399)

conservation (kahn sur VAY shuhn) protecting the environment. (p. 17)

constitution (kahn stih TOO shuhn) a basic plan for setting up and running a government. (p. 120)

construction (kuhn STRUHK shuhn) the way in which something is built. (p. 281)

consumer (kuhn SOO mur) someone who buys or uses goods or services. (p. 190)

continent (KAHN tuh nehnt) a large mass of land. (p. 7)

convention (kuhn VEHN shuhn) a meeting that brings many people together for a common purpose. (p. 200)

convert (kahn VURT) to persuade someone to change to a particular religion or belief. (p. 98)

cost (kawst) a loss or sacrifice. (p. 382)

council (KOWN suhl) a group of people who gather to give advice. (p. 66)

county (KOWN tee) a section of a state that has its own government. (p. 402)

culture (KUHL chur) the way of life shared by a particular group of people, including their beliefs, language, foods, and laws. (p. 56)

current (KUHR ehnt) the flow of wind or water. (p. 84)

decade (DEHK ayd) a period of 10 years. (p. 96)

declaration (dehk luh RAY shuhn) a statement of ideas. (p. 201)

defense industry (duh FEHNS IHN duh stree) businesses that sell goods and services to the military. (p. 322)

delegate (DEHL ih giht) someone chosen to represent others at a convention or in government. (p. 200)

delta (DEHL tuh) a flat, triangle-shaped area of land at the mouth of a river. (p. 16)

demand (dih MAND) the amount of a good or service that people will buy at a certain price. (p. 264)

democracy (deh MAWK ruh see) a form of government in which power belongs to the people. (p. 390)

depression (dih PREHSH uhn) a period when many people cannot find jobs and businesses fail. (p. 304)

desert (DEHZ urt) area with little rainfall. (p. 25)

diputación (dih PYOO tah see ohwn) an assembly, or group of citizens, under Mexican law that made laws. (p. 127)

discrimination (dih skrihm uh NAY shuhn) treating people unfairly or differently because they are part of a certain group. (p. 180)

diseño (dih SAYN yoh) a map of an area of land. (p. 128)

district (DIHS trihkt) an area set aside for a certain purpose, such as running schools. (p. 391)

diverse (dy VURS) varied; including many different groups or kinds. (p. 208)

diversity (dih VUR sih tee) difference or variety. (p. 42)

drought (drout) a long period when there is little or no rain. (p. 305)

Dust Bowl (duhst bohl) the area of the United States that suffered from a long drought in the 1930s. (p. 305)

earthquake (URTH kwayk) a shaking of the ground due to the movement of large plates that make up the earth's crust. (p. 15)

economy (ih KAHN uh mee) the way in which people use resources to make, buy, and sell goods and services. (p. 50)

emperor (EHM pur ur) the ruler of a group of lands or nations. (p. 120)

encyclopedia (ehn sy cloh PEE dee uh) a book or set of books with information about people, places, and events, arranged alphabetically. (p. 55)

engineer (ehn juh NEER) someone, usually trained in the math and science of engineering, who plans or builds machines or structures such as railroads or bridges. (p. 233)

entrepreneur (ahn truh pruh NUR) a person who takes a risk to start and run a business. (p. 192)

environment (ehn VY ruhn muhnt) the surroundings in which people, plants, and animals live. (p. 17)

equator (ih KWAY tur) the imaginary line around the middle of the earth. (p. 7)

erosion (ih ROH zhuhn) the process by which wind or water wear away the land over time. (p. 15)

exclusion (ehk SKLOO zhuhn) the practice of keeping people from entering a place or being included in something. (p. 253)

executive branch (ihg ZEHK yuh tihv branch) the part of a government that executes, or carries out, laws. (p. 389)

exhaust (ihg ZAWST) smoke and harmful chemicals that come from an engine. (p. 413)

expedition (ehk spih DIHSH uhn) a journey taken by a group of people for a certain reason, such as exploration. (p. 82)

export (EHK sport) a product that is sent out of a country to be sold or traded. (p. 123)

fact (fakt) information that is known to be true or can be proven. (p. 240)

fault (fawlt) the place where the edges of Earth's plates meet. (p. 15)

fertile (FUR tuhl) good for growing plants. (p. 262)

festival (FEHS tih vuhl) a day or period set aside for celebration. (p. 378)

fiesta (fee EHS tuh) a party or celebration, often in a Spanish-speaking country or region. (p. 133)

flow resource (floh REE sohrs) a resource that must be used when and where it is available. (p. 32)

forty-niner (FAWR tee NY nur) someone who came to California in 1849. (p. 173)

frontier (fruhn TYR) the edge of a country or a settled region. (p. 138)

geographer (jee AWG ruh fur) a person who studies geography. (p. 8)

geography (jee AWG ruh fee) the study of people, places, and environments on Earth. (p. 6)

ghost town (GOHST town) a town that people have abandoned. (p. 191)

glacier (GLAY shur) a large body of slowly-moving ice. (p. 40)

globe (glohb) a model of the earth that shows the planet's land and water. (p. 7)

gold rush (gohld ruhsh) a time when many people hurry to the same area to look for gold. (p. 173)

goods (gudz) products that people buy and sell. (p. 49)

government (GUHV urn muhnt) a system that makes and enforces laws in a certain area. (p. 66)

governor (GUHV ur nur) a person chosen to lead a colony, territory, or state. (p. 110)

grant (grant) money given to someone to pay the costs of college or other education. (p. 367)

headquarters (HEHD kwawr turz) a central place or office from which orders are given out by leaders. (p. 162)

hemisphere (HEHM ih sfihr) one half of Earth's surface. (p. 7)

high-tech (hy TEHK) very advanced technology. (p. 371)

hunter-gatherer (huhnt ur GATH ur ur) a person who collects food by gathering wild plants and hunting wild animals. (p. 64)

hydraulic mining (hy DRAWL ihk MY nihng) the use of powerful hoses to wash away earth and uncover gold. (p. 179)

hydroelectric power (hy droh ih LEHK trihk POW ur) electricity created from the power of flowing water. (p. 271)

immigrant (IHM ih gruhnt) someone who moves from one country to live in another. (p. 175)

immigration (ihm ih GRAY shuhn) the movement of people from one country to another. (p. 252)

import (IHM pawrt) a product brought from another country to be sold or traded. (p. 122)

independence (ihn duh PEHN dunhs) freedom from the rule of another country. (p. 119)

index (IHN dehks) an alphabetical list of the topics in a book and the pages on which they are found. (p. 55)

industry (IHN duh stree) all the businesses involved in making a product or providing a service. (p. 297)

international trade (ihn tur NASH uh nul trayd) trade between different countries. (p. 372)

internment camp (ihn TURN muhnt kamp) a place where a person is held captive, especially in wartime. (p. 321)

investor (ihn VEHS tur) a person who puts money into a business in the hopes of earning back more money in the future if the business succeeds. (p. 233)

irrigation

irrigation (ihr ih GAY shuhn) the use of ditches, pipes, or canals to bring water to dry land to help crops grow. (p. 262)

isthmus (IHS muhs) a narrow strip of land that connects two larger areas of land. (p. 174)

judicial branch (joo DIHSH uhl branch) the part of the government that decides the meaning of laws. (p. 389)

justice (JUHS tihs) applying laws to all people in a fair and equal way. (p. 208)

labor union (LAY bur YOON yuhn) an organization of workers who seek to improve pay and working conditions. (p. 346)

landfill (LAND fihl) a place where trash is buried in the ground. (p. 414)

landform (LAND fohrm) a shape or feature of the earth's surface. (p. 14)

land grant (LAND grant) a piece of land that is given away by a government. (p. 128)

latitude line (LAT ih tood lyn) an imaginary line that circles the globe from east to west. (p. 28)

leadership (LEE dur shihp) the guidance of a person or group of people. (p. 66)

legend (LEHJ uhnd) a box that tells what a map's symbols mean. (p. 13)

legislative branch (LEHJ ih slay tihv branch) the part of the government that legislates, or makes laws. (p. 389)

legislature (LEHJ ih slay chur) a group of people who make laws. (p. 400)

longitude line (LAHN jih tood lyn) an imaginary line that circles the globe from north to south. (p. 28)

Manifest Destiny (MAN uh fehst DEHS tuh nee) the belief that the United States should spread across the continent of North America. (p. 161)

manufacturing (man yuh FAK chur ihng) the process of using machines to make goods. (p. 322)

market (MAHR kiht) a place where goods and services are exchanged. (p. 264)

metropolitan area (meht ruh PAHL ih tuhn AIR ee uh) one or more cities and their surrounding suburbs. (p. 407)

military (MIHL ih tehr ee) people such as soldiers armed to protect a country. (p. 162)

minimum wage (MIHN uh muhm wayj) the least amount of money that the law allows a person to be paid. (p. 292)

migrant worker (MY gruhnt WUR kur) a person who moves from place to place to do farm work. (p. 263)

missile (MIHS uhl) a weapon that is propelled by a jet engine and can be dropped or launched at a target. (p. 332)

mission (MIHSH uhn) a settlement where people teach a particular religion. (p. 92)

missionary (MIHSH uh nehr ee) a person who travels to another country or region to teach a particular religion. (p. 92)

mountain pass (MOUN tuhn pas) a low space or gap between mountains. (p. 15)

movie palace (MOO vee PAL ihs) a fancy movie theater. (p. 298)

mutualista (myoo choo uh LEE stuh) a society formed by Mexican immigrants in the United States to help one another. (p. 257)

natural resource (NACH ur uhl REE sawrs) something found in nature that people use to make food, shelter, or other goods. (p. 30)

naturalized citizen (NACH ur uh lyzd SIHT ih zuhn) someone born in another country who becomes a United States citizen. (p. 360)

nonrenewable resource (nahn rih NOO uh buhl REE sawrs) something that cannot be replaced once it is used. (p. 32)

nonviolent protest (nahn VY uh luhnt PROH tehst) a way to protest, or fight against, injustice peacefully and without violence. (p. 345)

official (uh FIHSH uhl) a government worker who is in charge of an area or task. (p. 160)

opinion (uh PIHN yuhn) a belief or feeling that may or may not be supported by facts. (p. 240)

oral history (OHR uhl HIHS tuh ree) an account of past events passed down through speech. (p. 40)

orbit (AWR biht) to revolve around something, such as the earth. (p. 333)

party (PAHR tee) a group of people who gather for an activity. (p. 140)

peninsula (puh NIHN syuh luh) a piece of land attached to a larger body of land and surrounded by water on three sides. (p. 81)

petroleum (puh TROHL ee uhm) a thick liquid, also called oil, that forms underground. (p. 298)

pioneer (py uh NIHR) one of the first of a group of people to enter and settle a region. (p. 140)

point of view (poynt uhv vyoo) the way someone thinks about an issue, event, or person. (p. 184)

pollution (puh LOO shuhn) any substance in the air, water, or soil that harms the environment. (p. 340)

population density (pahp yuh LAY shuhn DEHN sih tee) the average number of people living in a certain area. (p. 406)

population distribution (pahp yuh LAY shuhn dih strih BYOO shuhn) the pattern of where groups of people live. (p. 405)

presidio (prih SEE dee oh) a fort built by the Spanish to protect their territory. (p. 109)

primary source (PRY mehr ee sawrs) an account of an event written by someone who experienced it. (p. 284)

prime meridian (prym muh RIHD ee uhn) the line of longitude located at zero degrees. (p. 28)

produce (PROHD oos) farm products such as fresh fruits and vegetables. (p. 264)

productivity (proh duhk TIHV ih tee) the rate at which goods or services are produced. (p. 334)

professional (pruh FEHSH uh nuhl) a person who has special knowledge and training. (p. 357)

profit (PRAWF iht) the amount of money a business has left over after all its costs have been paid. (p. 190)

progressive (pruh GREHS ihv) reformer who favors laws to protect workers', consumers', and citizens' rights. (p. 291)

property rights (PRAHP ur tee ryts) a person's claim to own certain land or property. (p. 214)

public (PUHB lihk) for the people. (p. 364)

pueblo (PWEH bloh) a Spanish town or settlement, often built of stone and adobe. (p. 110)

ranchera (ran CHAYR uh) a woman who owns a rancho. (p. 132)

rancheria (ran chay REE uh) land set aside for California Indians. (p. 402)

ranchero (ran CHAYR oh) a man who owns a rancho. (p. 132)

rancho (RAN choh) a cattle ranch owned by Californios. (p. 129)

rebel (rih BEHL) to go against the way things are, often to fight to be free from a government in power. (p. 162)

reclaim (ree CLAYM) to make land usable for farming. (p. 262)

recycle (ree SY kuhl) to re-use materials, such as glass and plastic, to make new goods. (p. 414)

reform (rih FOWRM) an action that makes something better. (p. 291)

refrigerate (rih FRIHJ uh rayt) to keep something, such as food, cooled or chilled. (p. 265)

refugee (REHF yoo jee) a person who flees war or danger to safety in another land. (p. 358)

region (REE juhn) an area that has one or more features in common. (p. 21)

religion (rih LIHJ uhn) people's belief in and worship of God or gods. (p. 60)

renewable resource (rih NOO uh buhl REE sawrs) something in nature that can be replaced after people use it. (p. 32)

report (rih PAWRT) a piece of writing that provides information about a topic. (p. 148)

republic (rih PUHB lihk) a form of government in which the citizens elect lawmakers and leaders. (p. 120)

reservation (rehz ur VAY shuhn) land set aside for American Indians by the United States government. (p. 216)

reservoir (REHZ ur vwahr) a human made lake for storing large amounts of water. (p. 270)

responsibility (rih sphahn suh BIHL ih tee) a duty that someone is expected to fulfill. (p. 390)

revolt (rih VOHLT) an uprising to take power away from a ruler. (p. 102)

right (ryt) something a person should have, according to law, custom, or nature. (p. 199)

rodeo (ROH dee oh) the round-up of a rancho's cattle for branding or sale. (p. 133)

satellite (SAT l yt) an object launched to circle the earth. (p. 333)

sawmill (SAW mihl) a place where lumber is sawed into boards. (p. 172)

scale (scayl) a ruler that shows how far places on a map are from each other. (p. 13)

school district (SKOOL dihs trihkt) an area that builds and runs public schools. (p. 365)

search engine (surch EHN jihn) a Web site that finds other Web sites related to key words and ideas. (p. 55)

secondary source (SEHK uhn dehr ee sawrs) an account of an event written by someone who did not experience it. (p. 284)

secularization (sehk yoo lahr ih ZAY shuhn) an action by a government to take control of property that belongs to a church. (p. 128)

segregation (sehg rih GAY shuhn) the practice of keeping different groups of people separate. (p. 344)

service (SUR vihs) work that a person or company does for another. (p. 49)

service industry (SUR vihs IHN duh stree) businesses that provide services, such as banks. (p. 408)

settler (SEHT lur) a person who moves to a new area to live. (p. 91)

shaman (SHAH muhn) an American Indian spiritual leader. (p. 60)

Sikh (seek) someone who practices the religion of Sikhism. (p. 254)

slate (slayt) a small chalkboard on which students once wrote. (p. 365)

slavery (SLAY vuh ree) the practice of buying and selling people who must work without pay. (p. 166)

smog (smahg) air pollution that is a mixture of smoke and fog. (p. 340)

solar energy (SOH luhr EHN ur jee) power that comes from sunlight. (p. 33)

space race (SPAYS rays) the competition between the United States and the Soviet Union to be the leader in space exploration. (p. 333)

special district (SPEHSH uhl DIHS trihkt) a local government set up to work on one particular issue. (p. 403)

special purpose map (SPEHSH uhl PUR puhs map) a map that uses symbols to show certain features of a place. (p. 330)

squatter (SKWAHT ur) a person who settles on land without having a legal claim. (p. 215)

stagecoach (STAYJ kohch) a horse-drawn carriage that carries mail and passengers. (p. 226)

strike (stryk) an action of refusing to work to win higher pay or better working conditions. (p. 235)

suburb (SUHB urb) a community near a city with many homes and few businesses. (p. 339)

suffrage (SUHF rihj) the right to vote. (p. 293)

summarize (SUHM uh ryz) the act of stating or writing the most important parts of another piece of writing. (p. 276)

supply (suh PLY) the amount of something that businesses will make available to sell at certain prices. (p. 191)

symbol (SIHM buhl) an image that stands for something on a map. (p. 88)

talkie (TAWK ee) slang for a movie with sound. (p. 298)

tallow (TAL oh) animal fat used to make candles or other goods. (p. 101)

tax (taks) money paid to a government. (p. 364)

technology (tehk NAWL uh jee) the use of tools, often improved by scientific knowledge, to do work. (p. 169)

telegraph (TEHL ih graf) a system for sending messages by electric signals through wires. (p. 229)

tenant farmer (TEHN uhnt FAHR mur) a farmer who farms land owned by someone else and pays the landowner rent and a share of crops. (p. 263)

territory (TEHR ih tawr ee) an area of land that belongs to a country. (p. 169)

tourism (TUR ihz uhm) the business of providing goods and services to people on holiday. (p. 299)

trade (trayd) the exchange, buying, or selling of goods, resources, or services. (p. 50)

tradition (truh DIHSH uhn) a custom or way of life that is handed down over many years. (p. 59)

transcontinental (tranz kahn tuh NEHN tl) crossing a continent. (p. 232)

transportation (trans pur TAY shuhn) any way of moving people or goods. (p. 227)

trapper (TRAP ur) a person who traps wild animals for fur. (p. 139)

treaty (TREE tee) a written agreement between nations to end fighting and follow certain rules. (p. 168)

trend (trehnd) a style or fashion that spreads quickly. (p. 377)

unemployment (uhn ehm PLOI muhnt) the number of people who are looking for a job but can't find one. (p. 305)

university (yoo nuh VUR sih tee) a school with several colleges. (p. 366)

vaquero (vah KAY roh) a cowhand who works on a rancho. (p. 133)

veteran (VEHT ur uhn) someone who has served in the military. (p. 338)

viceroy (VYS roy) a person who governs a region for a king or queen. (p. 118)

vigilante (vihj uh LAN tee) someone who captures and punishes people without a fair trial or respect for rights. (p. 209)

volcano (vawl KAY noh) an opening in the earth's surface through which lava, ash, and gas can escape. (p. 15)

wagon train (WAG uhn trayn) a group of wagons that travels together. (p. 140)

water rights (WAW tur ryts) the ability to control the use of water from a lake or river. (p. 270)

watershed (WAW tur shehd) a region that drains into a river. (p. 414)

weather (WEHTH ur) the condition of the air that surrounds a place. (p. 20)

wetland (WEHT land) a low area of land that has water on or near the surface. (p. 24)

Index

Page numbers with an *m* after them refer to maps. Page numbers in italics refer to pictures.

A

Acapulco, Mexico, 86
Adams, Ansel, 17
Adobe, 99, 134
Aerospace industry, 318, 333, 336
Africa, *7m, 317m*
    immigration, 110, 256
African Americans
    abolitionists, 166
    education, 345
    entrepreneurs, 155, 188, 208, 381
    and equal rights, 246, 257, 344–345
    in exploration, 82
    in the Gold Rush, 208
    freedom in free state, 202, 205
    leaders, *344, 345, 400, 404*
    in politics, *344, 345, 400,* 404
    settlement and, 110, 257
    slavery and, 166, 202, 205
    voting rights, 294
    women, 202, 205, 246, 404
    and World War II, 323
Agriculture
    agricultural industry, 260–263, 297, 298, 322, 334, 346–347
    California Indians and, 39, 65, 100–101, 103, 129, 135
    Central Valley, 24, 254–256, 261–262
    Central Valley Project, 307
    changes in, 261, 262, 297, 322, 334
    citrus, 101, 261, *262*
    Coachella Valley, *31*
    in the desert, 65
    and drought, 305
    and the economy, 264–265, 334
    farm workers in, 253–256, *262*, 263, 264, 334–335, 346–347, 350–351, 357
    festivals, 379
    Great Depression and, 305
    immigrants and, 253–256, 263, 335, 357
    Imperial Valley, 31, 254, 256, 266–267, 346
    irrigation and, 262, 266, 270, 271, 307
    large-scale, 261, 264, 322, 334
    at missions, 100–101, 103
    refrigerated railroad cars, 248, *264,* 265
    technology and, 261, *264,* 265, 334
    tenant farmers, 263
    United Farm Workers and, 346–347
    water control and, 262, 266, 270, 271, 307
    wheat, 261, 262
    World War I and, 297
    World War II and, 322
Airplane industry, 288, 297, 298, 322, 323, 332, 339
Alameda, California, 368
Alameda Corridor, 373
Alaska, 90, 130
Alcatraz Island, California, 348
Allen, Jane Bushton, *193*
Allensworth, Allen, 257
Alpine County, California, 365
American Indians in California. *See* California Indians.
Anaheim, California, 341, 407

Analysis Skills. *See* Map and globe skills; Study skills; Chart and graph skills; and Reading and thinking skills.
Angel Island, California, 253, *308m*
Anza, Juan Bautista de, 108
Aqueduct, Los Angeles, 248, 251, 270–271, 277
Architecture, 49, *56, 57, 59,* 65, 279, 281, *338,* 339
Argüello, Luís Antonio, 127
Argüello, Maria de la Concepción, 131
Arizona, 8, 169, 321
Armenia, immigration, 256, 323
Armstrong, Neil, *337*
Artists's colony, 279
Asia, *7m,* 40, 41, 80–81, 90, 91, 254, *255m, 316m,* 374–375
Asian Americans
    in agriculture, 254, 263
    entrepreneurs, 247, 254, 263, 359
    in the Gold Rush, 175, 180
    and railroads, 234–236, 254
    in science, *283*
    settlement, 253, 254, 359, 360
    in politics, 359, 405
    women, 381, 405
    in World War II, 321, 326–329
Asian immigration, 252–255, 263, 358–359
    Asian Indian, 254, *255m,* 357, 358
    Bangladeshi, 358
    Cambodian, 358–359, 360
    Chinese, 175, 180, 234–235, 252–253, *255m,* 357, 358
    Filipino, 255, 339, 357, 358, 360
    Hmong, 359
    Iranian, 357
    Japanese, 252, 254, 255, 263, 339
    Korean, 254, 255, 266, 339, 357, 358, 360
    Mien, 359
    Laotian, 358–359
    Pakistani, 358
    Sikh, 254, 255, 266
    Sri Lankan, 358
    Taiwanese, 357
    Vietnamese, 357, 358–359
Assembly, California, 400–401, 404
Australia, *7m, 16m*
Automobile industry, 298
    impact, 299, 342–343
    See also Cars.
Aztecs, 81

B

Baja California, Mexico, 81, 82, *83m, 88m,* 91, 113
Baker, Lily, *61*
Ball, Lucille, 340
Ballou, Mary, 154
Bandini, Arcadia, 160
Bangladesh, immigration, 358
Banks, 305, 306
Barrios, 319, 339
Barter, 51
Bartleson, John, 140

Bear Flag Republic, 163
Bear Flag Revolt, 162–163, 164
Beckwourth, James, 75, 139
Beckwourth Pass, 139
Beechey, Frederick William, 130
Benicia, California, 203, *223*
Bering Strait, 90
Bering, Vitus, 90
Berkeley, University of California at, 366, 377
Bidwell, John, 140, 142
Bidwell-Bartleson party, 77, 140, *142m*
Big Four, 233, 235, 291
    See also Railroads and Transcontinental Railroad.
Big Sur, California, 17
Bill of Rights
    California Constitution Declaration of Rights, 201
    United States Constitution, 390
Black, Shirley Temple, 306
Boom, economic, 190
Boom towns, 206–207
Boston, Massachusetts, *174m*
Boxer, Barbara, R4
Boycott, 347
Braceros, 335
Bradley, Tom, *344*
Brannan, Sam, 173, 191, 207
Burbank, California, 340
Burbank, Luther, 1, 261
Burke, Yvonne Braithwaite, 404
Bush, George H. W., 321
Butterfield, John, 228

C

Cable cars, 279, 281
Cabrillo, Juan Rodríguez, 76, 82, *83m*
Cahto, 42, *50m*
Cahuenga, Treaty of, 168, 170–171
Cahuilla, 42, 64, 65, 66, 67, 69
California
    borders, 8, 201
    climate, 20–25
    Constitution, 200–201, 291, 398–399
    counties, 402, R12–R14
    culture. *See* Culture *and individual countries and groups.*
    facts, R6–R7
    free state, 201, 202
    geographic isolation, 119, 126, 226–227
    geography, 6–9, 10–11, 14–17, 20–25, 30–33
    government, 398–403
    governors, 110, 127, 143, *198,* 199, 291, *401,* R10–R11
    immigrants. *See* Immigration.
    location within United States, 7–8
    Mexico and. *See* Mexican California *and* Mexico.
    natural resources, 30–33
    physical features, 10–11, 14–17, 22–25
    population, 42, 157, 160, 338, 406–407
    regions, 22–25, 31
    representatives, 349, 389, 400–401
    Spanish rule. *See* Colonial period.

R58 • Resources

state capital, 203, 207
state seal, R6
state symbols, R7
statehood, 199–200, 202
United States territory, 169, 198, 199
vegetation, 23
women in. See Women.
California Indians
adaptation to environment, 42, 43, 48, 49, 57, 58, 64, 65
agriculture, 39, 65, 100–101, 103, 129, 135
Alcatraz Island, California, 348
art, 68
artifacts, *38, 60, 62, 63, 65*
basketry, 38, 49, 61, 63
beliefs, 41, 60
ceremonies, 59–60
citizens, 214, 216–217
coastal peoples, 48–51
cultures of, 42–43, 49–53, 56–61, 62–63, 64–67, 68–69
dependence on environment, 48, 49, 57, 58, 64, 65
desert peoples, 64–67
diseases, 103, 216
diversity among, 42
economic activity, 49, 50–51, 52
and equal rights, 217, 348
fishing, 48–49, 57, 58, 65
foods, acorns, 43, 48–49, 50, 57, 58, 94
foods, corn, 39, 65
geographic distribution, *1m*, 48, *50m*, 56, 57, 64, *65m*
gold rush and, 173, 179, 180
government, 66–67, 402
housing, 49, *56*, 57, 59, 65
hunting and gathering, 57–58, 64–65, 100–101
land rights, 128, 216–217
land use, 43
language groups, 42
leadership, 66–67, 216
in Mexican California, 127, 128, 129, 133, 135, 136
miners, 173, 179, 180
missions to convert, 92, 93, 98–103, 104–107, *113m*
modification of environment, 43, 65
mountain and valley peoples, 56–61
oral history, 38, 41, 60
physical environment, 42, 48, 49, *50*, 57, 58, 59, 64, 65, 216
population, 42, 103, 216
in pueblos, 135
rancherias, 402
at ranchos, 129, 133, 135, 136
relations with United States government, 216–217, 348, 402
religions, 60
reservations, 216, 217, 348, 402
resistance, 102, 216–217
secularization and, 128, 129, 135
social organization, 66, 67
in Spanish California, 93, 98–103
town and village life, 49, 57, 58, 59, 60, 64, 65, 66
trade, 2, 50–51
treaties, 216
use of resources, 43, 48–51, 57–59, 64–65
voting rights, 201, 294–295

ways of life, 42, 48–51, 52–53, 56–61, 62–63, 64–67
See also individual groups.
California Institute of Technology, 333
California Trail, 140, *156m*
Californios
in American California, 199, 200, 214, 215
in the Gold Rush, 173
in Mexican California, 126, 128, 132–134, 160, 162, 164, 168
and property rights, 215
in Spanish California, 122, 123
Cambodia, 358
Cambodian Americans, 359
immigration, 358–359, 360
Canada
immigration, 252
trade with, 372, 375
Canals, 262, 266, 307, 414
Cape Mendocino, California, 86
Capital, California, 203, 207
Careers, 408–409
See also Jobs.
Carlsbad, California, 377
Cars, 281, 298–299, 340, 342–343
Cascade Range, 23
Cattle, 101, 128, 129, 132–133, 136, 261
Central America, 174, 361
Central Pacific Railroad Company, 233, 234, 237, 238, 239
Central Valley, 11, 21, *22m*, 24, 31, 56, 58–59, 139, 254, 256, 261, 262
Central Valley Project, 307
Chaffey, George, 266
Channel Islands, *11*, 50
Character Traits, R4–R5
caring, 130–131
civic virtue, 68–69, 404–405
courage, 380–381
fairness, 350–351
patriotism, 362–363
respect, 18–19
responsibility, 204–205, 392–395
Chart and graph skills
read a circle graph, 302–303
read a timeline, 96–97
Chavez, Cesar, 319, 346–347, 351
Chemehuevi, *65m*
Chew, Ng Poon, 258, R4
Child labor, 292
Chile, 372
China
Chinese Americans, 253, 258, 294
Chinese Exclusion Act, 253
immigration, 175, 180, 234–235, 252–253, *255m*, 357, 358
trade with, 372, 375
Chumash, 42, 49, 50–51, 52–53, 68, 82, 94
Cisneros, Evelyn, 380
Cities, growth of
Gold Rush and, 206–207, 278
Los Angeles, California, 269, 270, 360
migration and, 339, 407
Richmond, California, 322
Sacramento, California, 207
San Francisco, California, 206–207, 278–279
Stockton, California, 207
Citizenship
civic responsibility, 390
civic virtues, 390–391, R4–R5

common good, 390–391
democracy, 390
democratic values, 390–391, 399
make decisions, 382–383
participating, 390–391
patriotism, 362–363
point of view, 184–185
resolve conflicts, 418–419
See also Government.
Citizenship skills
make a decision, 382–383
point of view, 184–185
resolve conflicts, 418–419
Citrus industry, 261, 262
City council, 402
City government, 386, 402
City manager, 386, 402
Civic improvement, 391, 402
Civic responsibility, 390
Civic rights, 390
Civic virtues, 390–391, R4–R5
Civil rights, 293, 294–295, 345, 348–349, 390
Civil Rights Act, 345
Clapp, Louise, 181, 185, 205
Climate, 20–25, 34, 35
Coachella Valley, 30, 31, *266m*
Coast Miwok, *50m*, 83
Coast Ranges, 14, *15m*, 22
Colleges and universities, 354, 366
Colonial period, 91–93, 98–103, 108–111, 112–113, 118–119, 122–123
California Indians during, 93, 98–103
missionaries, 92, 94–95, 98–102
soldiers, 92, 99, 102, 108–109, 111, 112
See also Missions.
Colonization
influence of geography on, 99, 109
settlements, 92, 93, 99, 109, 110–111, *113m*
Colorado Desert, *267*
Colorado River, 16, 31, 65, 201, 266
Colton Hall, Monterey, 200
Columbus, Christopher, 80
Communication, 226–229, 232, 408
Communications industry, 408
Communities, 42
architecture, 279, 281, *338*, 339
climate, 34–35
land use, 34–35
population density, 34–35, 406
services, 34–35, 399, 402, 410–411
transportation, 34–35, 269, 340, 373
Community colleges, 366
Compass rose, 13
Compromise of 1850, 202
Computers, 370–371
Congress, United States, 389
Conquistadors, 81
Conservation, 17, 18, 33, 271, 414–415, 416–417
Constitution, California, 200, 201
Declaration of Rights, 201
document, *201*
history of, 199–201, 398
key principles, 201, 398, 399
reforms, 291
relationship to United States Constitution, 201, 399
Constitution, Mexico, 120, 127
Constitution, United States, 120, 201
Bill of Rights, 390

Constitutional Convention, California

content, 388, 398–399
importance, 388
structure, 389
Constitutional Convention, California, 200–201, 203
Cook, Captain James, 91
Cortés, Hernán, 78, 81
Costs and benefits, 382–383
Counties, 402, R12–R14
County government, 402
Crespí, Juan, 92, 93, 94
Crocker, Charles, 233, 235
Crowley, Patrick, *209*
Cry of Dolores, 119, 124
Culture
architecture, 49, *56*, 57, 59, 65, 279, 281, *338*, 339
art, 210–211, 279, 376–377
California and, 355, 376–377
customs, 60–61, 124, *125*, 175, 339, 378, 379
diversity, 42, 175, 208, 339
elements of, 56
festivals, 117, 124–125, 133, 134, 378–379
holidays, 378
immigration and, 175, 339, 361, 362
language, 24, 42, 69, 175, 339
literature, 181, 204, 205, 306, 380, 381
museums, 377
music, 377
oral history, 38, 41
religion, 60, 92, 98, 101, 175, 390
traditions, 59, 62–63, 378–379
See also individual countries and groups.
Culver City, California, 333
Cupertino, California, 371

Dams, 24, 262, 270, 307, 414, 416
Dana, Richard Henry, Jr., 74, 138
Death Valley, 25, 26–27
Decision making, 382–383
Declaration of Rights, 201
Defense industry, 322, 332
Demand, defined, 264
Democracy, defined, 390
See also Government.
Democratic values
caring, 130–131
equality, 127, 294–295, 344–349
fairness, 350–351
freedom, 390
justice, 189, 208–209, 291
opportunity, 140, 208, 252, 358–359, 361
responsibility, 204–205, 390, 399
Denmark, immigration, 378
Deserts, 25, 26–27, 31, 64, 65, 66, 228, 266
Development and construction
aqueducts, 248, 251, 270–271, 277
canals, 262, 266, 307, 414
dams, 24, 262, 270, 307, 414, 416
effects, 17, 262, 266, 271, 307, 414, 416
highways and roads, 299, 340
housing, 180, 281, 339
power plants, 271, 307
railroads, 232–237, 238–239, 269, 279, 373
reservoirs, 270, 414
Dinh, Viet, 359
Diputación, 127
Discrimination and reform, 180, 209, 253, 255, 257, 258, 288, 339, 345, 348, 349, 350
Diseño, 128
Disney, Walt, 341
Diversity, 42, 175, 208, 339
Dolores, 119
Dolores, Cry of, 119, 124
Dominguez, Manuel, 155, 201
Donner party, 141, 142
Drake, Sir Francis, 74, 83
Drakes Bay, California, 83
Drought, 305
Dust Bowl, 305, 306

Earthquakes, 15, 280–281, 282
East Los Angeles, California, 323, 348
Economics
consumers, 190
cost/benefit, 382
demand, 264
earning/income, 180, 323
entrepreneurs, defined, 192
goods, 49
income tax, 399
investing, 233
market, 264
money, 51
prices, 191, 227, 265
productivity, 334
profit, 190
sales tax, 399
services, 49
supply, 191
taxes, 364, 390, 399
trade, 50–51, 86–87, 372–373, 374–375
Economy, defined, 50
agricultural, 100–101, 260–265
boom, 190
California's economy, 370–373, 374–375, 408–409
depression, 304
education and, 366
employment. *See* Jobs.
Franciscan influence, 100–101, 103
hunter-gatherer, 49, 57–58, 64–65, 100–101
immigration and, 254–256, 359, 361
industrial, 297–298, 322–323, 332–333
industry, 297, 322, 323, 332, 333, 371, 408
unemployment, 305, 308
Edson, Katherine Philips, 292, 293
Education
community colleges, 366
effects, 366
grants, 367
public education, 364–367
reforms, 345, 348
San Diego State University, 366
school districts, 365
school system, 365–366
Stanford University, 371
universities, 354, 366
University of California at Berkeley, 366, 377
University of California system, 366
El Camino Real, 109, 112–113
El Salvador, immigration, 357
Elections, 291, 293, 389, 390, 392–395, 399
Electronics industry, 316, 370–372, 408

Elizabeth I, Queen of England, 83
Energy, 271, 307
England, 83, 91
Drake's raid, 83
exploration of the Pacific, 91
See also Great Britain.
Entertainment industry, 340–341
Entrepreneurs
Allen, Jane Bushton, *193*
Ball, Lucille, 340
Brannan, Sam, 173, 191, 207
Butterfield, John, 228
Crocker, Charles, 233, 235
defined, 192
Disney, Walt, 341
Ford, Henry, 298
Ghirardelli, Domenico, 192
Gibbs, Mifflin Wistar, 188, 208
Hopkins, Mark, 233
Huntington, Collis, 233
Hyung-soon, Kim, 254
Jobs, Steven, 370
Johnson, Eliza Steen, 154, 192
Kaiser, Henry J., 322
Lester, Peter, 155, 208
Loughead, Allan and Malcolm, 297
Mayer, Louis B., 297
Ngoy, Bun Tek, 359
Saint James, Synthia, 381
Shima, George, 247, 263
Stanford, Leland, 233, 235, 236
Stearns, Abel, 160, 161
Strauss, Levi, 192
Wakefield, Lucy Stoddard, 192
Weber, Charles, 207
Wilson, Luzena Stanley, 193
Wozniak, Stephen, 370
Environment, 17
effects of Gold Rush mining on, 179, 182–183
environmentalists, 17
how it affects people, 30–32, 42
how people affect, 17, 33, 43, 179, 182–183, 262, 266, 271, 307, 414, 413–416
pollution, 340, 413, 416
protection of, 17, 33, 411, 413–414
recycling, 414
water, 16, 262, 266, 270–271, 307, 414, 416–417
See also Geography.
Equator, 7, 28
Esselen, *50m*
Eu, March Fong, 405
Europe, *7m, 17m*
expeditions from, 80, 81, 83, 90, 91
immigration, 252, 256, 263
World War I, 296
World War II, 320, 321
Executive branch, 389, 400–401
Expeditions, 80–84, 90, 92–93, 139
Exploration
Anza, Juan Bautista de, 108
Beckwourth, James, 75, 139
Bering, Vitus, 90
British, 91
Cabrillo, Juan Rodriguez, 76, 82, *83m*
California Indians and, 82, 83, 100, 139
colonization. *See* Colonization.
Columbus, Christopher, 80
Cook, Captain James, 91
Cortés, Hernán, 78, 81
Crespí, Juan, 92, 93, 94

R60 • Resources

Drake, Sir Francis, 74, 83
Frémont, John Charles, 139, *142m*, 165
land routes, 85, 91, 92, 108, 139–141, *142m*
missionaries and, 92, 93, 94–95, 100
of North America, 80–85, 90–93
in the north Pacific, 90–91
Portolá, Gaspar de, 76, 92–93, 94
obstacles, 84–85, 108, 140–141
Russian, 90
sea routes, *76m*, 82–84, 86–87, *88m*
Serra, Junípero, 79, 92–93, 94–95
Smith, Jedediah Strong, 139, *142m*
soldiers and, 92, 108–109
space, 333, 336–337
Spanish, 80–82, 84–85, 92–93, 108–109
Ulloa, Francisco de, 88
Vizcaíno, Sebastián, 84, 85, 91

Factories
aerospace industry, 333, 336
airplane industry, 297, 322–323, 332
defense industry, 322, 332
shipbuilding industry, 322–323
steel industry, 322
Farming. *See* Agriculture.
Federal government. *See* National Government.
Feinstein, Dianne, 314, 349
Festivals
agricultural, 379
Cinco de Mayo, *124*, 378
Danish Days, 378
fiestas, 117, 133, 134
Mexican Independence Day, 124–125
Old Spanish Days, 378
Filmmakers, California
Disney, Walt, 341
Lucas, George, 377
Mayer, Louis B., 297
Fishing, 48, 49, 57, 58, 65
Florida, 120
Flow resources, 32
Ford, Henry, 298
Fort Ross, 122, 142
Forty-niners, 159, 173–175, *177*, 179–181, 216
France, 143, 296, 297, 320
Franciscan missionaries, 92–93, 94–95, 98–103
and the economy of California, 100–101, 103
Free states, 202
Freeways, 340
Frémont, Jessie Benton, 165
Frémont, John Charles, 139, *142m*, 162, 165, 168, 170–171
Fresno, California, 21, 254, 407
Fur trade, 90, 139

Gabaldon, Guy Louis, 323
Galvéz, José de, 91
Gandhi, Mahatma, 351
Garland, Judy, 324
Geographers, 8–9
Geographic terms, 7–9, 28–29
Geography, 6–9

climate, 20–25
coastal bays, 16
defined, 6
earthquakes, 15, 280–281, 282
environment and society, 17, 411, 412–414
erosion, 15
geographers, 8–9
harbors, 84, 85, 279
human-environment interaction, 17, 30–33, 43, 48–49, 57–59, 64, 65, 99, 179, 182–183, 262, 266, 271, 307, 411, 413–414, 416
influence on exploration, 84, 85
influence on settlement, 42, 99, 109, 134, 206–207, 278
landforms, 14–15
location, 6–8
mountain ranges, 14, 22, 23
natural resources, 30–33
questions about, 8–9
regions, 21–25
river deltas, 16
urban settlement, 22, 269, 278, 339, 407
volcanoes, 15
water, 16–17
See also Environment.
George, Ronald, *401*
Germany, 256, 320, 321
immigration, 252
Ghirardelli, Domenico, 192
Gibbs, Mifflin Wistar, 188, 208
Glenn, John, *336*
Gold Rush
businesses, 180, 190–193, 207
and California's culture, 175, 180, 208, 210–211
California Indians in, 173, 179, 180
changes in towns, 180, 191, 206–207, 278
claims, 180
crime, 208–209
daily life, 180–181, 191
economic conflicts during, 180, 215, 216
effects, 179, 180, 182–183, 190, 191, 199, 260, 278
entrepreneurs in, 192–193, 208
food and, 180, 191, 260
forty-niners, 159, 173–175, *177*, 179–181, 216
gold found at Sutter's mill, 172–173, 176
growth of cities and, 206–207, 278
hydraulic mining, 179, 182–183, 191
immigration, 174–175, 190, 199, 206–208
merchants, 190–193, 207
miners, 175, 177, 179–181, 191
mining camps, 180
mining technology, 179, 182–183, 191
physical environment, 180
population growth, 190, 199, 206–207, 278
production, 179, 180, 191
products during, 191–192
Sacramento and, 207
San Francisco and, 191, 192, 206–207, 278
travel, 174
vigilantes, 209
women in, 154, 181, 192, 193, 205

Golden Gate Bridge, 308–309
Golden Gate Strait, California, 308–309
Goods, defined, 49
Governance structure
counties, 402
local, 402
national, 389–389
rancherias, 402
reservations, 216, 217, 402
school districts, 365
state, 399–401
Government
Bill of Rights, 390
branches, 388–389, 400–401
California Indian, 66–67, 402
checks and balances, 389, 400
city government, 402
common good, 390–391
comparisons among, 120, 199, 201, 398, 399
Congress, United States, 389
Constitution, California, 200–201, 291, 398–399
Constitution, United States, 120, 201, 388–390, 398–399
counties, 402
defined, 66
democracy, 390
executive branch, 389, 400–401
functions, 389, 399–403
governor, 400–401
House of Representatives, 389
jobs in, 389, 399–403
judicial branch, 389, 400–401
legislative branch, 386, 389, 400–401
local, 402–403
mayor, 402
in Mexican period, 120, 126–129, 140, 143, 161–162, 199
national, 388–389, 398–399
President, 389
public services, 399, 402, 410–411
of rancherias, 402
reforms, 290–291
representative government, 120, 127, 389, 400, 402
republic, 120
rights and responsibilities, 390–391
school districts, 365
Senate, 389
in Spanish period, 98, 103, 110, 118–119, 122, 199
special districts, 403
state, 398–401
state Assembly, 400–401, 404
state Senate, 400–401, 404
state Supreme Court, 400–401, 405
Supreme Court, United States, 389
voting, 201, 293, 294–295, 345, 390, 392–395
See also Democracy; National Government; *and* State Government.
Governors, California, 400–401
Graves, Mary, 141
Great Britain
immigration, 252
in World War I, 296
in World War II, 320, 321
See also England.
Great Depression, 289, 304–307
Greece, immigration, 266, 277

Guadeloupe Hidalgo, Treaty of

Guadeloupe Hidalgo, Treaty of, 158, 169, 214, 216
Guatemala, immigration, 357
Guerrero, Vicente, 119
Gulf of California, *88m*

Hawaii, 320
Hawk, Tony, 377
Hemisphere, defined, 7
Hidalgo y Costilla, Miguel, 119
High-tech industry, 355, 370–371
Highways and roads, 299, 340
History
  California's first people, 41–43
  colonization, 91–93, 98–103, 108–111
  exploration, 82–85, 90–93, 139
  timelines. *See last page of lessons and chapter reviews.*
Hmong Americans, 24, 359
Holidays
  Cesar Chavez Day, 351, 378
  Chinese New Year, 378
  Cinco de Mayo, *124*, 378
  Martin Luther King Jr. Day, 378
  Mexican Independence Day, 124–125
Hollywood, California, 297, 340
Hoover, Herbert, 389
Hopkins, Mark, 233
House of Representatives, United States, 389
Huerta, Dolores, 346–347, 350
Human-environment interaction, 17, 30–33, 43, 48–49, 57–59, 64, 65, 99, 179, 182–183, 262, 266, 271, 307, 411, 413–414, 416
Hunter-gatherer economy, 49, 57–58, 64–65, 100–101
Huntington, Collis, 233
Hupa, 42, 69
Hydroelectric power, 271, 307
Hyung-soon, Kim, 254

Immigration
  accords, 335
  African, 110, 256
  Armenian, 256, 323
  Asian, 252–255, 263, 358–359
  Asian Indian, 254, *255m*, 357, 358
  Bangladeshi, 358
  Bidwell-Bartleson party, 140
  Cambodian, 358–359, 360
  Canadian, 252
  Chinese, 175, 180, 234–235, 252–253, *255m*, 357, 358
  communities, 253, 254, 359, 360
  conflicts, 180, 253, 255
  contributions, 175, 208, 234–236, 253, 254, 255, 256, 335, 359, 361
  and culture, 175, 339, 361, 362
  Danish, 378
  discrimination and reform, 180, 209, 253, 255, 257, 258, 339, 316, 356, 357, 358
  diversity, 175, 208
  Donner party, 141, 142
  employment and, 254–257, 335, 356–357, 359
  English, 252
  European, 175, 252, 256, 263
  Filipino, 255, 339, 357, 358, 360
  German, 252
  Gold Rush and, 174–175, 190, 199, 206–208
  Greek, 266, 277
  growth of towns and cities, 253, 254, 339, 359
  Guatemalan, 357
  Hmong, 359
  illegal, 360
  Iranian, 357
  Irish, 192, 236, 252
  Italian, 192, 252, 362
  Japanese, 252, 254, 255, 263, 339
  Jewish, 256
  Korean, 254, 255, 266, 339, 357, 358, 360
  Laotian, 358–359
  Latin American, 252, 360
  laws, 253, 255, 316, 356, 357, 358, 360
  Mexican, 256, 257, 263, 277, 335, 339, 357
  Mien, 359
  Pakistani, 254, 358
  politics and, 253, 255, 356
  reasons for, 174–175, 252–256, 357–358
  Russian, 175, 256, 323
  Salvadoran, 357
  Sikh, 254, 255, 266
  Sri Lankan, 358
  Swiss, 277
  Taiwanese, 357
  twentieth century, 254, 255, 256, 339, 356–361
  United States, 138–143, 160–161
  Vietnamese, 357, 358–359
Immigration Act of 1924, 255
Immigration and Naturalization Act, 356, 357
Imperial Valley, 31, 254, 256, 266–267, 346
Independence, 119, 120, 124
India, immigration, 254, *255m*, 357, 358
Individual rights, 201, 390
Industry
  airplane, 288, 297, 298, 322, 323, 332, 339
  aerospace, 318, 333, 336
  agriculture, 260–263, 297, 298, 322, 334, 346–347
  automobile, 298–299
  communications, 408
  defense, 322, 332
  electronics, 316, 370–372, 408
  employment and, 292, 323, 333, 336, 339, 356, 357, 360
  entertainment, 340–341
  high-tech, 355, 370–371
  manufacturing, 408
  movie, 249, 297–298, 300–301, 324, 339, 340, 376
  oil, 298, 305, 339
  Pacific Basin and, 372
  service, 408
  shipbuilding, 322, 323
  television, 340
  tourism, 269, 279, 299, 341
  transportation, 408
Internal migration, 256, 305–306, 407
Internment camps, 321, 326–329
Iran, immigration, 357
Ireland, immigration, 192, 236, 252
Irrigation, 250, 262, 266–267, 307
Isthmus of Panama, 158, 174
Italy, 320, 321
  immigration, 192, 252, 362
Iturbide, Agustín de, 120

Jackson, Helen Hunt, 204
Japan
  immigration, 252, 254, 255, 263, 339
  Japanese Americans, 247, 254, 255, 321, 326–329
  trade with, 372, *372*
  World War II and, 320, 321
Jet Propulsion Laboratory, 333
Jewett, William Smith, *161*, 279
Jewish Californians, 256
Jobs,
  in agriculture, 253–256, 263, 334, 335, 346–347
  in construction, 234–236, 238–239, 254, 270
  in industry, 292, 323, 333, 336, 339, 357, 360, 371, 408
  in ranching, 136–137
Jobs, Steven, 370
Johnson, Eliza Steen, 154, 192
Johnson, Hiram, 290, 291, 293
Jones, Julie Rodriguez, 377
Judah, Theodore, 233
Judicial branch, 389, 400–401

Kaiser, Henry J., 322
Kanamori, Hiroo, *283*
Karuk, 42, *50m*, 56, 60
Kawaiisu, 42, *57m*, *65m*
Kearny, Stephen Watts, 168
King, Martin Luther, Jr., 345, 378
King Philip II of Spain, 83
Kings Canyon National Park, 18
Kintpuash, 216
Kitanemuk, *57m*
Klamath Mountains, 23
Kumeyaay, *50m*, 64, *65m*, 67, 82
Kwan, Michelle, 377

L

La Brea Tar Pits, *40*
La Paz, Mexico, *88m*
Labor
  labor unions, 346
  See also Jobs.
Lake Tahoe, California, 16
Lakewood, California, 339
Lam, Tony, 359
Land Act of 1851, 215
Land Commission, 215
Land grants, 128–129, *134m*, 142, 215
Land rights, 214–217, 218–221
Land use, 31, 32, 34, 35, 128, 260, 262, 264
Landfills, 387, 414
Landforms, 14–15
Lange, Dorothea, 247, 306
Languages, California Indian, 42
Laos, immigration, 358–359
Lassen Peak, California, 15

Latin America, 103, 360
 immigration, 252, 360
Latitude, 28
Lava Beds National Monument,
 California, *217*
Lava fields, 216, 217
Laws, 189, 208, 209
 civil rights laws, 127, 293, 294–295, 345
 immigration laws, 253, 255, 316, 356,
  357, 358, 360
 land laws, 215
 trade laws, 122, 128, 317, 372
Leaders. *See* Politicians and leaders.
Legislative branch, 386, 389, 400–401
Leidesdorff, William, *364*
Lester, Peter, 155, 208
Lincoln, Abraham, 229
Lindbergh, Charles, 297
Literature
 diaries, 94, 141
 fiction, 44–47, 104–107, 194–197, 306,
  326–329,
 letters, 95, 181
 oral history, 44–47
Local government, 402–403
 city council, 402
 city government, 402
 city manager, 402
 mayor, 402
 special districts, 403
Long Beach, California, 35, *298,* 323,
 360, 373, 407
Longitude, 28
Los Angeles, California, 268–271
 aqueduct, 248, 251, 270–271, 277
 culture, 377
 discrimination and reform, 345
 founding, 110, 268
 growth, 269, 270
 hydroelectric power, 271
 immigration, 360
 location, 22
 movie industry, 297–298, 300
 oil industry, 298
 pollution, 340
 population, 111, 268, 269, 407
 pueblo, 110–111
 railroads and, 269, 373
 reforms, 292
 school district, 365
 trade, 16, 269, 372, 373
 water, 31, 270–271
 Watts, 345
 Watts Towers, 362–363
Loughead, Allan and Malcolm, 297
Lucas, George, 376
Luiseño, *50m*

Maidu, 42, 56, 57, 60, 61
Manifest Destiny, 161, 167
Manila, Philippines, 83, 86
Manila galleons, 83, 86, *87m*
Map and globe skills
 make a map, 88–89
 review map skills, 12–13
 use a special purpose map, 330–331
 use latitude and longitude, 28–29
Map legend, 13
Market, defined, 264
Marshall, James, 172

Martinez, Rueben, 315, 409
Mason, Bridget "Biddy," 202, 205
Massachusetts, 160, 205
Matthews, Miriam, 314
Mattole, *50m*
Mayer, Louis B., 297
Mayor, defined, 402
Merritt, Ezekiel, 162
Mexican-American War, 156, 163, 165,
 166–169, 170, 214
Mexican California, 120, 126–129, 132–
 135, 138–143
 land grants, 128–129, *134m,* 142, 215
 rancho economy, 129, 132–135
 secularization, 128, 129, 135
 settlements and, 134
Mexican Independence Day, 124–125
Mexican War for Independence, 118–
 120, 124, 126
 effects, 122–123
Mexico, *7m,* 8, 160
 Constitution of 1824, 120, 127
 government, 120, 126–129, 140, 143, 162
 immigration, 256, 257, 263, 277, 335,
  339, 357
 Mexican-American War, 156, 163, 165,
  166–169, 170, 214
 Mexican Americans, 256–257, 323, 346,
  348
 trade with, 372, 375
Mien Americans, 359
Migration, 256, 305–306, 407
Miller, Henry, 262
Mining camps, 180
Mining technology, 179, 182–183, 191
Missions
 daily life, 100–103, 104–107
 effects, 99, 100–103
 functions of, 93, 98, 100, 103, 111
 locations of, 99
 mapping, 99
 Mission La Purísima Concepción,
  99m, 104–107, *113m*
 Mission Nuestra Señora de la
  Soledad, *99m, 113m*
 Mission San Antonio de Padua, *99m,
  113m*
 Mission San Buenaventura, *99m,
  113m*
 Mission San Carlos Borromeo, 93, 95,
  99m, 113m
 Mission San Diego de Alcalá, 92, 93,
  98, *99m,* 102, *113m*
 Mission San Fernando Rey España,
  99m, 113m
 Mission San Francisco de Asís, 93,
  99m, 113m
 Mission San Francisco Solano de
  Sonoma, 99, *113m*
 Mission San Gabriel Arcángel, 93,
  99m, 102, 108, *113m,* 139
 Mission San José de Guadalupe, *99m,
  113m*
 Mission San Juan Bautista, *99m, 113m*
 Mission San Juan Capistrano, *99m,
  113m*
 Mission San Luís Obispo, *99m, 113m*
 Mission San Luís Rey, *99m, 113m*
 Mission San Miguel Arcángel, *99m,*
  102, *113m*
 Mission San Rafael Arcángel, *99m,
  113m*

North America

Mission Santa Barbara, 93, *99m, 113m*
Mission Santa Clara, *99m, 113m*
Mission Santa Cruz, *99m, 113m*
Mission Santa Inés, *99m, 113m*
and religion, 93, 98, 100, 101
secularization, 128, 129, 135
Spanish influence and, 98, 103
treatment of California Indians, 99,
 102
Missionaries, 92, 94–95, 98–103
Missouri, 140, 228
Miwok, 42, 56–61, 63
Modesto, California, 376
Modoc, 42, 216, 217
Mohave, 64, 65, 67
Mojave Desert, 25, 139, 270, 277, 332, 336
Molina, Gloria, *401*
Monache, *57m*
Mono Lake, California, 16
Monterey, California, 8, 93, 95, 108, 109,
 120, 127, *134m,* 167, 200
Monterey Bay, California, 84, 85, 91, 93
Morelos, José María, 119
Morgan, Julia, 377
Morse, Samuel F. B., 229
Mount Shasta, California, 15
Mount Whitney, California, 3, 21, 23
Mountain pass, 15, 139
Movie industry, 249, 297–298, 300–301,
 324, 339, 340, 376
Muir, John, 17, 18–19
Mulholland, William, 270
Municipal government, 402
Museums, 377
Music, 377
Mutualistas, 257

National government
 branches, 388–389
 checks and balances, 389
 functions, 389
 jobs in, 389
 purpose, 389
 state powers and, 389, 398
 under Constitution, 388–389
National parks, 18
Native Americans in California. *See*
 California Indians.
Natural resources, 30–33
 See also Resources.
Nebraska, 233, 236
Nevada, 8, 169
Nevada City, California, 193
Neve, Felipe de, 110
New Deal, 249, 306–307
New Helvetia, 142
New Mexico, 169
New Spain, 81, 108, 118–120, *121m,* 126
New York City, New York, 192
Newspapers, *173,* 176, 181, 208, 258–259
Ngoy, Bun Tek, 359
Nixon, Richard, 389
Noguchi, Isamu, 377
Nolan, Mae Ella, *293*
Nonrenewable resources, 32
Nonviolent protest, 319, 345, 347–349,
 351
North America, 7, 120, *316m*
 exploration, 80–85, 90–93
 first people, 40–43

North American Free Trade Agreement

settlers, 92, 93, 110, 111
Manifest Destiny, 161, 167
North American Free Trade Agreement (NAFTA), 317, 372
North Pole, 7
Northern Hemisphere, 7

Oakland, California, 279, *283,* 407
Ocean currents, 84, 86, *87m*
Ochoa, Ellen, 315, 366
Ohlone, *50m,* 51, 102
Oil, 31
discovery, 298
industry, 298, 305, 339
Ontiveros, Juan and Martina, *215*
Oregon, 8, 23, 140, *156m,* 321
Overland Mail Service, 228
Owens River, 270
Owens Valley, 270–271
Owings, Margaret, *17*
Oxnard, California, 379

Pacific Basin trade, 269, 279, 361, 372
Pacific Railway Act, 233
Pacific Rim, 372, 374–375
Paiute, Owens Valley, *65m*
Pakistan, immigration, 254, 358
Palm Springs, California, *66,* 299
Panama Canal, Panama, 269, 272
Paris, France, 297
Pasadena, California, 333
Patwin, *57m*
Pearl Harbor, Hawaii, 320
Pearl Harbor attack, 320, *321m*
Petroleum, 31, 298
See also Oil.
Philippines, 83, 86, *87m,* 255
Filipino Americans, 255, 346
immigration, 255, 339, 357, 358, 360
Philip II, King of Spain, 83
Photographers, California
Adams, Ansel, *17*
Lange, Dorothea, 247, 306
Physical features of California
bodies of water, 16–17
coast, 22
climate, 20–25
landforms, 10–11, 14–15
regions, 21–25
resources, 30–33
Pickford, Mary, 300, 314
Pico, Andres, 168, *169,* 170–171
Pico, Pío, 143, 161
Pioneers, 117, 140–143
Placerville, California, *191*
Pleasant, Mary Ellen, 246, 257
Poland, 256
Poles, North and South, 7
Politicians and leaders
Argüello, Luís Antonio, 127
Boxer, Barbara, R4
Bradley, Tom, *344*
Burke, Yvonne Braithwaite, 404
Bush, George H. W., 321
Chavez, Cesar, 319, 346–347, 351
Dinh, Viet, 359
Dominguez, Manuel, 155, 201

Eu, March Fong, 405
Feinstein, Dianne, 314, 349
Hoover, Herbert, 389
Huerta, Dolores, 346–347, 350
Johnson, Hiram, 290, 291, 292
King, Martin Luther, Jr., 345, 378
Lam, Tony, 359
Lincoln, Abraham, 229
Molina, Gloria, *401*
Neve, Felipe de, 110
Nixon, Richard, 389
Nolan, Mae Ella, *293*
Pico, Andres, 168, *169,* 170–171
Pico, Pío, 143, 161
Polk, James K., 161, 166, 167, 173
Reagan, Ronald W., *389*
Reynoso, Cruz, 405
Riley, Bennett, *198,* 199, 200
Roberts, Frederick, *400*
Roosevelt, Franklin D., 306, 307, 321
Roosevelt, Theodore, *19*
Schwarzenegger, Arnold, *401*
Semple, Robert, 188, 200
Vallejo, Mariano Guadalupe, 133, 162, 164, 200
Vuich, Rose Ann, 404
Polk, James K., 161, 166, 167, 173
Pollution, 340, 413, 416
Pomo, 42, 49, *50m*
Pony Express, 228, 230–231
Population
Anaheim, California, 407
of California, 42, 157, 160, 338, 406–407
California Indian, 42, 103, 216
changes in, 407
density, 387, 406
distribution, 407
Fresno, 407
growth of cities, 206, 207, 269, 278, 279, 322
growth and Gold Rush, 173, 175, 190, 199, 206–207, 278
growth and transcontinental railroad, 237, 269, 279
Long Beach, California, 35, 407
Los Angeles, California, 268, 269, 407
Oakland, California, 407
Redding, California, 34
Sacramento, California, 407
San Diego, California, 407
San Francisco, California, 206–207, 278–279, 407
San Jose, California, 407
Santa Ana, California, 407
Population density, 387, 406
Portolá, Gaspar de, 76, 92–93, 94
Ports
Long Beach, California, 35
Los Angeles, California, 16, 269, 372, 373
Sacramento, California, 207
San Francisco, California, 161, 206–207, 278–279
San Pedro, California, 269
Stockton, California, 207
Potatoes, 261, 263
Potato King, 247, 263
Power plants, 271, 307
Prehistoric animals, 40, 41
President, 389
Presidents, United States
Bush, George H. W., 321

Hoover, Herbert, 389
Lincoln, Abraham, 229
Nixon, Richard, 389
Polk, James K., 161, 166, 167, 173
Reagan, Ronald W., *389*
Roosevelt, Franklin D., 306, 307, 321
Roosevelt, Theodore, *19*
Presidios, 79, 109
daily life, 109
function, 99, 109, 111
placement, 109, *113m*
Primary sources, 94–95, 176–177, 181, 212, 258–259, 272–275, 284, 368–369
Prime meridian, 28
Problem solving, 413–415, 418–419
Progressives, 291–293
Promontory, Utah, 236
Public works, 306–307
Pueblos
daily life, 110, 134–135
function, 110–111, 134–135, 268
government, 110, 134, 198
trade, 134

Quechan, *65m*
Queen Elizabeth I of England, 83

Racism, 344–345, 348
Railroads, 227
Big Four, 233, 235, 291
Chinese contribution to, 234–236
Irish contribution to, 236
Judah, Theodore, 233
railroad companies, 233–237, 238, 264, 269, 291
railroad workers, 234–236, 238–239, 254
refrigerated cars, 248, *264,* 265
Sikh contribution to, 254
and trade, 236, 264–265, 279, 291, 373
transcontinental railroad, 232–237, 238–239
Rancherias, 402
Ranchos, 129
daily life, 133, 135, 136–137
herding economy and, 129, 132, 134
land, 129, 133, *134m,* 214, 218-221
Reading skills. See first page of each lesson.
Reading strategies. See pages at beginning of each chapter.
Reading and thinking skills
distinguish fact from opinion, 240–241
draw conclusions, 396–397
interpret historical images, 212–213
summarize, 276–277
Reagan, Ronald W., *389*
Recycling, 33, 414, 415
Redding, California, 34
Reform, 288, 290–293, 345, 348, 349
Refrigerated railroad cars, 248, *264,* 265
Refugees, 256, 358
Regions
Central Valley, 24, 31
climate, 20–25
coast, 22, 31
desert, 25, 31

R64 • Resources

landforms, 21–25
mountains, 23, 31
physical characteristics, 22–25, 31
resources, 31–33
Religion, 60, 92, 98, 101, 175, 339
freedom of, 390
Renewable resources, 32
Representative government, 120, 127, 389, 400, 402
Representatives
city council, 402
diputación, 127
governor, 400–401
mayor, 402
state Assembly members, 400–401, 404
state Senators, 400–401, 404
United States Representatives, 389
United States Senators, 389
Reservations, 216, 217, 348, 402
Reservoirs, 270, 414
Resources
conservation of, 32–33, 271, 414, 416–417
flow resources, 32
natural resources, 30–32
nonrenewable resources, 32
renewable resources, 32
sea resources, 32
Reynoso, Cruz, 405
Responsibility, personal and civic, 390
Rezanov, Count Nikolai, 131
Richmond, California, 322, 377
Rights, 199
guaranteed, 201, 390
land, 215
property, 189, 201, 214
voting, 200, 293, 294–295, 345, 390
water, 270
Rights and responsibilities, 390–391
Riley, Bennett, *198*, 199, 200
Risling, David, 69
Riverside, California, 261, *366m*, 407
Roberts, Frederick, *400*
Robles, Mitchell E., 68
Rockwood, Charles, 266
Rocky Mountains, 161, *227m*
Rodeos, 133
Rodia, Sabato, 362
Roosevelt, Franklin D., 306, 307, 321
Roosevelt, Theodore, *19*
Ruiz de Burton, Maria Amparo, 215
Ruiz de Rodriguez, Bernarda, 168, 170
Russia, 90, 91, 122, 256, 320
immigration, 175, 256, 323

S

Sacramento, California, 142, 203, 207, 233, 234, 254, 371, 377, *398*, 407
Sacramento River, 16, 24, 207, 307
Staint James, Synthia, 381
Salinan, *50m*
Salton Sea, California, *267*
San Andreas Fault, California, 15, *282*
San Diego, California, 82, *83m*, 84, 91, 92, 109, *134m*, *156m*, 167, 297, 366, 371, 407
San Diego State University, 366
San Francisco, California, 278–281
architecture, 279
climate, 22
culture, 279, 377

earthquakes, 280–281, 282
education, 365
Gold Rush and, 191, 192, 206–207, 278
Golden Gate Bridge, 308–309
government, 402
growth, 206–207, 278–279
immigration to, 253, 254
location, 22
mission, *99m*, *110m*, *113m*
population, 206–207, 278–279, 407
presidio, 109, *113m*
railroads, 233, 279
trade, 279
San Francisco Bay, California, 16, 93, 130, 131, 167, 253, 279, 322
San Gabriel, California, 102, 139
San Joaquin River, 16, 24, 207, 262
San Joaquin Valley, 140
San Jose, California, 203, 359, 366, 407
pueblo of San José, 110, *134m*
San Luis Obispo, California, *31*, 134
San Pedro, California, 269, 372
San Pedro harbor, California, 16
Santa Ana, California, 359, 407
Santa Barbara, California, 31, 84, 109, 134, 168, 371, 378
Santa Catalina Island, California, 50, 84
Santa Cruz Island, California, 50
Santa Fe Railway, 269
Santa Rosa, California, 261
Saroyan, William, 246
Saubel, Katherine Siva, 69
Scale, 13
School districts, 365
Schwarzenegger, Arnold, *401*
Secondary sources, defined, 284
Secularization, 128, 129, 135
Semple, Robert, 188, 200
Senate, California, 400–401, 404
Senate, United States, 389
Separation of powers, 388, 389, 398, 400–401
Sequoia National Park, California, 18
Serra, Junípero, 79, 92–93, 94–95
Serrano, *65m*
Service industry, 408
Services, defined, 49
Settlers, 91
Mexican, 128
Spanish, 91, 92, 108, 110, 268
United States, 117, 140–143, 160, 161, 215, 216
Shasta, California, 42, *57m*
Shasta Dam, 307
Shima, George, 247, 263
Shipbuilding industry, 322, 323
Shoshone, Panamint, *65m*
Sierra Club, 18
Sierra Nevada, 10, *11*, 14
Sikhs, 254, 255, 266
Silicon Valley, California, 371
Simons, Grace, 293
Sinkyone, *50m*
Situ, Mian, *236*
Slave states, 202
Slavery, 166, 201, 202, 205
Sledge and shovel army, 236, 238–239
Sloat, John D., 167
Smith, Jedediah Strong, 139, *142m*
Soldiers
in Mexican-American War, 166–168
in Spanish California, 92, 99, 102,

Switzerland, immigration

108–109, 111
in World War I, 296
in World War II, 321, 322, 323
Solvang, California, 378
Sonoma, California, 162, 164
Sonoma Valley, 133
Sonoran Desert, *85*, 108
South America, *7m*, 174, *316m*, 361
South Korea
Korean immigration, 254, 255, 266, 339, 357, 358, 360
trade with, 372, 375
South Pole, 7
Southern Hemisphere, 7
Southern Pacific Railroad, 269, 291
Soviet Union, 332–333
Space program, 333, 336–337
Spain
colonies in North America, 91, 93, 98–103, 108–111, 118–119, 122–123
exploration of North America, 80–82, 84–85, 92–93
government in California, 98, 103, 110, 118–119, 122, 199
Mexican War for Independence, 118–120, 124, 126
missions, 92, 93, 98–103, 111, *113m*
presidios, 79, 109, 111, *113m*
pueblos, 110–111
settlers, 92, 110
Spanish California, 98–103, 104–107, 108–111, 112–113, 118–119, 122–123
Spanish language, 24, 339, 350
Speech, freedom of, 390
Sports, 62–63, 377
Sri Lanka, immigration, 358
Stanford, Leland, 233, 235, 236
Stanford University, 371
State capital, 203, 207
State government
constitution, 200–201, 398–399
components of, 400–401
elected officials of, 400–401
functions, 400–401
services, 399, 410
state capital, 203, 207
structures, 400–401
See also Government.
State powers, 389, 398–401
Statehood, 198–203
Stearns, Abel, 160, 161
Steinbeck, John, 306, 380
Stockton, California, 207, 255, 350, 407
Stockton, Robert F., 167, 168, 207
Strauss, Joseph B., 308
Strauss, Levi, 192
Strikes, 235, 346–347
Study skills
identify primary and secondary sources, 284–285
use reference materials, 54–55
write a report, 148–149
Suburbs, 339–340
Suffrage, 293, 294–295
Supply, defined, 191
Supreme Court, California, 400–401, 405
Supreme Court, United States, 389
Sutter, John Augustus, 142, 172, *176*, 207
Sutter's Fort, 142, 144–147, *156m*
Sutter's Mill, 172, 173, 176
Swett, John, 364, 365
Switzerland, immigration, 277

T

Taiwan, immigration, 357
Tan, Amy, 381
Tataviam, *50m*
Taxes, 364, 390, 399
Tech Coast, California, 371
Technology, 159, 179, 182–183, 261, 265, 333–334, 370–371
Telegraph, 157, 229, 232, 236
Television industry, 340
Temple, Shirley, 306
Tenant farmers, 263
Terman, Frederick, 371
Territory
  of Mexico, 120, 12, 160, 161
  of Spain, 91, 98, 118
  of the United States, 169, 198, 199
Texas, 169
Tibbets, Eliza and Luther Calvin, 261
Timelines, read, 96–97
Tipai, 42
Tolowa, 42, *50m*
Tompkins, Rosie Lee, 377
Tongva, 42, 43, *50m*, 82, 102
Tourism industry, 269, 279, 299, 341
Toypurina, 102
Trade
  among California Indians, 50–51
  barter, 51
  between California and other states, 226–228, 236, 264–265, 269, 279, 373
  between countries, 122, 269, 279, 371, 372, 374–375
  Pacific, 83, 86–87, 279, 361, 372, 374–375
Transcontinental Railroad
  Big Four, 233, 235, 291
  building of, 234–236, 238–239
  Chinese workers and, 234–236
  Irish workers and, 236
  and trade, 236, 279
  See also Railroads.
Transportation and travel
  aviation, 297, 322, 332
  Cape Horn route, 174, 227
  freeways, 340
  highways and roads, 299, 340
  overland route, 108, 140, 141, *142m*, 174, 228
  Panama route, 174
  Pony Express, 228, 230–231
  railroads, 227, 232–237, 238–239, 265, 269, 279, 373
  stage coaches, 228, 232
  transportation industry, 408
Trappers, 139, 142, 161
Transverse Ranges, 23
Treaty of Cahuenga, 168, 170–171
Treaty of Guadalupe Hidalgo, 158, 169, 214, 216
Trinity County, California, 406
Tropics, 28
Tsnungwe, 42
Tubatulabal, 42, *57m*, *65m*

U

Ulloa, Francisco de, 88
Unemployment, 305, 308
Unions, 346
Union Pacific Railroad Company, 233, 236, 238
United Farm Workers, 346–347
United States
  Congress, 389
  Constitution, 120, 201, 388–390, 398, 399
  government, 388–389
  immigration to California, 138–143, 160–161
  President, 389
  Supreme Court, 389
Universities, 354, 366
University of California at Berkeley, 366, 377
University of California system, 366
Utah, 169

V

Vallejo, California, 203
Vallejo, Mariano Guadalupe, 133, 162, 164, 200
Vaqueros, 133, 136
Vegetation, 23
Vietnam, 358
  immigration, 357, 358–359
  Vietnamese Americans, 24, 359
Vietnam War, 358–359
Vizcaíno, Sebastián, 84–85, 91
Vocabulary strategies. *See first page of each lesson.*
Voting, 201, 293, 294–295, 345, 390, 392–395
Vuich, Rose Ann, 404

W

Wagon trains, 140–141, 174
Wakefield, Lucy Stoddard, 192
Walker, Joseph, 148
Wappo, 42
Washington, state, 321
Washington, D.C., 167
Water, 16–17, 23
  aqueducts, 248, 251, 270–271, 277
  canals, 262, 266, 307, 414
  ocean currents, 84, 86, *87m*
  conservation, 271, 414, 416–417
  dams, 24, 262, 270, 307, 414, 416
  irrigation, 250, 262, 266–267, 270, 307
  reclamation, 262
  reservoirs, 270, 414
  water rights, 270
  wetlands, 24, 262, 307
Watts Towers, 362, *363*
Wayne, John, 324, 381
Weber, Charles, 207

Western Union, 229
White Mountains, 23
Wildlife, 23, 411, 416
Wilson, Brian, 377
Wilson, Luzena Stanley, 193
Wind currents, 84, 86, *87m*
Wintu, *57m*
Wiyot, 42, *50m*
Women
  entrepreneurs, 154, 192, 193, 340, 381
  and equal rights, 292–293, 294–295, 349
  and Gold Rush, 154, 181, 192, 193, 205
  in politics, 293, 314, 349, *401*, 404, 405
  rancheras, 132, 133
  in sports, 377
  and voting rights, 293, 294–295
  in the workforce, 292, 323
  and World War II, 323
Woods, Daniel, 185
Works Progress Administration (WPA), 306
World War I
  effects on California, 297–298
  soldiers in, 296
World War II
  aviation, 322
  effects on California, 321–323, 338
  internment camps, 321, 326–329
  life during, 321–325
  military bases, 322, *330m*
  soldiers in, 321, 322, 323
Wozniak, Stephen, 370
Writers
  Clapp, Louise, 181, 185, 205
  Frémont, Jesse Benton, 165
  Jackson, Helen Hunt, 204
  Steinbeck, John, 306, 380
  Tan, Amy, 381

Y

Yana, 42, *57m*
Yeager, Charles E. "Chuck," *332*
Yerba Buena, *134m*, 167, 206
Yokut, 42, 56–60
Yorba, Maria de los Delores Ontiveros, 133
Yosemite National Park, California, 18, 306
Yosemite Valley, 17, 299
Yuki, 42, *50m*
Yurok, 42, 49, *50m*, 51

Primary Source References

Full citations for literary or primary source excerpts are given below. In many cases, the works can be found in sources other than those cited.

Page 1
For the quotation: McConahey, Meg. "Fifty Who Shaped Our Century: Luther Burbank." *The Santa Rosa Press Democrat*, 1998. For more information about Luther Burbank: American National Biography. http://www.anb.org/

Page 18
For the complete quotation by John Muir: Muir, John. *The Yosemite*. New York: Century, 1912.

Pages 44–47
For the complete story: Curry, Jane Louise. *Back in the Beforetime: Tales of the California Indians*. New York: Margaret K. McElderry Books, 1987.

Page 68
For more information about Mitchell E. Robles: Robles, Mitchell E. *Artistic Statement*. http://www.mitchrobles.com/

Page 74
For the complete quotation: Dana, Richard Henry. *Two Years Before the Mast*. New York: Harper & Brothers, 1840.

Page 82
For the complete quotation by Juan Rodríguez Cabrillo: Holder, Charles Frederick. *The Channel Islands of California; A Book for the Angler, Sportsman, and Tourist*. Chicago: A.C. McClurg & Co., 1910.

Page 84
For more information about early Europeans in California: Schwartz, Stephen. *From West to East: California and the Making of the American Mind*. New York: The Free Press, 1998.

Page 84
For the complete quotation by Sebastián Vizcaíno: Walker, Dale L. *Bear Flag Rising: The Conquest of California, 1846*. New York: A Forge Book, 1999.

Page 93
For the translated letter by Juan Crespí to Francisco Palóu: Bolton, Hubert Eugene. *Fray Juan Crespi: Missionary Explorer of the Pacific Coast, 1769–1774*. Berkeley: University of California Press, 1927.

Page 94
For the translation of Juan Crespí's diary: Beebe, Rose Marie and Robert M. Senkewicz, eds. *Lands of Promise and Despair: Chronicles of Early California, 1535–1846*. Berkeley: Heyday Books, 2001.

Page 95
For more of the letter by Junipero Serra: Beebe, Rose Marie and Robert M. Senkewicz, eds. *Lands of Promise and Despair: Chronicles of Early California, 1535–1846*. Berkeley: Heyday Books, 2001.

Page 102
For more on Toypurina: Monroy, Douglas. "The Prideful Mission and the Little Town: Los Angeles." *Common-Place*. Vol. 3, No. 4, July 2003. http://www.common-place.org/

Pages 104–107
For the complete story: Marvin, Mariah. "A Day in the Life of a Mission." *California Chronicles*, September 1999.

Page 141
For more of Mary Graves's diary: Chartier, JoAnn and Chris Enss. *With Great Hope: Women of the California Gold Rush*. Helena, Montana: Twodot, 2000.

Page 154
For the complete letter by Mary Ballou: Ballou, Mary B. *"I Hear the Hogs in My Kitchen": A Woman's View of the Gold Rush*. Archibald Hanna, ed. New Haven: Yale University Press, 1962.

Page 161
For the complete inaugural address by President James Polk: Polk, James. *Inaugural Address.* March 4, 1845. http://www.yale.edu/

Page 164
For the complete quote by Mariano Vallejo: "'More Like A Pig Than a Bear': Mariano Guadalupe Vallejo Is Taken Prisoner During the Bear Flag Revolt, 1846." *History Matters.* George Mason University. http://historymatters.gmu.edu/

Pages 170–171
For the English translation of the Treaty of Cahuenga: Denger, Mark J. "The Mexican War and California: The Treaty of Campo de Cahuenga." The California State Military Museum. http://www.militarymuseum.org/

For more information on Bernarda Ruiz: Rasmussen, Cecilia. "L.A. Then and Now: Woman Helped Bring a Peaceful End to Mexican-American War." *The Los Angeles Times.* May 5, 2002.

Page 172
For James Marshall's complete account of finding gold: Kowalewski, Michael, ed. *Gold Rush: A Literary Exploration.* Berkeley: Heyday Books, 1997.

Page 173
For more on Sam Brannan's announcement of the Gold Rush: Bancroft, Hubert. *History of California...* San Francisco: The History Company, 1884.

Page 176
For the complete article: "Gold Mine Found." *The Californian.* March 15, 1848. http://www.sandiego.edu/history/

Page 177
For the complete account: Colton, Walter. *Three Years in California.* New York: A.S. Barnes & Co., 1851.

Page 181
For the complete letter by Louise Clapp: Shirley, Dame. *The Shirley Letters: from the California Mines 1851–1852.* Marlene Smith-Baranzini, ed. Berkeley: Heyday Books, 1998.

Page 185
For the complete letter by Louise Clapp: Shirley, Dame. *The Shirley Letters: from the California Mines 1851–1852.* Marlene Smith-Baranzini, ed. Berkeley: Heyday Books, 1998.

Page 185
For the complete account: Woods, Daniel B. *Sixteen Months at the Gold Diggings.* New York: Harper & Brothers, 1851.

Page 193
For the complete memoirs: Wilson, Luzena Stanley. "Her Memoirs as Taken Down by her Daughter in 1881." *Archives of the West: Episode Three (1848–1856).* PBS. http://www.pbs.org/

Pages 194–197
For the complete book: Cushman, Karen. *The Ballad of Lucy Whipple.* New York: Clarion Books, 1996.

Page 201
For the complete California Constitution: California Secretary of State. http://www.ss.ca.gov/

Page 208
For the complete autobiography: Gibbs, Mifflin Wistar. *Shadow and Light: An Autobiography with Reminiscences of the Last and Present Century.* Washington, D.C.: 1902.

Page 215
For the complete quotation: Ruiz de Burton, Maria Amparo. *The Squatter and the Don: A Novel Descriptive of Contemporary Occurrences in California.* San Francisco: S. Carson & Co., 1885.

Page 230
For more information on the Pony Express: The Pony Express Museum. http://www.ponyexpress.org/ and the Virtual Museum of the City of San Francisco. http://www.sfmuseum.org/

Page 235
For the complete quotation: Stanford, Leland. *Central Pacific Railroad Statement Made to the President of the United States, and Secretary of the Interior, on the Progress of the Work.* October 10, 1865. Quoted on http://www.cprr.org/

Page 246
For the complete story: Saroyan, William. "The Pomegranate Trees." *My Name Is Aram.* New York: Harcourt, Brace & World, Inc., 1940.

Page 259
To learn more about Chinese newspapers: Library of Congress, *American Memory: The Chinese in California: 1850–1925.* http://loc.gov/

Pages 273–275
For the complete song: Frankenstein, A. F. (music) and F. B. Silverwood (lyrics). *I Love You, California.* 1913.

Page 284
For the complete article: Head, Lloyd. "One Boy's Experience." *Our Junior Citizens,* July 28, 1906.

Page 284
For the complete quotation: Rubey, William W. Introduction to the Reprinting of *The California Earthquake of April 18, 1906.* Washington, D.C.: The Carnegie Institution of Washington, 1969.

Page 314
For more of the interview with Miriam Matthews: Morris, Gabrielle. *Head of the Class: An Oral History of African-American Achievement in Higher Education and Beyond.* New York: Twayne Publishers, 1995.

Pages 326–329
For the complete book: Uchida, Yoshiko. *Journey to Topaz.* Berkeley: Creative Arts Book Company, 1985.

Page 351
For the complete quotation by Cesar Chavez: *"Can't We All Get Along?": A Peer Mediation and Awareness Campaign Project for Middle School Students.* http://chavezfoundation.org/

Page 366
For the complete quotation by Ellen Ochoa: "Ellen Ochoa, PhD, '85, MS, '81 Electrical Engineering: A Higher Education." *Stanford University School of Engineering.* http://soe.stanford.edu/

Page 409
For more of the interview with Rueben Martinez by Val Zavala: *Life and Times.* November 9, 2004. Available on http://www.kcet.org/

Acknowledgments

Permissioned Literature Selections

Excerpt from *The Ballad of Lucy Whipple,* by Karen Cushman. Copyright © 1996 by Karen Cushman. Reprinted by permission of Clarion Books, an imprint of Houghton Mifflin Company. Excerpt from *A Day in the Life of a Mission* from CALIFORNIA CHRONICLES' September 1999 issue: The California Missions, © 1999, Cobblestone Publishing, 30 Grove Street, Suite C, Peterborough, NH 03458. Reprinted by permission of Carus Publishing Company. All Rights Reserved. Excerpt from *Journey to Topaz,* by Yoshiko Uchida. Copyright © 1971 by Yoshiko Uchida. Reprinted by permission of The Bancroft Library, University of California, Berkeley. Excerpt from *Mountain-Making* from *Back in the Beforetime,* by Jane Louise Curry. Text copyright (1987) by Jane Louise Curry. Reprinted by permission of Margaret K. McElderry Books, an imprint of Simon & Schuster Children's Publishing Division.

Photography Credits

COVER (bridge) Ron Thomas/Getty Images. (bear) Art Wolfe/Getty Images. (nugget top) Jean-Claude Carton/ Bruce Coleman. (nugget bottom) Charles D. Winters/ Photo Researchers, Inc. (map bkgd) © MAPS.com/CORBIS. (seal) California State Archives. (bear spine) © Paul A. Souders/CORBIS. (back cover) © Richard Pasley/Ambient Images. (Cabrillo statue) © Kirkendall-Spring Photographers. **vi** (t) Thomas Hallstein/Alamy Images. (b) Jane Braxton Little. **vii** (t) © Richard Cummins/CORBIS. (b) © Cindy Charles/PhotoEdit. **viii** (t) Jonathan Wallen. (b) William S. Jewett, The Promised Land-The Grayson Family, 1850, oil on canvas, 50 3/4 X 64 inches, Terra Foundation for the Arts, Daniel J. Terra Collection, 1999.79; Photograph courtesy of Terra Foundation for the Arts. **ix** (t) Courtesy of the Bancroft Library, University of California, Berkeley, Landcase Map D-972. (b) © George H. H. Huey/CORBIS. **x** (t) Shades of L.A. Archives/Los Angeles Public Library, 0004293. (b) © David J. & Janice L. Frent Collection/CORBIS. **xi** Courtesy Anaheim Public Library, AN-001-832. (b) © Michael Newman/PhotoEdit. **xii** © AP/Wide World Photos. **xiii** © Nik Wheeler/CORBIS. **xiv** © William A. Blake/CORBIS. (Big Sur) Galen Rowell/ Mountain Light. **2** (l) © Bob Rowan/Progressive Images. **3** (t) © Galen Rowell/CORBIS. (m) © Richard Cummins/ CORBIS. (b) ©Frank Magallanes and Althea Edwards. **4** (l) Kevin Anthony Horgan/Getty Images. (r) © Mark E. Gibson/CORBIS. **5** (l) Thomas Hallstein/Alamy Images. (r) Monica Dalmasso/Getty Images. **6** www.WideImages. com. **7** Photodisc/Getty Images. **8** 111th Aerial Photography Sqd. www.the111th.com. **9** © Tim Zurowski/ CORBIS. **10** NASA **11** Jeff Schmaltz, MODIS Rapid Response Team, NASA/GSFC. **14-15** Mark E. Gibson/ CORBIS. **16** © John Elk III. **17** © Sissie Brimberg. **18** (t) Courtesy of the Bancroft Library, University of California, Berkeley, POR-11 Muir, John. (bl) © William A. Blake/ CORBIS. (bm) The Sierra Club. (br) California Historical Society, TN-5260. **19** © Underwood Archives. **20** © Krista Kennell/CORBIS. **21** © Galen Rowell/CORBIS. **22** Getty Images. **23** © Robert Holmes. **24** John Elk III. **25** Thomas Hallstein/Alamy. **26** John Cancalosi/Ardea London. **26-7** © Catherine Karnow/CORBIS. **30** © David Muench/CORBIS. **32** (l) Nik Wheeler. (m) © Joel W. Rogers/CORBIS. (r) © James Marshall/CORBIS. **33** Taxi/ Getty Images. **34** (t) Courtesy City of Redding. (b) © Philip James Corwin/CORBIS. **35** (t) © Douglas Slone/ CORBIS. (b) Courtesy City of Long Beach. **38** (l) © Spencer Grant/PhotoEdit. (r) John Bigelow Taylor/Art Resource, NY. **39** (l) © Frank Magallanes and Althea Edwards. (r) © Tom Myers/AGStockUSA. **40** © Phillip James Corwin/CORBIS. 42 © Galen Rowell/CORBIS. **43** Brand X Pictures/Getty Images. 48 © Frank Magallanes and Althea Edwards. **50** © Rich Reid/Animals Animals/ Earth Scenes. **54** © Frank Magallanes and Althea Edwards. **56** © Frank S. Balthis. **60** Phoebe Hearst Museum. **60** © Spencer Grant/PhotoEdit. (inset) Peabody Museum, Harvard University, Photo #05-7-10/64513. **61** Jane Braxton Little. **62** Marilyn "Angel" Wynn/ Nativestock.com. **63** (l) Peabody Museum, Harvard University, Photo T4848. (r) Courtesy of the Phoebe Apperson Hearst Museum of Anthropology and the Regents of the University of California, 1-10362, 1-10363a,b. **64** © John Elk III. **65** © Bob Rowan/ Progressive Images. **66** Courtesy Agua Caliente Band of Cahuilla Indians, Palm Springs. **67** Tim Stahl. **68** Courtesy Mitchell E. Robles. **69** (t) Courtesy Malki Museum, 11-795 Fields Road, PO Box 578, Banning, CA 92220. www. malkimusueum.org. (b) Dugan Aguilar. **74** (t) The Crown Estate/Bridgeman Art Library. (b) © Joel W. Rogers/ CORBIS. **75** (tl) Anaheim Public Library, P11598. (tr) Hulton Archive/Getty Images. (br) Photodisc/GettyImages. **76** (l) (detail) Sky Bonillo/PhotoEdit. (m) San Diego Historical Society. (r) The Granger Collection, New York. **77** (t) © Joel W. Rogers/CORBIS. (m) © Royalty-Free/ CORBIS. (bl) Newberry Library/Stock Montage. **78** (l) The Granger Collection, New York. (r) Stock Montage. **79** (l) © Richard Cummins/CORBIS. (r) National Park Service. **80** The Granger Collection, New York. **81** (l) Christie's Images Inc. (inset) © George H. H. Huey/CORBIS. **82** © Sky Bonillo/PhotoEdit. **84** San Diego Historical Society. **85** Christopher Talbot Frank/Ambient Images Inc./Alamy Images. **90** Dan Parrett/AlaskaStock.com. **91** Courtesy of the Oakland Museum of California. **93** Courtesy of the Bancroft Library, University of California, Berkeley. BANC PIC 1963.002:0672--A. **94** Craig Lovell/Eagle Visions Photography. **95** (t) Old Mission Santa Barbara Archive/ Library. (bkgd) © Lowell Georgia/CORBIS. **98** Peter Bennett/Ambient Images. **102** © Michael Newman/ PhotoEdit. (inset) © Robert Holmes/CORBIS. **108** San Diego Historical Society. **109** National Park Service. **113** Mike Mullen. **116** (l) The Granger Collection, New York. (r) California Historical Society, 78-37-1. **117** (l) © Gary Conner/PhotoEdit. (r) Newberry Library/Stock Montage. **119** © Danny Lehman/CORBIS. (inset) The San Jacinto Museum of History, Houston. **120** The Granger Collection, New York. **122** The Granger Collection, New York. **123** Photography Courtesy Peabody Essex Museum. M3547, NANCY ANN, American Brig, Watercolor attributed to M.F. Cornè. Photograph by Mark Sexton. **124** © Dennis MacDonald/PhotoEdit **125** © Gary Conner/PhotoEdit. **126-7** © Randy Faris/CORBIS. **127** (inset) California History Section, California State Library, Neg #7702. **128** Courtesy of the Bancroft Library, University of California, Berkeley, Landcase map D-972. **129** Craig Lovell/Eagle Visions Photography. **130** National Maritime Museum, London. BHC2543. **131** © Cindy Charles/PhotoEdit. **132** History Collections, Los Angeles County Museum of Natural History. **133** California Historical Society, FN-30660. **138** (l) California Historical Society, TN-5270. (r) California History Section, California State Library, Neg #8249. **139** (l) © Mark E. Gibson. (r) Hulton Archive/ Getty Images. **140-1** Newberry Library/Stock Montage. **143** Courtesy of the Bancroft Library, University of California, Berkeley. **154** (t) Courtesy of the Oakland Museum of California. (b) DK Images. **155** (tl) California Historical Society, FN-36171. (tr) British Columbia Archives, A-01626. (bl) Photodisc/Getty Images. (br) DK Images. **156** (l) © Jonathan Wallen. (r) Private Collection/ Bridgeman Art Library. **157** (l) Electricity Collection, NMAH, Smithsonian Institution, #74-2491. (r) Powder Monkeys, Mian Situ, Oil on canvas, 2001-2002, Museum of the American West collection, Autry National Center. **158** (l) © Jonathan Wallen. (r) © Planetary Visions Ltd/ Photo Researchers, Inc. **159** (l) Private Collection/ Bridgeman Art Library. (r) Hulton Archive/Getty Images. **160** Security Pacific Collection/Los Angeles Public Library, 00040880. **161** William S. Jewett, The Promised Land-The Grayson Family,1850, oil on canvas, 50 3/4 X 64 inches, Terra Foundation for the Arts, Daniel J. Terra Collection, 1999.79;Photograph courtesy of Terra Foundation for the Arts. **162** Courtesy of University of Southern California, on behalf of the USC Specialized Libraries and Archival Collection. **163** The Society of California Pioneers. **164** Courtesy of the Bancroft Library, University of California, Berkeley, Vallejo, Mariano POR 2. **165** (t) © Corbis. (b) Courtesy of the Autry National Center/Southwest Museum, Los Angeles. CT-18. **166** Printed Ephemera Collection/Library of Congress. **167** © Col. Charles Waterhouse, USMCR (Ret.)./U.S. Marine Corps Historical Center. **169** Courtesy of the Bancroft Library, University of California, Berkeley, Pico, Andres POR 3. **170** History Collections, Los Angeles County Museum of Natural History. **170-1** Courtesy of the Bancroft Library, University of California, Berkeley, BANC MSS C-B 72. **172** © Bettmann/CORBIS. **173** (l) The Beinecke Rare Book and Manuscript Library. **175** Courtesy of the California History Room, California State Library, Sacramento, California. Neg #23,162. **176 177** Private Collection/Bridgeman Art Library. **176** (l) © SuperStock, Inc./SuperStock. [National Gallery of Art, Washington, D.C.] **177** Private Collection/ Bridgeman Art Library. **180** Mary Evans Picture Library. **182** (l) Courtesy of the Oakland Museum of California. **182–183** Beinecke Rare Book and Manuscript Library. **188** (l) SCHOMBURG CENTER/ Art Resource, NY. (r) DK Images. **189** (l) California Historical Society, FN-12017. (r) Courtesy of the Bancroft Library, University of California, Berkeley, Landcase Map D-972. **191** Courtesy of University of Southern California, on behalf of the USC Specialized Libraries and Archival Collection. **192** Courtesy Levi Strauss & Co. **193** Colton Hall Museum, Monterey, California. **198** Courtesy of the Bancroft Library, University of California, Berkeley, Riley, Bennett, POR 1. **200** (l) California Historical Society, FN-12017. (r) © Dave G. Houser/CORBIS. **201** California State Archives. **203** Courtesy of the California History Room, California State Library, Sacramento, California. Neg # 27,298. **204** © Bill Aron/PhotoEdit. **205** (t) The Granger Collection, New York. (b) The Shirley Letters from California Mines, 1851-1852. Louise Amelia Knapp Smith Clappe. Paper 1922, Museum of the American West collection, Autry National Center. **206** The Granger Collection, New York. **208** (l) SCHOMBURG CENTER/ Art Resource, NY. (r) Courtesy of the California History Room, California State Library, Sacramento, California. Neg #26,989 **209** California Historical Society, FN-36170. **210** Courtesy of the Bancroft Library, University of California, Berkeley. **211** (t) Courtesy of the California History Room, California State Library, Sacramento, California, Neg # 1093. (ml) Courtesy PictureHistory. (mr) © Bettmann/ CORBIS. (b) Courtesy of the Bancroft Library, University of California, Berkeley. **212** San Francisco History Center, San Francisco Public Library, AAB-5275. **214-5** View South from Sonoma Hills, 1864 by Virgil Williams. The Bedford Family Collection. Photo courtesy Montgomery Gallery. **215** Anaheim Public Library, P11267. **216** The Granger Collection, New York. **217** Thomas Hallstein/ Outsight. **223** Courtesy of the Bancroft Library, University of California, Berkeley, F 861 C87:183. **224** (l) THE HAGGIN MUSEUM, Stockton, California. (r) Electricity Collection, NMAH, Smithsonian Institution, #74-2491. **225** (l) Courtesy Stanford University Archives, HART 356. (r) Private Collection. **226** Used by permission, Utah State Historical Society, all rights reserved. **228** Britton & Company, Britton & Rey, American active 19th century. California and Oregon Stage Company (View of Mount Shasta), 19th century color lithograph, 42.5 X 59.5 cm (image); 50.8 X 66 cm (sheet). Fine Arts Museums of San Francisco, Gift of the Estate of Natalie W. Peters, Harry T. Peters, Jr. and Natalie P. Webster, 57.6.11. **232** Courtesy of the California History Room, California State Library, Sacramento, California. Neg #650. **233** Private Collection. **235** Union Pacific Historical Collection, AJR0513. **236** Powder Monkeys, Main Situ, Oil on canvas, 2001-2002,

Museum of the American West collection, Autry National Center. **237** © Wolfgang Kaehler. **238-9** Hulton Archive/Getty Images. **239** (inset) © George H. H. Huey/CORBIS. **246** (t) San Francisco History Center, San Francisco Public Library, AAD-2996. (b) © Bettmann/CORBIS. **247** (tl) San Joaquin County Historical Society and Museum, 72-332-9. (tr) Copyright 1998 Rondal Partridge (bl) Iconotec.com. (br) Comstock, Inc. **248** (r) Brown Brothers. **249** (t) Mark E. Gibson. (b) Hot Ideas/Index Stock Imagery. **250** (l) Mark E. Gibson. (r) Brown Brothers. **251** (l) (detail) California Historical Society, FN-02046. (r) Courtesy of State Museum Resource Center, California State Parks. **253** National Archives, 90-G-124-519. **254** Gift of Tom Tsunoda, Japanese American National Museum, 92.73.5. (inset) National Archives, Pacific Region, San Bruno, CA. **256** Security Pacific Collection/Los Angeles Public Library, S-002-004. **257** California Department of Parks and Recreation, DPR#090-22001. **258** California Historical Society, FN-32735. **259** Courtesy of the Bancroft Library, University of California, Berkeley, ffF870.C5.5.C5 1998. **260** California History Section, California State Library, Neg #26,989. **261** Culver Pictures, Inc. **262** American Stock/Getty Images. **262-3** Joseph Sohm/Alamy Images. **266** Courtesy of the Bancroft Library, University of California, Berkeley, BANC PIC 1905.02719. **266-7** Jim Wark/Airphotona.com. **268** The Granger Collection, New York. **269** Shades of L.A. Archives/Los Angeles Public Library, 0004293. **270** California History Section, California State Library. **272** (l) © Lake County Museum/CORBIS. (r) © Galen Rowell/CORBIS. **272-3** Photodisc/Getty Images. **273** (l) Bill Brooks/Alamy Images. (r) © Lake County Museum/CORBIS. **274-5** © John Dittli. **278** © Bettmann/CORBIS. **279** The Granger Collection, New York. **280** (l) Arnold Genthe/Getty Images. (r) Tom Myers Photography. **282** (b) Tom Bean. **282-3** Mark E. Gibson. **283** (b) Courtesy Hiroo Kanamori. **285** (l) U. S. Air Force Photo, courtesy of National Museum of the United States. Airforce. (r) (detail) California Historical Society, FN-36176. **288** (l) California Historical Society, FN-19319. (r) (detail) California Historical Society, FN-36176. **289** (l) California State Railroad Museum, 24573T. (r) American Stock/Getty Images. **290** (l) © David J. & Janice L. Frent Collection/CORBIS. (r) San Francisco History Center, San Francisco Public Library, Neg#10976. **291** Tom Myers Photography. **292** (l) Brown Brothers. (r) Popperfoto/Retrofile.com. **293** California History Section, California State Library, Neg #8537. **294** (r) © Underwood & Underwood/CORBIS. **295** (t) California Historical Society, FN-19319. (b) AP/Wide World Photos. **296** American Stock Photography/Retrofile.com. **297** (l) U. S. Air Force Photo, courtesy of National Museum of the United States. Airforce. (r) California Historical Society, FN-36176. **298-9** © CORBIS. **299** © Ron Kimball/Ron Kimball Stock. **300-1** Culver Pictures, Inc. **304-5** © CORBIS. **306** www.nakamichiphoto.com. **307** © Philip James Corwin/CORBIS. **308-9** © Bettmann/CORBIS. **314** ©Roger Ressmeyer/CORBIS. (b) Photodisc/Getty Images. **315** (tl) Courtesy of The John D. and Catherine T. MacArthur Foundation. (tr) NASA. (bl) Comstock. (br) NASA. **316** (l) © Minnesota Historical Society/CORBIS (r) Courtesy of Apple Computer, Inc. **317** (l) David R. Frazier. **318** (l) Library of Congress, LC-USW33-028624-C DLC. (r) © NASA/Roger Ressmeyer/CORBIS. **319** © Shepard Sherbell/CORBIS SABA. (r) © 1976 George Ballis/Take Stock. **320** © CORBIS. **322** © CORBIS. **323** Library of Congress, LC-USW33-028624-C DLC. **324** Library of Congress, LC-USF34-72477-D. **325** © Stock Montage. **332** © Bettmann/CORBIS. **333** © NASA/Roger Ressmeyer/CORBIS. **334** Courtesy California History Room, California State Library, Sacramento, California, Neg #27,923. **335** USDA Photo, N-27265. **336** (l) Getty Images. (r) © 1996 CORBIS; Original image courtesy of NASA/CORBIS. **315** (tl) Courtesy of The John D. and Catherine T. MacArthur Foundation. (tr) NASA. (bl) Comstock. (br) NASA. **316** © Minnesota Historical Society/CORBIS (r) Courtesy of Apple Computer, Inc. **317** (l) David R. Frazier. **338** Time Life Pictures/Getty Images. **339** Courtesy Anaheim Public Library, AN-001-832. **341** © Reuters/CORBIS. **342** Hulton Archive/Getty Images. **343** (t) Hulton Archive/Getty Images. (b) Image Port/Index Stock Imagery. **344** © Henry Diltz/CORBIS. **345** (l) © Ted Streshinsky/CORBIS. (r) Time Life Pictures/Getty Images. **346** (l) Courtesy of the Oakland Museum of California. (r) © Bettmann/CORBIS. **347** (l) © 1976 George Ballis/Take Stock. (r) AP Wide World Photos. **348** © Bettmann/CORBIS. **350** Library of Congress, LC-USZC4-2420. **350-1** © 1976 Bob Fitch/Take Stock. **354** (l) © Jeff Greenberg/PhotoEdit. (r) Mark E. Gibson. **355** (l) © Spencer Grant/PhotoEdit. (r) Joe McBride/Getty Images. **356** © Larry Hirshowitz/CORBIS. **358** © Bettmann/CORBIS. **360** (l) © Kayte M. Deioma/PhotoEdit. (r) © Becky Luigart-Stayner/CORBIS. **361** © Spencer Grant/PhotoEdit. **362** (t) Hulton Archive/Getty Images. (b) © Bettmann/CORBIS. **363** © Michael Newman/PhotoEdit. **364** African American Library and Museum at Oakland. **365** Underwood Archives. **367** © Jose Luis Pelaez, Inc./CORBIS. **368** (pencil case, book, lunch pail) © Raymond Bial Photography. **368-9** Trove.net Ã–/Index Stock Imagery. **370** © Roger Ressmeyer/CORBIS. **371** Courtesy the Tech Museum, Photo: Kathy Howe. **372** David R. Frazier. **373** Courtesy Alameda Corridor Transport Authority. **376** The Kobal Collection/Picture Desk, Inc. **377** © Morton Beebe/CORBIS. **378** © Chuck Place Photography. **379** © Peter Beck/CORBIS. **380** (t) Ron Scherl/Stage Image. (b) Culver Pictures. **381** (tl) © Bettmann/CORBIS. (tr) © Najlah Feanny/Corbis. (b) Courtesy Synthia Saint James. Photography by Leroy Hamilton. **386** (l) © Spencer Grant/PhotoEdit. (r) Photo by Rick Meyer for the City of Burbank. **387** (l) Jim Wark/Airphotona.com. (r) © Tony Freeman/PhotoEdit. **389** © Wally McNamee/CORBIS. **390** © David Young-Wolff/PhotoEdit. **391** © Tony Freeman/PhotoEdit. **398** © Nik Wheeler/Corbis. **400** Courtesy of African American Museum and Library at Oakland. **401** (tl) (tr) (br) AP/Wide World Photos. (ml) Courtesy California State Assembly. (mr) © Michael Newman/PhotoEdit. (bl) Courtesy Judicial Council of California, Administrative Office of the Courts. **402** Photo by Rick Meyer for the City of Burbank. **403** © Wolfgang Spunbarg/PhotoEdit. **404** (l) © Amanda Edwards/Getty Images. (r) California State Archives. **405** (t) California State Archives. (b) © Cruz Reynoso. **406-7** Courtesy of the San Jose Convention & Visitors Bureau. **408** Photodisc/Getty Images. **409** © Michael S. Yamashita/CORBIS. **410** © Dwayne Newton/Photo Edit. **411** (t) Tom Vezo/Minden Pictures. (b) © Spencer Grant/Photo Edit. **412** © Thomas Wiewandt; Visions of America/CORBIS. **413** © Kim Kulish/CORBIS. **415** © David Sanger Photography. **416** AP Wide World Photos. **417** © Randy Wells/CORBIS. (Lake Tahoe) Gerald L. French/Panoramic Images. **R4** (t) Courtesy of the California History Room, California State Library, Sacramento, California. Neg #11,033. (b) AP Wide World Photos. **R6** California Secretary of State. **R7** (tl) © North Wind Picture Archives. (tr) Brand X Pictures/PictureQuest. (mr) (br) © Ken Lucas/Visuals Unlimited. (bl) © Galen Rowell/CORBIS. (bm) Jean-Claude Carton/Bruce Coleman. **R8** (t) Seaver Center for Western History Research. (b) Hulton Archive/Getty Images. **R9** (t) Courtesy California History Room, California State Library, Sacramento, California, Neg #1102. (m) Courtesy of the Bancroft Library, University of California, Berkeley, BANC PIC 1945.010:45. (b) © Spencer Grant/PhotoEdit. **R12** © John Elk III. **R13** Mike Mullen.

Assignment Photography

All assignment photography © HMCo./Coppola Studios, Inc.

Illustration Credits

44-47 Jennifer Hewitson. **50-51** Karen Minot. **52-53** Inklink. **56-57** Luigi Galante. **100-101** Will William. **104-107** Greg Ruhl. **112-113** Karen Minot. **136-137** Wood Ronsaville Harlin, Inc. **144-147** Steve Patricia. **194-195** Joel Spector. **218-221** Will Williams. **256-257** Bill Farnswort. **234-235** Derek Grinnell. **264** Patrick Gnan. **273-275** Will Brinkley. **326-327** Winson Trang. **366** David Coulson. **392-395** John Ceballos.

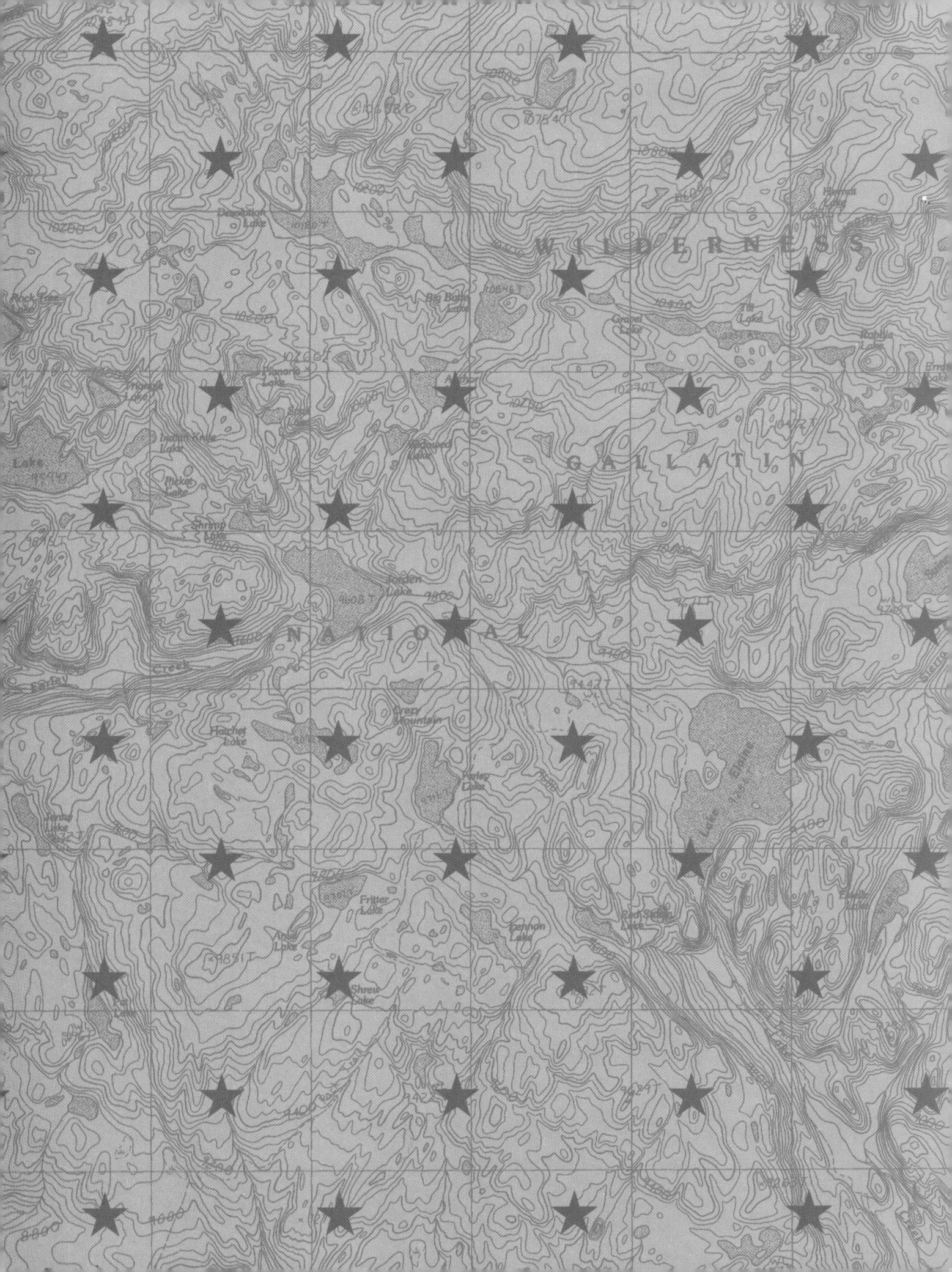

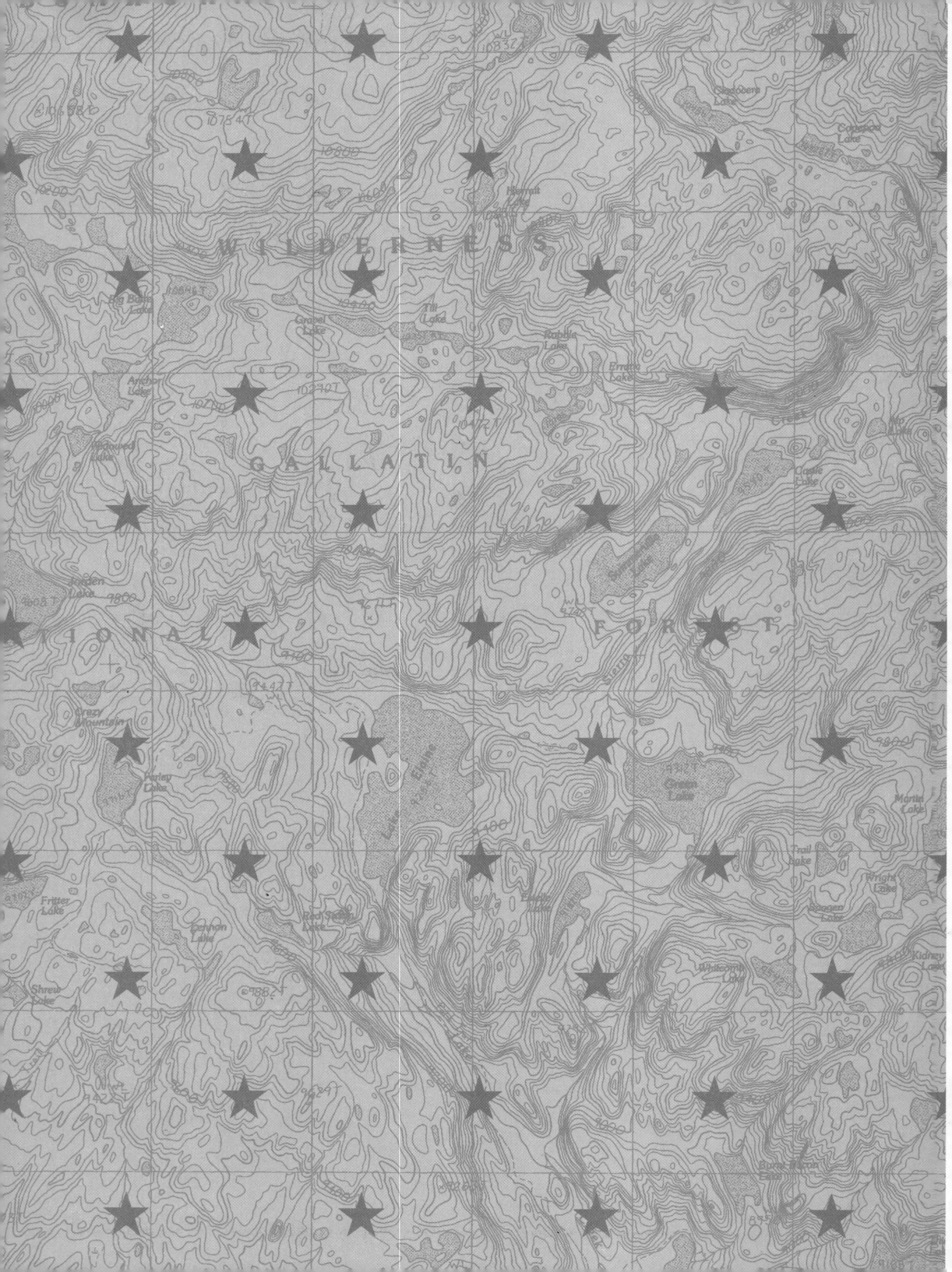